COLORADO POLITICS AND GOVERNMENT

THOMAS E. CRONIN AND ROBERT D. LOEVY

Colorado Politics & Government

GOVERNING THE CENTENNIAL STATE

UNIVERSITY OF NEBRASKA PRESS
LINCOLN & LONDON

The paper in this book
meets the minimum requirements of
American National Standard
for Information Sciences—Permanence of
Paper for Printed Library Materials,
ANSI Z39.48–1984.

Library of Congress
Cataloging-in-Publication Data
Cronin, Thomas E.
Colorado politics and government:
governing the Centennial State /
Thomas E. Cronin and Robert D. Loevy.
p.   cm.—(Politics and governments
of the American states)
Includes bibliographical references
(p.   ) and index.
ISBN 0-8032-1451-0 (cl: alk. paper).
ISBN 0-8032-6358-9 (pb: alk. paper)
1. Colorado—Politics and government.
I. Loevy, Robert D., 1935–.
II. Title. III. Series.
JK7816.C76   1993   320.9788—dc20
93-6587   CIP

CONTENTS

TABLES, MAPS, AND FIGURES

JOHN KINCAID

Series Preface

The purpose of this series is to provide intelligent and interesting books on the politics and governments of the fifty American states, books that are of value not only to the student of government but also to the general citizen who wants greater insight into the past and present civic life of his or her own state and of other states in the federal union. The role of the states in governing America is among the least well known of all the 83,217 governments in the United States. The national media focus attention on the federal government in Washington, D.C., and local media focus attention on local government. Meanwhile, except when there is a scandal or a proposed tax increase, the workings of state government remain something of a mystery to many citizens—out of sight, out of mind.

In many respects, however, the states have been, and continue to be, the most important governments in the American political system. They are the main building blocks and chief organizing governments of the whole system. The states are the constituent governments of the federal union, and it is through the states that citizens gain representation in the national government. The national government is one of limited, delegated powers; all other powers are possessed by the states and their citizens. At the same time, the states are the empowering governments for the nation's 83,166 local governments—counties, municipalities, townships, school districts, and special districts. As such, states provide for one of the most essential and ancient elements of freedom and democracy, the right of local self-government.

Although, for many citizens, the most visible aspects of state government are state universities, some of which are the most prestigious in the world, and state highway patrol officers, with their radar guns and handy ticket books, state governments provide for nearly all domestic public services.

Whether elements of those services are enacted or partly funded by the federal government and actually carried out by local governments, it is state government that has the ultimate responsibility for ensuring that Americans are well served by all their governments. In so doing, all of the American states are more democratic, more prosperous, and better governed than most of the world's nation-states.

This is a particularly timely period in which to publish a series of books on the governments and politics of each of the fifty states. Once viewed as the "fallen arches" of the federal system, states today are increasingly seen as energetic, innovative, and fiscally responsible. Some states, of course, perform better than others, but that is to be expected in a federal system. Each state is unique in its own right. It is our hope that this series will shed light on the public life of each state and that, taken together, the books will contribute to a better, more informed understanding of the states themselves and of their often pivotal roles in the world's first and oldest continental-size federal democracy.

Acknowledgments

We are indebted to Daniel J. Elazar, who first proposed we write this book. He also provided helpful suggestions at the early stages of our research efforts. John Kincaid and state Senator Mike Bird provided especially helpful critiques of our first draft. The manuscript benefitted, too, from suggested improvements and corrections from Ann Armstrong, Richard Beidleman, Richard Lamm, Ed Marston, and John Parr.

Research assistants John Calhoon, Walter Keller, Michael Shaver, and Michael Trevithick all contributed in important ways. Sally Hegarty helped us present some of our data in more visually pleasing ways.

We interviewed over one hundred Coloradans on various aspects of Colorado history, politics, government, and public policy. Among those we especially want to thank are Governors Richard Lamm and Roy Romer; former U.S. Senator Floyd Haskell; Chief Justice Luis Rovira; Justices Joseph Quinn and Jean Dubofsky; Judge John Gallagher; state legislators Chuck Berry, Mike Bird, Ralph Cole, Terry Considine, Renny Fagan, Hugh Fowler, Peggy Kerns, Wayne Knox, and Jana Mendez; former legislator and Lieutenant Governor Nancy Dick; Mayors Robert Issac, Federico Pena, and Linda Shaw; County Commissioner Pat Montgomery; historians Duane Smith, Robert Smith, and Marshall Sprague; Chuck Green, Bob Ewegen, and Fred Brown of the *Denver Post;* Vincent Carroll and Charles Roos of the *Rocky Mountain News;* statehouse Associated Press bureau chief Carl Hilliard; former *Denver Post* editor Carl Miller; lobbyists Stanley Dempsey, Briggs Gamblin, Pat Ratcliffe, and Roger A. Walton; and Marshall Kaplan, Conrad McBride, Dan Sloan, Floyd Ciruli, Bob Drake, Eric Sondermann, Paul Talmey, Robert Dunlap, Robert Lackner, Dick Freese, Buie Seawell, Hank Hahne, John Britz, Walt Klein, Stewart Bliss, B. J. Thornberry, Eugene Petrone, Larry Kallenberger, Wade Buchanan, Dewitt John, Bill Porter, Reid Reynolds, Jim Westkott, John Suthers, Douglas Bruce, David Hite, Douglas Brown, Ed Bowditch, Harriet LaMair, Geraldine Hughes, Carll Jarrett, John Pan, William Hybl, Cathy Reynolds, Elayne Gallagher, James Pierce, Donneta Davidson, Martha Romero, David Wood, Katherine Tamblyn, Douglas Haxton, Daniel Hall, Nancy Jordon, Mac Danford, Michael Valdez, Kenneth McClelland, Art Osier, Jerrye Gilmore, Kenneth Bueche, Harry Bowers, Romona Garcia, and Grace Broyles.

We thank all our colleagues in the Department of Political Science at Colorado College for advice and support. We express special thanks to Jane Stark for both her wonderful secretarial assistance and her cheerful encouragement as draft chapters passed through her hands and word processor. Thanks also to the staff at Colorado College's Tutt Library.

We are especially grateful to Tania and Alex Cronin, and Constance, Walt, and Katie Loevy—our favorite Coloradans.

As we record thanks to all of the above for help in making this a better, more informed book, we also absolve everyone of them of any responsibility for what we have written here.

DANIEL J. ELAZAR

Series Introduction

The more than continental stretch of the American domain is given form and character as a federal union of fifty different states whose institutions order the American landscape. The existence of these states made possible the emergence of a continental nation where liberty, not despotism, reigns and where self-government is the first principle of order. The great American republic was born in its states, as its very name signifies. America's first founding was repeated on thirteen separate occasions over 125 years, from Virginia in 1607 to Georgia in 1732, each giving birth to a colony which became a self-governing commonwealth. Its revolution and second founding was made by those commonwealths, now states, acting in congress, and its constitution was written together and adopted separately. As the American tide rolled westward from the Atlantic coast, it absorbed new territories by organizing thirty-seven more states over the next 169 years.

Most of the American states are larger and better developed than most of the world's nations. Each has its own story. Each is a polity with its own uniqueness. The American states exist because they are civil societies. They were first given political form and then acquired their other characteristics. Each has its own constitution, its own political culture, its own relationship to the federal union and to its section. These in turn have given each its own law and history. The longer that history, the more distinctive the state.

It is in and through the states, no less than the nation, that the great themes of American life play themselves out. The advancing frontier and the continuing experience of Americans as a frontier people, the drama of American ethnic blending, the tragedy of slavery and racial discrimination, the political struggle for expanding the right to vote—all found, and find, their expression in the states.

The changing character of government, from an all-embracing concern with every aspect of civil and religious behavior to a limited concern with maintaining law and order to a concern with providing the social benefits of the contemporary welfare state, has been felt in the states even more than in the federal government. Some states began as commonwealths devoted to establishing model societies based on a religiously informed vision (Massachusetts, Connecticut, Rhode Island). At the other end of the spectrum, Hawaii is a transformed pagan monarchy. At least three states were independent for a significant period of time (Hawaii, Texas, and Vermont). Others were created from nothing by hardly more than a stroke of the pen (the Dakotas, Idaho, Nevada). Several are permanently bilingual (California, Louisiana, and New Mexico). Each has its own landscape and geographic configuration, which time and history transform into a specific geohistorical location. In short, the diversity of the American people is expressed in no small measure through their states, and each state's politics and government have their own fascination.

Cronin and Loevy's *Colorado Politics and Government* is the eighth book in the Center for the Study of Federalism and the University of Nebraska Press series Politics and Governments of the American States. The aim of the series is to provide books on the politics and government of the individual states of the United States that will appeal to three audiences: political scientists, their students, and the wider public in each state. Each volume in the series examines the specific character of one of the fifty states, looking at the state as a polity—its political culture, traditions and practices, constituencies and interest groups, and constitutional and institutional frameworks.

Each book in the series reviews the political development of the state to demonstrate how the state's political institutions and characteristics have evolved from the first settlement to the present, presenting the state in the context of the nation and section of which it is a part, and reviewing the roles and relations of the state vis-à-vis the other states and the federal government. The state's constitutional history, its traditions of constitution making and constitutional change, are examined and related to the workings of the state's political institutions and processes. State-local relations, local government, and community politics are studied and the state's policy concerns are reviewed. Each book concludes by summarizing the principal themes and findings in order to draw conclusions about the current state of the state, its continuing traditions, and emerging issues. Each volume also contains a bibliographic survey of the existing literature on the state and a guide to the use of that literature and state government documents.

Although the books in the series are not expected to be uniform, they do focus on the common themes of federalism, constitutionalism, political culture, and the continuing American frontier, providing a framework within which to consider the institutions, politics, and policy processes of state government.

FEDERALISM

Both the greatest conflicts of American history and the day-to-day operations of American government are closely intertwined with American federalism—the form of American government (in the eighteenth-century sense of the term, which includes both structure and process). American federalism has been characterized by several basic tensions. One is between state sovereignty—the view that in a proper federal system, authority and power over most domestic affairs should be in the hands of the states—and national supremacy—the view that the federal government has a significant role to play in domestic matters affecting the national interest. The other tension is between dual federalism—the idea that a federal system functions best when the federal government and the states function as separately as possible, each in its own sphere—and cooperative federalism—the view that federalism works best when the federal government and the states, while preserving their own institutions, cooperate closely on the implementation of joint or shared programs.

Colorado, the first of the Rocky Mountain states to be admitted to the Union, was, like all western states, carved out of the public domain that since the Articles of Confederation has been under the control of the federal government for the use of the American people as a whole. As such, Colorado is both a creature of the United States and, constitutionally, a sovereign state equal to any of the original thirteen that antedated the American founding. This mixed reality has shaped Colorado's relationships with the federal government in every way. A beneficiary of federal activity to promote settlement and development since its beginnings, it nevertheless has asserted its independence as a state whenever Coloradans have felt it necessary to do so. At the same time, as Cronin and Loevy discuss, Coloradans have never hesitated to call upon the federal government for more assistance in one way or another.

As with the other western states, control over land and natural resources has been a major point of contention and negotiation between Colorado and Washington. Otherwise, in general, Colorado rather easily fits into the pattern of intergovernmental cooperation which was developed in the public land states from the earliest part of the nineteenth century. Even on land and resource issues, intergovernmental cooperation rather than conflict has been the norm, whereas in the near western and northwestern states to the east of it, especially those of the prairie-plains, federal activity was more often formally shared with the states through cooperative programs involving land grants in the nineteenth century and moving smoothly into cash grants in the twentieth. Colorado is a typical western state in that it relied more upon direct federal activity in its early days because of its large area and sparse settlement, a practice which continued into the twentieth century through federal installations and projects administered directly.

CONSTITUTIONALISM

Representatives of the Connecticut River valley towns of Hartford, Windsor, and Wethersfield met in January 1639 to draft a constitution. That document, the Fundamental Orders, established a federal union to be known as Connecticut and inaugurated the American practice of constitution making as a popular act and responsibility, ushering in the era of modern constitutionalism. The American constitutional tradition grows out of the Whig understanding that civil societies are founded by political covenant, entered into by the first founders and reaffirmed by subsequent generations, through which the powers of government are delineated and limited and the rights of the constituting members are clearly proclaimed in such a way as to provide moral and practical restraints on governmental institutions. That constitutional tradition was modified by the federalists, who accepted its fundamental principals, but strengthened the institutional framework designed to provide energy in government while maintaining the checks and balances that they saw as needed to preserve liberty and republican government. At the same time, they turned nonbinding declarations of rights into enforceable constitutional articles.

American state constitutions reflect a melding of these two traditions. Under the U.S. Constitution, each state is free to adopt its own constitution, provided that it establishes a republican form of government. Some states have adopted highly succinct constitutions, like the Vermont constitution of 1793 with 6,600 words, which is still in effect with only fifty-two amendments. Others are just the opposite. For example, Georgia's Ninth Constitution, adopted in 1976, has 583,000 words.

State constitutions are potentially far more comprehensive than the federal constitution, which is one of limited, delegated powers. Because states are plenary governments, they automatically possess all powers not specifically denied them by the U.S. Constitution or their citizens. Consequently, a state constitution must be explicit about limiting and defining the scope of governmental powers, especially on behalf of individual liberty. So state constitutions such as the Colorado constitution normally include an explicit declaration of rights, almost invariably broader than the first ten amendments to the U.S. Constitution.

The detailed specificity of state constitutions affects the way in which they shape each state's governmental system and patterns of political behavior. Unlike the open-endedness and ambiguity of many portions of the U.S. Constitution, which allow for considerable interpretative development, state organs, including state supreme courts, generally hew closely to the letter of their constitutions because they must. This means that formal change of the constitutional document occurs more frequently through constitutional amendment whether initiated by the legislature, special constitutional commissions, constitutional conventions, or direct action by the voters, and, in a number of states, the periodic writing of new constitutions. As a result, state constitutions have come to reflect quite explicitly the changing conceptions of government which have developed over the course of American history.

Overall, six different state constitutional patterns have developed. One is the commonwealth pattern, developed in New England, which emphasizes Whig ideas of the constitution as a philosophic document designed first and foremost to set a direction for civil society and to express and institutionalize a theory of republican government. A second is the constitutional pattern of the commercial republic. The constitutions fitting this pattern reflect a series of compromises required by the conflict of many strong ethnic groups and commercial interests generated by the flow of heterogeneous streams of migrants into particular states and the early development of large commercial and industrial cities in those states.

The third is that found in the South, which can be described as the southern contractual pattern. Southern state constitutions are used as instruments to set explicit terms governing the relationship between polity and society, such as those which protected slavery or racial segregation, or those which sought to diffuse the formal allocation of authority in order to accommodate the swings between oligarchy and factionalism characteristic of southern state politics. Of all the southern states, only Louisiana stands somewhat outside this pattern, since its legal system was founded on the French civil code. Its constitutions have been codes—long, highly explicit documents that form a pattern in and of themselves.

A fifth pattern is found frequently in the less populated states of the Far West, including Colorado, where the state constitution is first and foremost a frame of government explicitly reflecting the republican and democratic principles dominant in the nation in the late nineteenth century, but emphasizing the structure of state government and the distribution of powers within that structure in a direct, businesslike manner. Finally, the two newest states, Alaska and Hawaii, have adopted constitutions following the managerial pattern developed and promoted by twentieth-century constitutional reform movements in the United States. Those constitutions are characterized by conciseness, broad grants of power to the executive branch, and relatively few structural restrictions on the legislature. They emphasize natural resource conservation and social legislation.

Colorado's constitution, based on the frame-of-government model, is among those conventional ones that attract little public attention, remaining more the concern of judges and lawyers or, less frequently, governors and legislators, and only rarely becoming a public issue. Recent efforts to replace the Colorado constitution (still the original one adopted in 1876) did become a public issue, but the public response speaks for itself. Constitutional change in Colorado has been accommodated through appropriate amendments to the original document that seem to have accommodated public concerns, sometimes in far-reaching ways, often in more modest ones. Thus while Colorado's constitution is not revered, it is considered quite serviceable and does not evoke negative response on the part of the broad public either.

THE CONTINUING AMERICAN FRONTIER

For Americans, the word *frontier* conjures up the images of the rural-land frontier of yesteryear—of explorers and mountain men, of cattle drivers and Native Americans, of brave pioneers pushing their way west in the face of natural obstacles. Later, Americans' picture of the frontier was expanded to include the inventors, the railroad builders, and the captains of industry who created the urban-industrial frontier. Recently television has begun to celebrate the entrepreneurial ventures of the automobile and oil industries, portraying the magnates of those industries and their families in the same larger-than-life frame as once was done for the heroes of that first frontier.

As is so often the case, the media responsible for determining and catering to popular taste tell us a great deal about ourselves. The United States was founded with a rural-land frontier that persisted until World War I, more or less, spreading farms, ranches, mines, and towns across the land. Early in the nineteenth century, the rural-land frontier generated the urban frontier based on industrial development. The creation of new wealth through industrialization transformed cities from mere regional service centers into generators of wealth in their own right. The frontier persisted for more than one-hundred years as a major force in American society as a whole and perhaps an additional sixty years as a major force in various parts of the country. The population movements and attendant growth on the urban-industrial frontier brought about the effective settlement of the United States in freestanding cities from coast to coast.

Between the world wars, the urban-industrial frontier gave birth in turn to a third frontier stage, one based on the new technologies of electronic communication, the internal combustion engine, the airplane, synthetics, and petrochemicals. These new technologies transformed every aspect of life and turned urbanization into metropolitanization. This third frontier stage generated a third settlement of the United States, this time in metropolitan regions from coast to coast, involving a mass migration of tens of millions of Americans in search of opportunity on the suburban frontier.

In the 1970s, the first post–World War II generation came to a close. Many Americans were speaking of the "limits of growth." Yet despite that antifrontier rhetoric, there was every sign that a fourth frontier stage was beginning in the form of the rurban, or citybelt-cybernetic, frontier generated by the metropolitan-technological frontier, just as the latter had been generated by its predecessor.

The rurban-cybernetic frontier first emerged in the Northeast, as did its predecessors, as the Atlantic Coast metropolitan regions merged into one another to form a six-hundred-mile-long megalopolis—a matrix of urban and suburban settlements in which the older central cities came to yield importance if not prominence to smaller ones. It was a sign of the times that the computer was conceived at MIT in Cambridge, Massachusetts, and was developed at IBM in White Plains, New York, two medium-sized cities in the megalopolis that have become special centers in their own right. This in itself is a reflection of the two primary characteristics of the new frontier. The new locus of settlement is in medium-sized and small cities and in the rural interstices of the megalopolis.

The spreading use of computer technology is the most direct manifestation of the cybernetic tools that make such citybelts possible. In 1979, the newspapers in the Northeast published frequent reports of the revival of the small cities of the first industrial revolution, particularly in New England, as the new frontier engulfed them. Countrywide, the media focused on the shifting of population growth into rural areas. Both phenomena are as much a product of direct dialing as they are of the older American longing for small-town or country living. Both reflect the urbanization of the American way of life no matter what lifestyle is practiced, or where.

Although the Northeast was first, the new rurban-cybernetic frontier, like its predecessors, is finding its true form in the South and West, where these citybelt matrices are not being built on the collapse of earlier forms, but are developing as an original form. The present sunbelt frontier—strung out along the Gulf Coast, the southwestern desert, the valleys of the Rocky Mountains, and the fringes of the California mountains—is classically megalopolitan in citybelt form and cybernetic with its aerospace-related industries and sunbelt living made possible by air conditioning and the new telecommunications.

The continuing American frontier has all the characteristics of a chain reaction. In a land of great opportunity, each frontier, once opened, has generated its successor and, in turn, has been replaced by it. Each frontier has created a new America with new opportunities, new patterns of settlement, new occupations, new challenges, and new problems. As a result, the central political problem of growth is not simply how to handle the physical changes brought by each frontier, real as they are—it is how to accommodate newness, population turnover, and transience as a way of life. That is the American frontier situation.

Located as it is at the intersection of the Rocky Mountains and the Great Plains, Colorado is part of the country that most fully presents the western frontier myth in all of its facets. Colorado was initially explored by fur trappers, many from French Canada, then by mountain men who inaugurated trade between the American states and the Hispanic Southwest. After the Native Americans, the first permanent settlers of Colorado came from Hispanic New Mexico, while the first settlers from the eastern and midwestern United States came west as part of a gold rush. The mining frontier dominated Colorado's public image for the next generation, while at the same time east of the Rockies, Colorado was very much a part of the cattle growers' frontier, with the major cattle trails from Texas northward passing through the state. In the process, Colorado had its share of wars with Native Americans, featuring some of the major Plains Indian tribes, especially the Cheyenne, perhaps the most romantic of the Plains Indians in the western myth. Finally, Colorado had its homesteaders, its wars between cattle and sheep ranchers and between ranchers and farmers, and even efforts at communal settlement, particularly in the state's northeastern quadrant. From the

Sand Creek massacre to the burying of Buffalo Bill on Lookout Mountain west of Denver following his death in 1917, Colorado lived up to both the worst and the best elements of the image of the western frontier myth.

On the other hand, the urban industrial frontier had relatively little separate impact on Colorado. In fact, whatever there was of it was part of the state's frontier of settlement. As with the other Far Western states, settlement was predominantly urban from the first, particularly because of the mining frontier. Such industrialization as reached Colorado also was mostly a product of the mining frontier—e.g., smelters—or the exploitation of non-precious metal resources such as coal and iron found in the state—e.g., Colorado Fuel and Iron. Colorado's railroads developed primarily to serve the mining industry. The state's extraordinarily rugged terrain prevented it from becoming a major link on the transcontinental railroad. As a result, during the heyday of the urban industrial frontier nationally, Colorado suffered its worst period of colonialism—it not only had to import most manufactured goods from the East, but under the "basing point" system its residents had to pay eastern prices even for those goods produced within the state or region. Most products sold in the state were from 10 to 25 percent higher in price from Colorado westward.

All of this changed after World War II. The influx of large numbers of military personnel into military installations constructed in Colorado during the war stimulated a postwar population boom which propelled Colorado squarely onto the metropolitan-technological frontier, particularly in the Denver area and along the Front Range of the Rockies. With the mass migration westward of people seeking the benefits of Colorado's climate and topography came space-age industries taking advantage of the skills that those migrants possessed. It was as if one day Colorado was a remnant of the Old West and the next it was propelled onto the farthest reaches of the metropolitan frontier. This transition, which took place in the decade following 1946, permanently changed the state.

Nevertheless, Colorado's economy remained what it had always been, a cyclical one in which periods of boom were followed by great periods of bust. Thus, the closing of the metropolitan frontier in the early 1970s left Colorado divided. Mountain resorts west of Denver along Interstate 70, (covered in books in greater detail) dedicated to summer and winter leisure-time activities, whether skiing at Breckenridge or music and the arts at Aspen, were tailor-made for the rurban-cybernetic frontier and continued to develop along the lines of that fourth frontier stage. The Denver area, on the other hand, based on oil and defense industries, entered a period of bust from which at this writing it is only beginning to recover. Thus, as the fourth frontier stage emerges, Colorado's mountain areas have found a role for themselves that they have not had since the first frontier, while the area which embraced the previous two frontier stages has yet to cross the divide.

THE PERSISTENCE OF SECTIONALISM

Sectionalism—the expression of social, economic, and especially political differences along geographic lines—is part and parcel of American political life. The more or less permanent political ties that link groups of contiguous states together as sections reflect the ways in which local conditions and differences in political culture modify the impact of the frontier. This overall sectional pattern reflects the interaction of the three basic factors. The original sections were produced by the variations in the impact of the rural-land frontier on different geographic segments of the country. They, in turn, have been modified by the pressures generated by the first and subsequent frontier stages. As a result, sectionalism is not the same as regionalism. The latter is essentially a phenomenon—often transient—that brings adjacent state, substate, or interstate areas together because of immediate and specific common interests. The sections are not homogeneous socioeconomic units sharing a common character across state lines, but complex entities combining highly diverse states and communities with common political interests that generally complement one another socially and economically.

For example, New England is a section bound by the tightest of social and historical ties even though the differences between the states of lower and upper New England are quite noticeable, even to the casual observer. The six New England states consciously seek to cooperate with one another in numerous ways. Their cooperative efforts have been sufficiently institutionalized to create a veritable confederation within the larger American Union. It is through such acts of political will that sectionalism best manifests itself.

Intrasectional conflicts often exist, but they do not detract from the long-term sectional community of interest. More important for our purposes, certain common sectional bonds give the states of each section a special relationship to national politics. This is particularly true in connection with those specific political issues that are of sectional importance, such as the race issue in the South, the problems of the megalopolis in the Northeast, and the problems of agriculture and agribusiness in the Northwest.

The nation's sectional alignments are rooted in the three great historical, cultural, and economic spheres into which the country is divided: the greater Northeast, the greater South, and the greater West. Following state lines, the greater Northeast includes all those states north of the Ohio and Potomac rivers and east of Lake Michigan. The greater South includes the states below that line but east of the Mississippi plus Missouri, Arkansas, Louisiana, Oklahoma, and Texas. All the rest of the states compose the greater West. Within that framework, there are eight sections: New England, Middle Atlantic, Near West, Upper South, Lower South, Western South, Northwest (including Colorado), and Far West.

From the New Deal years through the 1960s, Americans' understanding of sectionalism was submerged by their concern with urban-oriented socioeconomic categories, such as the struggle between labor and management or between the haves and have-nots in the big cities. Even the racial issue, once the hallmark of the greater South, began to be perceived in nonsectional terms as a result of black immigration northward. This is not to say that sectionalism ceased to exist as a vital force—only that it was little noted in those years.

Beginning in the 1970s, however, there was a resurgence of sectional feeling as economic and social cleavages increasingly came to follow sectional lines. The sunbelt-frostbelt contribution is the prime example of this new sectionalism. *Sunbelt* is the new code word for the Lower South, Western South, and Far West. *Frostbelt* is the code word for the New England, Middle Atlantic, and Great Lakes (Near Western) states. Sectionalism promises to be a major force in national politics, closely linked to the rurban-cybernetic frontier.

A perennial problem of the states, hardly less important than that of direct federal-state relationships, is how to bend sectional and regional demands to fit their own needs for self-maintenance as political systems. One of the ways in which the states are able to overcome this problem is through the use of their formal political institutions, since no problems can be handled governmentally without making use of those formal institutions.

Some would argue that the use of formal political institutions to deflect sectional patterns on behalf of the states is "artificial" interference with the "natural" flow of the nation's social and economic system. Partisans of the states would respond not only by questioning the naturalness of a socioeconomic system that was created by people who migrated freely across the landscape as individuals in search of opportunity, but by arguing that the history of civilization is the record of people's efforts to harness their environment by means of their inventions, all artificial in the literal and real sense of the term. It need not be pointed out that political institutions are among the foremost of those inventions.

From a sectional perspective, the popular image is of Colorado as one of the states of the Far West, from the Rockies through the Great Basin to the Pacific. It is more accurate, however, to see Colorado as part of the Northwest Central region that extends from the Mississippi Valley across to the Rockies. As always, most of the predominant patterns of transportation and communication tell the story. Denver in the nineteenth century was a dead end for the railroads heading westward from Chicago and St. Louis and had only difficult and round-about transportation ties with the area to the west of it. Today, the U.S. West telephone conglomerate reflects the dominant lines of communication for the current frontier. Its two anchors are Minneapolis– St. Paul and Denver. Colorado remains the playground of the prairie-plains states and part of the western Mississipi/Missouri Basin. Its connections to Utah and westward are no more or even less than those it has with the rest of the country. Both its natural and developed ties are eastward. Nevertheless, governmentally it tends to be part of a web of organizations of the western states, detached from its neighbors to the east.

THE VITAL ROLE OF POLITICAL CULTURE

The United States as a whole shares a general political culture that is rooted in two contrasting conceptions of the American political order that can be traced back to the earliest settlement of the country. In the first, the polity is conceived as a marketplace in which the primary public relationships are products of bargaining among individuals and groups acting out of self-interest. In the second, the political order is conceived to be a commonwealth—a polity in which the whole people have an undivided interest—in which the citizens cooperate in an effort to create and maintain the best government in order to implement certain shared moral principles. These two conceptions have exercised an influence on government and politics throughout American history, sometimes in conflict and sometimes complementing each other.

The national political culture is a synthesis of three major political subcultures. All three are of nationwide proportions, having spread, in the course of time, from coast to coast. At the same time, each subculture is strongly tied to specific sections of the country, reflecting the streams and currents of migration that have carried people of different origins and backgrounds across the continent in more or less orderly patterns. Considering their central characteristics, the three are called *individualistic, moralistic,* and *traditionalistic*. Each of the three reflects its own particular synthesis of the marketplace and the commonwealth.

The *individualistic political culture* emphasizes the democratic order as a marketplace in which government is instituted for strictly utilitarian reasons, to handle those functions demanded by the people that it is created to serve. Beyond the commitment to an open market, a government need not have any direct concern with questions of the good society, except insofar as it may be used to advance some common view formulated outside the political arena, just as it serves other functions. Since the individualistic political culture emphasizes the centrality of private concerns, it places a premium on limiting community intervention—whether governmental or nongovernmental—into private activities to the minimum necessary to keep the marketplace in proper working order.

The character of political participation in the individualistic political culture reflects this outlook. Politics is just another means by which individuals may improve themselves socially and economically. In this sense politics is a business like any other, competing for talent and offering rewards to those who take it up as a career. Those individuals who choose political careers may rise by providing the governmental services demanded of them and, in return, may expect to be compensated adequately for their efforts. Interpretations of officeholders' obligations under this arrangement vary. Where the norms are high, such people are expected to provide high-quality public services in return for appropriate rewards. In other cases, officeholders' primary responsibility is to serve themselves and those who have supported the officeholders directly, favoring such supporters even at the expense of the public.

Political life within the individualistic political culture is based on a system of mutual obligations rooted in personal relationships. In the United States, political parties serve as the vehicles for maintaining the obligational network. Party regularity is indispensable in the individualistic political culture because it is the means for coordinating individual enterprise in the political arena and is the one way of preventing individualism in politics from running wild. Such a political culture encourages the maintenance of a party system that is competitive, but not overly so, in the pursuit of office.

Since the individualistic political culture eschews ideological concerns in its businesslike conception of politics, both politicians and citizens look upon political activity as a specialized activity, essentially the province of professionals, of minimum and passing concern to the lay public, and with no place for amateurs to play an active role. Furthermore, there is a strong tendency among the public to believe that politics is a dirty—if necessary—business, better left to those who are willing to soil themselves by engaging in it. In practice, then, where the individualistic political culture is dominant, there is likely to be an easy attitude toward the limits of the professionals' perquisites. Since a fair amount of corruption is expected in the normal course of things, there is relatively little popular excitement when any is found, unless it is of an extraordinary character. It is as if the public is willing to pay a surcharge for services rendered and rebels only when it feels the surcharge has become too heavy. (Of course, the judgments as to what is normal and what is extraordinary are themselves subjective and culturally conditioned.)

Public officials, committed to giving the public what it wants, normally will initiate new programs only when they perceive an overwhelming public demand for them to act. The individualistic political culture is ambivalent about the place of bureaucracy in the political order. Bureaucratic methods of operation fly in the face of the favor system, yet organizational efficiency can be used by those seeking to master the market.

To the extent that the marketplace provides the model for public relationships in American civil society, all Americans share some of the attitudes that are of first importance in the individualistic political culture. At the same time substantial segments of the American people operate politically within the framework of two political cultures.

The *moralistic political culture* emphasizes the commonwealth conception as the basis for democratic government. Politics, in the moralistic political culture, is considered one of the great activities of humanity in its search for the good society—a struggle for power, it is true, but also an effort to exercise power for the betterment of the commonwealth. Consequently, both the general public and the politicians conceive of politics as a public activity centered on some notion of the public good and properly devoted to the advancement of the public interest.

In the moralistic political culture, there is a general commitment to utilizing communal—preferably nongovernmental, but governmental if necessary—power to intervene in the sphere of private activities when it is considered necessary to do so for the public good or the well-being of the community. Accordingly, issues have an important place in the moralistic style of politics, functioning to set the tone for political concern. Government is considered a positive instrument with a responsibility to promote the general welfare, though definitions of what its positive role should be may vary considerably from era to era and place to place.

Politics is ideally a matter of concern for every citizen. Government service is public service, placing moral obligations on those who serve in government that are more demanding than those of the marketplace. Politics is not considered a legitimate realm for private economic enrichment. A politician is not expected to profit from political activity and, in fact, is held suspect if he or she does.

The concept of serving the commonwealth is at the core of all political relationships, and politicians are expected to adhere to it even at the expense of individual loyalties and political friendships. Political parties are considered useful political devices but are not valued for their own sakes. Regular party ties can be abandoned with relative impunity for third parties, special local parties, nonpartisan systems, or the opposition party if such changes are believed helpful in gaining larger political goals.

In practice, where the moralistic political culture is dominant today, there is considerably more amateur participation in politics. There is also much less of what Americans consider corruption in government and less tolerance of those actions that are considered corrupt, so politics does not have the taint it so often bears in the individualistic environment.

By virtue of its fundamental outlook, the moralistic political culture creates a greater commitment to active government intervention in the economic and social life of the community. At the same time, its strong commitment to communitarianism tends to keep government intervention local wherever possible. Public officials will themselves initiate new government activities in an effort to come to grips with problems as yet unperceived by a majority of the citizenry.

The moralistic political culture's major difficulty with bureaucracy lies in the potential conflict between communitarian principles and large-scale organization. Otherwise, the notion of a politically neutral administrative system is attractive. Where merit systems are instituted, they tend to be rigidly maintained.

The *traditionalistic political culture* is rooted in an ambivalent attitude toward the marketplace, coupled with a paternalistic and elitist conception of the commonwealth. It reflects an older, precommercial attitude that accepts a substantially hierarchical society as part of the ordered nature of things, authorizing and expecting those at the top of the social structure to take a special and dominant role in government. Like its moralistic counterpart, the traditionalistic political culture accepts government as an actor with

xxx   Series Introduction

a positive role in the community, but it tries to limit that role to securing the continued maintenance of the existing social order. To do so, it functions to confine real political power to a relatively small and self-perpetuating group drawn from an established elite who often inherit their right to govern through family ties or social position. Social and family ties are even more important in a traditionalistic political culture than personal ties in the individualistic, where, after all is said and done, one's first responsibility is to oneself. At the same time, those who do not have a definite role to play in politics are not expected to be even minimally active as citizens. In many cases, they are not even expected to vote. As in the individualistic political culture, those active in politics are expected to benefit personally from their activity, although not necessarily by direct pecuniary gain.

Political parties are not important in traditional political cultures because they encourage a degree of openness that goes against the grain of an elitist political order. Political competition is expressed through factions, an extension of the personal politics characteristic of the system. Hence political systems within the culture tend to have loose one-party systems, if they have political parties at all. Political leaders play conservative and custodial rather than initiatory roles unless pressed strongly from the outside.

Traditionalistic political cultures tend to be antibureaucratic. Bureaucracy by its very nature interferes with the fine web of social relationships that lies at the root of the political system. Where bureaucracy is introduced, it is generally confined to ministerial functions under the aegis of the established powerholders.

Colorado's geographic location has meant that all three political subcultures are represented in the state. Its first settlers were from traditionalistic political cultures, both Hispanic (who originally were part of a traditional political culture outside of the American cultural synthesis) and from the American South. Within a very short time, the gold rushes brought in people from the other political subcultures. Agricultural settlement in the northeastern quadrant of the state was strongly moralistic, while the mining camps were predominantly individualistic. These other two subcultures soon dominated the state.

The representatives of the moralistic subculture took the lead in civic and political life in the early days of Colorado settlement and made their political culture dominant in state politics. But because there were so many people coming in from the individualistic political culture, the moralistic leadership had to make its peace with that subculture to a large degree. Representatives of the traditionalistic subculture were left out and from time to time have been the source of what is considered political corruption in Colorado. Such phenomena as courthouse gangs, open manipulation of government for benefits of questionable legality, and outright bribery and corruption since Colorado's early days have been found in predominantly traditionalistic or mixed traditionalistic-individualistic areas, while reform movements have normally gained their strength in moralistic or a combination of moralistic-individualistic areas.

Colorado's political culture, like that of the West generally, is populistic and remained so even in those years when the state was led by a business "establishment" that constituted an economic elite. By and large, Colorado's politics is open and activist. Its populist-cum-moralistic bent has been further strengthened by the settlement in the state of people looking for the famed Colorado quality of life and who are thereby actively involved in the kind of "quality of life" issues associated with the wave of "green" politics that has grown up in the developed world. Quality-of-life issues normally lead to a full-fledged mobilization of this kind of moralistic "green" populism with telling results. See chapter 1 and chapter 5 for additional discussions on the character and culture of contemporary Colorado.

SUMMING UP

Colorado's image is compounded of its high, snow-capped mountains, a robust "Western" past focused on gold and silver rushes, and a present and future emphasizing skiing. But Colorado is a state of other contrasts as well: a boom-and-bust economy, high mountains where the people play and high plains where the people live. By and large these contrasts are as politically balanced as the Democratic and Republican parties have been for the last four generations or since the beginnings of political life in Colorado Territory. At the same time, Colorado has been transformed from an expression of the Old West to the cutting edge of the leisure-oriented aspects of the rurban-cybernetic frontier. If the post–World War II metropolitan-technological frontier created a belt of settlement running north to south from Fort Collins to Pueblo, the rurban-cybernetic frontier is developing a crossbelt running from Denver and Colorado Springs on the east through the Rockies along the I-70 corridor, now as far as Glenwood Springs, and moving westward—a whole new world of small towns that live off high-grade, costly culture and sports activities. Thus the Colorado mountains are either emptying out or are becoming more like Switzerland, with a permanent settlement at the lower elevations and a commitment to preserving at least the illusion of wildness at higher ones. This is likely to be Colorado's immediate future, both economically and politically.

Colorado today is very definitely part of the "New West," a term that has been used to refer to the changes that have taken place since the beginning of the postwar generation, as the mining frontier gave way to the metropolitan frontier, to replace the "Old West" of cowboys and Eastern colonialism. "New West" suggests within it a civilization coming of age, no longer marginal and impermanent, in which exploitation of the state's resources has been replaced by advanced environmentalism and the Grand Old Opry has been replaced by grand opera as a cultural benchmark. Colorado politics and government have reflected these changes: in a sense Colorado progressivism today is a kind of continuing attack on the attitudes attributed to the Old West, while Colorado conservatism sees itself as a defense of precisely those values.

COLORADO POLITICS AND GOVERNMENT

CHAPTER ONE

The Character and Spirit of Colorado

Colorado is big and mountainous and beautiful and has a history of booms and busts. This nearly perfect rectangle of a state measures almost 400 miles east to west and nearly 300 miles north to south.

It is twice the size of England, half the size of France, and at least ten times the size of Massachusetts. It is the eighth largest state in the United States in terms of land area on the map. Colorado is said to be the number one state in *surface* land area. That is, if you flattened out all of Colorado's mountains and foothills (which no one is advocating), there would be more land area than either Alaska or Texas (if they, too, were flattened out).

Colorado ranks twenty-sixth in population in the United States. Still, its more than 3.5 million people make it larger than fifty nations in the United Nations. Its great distance from the two coasts and even the hundreds of miles between it and Kansas City, Omaha, Dallas, Salt Lake City, and Albuquerque make it appear even larger and more removed. In many respects the Centennial State, so-called because it was admitted to the Union in 1876, is a small separate nation, isolated in high plains, grasslands, plateaus, and rugged mountain splendor.

Colorado is the nation's highest state, with a mean altitude of 6,800 feet above sea level. It ranges from a spectacular 14,431 feet atop Mt. Elbert, in the center of the state, to a respectable 3,385 feet near the farming community of Holly, in southeastern Colorado close to the Kansas border.

This "Switzerland of America" is a magnet for more than 25 million out-of-state tourists and visitors each year. The mountains of Colorado provide a scenic splendor that is hard to match anywhere in the world, and that helps explain the upbeat, optimistic, and generally positive opinion most Coloradans have toward their state and its rich natural resources.

What do people think of when they think of Colorado? Coloradans and many who know the state answer with the following: fabulous mountains, sunshine, blue skies, wonderfully dry and fresh air, great skiing, excellent fishing and hunting, outdoor sports, cattle and ranching, mines, ghost towns, billions of conifers and aspen trees, Rocky Mountain National Park, Pike's Peak, Mesa Verde, the U.S. Air Force Academy, Denver, Aspen and Vail, the Continental Divide, one-time presidential candidate Gary Hart, former Governor Richard Lamm, U.S. Representative Patricia Schroeder, Native American U.S. Senator Ben Nighthorse Campbell, country and pop singer John Denver, Coors beer, the Denver Broncos, the Colorado Rockies baseball team, and also the controversial 1992 Amendment 2 that prohibited passage of laws to protect homosexuals from discrimination. Colorado, of course, is far more than the Rocky Mountains or beautiful scenery or any of the above-mentioned places, pastimes, events, or people.

Colorado has a diversified economy. The state is forever trying to avoid the cycles of booms and busts that have dominated its economic and political past. Coloradans are painfully aware of these cycles in mining gold, then silver, then gold again, coal, molybdenum, oil and gas, oil shale, in military spending, and in real estate speculation.

What follows in this chapter is a review of the geographical, political, economic, and social realities that have to be appreciated before one can come to terms with the character of Colorado. They are not in any strategic order, and no one factor alone can explain political behavior in the Centennial State. Yet collectively they go a long way in helping us understand the views, values, and political culture of those who live, vote, and pay taxes in Colorado.

One last note of introduction. In interviews, several of the leading pollsters, political analysts, and political reporters in the state were asked to reflect on what unifies Colorado. "What brings the citizens of the state together and makes them Coloradans?" After a long pause, many interviewees wondered whether there was much, if anything, that unifies the people of the state. Some pointed to the mountains, or a frontier outlook, or a spirit of independence. On the other hand, everyone could list, and did list, a large number of factors or forces that divide the people of Colorado, including east versus west, urban versus rural, urban versus suburban, Denver versus the rest of the state, Anglo versus Hispanic, natives versus newcomers, developers versus environmentalists, Republicans versus Democrats, black interests versus white interests, the "religious right" versus the "politically correct" left, the legislature versus the governor, and on and on.

Paradoxically, much that unifies Colorado also divides it. Thus Coloradans revere the mountains even as those same mountains create a huge barrier between the Front Range and the western slope. Everyone wants everyone else's water, yet Coloradans are united, usually, in not wanting to let Texans, Californians, Nebraskans, or anyone else get more of Colorado's water. And most Coloradans who live far from Denver view the state's largest city as a mixed blessing at best, yet sports fans from Julesburg to Cortez and from Springfield to Rangely root for the Denver Broncos on Sunday afternoons each autumn, especially when the Broncos have won a few games.

Here then are the forces, factors, or realities that shape Colorado politics, past and present.

THE MOUNTAINS AND THEIR MYSTIQUE

"Very little in the world can compare to the scenery of Colorado," wrote journalist John Gunther in 1947. "The vistas here stretch the eyes, enlighten the heart, and make the spirit humble."[1] Katherine Lee Bates wrote her famous poem, "America the Beautiful," after she visited the top of Pike's Peak (14,110 feet above sea level):

O beautiful for spacious skies,
    For amber waves of grain,
For purple mountain majesties
    Above the fruited plain!

The mountains dominate Colorado as they do no other state. A mountainless Colorado is impossible to imagine, although geologists have determined that about 70 million years ago much of Colorado was part of an ocean bed. These mountains are the state's greatest natural asset, yet they also have drawbacks. It snows a lot, both in the mountains and on the prairies at the foot of the mountains. It snows somewhere in the state every month of the year, and perhaps even every day of the year. One of the authors, for example, was snowed on while hiking on Lost Man Trail near Independence Pass (between Twin Lakes and Aspen) at high noon in mid July. The other was late to a meeting in Vail because a late June snowstorm closed Vail Pass.

The apex of the Rocky Mountain chain is in Colorado. More than a thousand summits in the state rise above 10,000 feet. The most famous of Colorado's peaks are the fifty-four over 14,000 feet, known as Fourteeners. Colorado contains about 80 percent of the Fourteeners in the contiguous United States.

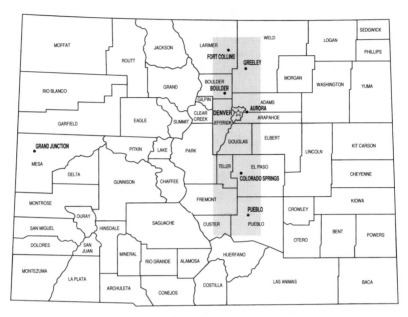

Map 1.   Colorado's Predominant Population Corridor

The impressive and rugged Rockies are also the great divider of waters, as the Continental Divide winds through the heart of Colorado's mountains. Streams flow east to the Atlantic or west to the Pacific, depending on the side of the divide, at this "crest of the continent."

The mountains have always been a major obstacle for east-west transportation, dividing the state and making it hard to fashion a statewide sense of community. The daunting mountain passes and unpredictable weather help explain why Colorado was one of the last states to be settled by Anglo-Americans.

The state's official borders are unnatural and arbitrary. What really define Colorado, its signature, are the Rocky Mountains. Fully 95 percent of Colorado's current population can see the mountains, although perhaps only 5 percent or so actually live in them, that is, live in real mountain towns like Silverton, Leadville, Fairplay, Garfield, Tincup, Granby, Rico, Estes Park, Somerset, and Cripple Creek.

The mountains are the jewels of Colorado, and they perhaps justify the sometimes harsh and forbidding winter weather. When Coloradans are asked why they live in the state, the predictable answer is that they love the mountains. Coloradans hike, backpack, fish, ski, cycle, jog, hunt, raft, canoe, windsurf, and in other ways relax and enjoy themselves in and around the mountains, rivers, lakes, and valleys of their state.

People from the eastern United States came to Colorado to extract gold and silver and, later, scores of other treasures in the mountains. Colorado is a mineral-rich state. It has more than 250 metallic and nonmetallic minerals and produces more tin, molybdenum, uranium, granite, sandstone, and basalt than any other state. Experts say Colorado has a potential supply of 80 billion tons of bituminous coal and perhaps as much as 500 billion barrels of oil that could be extracted from oil shale in the state. Petroleum and natural gas are also a major part of the Colorado economy.

Once-defunct or near-defunct mining villages in the mountains, such as Aspen, Crested Butte, and Breckenridge, are now tourist meccas that thrive on the beauty and recreational assets of the mountains.

The mountains also leave a psychological impact on Coloradans. They are rugged and rocky. They test one's independence as well as one's character. Climbers and skiers view them as a challenge. In many ways the mountains both inspire Coloradans and separate them from the rest of the country. The mountains give Coloradans a superiority complex and encourage a sense of freedom, space, and separateness. They remain a frontier, a temptation for escapism, and they remind Coloradans in various ways that the rugged individualism and independent spirit once necessary just to ascend and "tame" these mountainous areas are also qualities that need to be celebrated and encouraged today.

The "every man for himself" ethos of the 1850s and 1870s is still a part of the character of Colorado, even if it was once exaggerated into legends by historians of the romantic school.[2] Although large numbers of Coloradans do not hunt, fish, ski, or rock climb, the spirit of the Native Americans, the fur trappers, and the mountain men and women is still a part of the mountain "mystique" that helps shape the political outlook of contemporary Coloradans.

Colorado, of course, is much more than mountains. The mountainous portions of the state comprise less than two-fifths of the state's land. But the remainder of the state is dwarfed by the mountains and their worldwide reputation.

WATER AND WATER POLITICS

The Colorado Rockies contain the source of many rivers, and water has been indispensable to the economic growth and prosperity of the state. The avail-

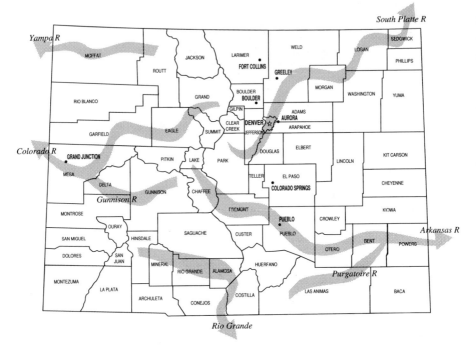

Map 2.   Rivers of Colorado

ability, diversion, and proper use of water has been a political issue throughout the history of Colorado.

Both the eastern plains and the western plateaus and canyonlands are
semiarid. The state averages ten to eighteen inches of rain annually in most
areas, a bit higher in the mountains. Annual rainfall in Colorado Springs, for
example, averages fifteen to sixteen inches, compared to Chicago's twenty-
three, Boston's forty-two, and Miami's sixty-one inches a year. What is sel-
dom understood, moreover, is that thirty inches of dry snow is the equivalent
of only one inch of rainwater.

As the rain and melted snow flow down the Colorado Rockies onto the
eastern plains and the western deserts, much of the water is dammed and diverted through canals to irrigate croplands. About 80 percent of diverted water in the Rocky Mountain West is used for agricultural purposes. Also, water is stored in mountain reservoirs and then piped into the water supply
systems of major cities along the Front Range urban corridor, such as Denver, Fort Collins, Colorado Springs, Lakewood, Aurora, Boulder, and
Pueblo.

Four major river systems begin in Colorado, all four with headwaters located high in the Rockies (see map 2). The north and south branches of the Platte River originate in the mountains west of Denver. The North Platte flows northward out of the state toward Laramie, Wyoming, eventually joining the South Platte at North Platte, Nebraska. The South Platte flows northeastward through Denver and northeast Colorado (and through James A. Michener's novel *Centennial*) into Nebraska, eventually emptying into the Missouri River near Omaha. The Arkansas River also rises in the mountains west of Denver, descending southeast before turning due east and flowing through the cities of Pueblo, La Junta, and Lamar into Kansas. It eventually flows into the Mississippi River in Arkansas. The Rio Grande begins in the mountains of south central Colorado. It flows due south through the San Luis Valley and the city of Alamosa to New Mexico, eventually forming the Texas-Mexico boundary as it flows into the Gulf of Mexico.

The Platte, Arkansas, and Rio Grande rivers are all on the eastern slope of the Continental Divide and eventually flow into the Atlantic Ocean. A fourth river, the Colorado River, rises on the western slope of the Continental Divide near the resort community of Grand Lake and flows westward across the state into Utah. The Colorado and its many tributaries (the Yampa, Gunnison, San Miguel, Dolores, Animas, and San Juan rivers) drain the entire western slope of Colorado. From Utah the mighty Colorado River flows through Lake Meade and the Hoover Dam into Arizona, eventually forming the Arizona-California boundary before entering Mexico and emptying into the Gulf of California and the Pacific Ocean.

An overriding fact of political and economic life in Colorado is that water is scarce. "Whiskey is for drinking," a saying in this region has it, "but water is for fighting over." Another old saw in the West holds that "water runs uphill toward money." Both tell a lot about Colorado politics.

Farmers on both the eastern plains and the western slope always want more water, and they have been the beneficiaries of some of the largest U.S. government public works projects, giant dams and diversions, in our country's history. The U.S. Reclamation Act of 1902 brought cheap water to the farmers, thereby helping to transform Colorado as well as other states in the West.

Farmers received large amounts of water first. Later developers, manufacturers, and the energy and ski industries also would get water. In the early 1990s the tourist industry began to argue it is in the best long-term interest of the state to leave as much water as possible in the streams, lakes, and rivers that make Colorado so attractive for visitors.

Developers, as well as many economists, say farmers use water much too inefficiently. Water boards and water providers, such as the Denver Water Board and the Colorado Water Congress, lament the recent halt in the building of dams and diversion projects and claim the state is losing water to which it is entitled because of the lack of adequate structural storage facilities. Environmentalists, not surprisingly, want Coloradans to change their consumption habits and to grow low-water, low-maintenance lawns so the state might retain its water in mountain streams and not divert it to water Kentucky bluegrass lawns in Front Range cities.

Coloradans have continually battled other Coloradans over water diversion schemes. Denver's populous suburbs and the city of Colorado Springs have wanted and need high-country water and water from the western slope. But since water is virtually blood in Colorado, western Coloradans resent the financial and legal deals concocted by Front Range Coloradans to get at their water.

Water management, legal rulings, and policy decisions have historically been the preserve of a relatively small group of water experts. Key questions are: What are the most efficient uses of water? How can the state provide for them? What price should be paid for water? And should water policy decisions be left, as they have in the past, to a small band of water experts?[3] To understand Colorado politics and political leaders, one has to understand the longstanding fights over water rights and the "proper" use of water.

THE DEVELOPMENT-VERSUS-ENVIRONMENT DIALECTIC

Virtually everyone in Colorado agrees on the importance of a healthy, expanding economy that can provide jobs and reasonable prosperity for everyone who lives in the state. Most Coloradans also want more open-space wilderness areas and want government to impose fines on industries that pollute the air and water or damage the scenery. And most Coloradans claim to be "environmentalists."

But when abstract considerations are brought down to specific problems, the people of Colorado invariably divide into two groups. One group believes Colorado is obliged to use its resources to provide jobs and expand business opportunities. The other believes that preservation, conservation, and regulations that limit development are both desirable and, in the long run, in the vital economic interest of the state.

Many Coloradans want the U.S. government to designate more open-space wilderness areas. Yet *open space* means different things to different people. To conservationists it means a place where backpackers can go to appreciate the spectacular mountains and parks of the state. To ranchers on the western slope it means more regions for grazing cattle or sheep. To the tourism industry it means more regions to promote as fishing, rafting, skiing, or camping sites.

An issue arose in 1990 that illustrates this dialectic. Several people in Colorado Springs and in some of the counties in the western suburbs of Denver thought there should be stronger environmental restrictions placed on firms that quarry rock for cement and building use. A few notably ugly quarry scars had been left, especially near Colorado Springs. Local business leaders complained the scars were so noticeable that they were an enduring detriment to attracting tourists and businesses to the area, not to mention the permanent loss of visual beauty to the thousands who regularly had to drive near or past those scars. A bill was introduced in the Colorado legislature requiring certain modest changes in quarry approval. Immediate opposition came from lobbyists for the Colorado Rock Products Association. Even these modest changes, the lobbyists claimed, would increase the costs of home building in Colorado, would cost jobs, and would lead to increased importation of rocks for cement from nearby states, such as Wyoming, that had fewer restrictions on quarry operators. The bill died in a legislative committee.[4]

The Rocky Flats nuclear warhead plant, located northeast of Denver, likewise divided public opinion. Operated at various times by a series of companies, including Dow Chemical and Rockwell International, it was the only U.S. plant equipped for the mass production of plutonium parts needed for triggers in hydrogen bombs. Problems arose because plutonium is both flammable and radioactive. A number of accidents, leaks, and contaminations occurred over the years, yet the Colorado political establishment and Colorado business and labor leaders fought to keep the plant open because it provided thousands of jobs and infused much desired federal monies into the metropolitan Denver economy.

Virtually every boom in Colorado's history has had its environmental costs, from the radioactive uranium tailings in Durango to the range erosion often caused by opportunistic, yet short-sighted, ranchers. "The rancher is a man who supplants the native grasses with tumbleweed, snakeweed, mud, dust and flies," wrote the late novelist Edward Abbey. "He drives off elk and antelope and shoots eagles, bears and cougars on sight. And then he leans back and grins at the TV cameras and talks about how much he loves the American West."[5]

Business and political leaders deny Colorado has to choose between unrestrained economic growth and zealous environmentalism. "Balance economic development with concern for the environment" is what the Colorado Association of Commerce and Industry (CACI) urges. Its *Blueprint for Colorado: A Look at the 90s* almost sounds as if there are no environmental crises in Colorado's future: "Besides our people, Colorado's greatest asset is its unique physical environment, which is being protected, maintained, and preserved. A long-range environmental plan, based on scientific data and technical feasibility, has been embraced by all segments of society. . . . Coloradans recognize the link between a healthy environment and a strong economy."[6]

What CACI's *Blueprint* said is valid, up to a point. Many programs, such as the statewide Land Use Commission, are in place, but these programs have been very much unfunded in recent years. Environmental programs have been adopted yet inadequately implemented.

Coloradans do appreciate the link between a healthy environment and a healthy economy. Statewide polls indicate, however, that people divide sharply on how much they are willing to change their lifestyles or pay increased taxes to ensure an improved quality of life. Most Coloradans are now opposed to building more dams, but they still want cheap water for their extensive green lawns. Most Coloradans want clean air, but they also want to drive their cars whenever and wherever they want. Coloradans, like people most places, want it both ways.

These divisions are even more sharply observed in the state legislature as it debates proposed laws on the environment and economic development. The legislature is usually pro-business, pro-jobs, and pro-growth. Groups such as the Greater Denver Chamber of Commerce, the Colorado Water Congress, homebuilders, unions, the Colorado Association of Commerce and Industry, and kindred associations typically prevail over the Sierra Club, the Western Colorado Congress, the Colorado Open Space Council, and other conservation- or preservation-oriented groups. The major political action committees and the lobbyists with the highest salaries and reputed "clout" are commonly on the side of economic development. Environmentalist groups and environmentalist legislators are invariably on the defensive at the state capitol.

A LARGE FEDERAL GOVERNMENT PRESENCE

Thirty-seven percent of modern-day Colorado is owned by the U.S. government. Moreover, virtually two-thirds of Colorado west of Denver and the Front Range is designated "federal land." The federal government has been in Colorado early and often, and its impact is enormous. Only a handful of states, such as Alaska and Nevada, are more influenced and regulated by the national government.

Nowadays national forests, national parks, Bureau of Land Management (BLM) holdings, and major military installations are found all over the state. The Denver metropolitan area has one of the largest concentrations of federal employees outside of the Washington, D.C., metropolitan area. There are 115,000 federal employees living and working in Colorado, nearly 30 percent in defense-related work. Denver is the seat of both the federal District Court for Colorado and the Tenth Circuit U.S. Court of Appeals. It is home to a major federal mint and houses regional offices of many federal cabinet-level departments. Colorado also has a large contingent of forest rangers and other officials of the Interior and Agriculture departments who work in the national parks, forests, and monuments in the state. The Defense Department has a variety of installations, including the U.S. Air Force Academy, the North American Aerospace Defense Command (NORAD), a major army base, Fort Carson, and the U.S. Space Command.

The federal government provided major subsidies and concessions to bring the railroads to Colorado. And, as noted, it has been indispensable to the building of scores of dams, diversion projects, and related reclamation projects. A rash of federal subsidies in various forms also came to the cattle growers, the wheat growers, the sugar beet farmers, and others who make agricultural production one of Colorado's leading industries.

In recent years, however, Coloradans have often fought with federal Environmental Protection Agency (EPA) officials over what they think are excessive air, water, and chemical regulations. Thus farmers were annoyed when the EPA outlawed or limited the use of weed spray and animal poison in areas where farmers and ranchers viewed these chemicals as essential.

A "sagebrush rebellion" brewed in the early 1980s in Colorado and other western states in an attempt to force the federal government to turn over large tracts of land to the states. Self-determination and freeing up land for development were the twin goals of the movement. In Colorado, the sagebrush rebellion was strongly backed by energy and cattle interests, and their motto was "resources have been put on earth for men to develop."

In the spring of 1981 a bill was introduced in the Colorado legislature calling for the U.S. government to turn over 16 million acres of national forest and 8 million acres of BLM land to the state by 1983. The bill's supporters argued that "lands held by the federal government are a burden on the state of Colorado" and that "the state could administer them better than the absentee federal 'landlord.'"[7] The bill was vetoed by the Colorado governor, and urban and suburban legislators helped sustain the veto, but the sagebrush rebellion symbolized discontent about the way the federal government dominates much of the Centennial State.

Coloradans are in a long-term, awkward embrace with the U.S. government. The state and its businesses and universities want all the federal grants, subsidies, and assistance possible, yet they do not want, or like, federal standards and controls. Colorado and the federal government need each other, and the question is always one of balance, fine-tuning the relationship, and tactfully negotiating compromises on a whole range of public policy questions.

THE MULTIPLE STATES OF COLORADO

Colorado was born of multiple parents. Native Americans, Spaniards, French, Mexicans, and Anglo-Americans all made a contribution. Colorado remains today a more diverse state than most. Geographical, ethnic, and social divisions abound.

It did not take long after the Anglo-Americans arrived for Denver to dominate territorial and, later, state politics. Denver soon became the financial, political, and cultural capital of the state and remains so today. One consequence of Denver's concentration of population and economic importance is that the rest of the state is at least a little disaffected and sometimes jealous of Denver's multiple powers. Such a relationship lends itself to a "we-they" alienation. Residents of the western slope, especially, believe they are neglected by "the powers that be" over in the big city of Denver. Rural residents often have an anti-Denver attitude. The cities of Colorado Springs, Pueblo, Fort Collins, and more recently Lakewood and Aurora have viewed Denver as a rival, sometimes a bitter one, when it comes to patronage, state projects, federal projects, and other valued commodities. For example, all these communities have economic development councils that compete with Denver to recruit new businesses and more tourism.

Socially and politically, a north-south division also exists in Colorado. Northern Coloradans, probably unwittingly yet nonetheless overtly, look down on Pueblo and many of the southern-tier counties of the state, which are poorer and contain more Hispanics. On more than one occasion it has been suggested that all concerned would be happier if the southern counties were detached from Colorado and merged with New Mexico.[8]

In recent years the development of resort communities in Aspen, Vail, and Steamboat Springs has lured wealthy newcomers who have little or no identification with, nor much interest in, the rest of Colorado. Residents

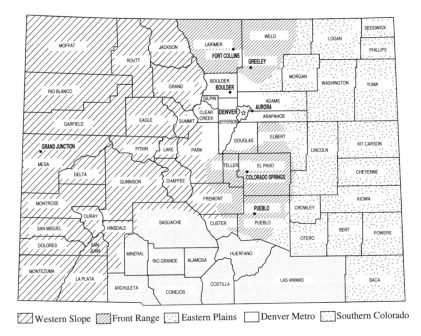

Western Slope [ ] Front Range [ ] Eastern Plains [ ] Denver Metro [ ] Southern Colorado

Map 3.   "The Five States of Colorado"

there often function as foreign enclaves divorced from the central issues and policy debates of the state.

Many analysts have long referred to the distinctive, decentralized sections or regions within Colorado. In the late 1980s several historians and policy analysts suggested the concept of "The Five States of Colorado" as a means of explaining the state's complex cultural and geographical mix (see map 3). The division is a useful one, although it differs from various other divisions of the state used for economic development, congressional districts, tourism, or media markets.

"The Five States of Colorado" project holds that the Eastern Plains, the Front Range, Metro Denver, Southern Colorado, and the Western Slope are the best way of looking at the state's distinctive regions. The project left the boundaries a bit blurry. The Colorado Endowment for the Humanities, which developed the "Five States" concept, noted that many people "in the southeastern corner of the state preferred to be in the Eastern Plains designation rather than Southern Colorado and there is some justification for that."[9]

The *Eastern Plains* comprise nearly 40 percent of the state and consist mainly of high, rolling prairies. This is farm and ranch country, an area resembling popular images of western Kansas more than Colorado. Irrigated farm communities developed in eastern Colorado to feed the massive gold rush migration. These communities grew up mainly along the flood plains of the Arkansas and South Platte rivers. Large cattle ranches also developed in these areas. The U.S. Homestead Act of 1862 brought a large number of farmers and would-be farmers to this region, where farming was (and is) always precarious, subject to drought, prairie fires, grasshoppers, hailstorms, and tornadoes. Diverted water, as well as a major underground water supply (the Ogallala aquifer), and various soil conservation efforts have allowed increased production per acre in this area. But automation and farm foreclosures have had the same effect in eastern Colorado as they have everywhere—a decline in population and a decline in political clout. Less than 10 percent of the state's population lives on the eastern plains.

The *Front Range* (excluding Metro Denver) consists of a string of cities from Fort Collins and Greeley, not far from the Wyoming border, to the major cities of Colorado Springs (270,000 population) and Pueblo (100,000), south of Denver. Some farming goes on in this region, but its altitude of between 4,500 to 7,000 feet makes farming unrewarding. Manufacturing, military installations, space and technology research and development, tourism, and higher education are the main sources for jobs and economic stability. Most of these cities along the Front Range grew dramatically in the post–World War II years, and Fort Collins and Colorado Springs were among the fastest-growing communities in the nation in the 1970s and 1980s.

Metro Denver is the city of Denver plus the suburban counties of Jefferson, Adams, Arapahoe, Boulder, and Douglas. It is, and has been since 1858, the center of the state's population. Over 60 percent of the people in the state live in this Greater Denver area. Colorado's wealth is here. Most of its major universities and businesses are located here, and many of the state's political leaders, not surprisingly, also come from Greater Denver. It is now an accepted rule of thumb in contemporary politics that anyone who can win this region, especially the crucial suburban vote, wins statewide Colorado elections. Of course, many of the greatest policy problems are also located in Metro Denver, such as air pollution, water pollution, hazardous waste, crime, homelessness, and transportation problems.

Southern Colorado comprises the quarter of the state located immediately north of the New Mexico border. In the heart of Southern Colorado is the San Luis Valley, one of the largest and visually most spectacular valleys in America. A large Spanish-speaking population still resides in this valley and around the old mining districts of Trinidad and Walsenburg. The political history of the southern Colorado region is a tale of water rights battles, poverty, and disgruntlement with being ignored by the political leaders in Denver. There has been a certain amount of cultural assimilation among Hispanics, Native Americans, and Anglo-Americans. Population in this region is declining, and poorly financed county and city governments struggle to operate in this sparsely populated area (only about 5 percent of the state's population).

Finally, there is the *Western Slope,* the area from the Continental Divide westward to the Utah border, stretching from New Mexico on the south all the way north to the Wyoming border. This westernmost section of Colorado contains about 12 to 15 percent of the state's population, a third or more of the land, and nearly 70 percent of the state's water. This region contains prodigious mineral deposits and has experienced more than its share of the boom and bust cycle, most recently in the 1980s oil shale boom and bust in the Grand Junction and Rifle regions. Most of the celebrated ski resorts are also on the western slope.

There is a distinct western slope attitude, partly one of feeling exploited by Front Range water boards, developers, and the state's political leadership. Duane Vandenbusche and Duane A. Smith call the western slope region "A Land Alone" in their excellent study of this region.[10] Tourism, mining, and agriculture provide the employment for this part of the state. But few important political leaders come from the western slope, and this leaves residents there with an enduring sense of being unrepresented and even unheard. The western slope is to Colorado what the Berkshire region is to Massachusetts, or even what Quebec is to Canada. These Coloradans are the outside people, and the rugged mountains make them separate, if not separatists, in Colorado political life. Back around the beginning of statehood there was, in fact, a short-lived effort on the part of some southwestern Coloradans to secede from the new state.

In short, Colorado can be divided conveniently into at least five regions, and even these regions are not homogeneous. Aspen, for example, has little in common with Leadville; Rifle is dissimilar to Vail; Colorado Springs and Pueblo differ sharply; and Jefferson and Adams counties are contrasting suburban Denver communities. State leaders are forever challenged by the task of building morale and community across the state for new initiatives. And since the state legislature is a product of these diverse sections of the state, it often falls as a burden on governors to provide unifying statewide leadership.

Colorado "is conservative politically, economically, financially," wrote John Gunther over forty years ago. "I do not mean reactionary. Just conservative, with the kind of conservativeness that does not budge an inch for anybody or anything unless pinched or pushed."[11] This characterization is still true in the 1990s. Colorado is a pro-business, pro-work, antigovernment, and antitax state.

The only governors in Colorado who have been returned to office and accomplished much have been those who built strong ties with the business community. One of the few exceptions was Governor Stephen McNichols, who introduced a number of reform measures in the late 1950s. He was thrown out of office rather unceremoniously in 1962 (after six years in office) for having raised taxes and for being too much of a programmatic liberal.

These days everyone is a fiscal conservative, and as one writer told us, "there is virtually no left left." Neither Governor Richard Lamm nor Roy Romer was a liberal. Indeed, Governor Romer, former Senator Tim Wirth, and Senator Ben Nighthorse Campbell could all be considered "Chamber of Commerce Democrats" on many matters of business and growth. There is a long tradition of conservative Democrats holding statewide office. Governor and U.S. Senator Edwin "Big Ed" Johnson especially typified this tradition from the 1930s to the mid 1950s.

There is an old saying in American politics that the only extreme that regularly wins is the extreme middle. Well, in Colorado the middle is slightly right of center. Normally a conservative or moderately conservative Republican will win statewide elections. Thus Republican candidates for the presidency have usually carried Colorado. Democrats have won only in 1948, 1964, and 1992, but it should be noted that Bill Clinton won only 40 percent of the popular votes in 1992's three-person race for president. "The safe party in Colorado state elections for most people here," says pollster Paul Talmey, "is the Republican party."[12] That is to say, Republicans are more predictably conservative and are the least likely to rock the boat, raise taxes, or introduce real change.

Political observers say there are three parties in Colorado, especially in the state legislature: the conservative Republicans, the moderate Republicans, and the Democrats. This is a useful description. In recent years, Democrats often have been outnumbered in the state's General Assembly by a 2-to-1 margin. However, Democrats have done better than the Republicans at winning the governorship.

Denver Post editor Bob Ewegen quotes the accurate saying that "the differences within the parties in Colorado are greater than between the parties."[13] There are Libertarians and John Birch types loosely affiliated with the Republicans, and a good number of national Democrats and Jesse Jackson-style liberals within the ranks of the Democrats. Yet there are large numbers of conservative Democrats who are just as moderate, centrist, or even conservative as countless Republicans in and out of public office in Colorado. Pueblo and Adams counties are noted for having sizable numbers of conservative Democrats, folks who are probably more conservative on many policy issues than many Fort Collins, Boulder, or Evergreen Republicans.

Colorado's conservatism is well illustrated by the voting patterns in the state legislature, which tends to be cautious about new social and spending programs and generally against taxes. The frequency, and success, of antitax citizen initiatives is yet another indication of the state's conservative attitude. Coloradans favor law and order, but otherwise they merely tolerate government.

Similarly, governor after governor has failed to win much support for major high-cost investments in the state's infrastructure, such as prisons, highways, state parks, or higher education. Yes, occasional victories are won, but only after everyone is "pinched or pushed," to borrow John Gunther's apt phrase.

Colorado politics is also marked by a streak of independence. There is a widespread "leave me alone" attitude among Coloradans. It is partly a "you do what you want to do, but I'll do what I want to do" disposition. A "Make My Day" law, passed and signed into law in 1985, made it legal in Colorado to shoot and kill threatening intruders in one's home.

It is probably true that prior to the 1960s Coloradans were even more antigovernment and antitaxes than is currently the case. Old-timers often dwell on the "frontier ethos" of the Centennial State's past and the appropriate images of rugged individualism and a do-it-yourself society. These legends are probably more mythical and idealized than accurate, as historian Patricia Nelson Limerick has pointed out.[14] Perceptions and attitudes often are different from and exaggerations of reality. Still, the vast in-migration of over a million residents in the past generation has transformed Colorado into a more moderate state. Even newcomers, however, take on some of the coloration of the dominant political values, which include skepticism toward establishments of all kinds, especially elected and party leadership establishments.

One trait of Coloradans that carries over to politics is their fondness for the outdoors. The mountains are the state's icon, and without doubt this love of the outdoors is somehow correlated with a love of freedom and a spirit of independence. It is hard to quantify. But nearly all of the pollsters and political analysts interviewed agreed that this intangible value characterizes the political mood in Colorado.

Political consultant Walt Klein sees Coloradans as having "a streak of independence." You do not have to live in Colorado very long, he argues, before you feel it. Klein believes the independent nature of Colorado voters explains why there is so much ticket splitting in the state. He concludes: "People in Colorado like their state, like their situations far more than in other states, and there is optimism and upbeat good feeling about living in the region."[15]

Colorado ranks third highest in the United States in the percentage of registered independents or unaffiliateds. Only Alaska and Massachusetts have a higher percentage. Political parties are weak in Colorado, and a large number of people who move into the state prefer to wait and watch politics for awhile before affiliating with one or the other party.

Coloradans are independent in other ways, too. They have thrown more judges out of office in judicial retention elections than has any other state of the twenty or more using the Missouri Plan for selecting and electing judicial officials. Colorado also has a larger number of initiative and recall elections than all but a handful of states, such as California, Oregon, and North Dakota. Moreover, it is not uncommon for elected officials to switch party affiliation.

Political parties mean a lot in the state legislature, however, and they still count when people have to vote for candidates they do not know. At least 60 percent of registered voters do have a preference, and even many of the so-called independents lean regularly one way or the other in their partisan preferences. Party orientation, however, declines as a crucial factor in statewide and presidential elections when issues and character qualities are enlarged by television ads, debates, news, and media coverage.

Colorado has a populist tradition as well. Thus miners together with farmers and pro-silver forces helped elect Populist party candidates to Congress and to the statehouse in 1892. The Populist candidate for president also won Colorado's electoral votes that year.

A progressive movement, although different in its bases of support and its goals from the Populist party of the 1890s, also developed in Colorado. Progressive candidates received support from those who believed the existing two political parties (Republicans and Democrats) failed to respond to new and necessitous conditions. Later efforts, such as the anti-Olympics campaign of 1972, the legislature's "sagebrush rebellion" legislation in the 1980s, the tax-limitation and term-limitation campaigns in the 1990s, and the reasonably strong support for Ross Perot in 1992, were illustrative of populist or semipopulist outbursts.

The 1990 campaign for governor opened with a debate before the Colorado Municipal League in which both the incumbent Democrat and the challenging Republican claimed to be the true populist. "I'm probably the most populist governor in the past fifty years in this state," said Democrat Roy Romer. John Andrews, his Republican opponent, replied: "I'm a small 'd' Jeffersonian. I trust the people. I'm a decentralizer. I'm a reformer . . . and I'm an outsider to the political and government establishments. I'm a citizen candidate." And Andrews suggested his stands on issues made him, not Romer, the real populist. "You'll find out, as this campaign proceeds, who really trusts the people," said Andrews. He pointed out that on taxes, voucher systems for school choice, and abortion, he, Andrews, would in effect let the people decide.[16] Populist Romer defeated populist Andrews on election day.

INSTANCES OF INTOLERANCE

Racial and social intolerance are also, sadly, part of Colorado's political heritage. It was first noticeable, of course, in the treatment of Native Americans. Federal treaties that were supposed to be "forever" typically lasted four or five years. In addition to countless broken treaties, there were some instances when early Anglo-Americans in Colorado treated the Native Americans unfairly and denied them the most basic of human rights.

Nativism, at least as it can be used in the context of Colorado history, has an ironic twist to it. The term generally refers to a policy of favoring native inhabitants as opposed to aliens or immigrants. Nativism can also refer to an intolerance or prejudice toward foreigners or those without original or indigenous roots. In the case of Colorado, of course, the Native Americans were resident in the area long before the Anglo-Americans arrived. It was the miners and farmers from New England, Ohio, Illinois, Missouri, Kansas, Texas, and elsewhere who were the newcomers. But many Anglo-Americans assumed a status of superiority and, in the shortest of time imaginable, developed attitudes of exclusion, discrimination, and ill-treatment of anyone not like themselves.

There is a contemporary version of nativism in Colorado. It takes the form of dislike for the large numbers of people who have been moving into

Colorado since the end of World War II. This form of nativism is not usually directed at individuals—people who move to Colorado are personally welcome and are treated like everyone else. The dislike is directed at the effect on the state of having so many newcomers. Among some groups in Colorado, rapid population growth is blamed for causing open fields to turn into housing developments and shopping centers, quiet suburban roads to turn into automobile-jammed highways, and the beautiful mountains of Colorado to be speckled with too many vacation homes and crowded resort communities. The best reflection of this dislike for new arrivals as a group is the large number of Coloradans in the 1980s who drove around with a bumper sticker displaying a ridgeline of the Colorado rockies (similar to the state license plate) with the word *native* printed on it.

It is curious that a state that was reasonably sophisticated in several other ways was discriminatory in its treatment of Native Americans and, to a lesser degree, Mexican-Americans. James A. Michener perhaps overstated the problem, but caught its flavor in his historical novel *Centennial:* "For more than half a century this condition prevailed. No church, no crusading newspaper, no band of women sought to correct this basic evil, and across Colorado, Anglo children who once had been raised to believe that Indians were not humans were now raised to think that Mexicans were even less so."[17]

No matter that this form of discrimination also thrived in neighboring states. It happened in Colorado, and this is a reality in the state's past. Over the years there were countless instances of discrimination against outcast groups, including Catholics, Chinese, and Japanese. One of the worst episodes of outright racism occurred in late 1880 when working-class Anglos literally burned down Denver's small "Chinatown" and lynched at least one Chinese resident in an ugly act of terrorism now known as the Hop Alley riots.

A strong state chapter of the American Protective Association emerged in the 1890s. "Behind the patriotism and morality which the organization preached, there were few who misunderstood its anti-Catholic message."[18] It urged its members to vote Catholics out of office and called for boycotts of Catholic-owned businesses. It gained considerable influence in the Republican party, and it had some support within the Democratic party as well.

Another episode of discrimination in Colorado was the partial takeover of the Republican state party in 1924 by the state Ku Klux Klan. The Republicans nominated and elected a Klansman, Clarence J. Morley, as governor. Several other Klan-backed candidates were elected to major positions, including U.S. Senator Rice Means. Once in office, the Klan members tried to repeal civil rights laws and strengthen enforcement of laws prohibiting alcoholic beverages. They urged measures such as a ban on marriages between whites and Asians and tried to require Catholic children to attend public schools rather than Catholic schools. Fortunately, Republicans opposed to the Ku Klux Klan maintained majority control of the Colorado state senate and voted down most of the discriminatory legislation presented by the Klan.

Colorado was by no means alone in having Klan activity. Along with Indiana and Oregon, however, Colorado was said to be the strongest Klan center outside of the South.[19] It is also a part of Colorado's history that there were at least sixty-eight lynchings in the period 1880 to 1944, one of the highest number outside of the South and border states.

Occasional Ku Klux Klan rallies still are held in Colorado, often on the west steps of the state capitol in Denver, a traditional spot for holding large outdoor political gatherings. Two such rallies, held on the Martin Luther King holiday in January of 1992 and 1993, resulted in ugly confrontations between Klan members and anti-Klan demonstrators. In 1992, in an ensuing street riot, several police cars were overturned and a number of police officers and bystanders slightly injured.

By the early 1990s the Klan had refined its message with such slogans as, "Equal rights for all; special privileges for nobody." The *New York Times* and other national news media interviewed a Klansman from Aurora, Shawn Slater, who led the group that disrupted Denver's Martin Luther King Day celebration in 1992. Slater said that he was not a white supremacist and that he had many black friends. Yet he had been arrested a few years earlier for wearing Nazi emblems. He called his organization "white Christian" and said "there's no way a Jew could get in." He proudly talked of his pilgrimage to Tennessee to help celebrate the 125th anniversary of the founding of the Ku Klux Klan. On his telephone answering machine, the *New York Times* reported, Slater recorded a message saying he wanted to run for governor of Colorado someday, asked callers to leave a message, and then cheerfully added, "Have a nice day for white America."[20]

At one point in Colorado there was an attempt to exclude outsiders for economic reasons. In 1936 Governor Ed Johnson "closed" Colorado's southern border to prevent migrant farm laborers and other "unwanted" individuals from entering the state. Members of the National Guard were sent to the border crossing to repel "aliens, indigents, and invaders." Governor Johnson argued that Mexican beet workers were depriving Coloradans of jobs. "Jobs in this state are for our citizens," he said. "Barricades went up;

trains, busses, cars, and trucks were stopped and occupants questioned. . . ." A headline in the *Durango Herald-Democrat* proclaimed: "Governor Calls Out National Guard to Halt Influx of Undesirables into Colorado."[21] Dozens of non-Coloradans were turned away over a ten-day period. Eventually, this unconstitutional "foreign policy" was rescinded and the border with New Mexico reopened. Still, it was another manifestation of how some people in Colorado feel about "outsiders."

In 1992 nativism again was expressed when Colorado voters approved an initiated constitutional amendment that declared unconstitutional state and local laws prohibiting discrimination against gays. This was a measure sponsored by the religious right—yet it was approved by a majority of Coloradans in one of the largest voter turnouts in Colorado history.

"Coloradans are basically pragmatic," says former Governor Richard D. Lamm. "They are sometimes conservative, sometimes populist. They find neither party always to their satisfaction, and they cross over and switch parties a lot at election time." Then how do things ever get done? Lamm's answer: "Good people have to put coalitions together across party lines and try to bring about progress, and this does happen."[22]

INDIVIDUALISTIC AND MORALISTIC POLITICAL CULTURES

Political scientists use the term *political culture* to refer to a set of widely shared beliefs, values, and norms concerning the relationship of citizens to government and to one another. For example, Coloradans, like most Americans, have always been united by their commitment to liberty and more or less united by their commitment to equal rights and equality of opportunity. Another shared belief is that the government should exist to serve the people rather than the other way around.

Daniel J. Elazar, a student of state politics and federalism, suggested several years ago that there are three dominant types of political cultures or subcultures in the United States—the moralistic, the individualistic, and the traditionalistic.[23] Each of these three cultures first developed on the East Coast and then spread westward as pioneer settlers moved to the Midwest and then to the Mountain West.

The *moralistic political culture* first developed in colonial New England. Mainly because of the influence of the Puritan religion, New Englanders came to view politics and government as existing to promote the public good. They believed it was the job of government to improve society and to build a "commonwealth" in which government would work to better social and economic conditions in the society.

The moralistic political culture came to Colorado as New Englanders spread westward across Ohio and Michigan to Illinois and Iowa and then came up the South Platte River into northeast Colorado and the Denver area. The moralistic political culture was probably best represented in Colorado history in the founding of "colony towns," such as Greeley and Colorado Springs. These towns were specifically founded to be ideal places to live, communities with extensive parks, excellent schools, and other public facilities that would provide what now is known as "a high quality of life."

Sharply contrasting with the moralistic political culture is the *individualistic political culture,* which developed in the Middle Atlantic states, particularly New Jersey, Pennsylvania, Delaware, and Maryland. Free of the moralistic and reformist influences of the Puritan church, the individualistic political culture emphasized the idea that governments should do only those things individuals cannot do for themselves. Thus, government should have no lofty goals or purposes, the individualist culture holds, and should simply create a "marketplace," rather than a "commonwealth," in which individuals are free to compete fairly with one another as they go about leading their individual lives.

The individualistic political culture spread westward to Colorado from the mid-Atlantic states through southern Ohio and Illinois, then across Missouri and Kansas and up the Arkansas River into southeastern and central Colorado. The individualistic political culture was particularly strong among the gold and silver miners who came to Colorado during the gold and silver rushes occurring throughout the state's history. With their willingness to move frequently and to take great risks in hopes of finding a fortune, the gold and silver miners were naturally inclined to the individualistic political culture. Cattle growers, and the nomadic cowboys who worked for them, also represented the individualistic philosophy in Colorado.

The third type of political culture, the *traditionalistic,* is present in Colorado, yet is relatively weak. It came into the state two ways—with the Spanish settlers who came up the Rio Grande from New Mexico, and with former Southerners who came up the Arkansas River.

The Spanish settlers who came into Colorado from Mexico and New Mexico brought with them the political and social conventions of Spain. The Spanish tradition emphasized preservation of the status quo, particularly the idea that the dominant role in society and government should be played by a limited number of socially prominent families with large landed estates. Elements of this Spanish tradition can still be found in southern Colorado, yet it plays a relatively modest part in the state's overall political life.

The traditionalistic political culture of the American South was brought into Colorado by a number of immigrants who traveled up the Arkansas River valley, some of them from Missouri. Similar to Spanish attitudes, the traditionalistic political culture of the southern United States emphasized opposition to rapid change and reliance on well-established groups to govern the society.

The notion of political cultures provides a means for analyzing various patterns of political behavior in Colorado. One of the major enduring divisions in Colorado politics is between the individualistic and the moralistic political cultures. The traditionalistic culture is rapidly fading from Colorado, although some last vestiges of it may be seen in Hispanic communities scattered around the state.

Individualists in Colorado are noted for their strong embrace of economic freedom and their strong opposition to taxes and big government. The moralists in Colorado generally try to make Colorado a better place by using government as a means toward these ends. Thus moralists want better public schools and are willing to pay more for them. Moralists also back reforms of the political process, such as open-meeting laws and campaign finance reform. Where individualists fear and oppose government intrusions, moralists often view governmental programs in a wholly affirmative light.

The Republican-controlled state legislature in Colorado more or less typifies the individualistic culture. Many of the governors in the past two generations, especially Stephen McNichols, Richard Lamm, and Roy Romer, as well as John Love to some extent, have often acted as agents of a moralistic political culture. In broad, general terms the Republican party can be viewed as embodying the individualistic culture, whereas the Democratic party is usually illustrative of the moralistic. Of course, there are various cross-culture political figures in the state, and they are of special interest because of their balancing and perhaps integrating activities. Governor Lamm often reflected this mixed stance.

Neither the individualistic nor the moralistic political culture has succeeded in completely dominating Colorado politics, although the more conservative and sometimes libertarian individualistic culture has enjoyed more success in the past two or three decades. Still, moralism and individualism appear locked in a continuing struggle, one side winning on certain issues and the other winning on yet different issues.

No one individual, leader, party, interest group, or lobbyist rules Colorado. On the contrary, the state's public policy agenda is shaped by a multiplicity of competing interests. As pollster Paul Talmey put it: "There is no one in the state who can say let's do X and it gets done. A few people can veto things. An example was when Speaker of the Colorado House of Representatives Carl 'Bev' Bledsoe was in power in the 1980s, but his power was limited to certain matters."[24] Or as former Governor Lamm remarked, "There is no epicenter" in Colorado politics.

It is not that there are no leaders in Colorado; rather it is just that no one leader in and out of government has great amounts of authority or influence over public policy matters. Colorado's governorship has certain powers, such as the veto and the item veto, and considerable influence in appointing state and district judges, yet Colorado's governor is weak when it comes to shaping the state's budget. The legislature is strong on budget matters, yet few legislators are noted for shaping overall state policy in more than one or two areas, usually the policy areas reflected by their committee assignments.

Interest groups and lobbyists are influential in Colorado, yet, according to one study, they are not as influential or powerful as in many states.[25] Unlike the Anaconda Copper Company's once-strong influence in Montana, or gambling and hotel interests in Nevada, or farming interests in Kansas and Nebraska, Colorado's economy is diversified. Mining and agricultural interests may have once dominated Colorado political decision making, but today tourism, manufacturing, high-tech, space research, and a host of other interests have eclipsed their influence.

In years past, noted lobbyists such as Dave Rice of the Colorado Cattlemen's Association, Ray Kimball of the Colorado Association of Commerce and Industry, John A. Schwartz of the Colorado Fuel and Iron Company, and a handful of lobbyists for AMAX (a major mining concern) were viewed as decidedly influential on matters of state legislation. In the 1990s, more than five hundred individuals were registered lobbyists, and no one or two or even a dozen persons could be singled out as dominant.

Some interest groups are important because they represent significant numbers of people. Thus the Colorado Education Association represents large numbers of teachers, and various public employee organizations represent state and local government workers.

As elsewhere, money in the form of campaign contributions buys access and usually a careful hearing, if not votes. Former state Representative Miller Hudson said, "Colorado's legislators frequently tailor their votes to suit the whims of lobbyists."[26] Among the groups that regularly donate several hundreds of dollars to a large number of legislative candidates are the Colorado Association of Realtors, the Colorado Education Association, U.S. West (telephone company), Colorado AFL-CIO, Colorado Home Builders Association, Coors, Colorado Association of Commerce and Industry, Colorado Rock Products Association, Colorado Trial Lawyers Association, Colorado Association of General Contractors, and various transportation, communication, insurance, financial, and medical associations. It is not uncommon for key legislators to receive $25,000 or more in contributions from political action committees, even though they have relatively safe seats.

Cities and counties and their elected officials are also an important voice in state public policy matters. Groups such as the Colorado Municipal League, Colorado Counties, and the Colorado District Attorneys Council are often cited by state legislators and their aides as "major players" in the way legislation gets written. The Colorado Bar Association is also, on occasion, an influence.

Various citizen and "good government" associations have grown in strength in recent years, and although they are not viewed as "powerful" at the statehouse, they are nonetheless a presence there in raising consciousness about certain issues, demanding hearings, and rallying public support in initiative elections. Groups such as the League of Women Voters, the Sierra Club, Common Cause, the Colorado Open Space Council, and the Colorado Public Interest Research Group, all decidedly rooted in the moralistic political culture, serve as watchdogs for their members. They act as a counterweight to the more dominant financial and business interest groups.

Plainly, certain interests are more powerful than others. Well-known businesspeople and lawyers in or near Denver who successfully solicit large campaign contributions for the governor and key state legislators get a more careful hearing than does a concerned yet average citizen from Conejos, Crawford, Cortez, or Craig. So, too, building contractors and cattle growers are better represented in the state legislature than are the homeless and disabled. Further, those who can afford to hire on retainer certain of the best statehouse lobbyists, such as Frank Hays, Bob Kirscht, or Roger Alan Walton, or who can hire senior partners in the top "Seventeenth Street" law firms to prepare bills and lobby for their interests are in a better position than those who just write letters. But legislators and statewide elected officials do read their mail, and many also hold local town meetings around the state.

Complicating matters further is the fact that for a long while one party, the

Republican party, has controlled the state legislature, and the other party, the Democratic party, has controlled the governor's office. The state's congressional delegation has also been split, often fifty-fifty, in recent years. Similarly, party registration in recent years has been divided approximately three ways, with a third of the voters registered as Republicans, a third registered as Democrats, and a third registered as unaffiliated or independent.

Critics might justifiably call it a "nobody's-in-charge" system. In reality, Colorado has a system of multiple vetoes and a system that forces alliance building and the forging of coalitions across party, ideological, and regional lines. In a state that has distinctive regional barriers and competing political cultures, it is accurate to say leadership in Colorado is dispersed and decentralized.

On occasion, however, a strong governor with a lot of help from leading legislators, interest groups, local officials, and supportive media can bring about innovations and achieve desired breakthroughs. This happened for a few years in the late 1950s under the leadership of Governor Steve McNichols. Sometimes it is the business leaders in and around Denver who lead the way as they, along with the governor, the mayor of Denver, and countless elected and other officials, push for and help achieve a new convention center in Denver and a major new international airport. At other times important water projects have resulted from similar alliances. Also, improvements in air and water quality have been realized only when broad coalitions have been formed to promote these goals.

In sum, citizens in Colorado are represented by elected officials, by political parties, by interest and lobbying groups, by citizen activist organizations, and through regular and direct democratic elections. Colorado politics are characterized by a conservative and partisan legislature, by two statewide newspapers that can be described generally as centrist (with the *Denver Post* generally in the middle and the *Rocky Mountain News* generally somewhat right of center), by constitutionally weak yet entrepreneurial governors, and by an openness and porousness in the policy process. Pro-business and other "inside" lobbyists have a large say in how laws get written and budgets are allocated, but "citizen power" can also be a force in Colorado politics. On a number of matters, such as environmental issues, English as the official language, term limits for elected officials, and antitaxes (to mention just a few), the voice of the people can be influential.

Political and policy leadership in Colorado is fragmented or simply diverse, depending on your perspective. For those who prefer neat, well-organized, predictable statewide leadership, it often looks pretty fragmented. On the other hand, leadership in Colorado can also be described as merely diverse, and thus democratically reflective of the state and its multiple organized interests and representative institutions.

CONCLUSION

Colorado may have an image as a rural state with much of its population living on ranches or farms or in small mountain communities. In fact, however, Colorado is one of the more urban states in the country, with more than 80 percent of its residents living in metropolitan Denver and a group of nearby Front Range cities.

Colorado is a pro-business state, yet it is home to few corporate headquarters. Just as its major mines were once almost wholly owned and operated by out-of-state interests, today Colorado's major businesses, with few exceptions (such as Coors beer), are owned by out-of-state financial concerns.

Colorado is a many-splendored as well as a many-splintered state. It is decidedly remote from most of the major centers of commerce in the nation, and it is also a decentralized and diverse state. Its diversity reflects a citizenry of varied backgrounds and political views.

Still, the state's enormous assets, such as its people, its spectacular beauty, and its wealth of minerals and tourism opportunities, considerably outweigh the state's liabilities. Colorado's problems are viewed by most of its citizens as challenges, or even as opportunities, not as paralyzing burdens. Unifying leadership may be hard to come by and hard to exercise in Colorado, yet somehow it emerges, at least from time to time.

CHAPTER TWO

A Sociopolitical History of Colorado

NATIVE AMERICANS

Among the first permanent residents of what is now Colorado were Native Americans living at Mesa Verde in the southwest corner of the state. Called the Anasazi, or ancient ones, they first occupied the area in the first century A.D. Initially they lived in pit houses dug into the earth and covered with a thatched roof. Later, they built masonry-style villages on the mesa tops. They then moved to cliff dwellings, elaborate structures built in large niches halfway up the walls of canyon cliffs. Frequently, high solid rock overhangs protected these cliff communities from the elements. To most people, these early Coloradans are known as the cliff dwellers.

For some unknown reason, the cliff dwellers departed Mesa Verde by 1300, and what was once a booming native culture, now noted for its basket weaving and pottery, was abandoned.[1] The cliff dwellings at Mesa Verde, the first of Colorado's many ghost towns, today are preserved as Mesa Verde National Park.

Up until the late 1800s, more nomadic tribes of Native Americans were moving in and out of present-day Colorado. The Apaches, Navajos, Comanches, Pawnees, Kiowas, Cheyennes, Sioux, and Arapahoes all hunted and lived in the area at one time or another. The most permanent Native American residents were the Utes, whose language was similar to the Shoshones. The Utes were not agricultural, living instead by hunting and enjoying the spoils of war making. They inhabited and in effect possessed the major mountain areas of Colorado at the time of the earliest European explorations and remained there for many years to come.

The first European nation to claim a portion of what is now Colorado was Spain. After conquering Mexico under the leadership of Hernando Cortez, the Spaniards explored and colonized to the north, working their way up the Rio Grande through what is now New Mexico to Santa Fe and Taos. Probably one of the first persons of European origin to enter Colorado was Juan de Archuleta. Sometime between 1664 and 1680 he traveled through southeastern Colorado while searching for runaway Native Americans who had escaped from their Spanish masters in Taos. Archuleta found his way to the Arkansas River and explored the general area along the Colorado-Kansas border.

Over the next century the Spanish occasionally entered what is now Colorado to chase runaway Pueblo Native Americans or to fight the roaming Native American tribes that periodically attacked the Spanish pueblos from the north. In 1776, the year of the Declaration of Independence and the early stages of the American Revolution, two Spanish priests, Francisco Dominguez and Silvestre Escalante, led a major expedition that explored much of western Colorado, particularly the area around the present-day cities of Durango, Paonia, and Grand Junction.

In 1787, in an effort to get the Comanches to lead a more settled and less-warlike life, the Spanish governor at Santa Fe, Don Juan Bautista de Anza, founded a settlement for the Comanches on the Arkansas River near the present-day city of Pueblo. The first attempt to establish a permanent settlement in what is now Colorado was underway. Governor Anza sent workers and supplies to build houses. Seeds were provided to plant crops, and cattle and sheep were sent to provide the new community with milk, meat, and clothing.

This first European-originated settlement in Colorado was named San Carlos. During its first year, a Comanche woman died at the village, and the other Comanches took this to be a sign of divine disapproval of the new community and quieter way of life. The Comanches abandoned San Carlos, and the Spaniards were unable to convince them to return. Thus Spain's first attempt to found a settlement in Colorado ended in failure. It would not be the last town in Colorado to "give up the ghost" and disappear.

In 1762 the French ceded all of their claims west of the Mississippi River, known as Louisiana, to the Spaniards. In 1800, however, Spain traded Louisiana back to France in return for a kingdom in Italy. Thus Spain, which had claimed most of what is now Colorado since the 1500s, traded away its title to much of the area. Despite its avowed interest in precious metals, particularly gold, Spain had done little with its claim to Colorado. It never pushed its settlements significantly north of Santa Fe and Taos. The great gold and silver wealth of Colorado, which Spain had "owned" for almost three hundred years, would be discovered, mined, and spent by others.[2]

THE LOUISIANA PURCHASE

By the year 1800, domination of North America by Europe was coming to an end. The thirteen British colonies on the Atlantic seaboard had won their Revolutionary War and established the United States as an independent nation. Napoleon Bonaparte, the ruler of France, was having trouble maintaining control of France's many possessions in the New World, so he offered to sell all of his Louisiana territory to the United States. The Louisiana Purchase, completed in 1803, brought the vast lands west of the Mississippi River and north of the Arkansas River under U.S. control. Because the Arkansas River runs through southern Colorado, the northern two-thirds of what is now Colorado became part of the United States.

President Thomas Jefferson quickly dispatched official expeditions, paid for by the U.S. government, to explore the vast, unknown territory that the young nation had acquired. The famed Lewis and Clark expedition explored the northern part of the Louisiana Purchase by traveling up the Missouri River. On July 15, 1806, U.S. Army Lieutenant Zebulon Montgomery Pike and a party of men set out from Fort Belle Fontaine, north of St. Louis, to explore the southwestern portion of the purchase.

Pike traveled by horseback across what is now central Kansas and then advanced up the Arkansas River to present-day Pueblo. As he crossed the prairie, he noticed a mountain peak to the northwest that stood alone as a prominent landmark. For two and a half days Pike and his party attempted to climb the great mountain, but eventually they had to give up because of their light clothing and the waist-deep snows surrounding the mountain top. Since Pike was the first American to describe the mountain and attempt to climb it, those who came after him called it Pike's Peak.

Pike continued his explorations in the general area of southern Colorado. His party encountered Spanish soldiers from New Mexico, who detained and questioned them but eventually released them. Zebulon Pike's distinguished military career ended during the War of 1812, when he was fatally wounded in Canada leading the U.S. attack on the British at Toronto, Ontario. The easternmost 14,000-foot peak of the Rocky Mountains bears his name, however, and it was the name *Pike's Peak,* not *Colorado,* that first identified the general region that is now Colorado.

Another U.S. explorer was Major Stephen H. Long, who set out from Council Bluffs, Iowa, in 1820 and advanced up the Platte River to the South Platte. The spectacular 14,000-foot peak he saw and described, considerably north of Pike's Peak, would later be known as Long's Peak. The Long party passed through the present sites of the cities of Denver and Colorado Springs. Three members of the group, led by scientist Dr. Edwin James, succeeded in climbing Pike's Peak.

BEAVER TRAPPERS AND BUFFALO HUNTERS

Throughout the early 1800s the area that is now Colorado belonged to the "mountain men"—the beaver trappers and fur traders who explored the Rocky Mountain regions but did not settle there. It was European fashions that brought these "lone explorers" to the edge of the mountain frontier. Hats made from beaver pelts were popular with European men at the time.

The trappers worked out of Santa Fe and Taos in New Mexico. Many of them were French and gave French names, such as St. Vrain and Cache La Poudre, to many of the rivers in northern Colorado. The closest the beaver trappers and fur traders came to settling in the Rocky Mountains was holding periodic "rendezvous," large encampments where they would sell and trade furs, restock their provisions, and socialize, mainly by telling stories of their explorations and exploits in the mountains. The fur trade faded when beaver hats were no longer popular in Europe, but many of the trappers switched to hunting buffalo on the eastern plains and selling "buffalo robes."

THE SANTA FE TRAIL

In 1820 Mexico revolted from Spain and became an independent nation. Unlike the Spanish, who wanted to keep U.S. commercial interests out of New Mexico, the newly independent Mexicans welcomed trade with the United States. Wagon trains set out from Independence, Missouri, carrying U.S. goods to Santa Fe, where they could be sold for large profits.

The shortest route of the Santa Fe Trail crossed Oklahoma into New Mexico, but the Mountain Branch, which was longer yet had more reliable water supplies and less danger from Native Americans, crossed through southeastern Colorado. In 1833, between the present-day cities of La Junta and Las Animas, the trading firm of Bent, St. Vrain and Company built Bent's

Fort on the Mountain Branch of the Santa Fe Trail. The fort, constructed of thick adobe with high watchtowers at two corners, served buffalo hunters and beaver trappers as well as wagon traders traveling the Mountain Branch of the Santa Fe Trail. Bent, St. Vrain and Company later built Fort St. Vrain on the South Platte River near the present town of Platteville to serve as a trading post for northeastern Colorado.

Although the trappers, traders, hunters, and trading post operators did not found permanent settlements in the area, they made significant contributions. The valleys and passes of the mountain regions were explored by these mountain men, and later their maps and stories would help guide other men and women into these once-remote regions. Contact had been made with the Native American tribes of the area, and in many instances trade had been established between the Native Americans and the newcomers. Most important, these frontier people demonstrated the mountain and prairie wilderness of Colorado was liveable.

SAN LUIS

In 1845 the United States annexed Texas from Mexico, thereby gaining the land south of the Arkansas River claimed by Texas. Following the Mexican War, at the Treaty of Guadalupe Hidalgo in 1848, the United States gained from Mexico virtually all of the remaining land that comprises the southwestern United States, including southwestern and western Colorado. Thus the entire land area of what is now the state of Colorado belonged to the United States beginning in 1848.

In 1851 New Mexican settlers came up the Rio Grande valley and established a permanent settlement at what is now San Luis, Colorado. Of Spanish origin, these settlers constructed homes and public buildings of adobe. They also dug the San Luis People's Ditch, the oldest irrigation canal in Colorado in continuous operation. The oldest water rights recognized in Colorado were claimed by these first settlers at San Luis. In 1858 the first church in Colorado was constructed at the nearby town of Conejos.

Other New Mexican settlers soon followed the founders of San Luis. They brought with them the Spanish names (such as Alamosa, Antonito, and Conejos), architecture, and lifestyle that had come from Spain through Mexico to New Mexico. A distinctive and rich Spanish influence still exists in southern Colorado today.

San Luis is the oldest permanent settlement in the state. It is noteworthy, however, that almost two hundred years passed between the time Juan de Archuleta entered Colorado in the middle 1600s and the time when the first permanent Euro-American settlement was established in 1851.

GOLD

The Colorado region was a quiet place in the mid 1850s. The fur trade had faded almost completely, and most of the trading posts on the Arkansas and Platte rivers were abandoned. The only permanent settlements of European origin were the small New Mexican colonies in southern Colorado. The vast area of mountains and plains surrounding Pike's Peak mainly belonged to the mountain Utes and the nomadic Native Americans on the eastern plains.

In February of 1858 William Green Russell and his two brothers, Oliver and Levi, left their home in Georgia with the intent of prospecting for gold in the Rocky Mountains. William Russell had found and mined gold both in Georgia and in the California gold rush of 1849. He and his brothers accumulated a sizable party of would-be miners and came up the Arkansas River into present-day Colorado. They continued north until coming to the spot, just east of the Front Range of the Rocky Mountains, where Cherry Creek flows into the South Platte River.

There was no gold at Cherry Creek. A short distance away, however, at the mouth of Dry Creek, the Russell party panned out several hundred dollars worth of gold dust. The small pocket was soon exhausted. As recounted later by historians, "The quantity was insignificant, but it was, perhaps, the most important discovery ever made within the region, for from this meager showing the great Pike's Peak gold rush developed."[3]

Word of the Russell party's discovery quickly spread eastward, and Colorado's first great mineral rush was underway. It was called the Pike's Peak gold rush because the prominent mountain seventy miles to the south served to guide the prospectors to the mining areas. In 1859 additional and more lucrative gold strikes were made along Clear Creek and Boulder Creek (South Platte River tributaries) at Central City, Idaho Springs, and Boulder.

To serve these booming mining areas, supply towns were built at the foot of the Front Range of the Rocky Mountains. The most important of these supply towns, Denver, grew up at Cherry Creek and the South Platte River. Denver was near the site where gold was first discovered; therefore, Denver was the starting point for everyone looking for gold of their own. Other important supply towns were founded at Golden (west of Denver), Colorado City (now part of Colorado Springs), and Canon City (on the Arkansas River west of Pueblo).

The importance of the Russell brothers' striking gold near the present-day city of Denver cannot be minimized. The major effect of the strike was to draw large numbers of people into what is now Colorado from the eastern, midwestern, and southern United States. Although not so numerous or famous as California's "forty-niners," Colorado's "fifty-niners" came in large numbers and began the process of populating a previously remote and forbidding area. The number of people from the East, Midwest, and South who came to search for gold, or to service those who were doing the searching, soon greatly outnumbered the persons of New Mexican origin who settled in southern Colorado.

It was the miners who were generally responsible for the way the Utes and other Native American tribes were pushed out and away from the mineral-rich mountains and the prairie and foothill trails that led to the mountains. The Utes were pushed ever westward, particularly when additional minerals were discovered on lands once ceded to the Utes. For the miners it was "the Ute Problem," and eventually the cry of the day became "The Utes Must Go!" "Wherever Anglo-Americans contended with the Indians for land, conflicting interests led to disputes and the triumph of the former's overwhelming number, resources and superior technology."[4]

At the time of the 1858 gold strike in Colorado, the "agricultural frontier" was still back in the general area of the Missouri River. Homesteaders, those sturdy farmers who took virgin lands, broke them with the plow, and turned them into productive agricultural areas, had not advanced anywhere near Colorado. This meant that Colorado was not founded as a rural-agrarian community of farmers, which is the way most other states in the United States were first populated and developed.

The people who rushed to Colorado in and shortly after 1858 were interested in pursuing an urban-industrial process, the mining of precious minerals. Instead of founding small rural towns, as happens in rural-agrarian areas, they founded towns and cities (i.e., urban areas) that served as either mining camps or supply towns. Except in San Luis and the other Spanish-oriented towns of southern Colorado, where the lifestyle was rural-agrarian, Colorado bypassed the rural-agrarian stage and, through mining and city founding, went directly to the urban-industrial stage.

The increase in population caused by the Pike's Peak gold rush led almost immediately to various proposals for organizing as a territory the area that is now Colorado. In 1861, only three years after gold was discovered at Dry Creek, Congress enacted the necessary legislation creating the Territory of Colorado. Fifteen years later, in 1876, Colorado became a state.

Gold mining in Colorado boomed throughout the early 1860s, and Colorado gold stocks boomed on the New York Stock Exchange. At one point the stocks of more than two hundred Colorado mining companies were being traded on major eastern stock exchanges. Adding to the Colorado gold euphoria, which was turning into investment madness, was the fact that gold found in Colorado during this period was largely free gold, chemically separate from other elements. Only a minor amount of crushing and washing was required to redeem the gold and prepare it for sale.

By early 1864, however, the rumor began to spread that the gold-bearing ores were beginning to dwindle in Colorado. Further, it appeared that the "easy" gold had run out. Now the ores being brought out of the ground had their gold mixed with other elements, and simple mechanical procedures were no longer sufficient to set the gold free. In April of 1864, the Colorado gold-mining bubble burst. The price of Colorado gold-mining stocks collapsed on the eastern stock exchanges. Colorado, famous for its giant boom, was experiencing its first major bust.

Colorado's first mineral depression began to ease in 1868 when Nathaniel P. Hill, a professor of chemistry at Brown University, developed an efficient and profitable process for separating gold from gold ore. He organized Colorado's first ore-reduction company, the Boston and Colorado Smelting Company, and built the state's first gold smelter at Black Hawk, a mining town adjacent to Central City. As Colorado entered the 1870s, the gold-mining industry began to revive.

SILVER

In the 1870s the renewed gold boom in Colorado was joined by a silver boom. Similar to the deeper gold ores, the problem with silver was that it was tightly mixed with other materials. By 1870, however, working silver smelters were in operation, and one mountain town after another boomed as silver discoveries were made and publicized. With each new find, the word spread, excitement built, and people rushed to the new "El Dorado." There seemed to be a promise of wealth for everyone. This process repeated itself in the silver areas of Colorado over and over again. As the mines and enthusiasm played out in one area, another strike somewhere else would reinitiate the entire process.

The first of the "silver queens" was Georgetown, located west of Denver in a scenic valley just east of the Continental Divide. Soon silver camps were everywhere in the mountains of Colorado, from Caribou, in Boulder County northwest of Denver, to Aspen, in the central mountains, to Silverton, in southwestern Colorado. Another major silver area was Creede, which boomed in the early 1890s. Yet another silver mine blossomed just south of Crestone at the eastern edge of the San Luis Valley. Perhaps the most notable silver strikes of all, however, were in Leadville, in the mountains nearly one hundred miles southwest of Denver, where lucky finds and smart deals made millionaires, and men such as Horace Tabor and Leadville Johnny Brown became national personalities.

Horace Tabor was a veteran prospector and storekeeper. As a storekeeper, he grubstaked (gave provisions and mining tools for free) two miners in return for an interest in whatever they found. What they found was the Little Pittsburg, a silver mine in Leadville that produced handsomely and lifted Horace Tabor and his wife, Augusta, from middle-class respectability to millionaire status. Tabor subsequently bought the Matchless Mine, which produced millions in silver for almost a decade.[5]

Like many of Colorado's gold and silver millionaires, Tabor gave part of his money to the mining town that had made him wealthy. He built the Tabor Opera House in Leadville and sought the best-known performers in the eastern United States and Europe to perform in it. In the most famous social scandal in Colorado history, he divorced Augusta, his first wife, and married a younger woman, Elizabeth McCourt, who was nicknamed Baby Doe.

Tabor used his money and his fame to enter politics. He served as the first mayor of Leadville; later he was elected lieutenant governor of Colorado and served briefly as U.S. Senator. Eventually his wild speculations and the collapse of the silver-mining industry exhausted his wealth. He died penniless, and his wife, Baby Doe, lived the remainder of her life in poverty at the Matchless Mine, waiting for a silver revival that never came.

In a very real sense, Baby Doe Tabor was like tens of thousands of Coloradans, living in bleak, difficult conditions, hoping against hope that a boom would transform their lives. Centennial State residents thrive on the booms and the hope of booms and simply mark time during the periodic busts.

Tabor himself was, in many ways, the living symbol of Colorado in the late nineteenth century. A respectable middle-class man, he gained fabulous wealth through a series of lucky mineral strikes. That wealth, however, led to an almost reckless and unrestrained lifestyle and, eventually, to disastrous overspeculation. Tabor's life "boomed" and "busted" much as the gold and silver mines did. The Tabor legend is nicely captured in the modern opera *The Ballad of Baby Doe*.

Leadville Johnny Brown, a second prominent mining personality, struck it rich at Leadville. He and his wife, Molly, moved to Denver and used Johnny's millions to try to buy their way into respectable Denver society. Molly was on board the ocean liner *Titanic* the night it struck an iceberg and sank in the North Atlantic. Although most of the passengers drowned, Molly succeeded in getting to a lifeboat and survived this great maritime tragedy. Her ocean adventure earned her the nickname "Unsinkable," and her life with Leadville Johnny Brown was romanticized in the New York musical *The Unsinkable Molly Brown*.

As the years passed, the day of the individual prospector rapidly gave way to large corporate mining operations. Solo prospectors with picks and shovels were displaced by mining companies using expensive steam and electrical appliances, especially steam drills. Wrote Emma F. Langdon, an activist historian in Cripple Creek: "The speculators and capitalists came to get that which the prospector had found, and from then until now every inch of valuable ground, staked as a claim by the miner, has in some manner found its way into the hands of corporation capital."[6]

RAILROADS

The famed mining era in Colorado corresponded to the railroad era. In 1869 the Union Pacific Railroad and the Central Pacific Railroad joined their rails at Promontory, Utah, thereby completing the first transcontinental railroad. Because of the high mountain barrier west of Denver, the railroad had been built to the north of Colorado, through Cheyenne, Wyoming, on a route with a lower and easier crossing of the Continental Divide. Suddenly it appeared that Cheyenne, on the Union Pacific's transcontinental main line, and not Denver, which had no railroad at all, was going to be the major metropolis of the Rocky Mountain region.

Not to be outdone, Denver political and business leaders organized a Board of Trade and began raising money to build a branch line off the Union Pacific from Cheyenne to Denver. The project was linked with a plan to lay rails east from Denver and to connect with the western terminus of the Kansas Pacific Railroad in western Kansas. The Union Pacific and Kansas Pacific railroads supported the combined plan, both hoping to profit by serving the mining industry in Colorado. In June of 1870 the Cheyenne-to-Denver line was completed, and in August of 1870 the final spike was driven on the line joining Denver and Kansas City. Colorado now had two railroad connections to the rest of the United States.

The completion of the Kansas Pacific Railroad earned Colorado a spot in U.S. railroad history. At the same time one construction crew was laying track eastward from Denver, a second crew went to work in western Kansas building westward toward Denver. A friendly competition developed between the two crews. On the last day before the rails were joined, the two crews laid more than ten miles of track in ten hours time, a construction rate of one mile per hour.

More significantly, the completion of the Kansas Pacific Railroad across eastern Colorado meant there now existed an *all-rail* connection between the East Coast and the West Coast of the United States. Although the Union Pacific and Central Pacific went into the record books as the first transcontinental railroad, the Union Pacific used ferryboats rather than a railroad bridge to move its trains across a major river. That meant there was a break in the rails. The Kansas Pacific Railroad, however, had a railroad bridge over every river and thus no break in the rails. Not until the Kansas Pacific was completed at Strasburg, a small farming community in eastern Colorado, was there a *continuous* rail connection from one coast to the other. A small monument and city park in Strasburg commemorate this Colorado contribution to railroad history.

At the same time the Kansas Pacific Railroad was completed, William J. Palmer, who had been a Union general in the Civil War, began the construction of the Denver and Rio Grande Railroad. He built his main line southward from Denver down the foot of the Front Range. Later branch lines running westward into the mountains were added to serve the mining camps.

Because he intended to route his railroad through mountains and canyons, General Palmer built his tracks "narrow gauge," with only three feet between the rails, instead of the "standard gauge," four feet, eight and one-half inches. This "baby railroad" would be able to climb steep mountain grades and twist around tight canyon curves that standard-gauge tracks and trains could not handle. Other railroad builders decided to follow Palmer's example, and soon the mountains of Colorado were laced with narrow-gauge track.

As the Denver and Rio Grande Railroad was being built southward from Denver, the Santa Fe Railroad entered Colorado by building a line up the Arkansas River from Kansas. Soon the Rio Grande and the Santa Fe were locked in a bitter and well-publicized "railroad war" to see which company could first lay track through the Royal Gorge west of Canon City. The Arkansas River canyon was so narrow in the Royal Gorge area there was barely room for one railroad track, let alone two. According to legend, the rival railroad construction crews fought over the Royal Gorge, one crew secretly tearing up at night the track that had been laid by the other crew during the day. Actually, before much violence took place, the conflict was transferred to the courts. After much arguing and many meetings (a key one in Boston), the Rio Grande won the right to build westward through the Royal Gorge in return for allowing the Santa Fe the exclusive right to build southward into New Mexico over Raton Pass.

The railroad industry was an ideal companion to the mining industry. As word of new gold and silver strikes spread to the East, would-be prospectors and miners could ride the train to Colorado instead of having to come by horseback, wagon, or stagecoach. This facilitated population growth during the gold and silver era. Once mineral strikes were made, railroads could make money hauling in the heavy machinery used in large-scale mining operations. Railroads also could haul out of the mining camps the gold and silver ore and carry it to the smelters, many of which were located in the supply cities, such as Denver and Colorado City, at the foot of the Front Range.

With each new gold or silver strike, the various railroad companies in Colorado would race to see which one could build the first rail line into the new mining camp. The company that reached a major strike area first would reap handsome profits hauling in people and supplies and hauling out the mineral ore. Railroaders became prospectors themselves, laying tracks into the mountains of Colorado and gambling that sometime in the near future a major gold or silver strike would be made close to their line. The Denver and Rio Grande Railroad and its founder, General William J. Palmer, seemed particularly bold and adventurous in this regard. "It was a railroad with a master prospector at the helm, one that followed the miner and his burro, bound for where they were headed, looking for the same thing, wherever it was."[7]

The coming of the smelters and the railroads added to the urban-industrial character of early Colorado. Denver in the north and Pueblo in the south became major rail junctions on the Front Range, and their urban populations increased accordingly. Because of the smoke and cinders of puffing steam engines, and the smoke pouring from the smokestacks of the smelters, many Colorado cities and towns developed a decidedly industrial look.

LABOR UNREST

Along with the mines, the smelters, and the railroads came labor unions, and with the unions came labor strikes and labor unrest. Some of the union strikes at the gold and silver mines were particularly bitter, resulting in violence on the part of both strikers and strikebreakers and attracting national attention. In one incident in 1904, thirteen people were killed when a railroad station was dynamited during a miners' strike at Cripple Creek, a booming gold camp southwest of Colorado Springs.[8] In an ugly 1914 clash between striking coal miners and the state militia at Ludlow, a coal-mining area north of Trinidad, nineteen people were killed, including two women and eleven children.[9] A poignant United Mine Workers of America memorial, less than a mile off today's Interstate 25, marks the site of what laboring men called "the Ludlow Massacre."

The Cripple Creek and Ludlow episodes were only two among many clashes between the mineworkers and the mine owners. Whom one favored in these struggles usually shaped one's political values and election preferences. State politics for nearly fifty years was affected by the politics of mining and the political and economic struggles between workers and their employers. During much of this time Republicans, aided by mining money, controlled state government.

A different approach was taken by Josephine Roche, a mine heiress who had seen firsthand the indecent conditions of the miners. She vowed to be a fair-minded and responsible mine owner and set out to prove one did not have to mistreat mineworkers as other absentee mine owners regularly did. She paid her miners $7 a day, a very high wage at the time, and they responded with high rates of production. In 1934 Josephine Roche was a candidate for governor (the first woman to run for governor in Colorado), but she failed to be elected.[10]

COLONY TOWNS

Not everyone who came to Colorado in the 1870s came to be a miner, a merchant, or a railroader. Some came to found new communities, often with a religious or philosophical theme. Most of these settlements were intended to be agricultural, or at least agricultural centers, but others were founded as resort and vacation communities. In most cases these "colonies," as they liked to be called, were located on the Front Range and relied on irrigation from nearby rivers to provide water for both agricultural and human needs.

Usually the colony was organized and promoted in some eastern or midwestern city. A large tract of land would be purchased, houses and stores would be built, and people would begin coming to the colony, usually by train. In fact, many of the colony towns were aided in their development by the railroads, which had land along their tracks to sell and made money hauling goods and people to and from the new communities.

One of the more famous colony towns was Greeley. Organized by Nathan C. Meeker, the agriculture editor of a New York newspaper, the town was named for Meeker's well-known editor and publisher, Horace Greeley. At a meeting in 1869 in New York City, the colony was organized, a constitution was drafted, and memberships were offered for sale to "temperance men of good character."

Greeley was located on land purchased from the Denver Pacific, the rail line from Cheyenne to Denver. Nearby was the point at which the Cache La Poudre River flowed into the South Platte, so there was an ample supply of water for irrigated agriculture. The town prospered and, as its temperance-oriented founders intended, became a cultural center with a library and a theater association.

Colorado Springs was an interesting variant of a colony town. General William J. Palmer founded the city at the foot of Pike's Peak along the Denver-Pueblo main line of his Denver and Rio Grande Railroad. Palmer intended his new community to be a Rocky Mountain resort city for well-to-do Americans from the East Coast. Colorado Springs indeed became the first genuine resort west of Chicago. "Though it had no springs, Palmer named it Colorado Springs because most of the fashionable resorts back East had the word *springs* attached to their name."[11] He hired a city planner to design a community of wide streets and beautiful parks. He provided space for the development of future artistic, cultural, and educational institutions, including a college. His theory was that Colorado Springs should be the most attractive place for homes in the West.

Similar to Greeley, Colorado Springs prospered and became an important city. Two other successful colony-type towns were Longmont and Fort Collins, located at the foot of the Front Range north of Denver. Many other colony towns did not succeed, however, either because they were poorly planned and located or because they were, or became, semifraudulent real estate promotions. Similar to the mining towns, some colony towns boomed, and some went bust.

CATTLE

As prospectors and miners poured into Colorado, closely followed by merchants and railroaders, there suddenly was a market for agricultural produce. As the various gold and silver strikes changed the mountains, they also changed the eastern plains, because it was there that some of the new arrivals began attempting to grow food to take to market in the mountain mining camps and the supply cities at the foot of the Front Range.

At first it was not believed that the high, dry prairies in eastern Colorado could support large cattle herds. A popular legend holds that many prospectors and freight wagon drivers, after arriving in Denver or Colorado City, would turn their oxen loose on the eastern plains, certain that the animals would meet an early death from starvation. The oxen flourished on the native grasses of the high prairies, however, thus demonstrating that Colorado's eastern plains had the potential to be good cattle country.[12]

Almost from the moment of the first gold strike at Dry Creek, Texas cattle growers began driving cattle northward from Texas to supply meat to the gold and silver camps. The first official report of a Texas herd reaching what is now Colorado was in 1859. By the 1870s, when the railroads reached as far west as Denver, Texas cattle growers would drive their herds north into Colorado, fatten the animals on the prairie grasses of the eastern plains, and then ship the cattle eastward to market by rail. Two of the best-known cattle-drive trails entering Colorado were the Dawson Trail and the Goodnight Trail.

Colorado soon developed its own "Cattle Kings," men in the Texas tradition who owned giant herds grazing on large spreads of both public land and privately owned land. John Wesley Iliff, who supplied beef to Union Pacific Railroad construction crews, owned 15,000 acres of rangeland stretching along the South Platte River from Greeley to Julesburg. John Wesley Prowers owned forty miles of river frontage on the Arkansas River, enough land and water to graze herds of 10,000 cattle.

The cattle industry on the eastern plains and elsewhere in Colorado became so big that laws had to be passed to regulate it. In 1871 the territorial legislature passed a "roundup law" regulating the rounding up and branding of cattle grazing on Colorado's millions of acres of public land. A "brand law" was passed in 1872 requiring county clerks to eliminate duplicate brands. In 1879 the state legislature divided Colorado into sixteen "roundup districts" because the counties were too small for effectively rounding up the large herds grazing on the open range at that time. In 1885 the legislature passed a law requiring that all cattle brands be registered with the secretary of state of Colorado.

As farmers began to fence the open range, cattle growers began to do the same thing. What once was "cattle ranging" on public land became "cattle ranching" on private land. Although the giant herds grazing on vast stretches of public land are a thing of the past in Colorado, the cattle industry remains today an important part of the state's economy.

Colorado lies well west of the 100th meridian, that north-south line in western Kansas and Nebraska that marks the boundary between the Midwest and West. West of the 100th meridian, annual rainfall is so low that it becomes a major problem where agriculture is concerned. In Colorado the rainfall averages only ten to eighteen inches a year, considerably less than the minimum requirements for "traditional farming" as it is practiced in the more humid sections of the United States.

The first Europeans to settle in Colorado, those of Spanish origin who moved into the San Luis Valley from New Mexico, had little difficulty adjusting to farming under such dry conditions. They copied the dams and irrigation ditches that were used to irrigate crops throughout the Rio Grande valley in New Mexico. If there had been more contact between the two groups, the Hispanic settlers of southern Colorado could have taught their new northern neighbors much about successful irrigation techniques.

In northern Colorado many disappointed prospectors and miners, failing to strike it rich in either gold or silver, turned to the trade they had grown up with—agriculture. Having learned farming in the East, however, they had to unlearn much of their previous agricultural knowledge and begin anew.

In 1859 David K. Wall diverted water from Clear Creek near the town of Golden and successfully grew two acres of vegetables. Others soon copied this idea of irrigating nearby lands with diverted river water, and lands accessible to both the South Platte and Arkansas rivers were dotted with small irrigation systems and small farms.

Soon farmers were banding together to form cooperatives and corporations for building more elaborate irrigation systems with larger and longer canals that could irrigate the tablelands or "bench" lands a considerable distance from the riverbeds. Large reservoirs were constructed to store the precious river water so that it could be released for irrigation at exactly the time in the growing season that the farmers needed it. As previously noted, the promoters of colony towns, such as Greeley, relied on community irrigation systems to make their agricultural utopias bloom.

As might be expected, water regulation and water law became a crucial part of early Colorado legal history. The doctrine of "prior appropriation," the idea that water in a river or stream "belonged" to the first person who found and used it, was written into the new state constitution when Colorado Territory became a state. In 1879 the legislature divided Colorado into water districts and provided for state administration of water rights. In 1901 the legislature passed a law permitting landowners to organize and finance irrigation projects through state-sanctioned "special irrigation districts." At the same time, the office of the state engineer was created to determine water availability in Colorado and to gather information that could be used in settling water disputes and making water policy.

Although irrigated agriculture became widespread in Colorado, millions of acres of land on the eastern plains remained high and dry prairie grass. Many attempts to plow and plant these lands were made during the 1880s and 1890s, particularly in small communities located along and promoted by the various east-west railroad lines. In periodic "wet" periods when rainfall would increase, prairie farmers would bring in a grain crop or two and make some money. The "wet" periods were soon followed by "dry" periods and widespread crop failures, however, and disappointed farm families would attempt cattle ranching or give up and move away. Boom and bust became a part of life on the dry prairies, just as it was in the gold and silver camps.

In the early 1900s, however, farmers made a new attempt at dryland farming on the prairies of Colorado. The state Agricultural College at Fort Collins experimented with various methods and techniques of getting crops to survive on low amounts of annual rainfall. The Colorado state dryland experiment station, founded at Cheyenne Wells in 1893, aided in the development of drought-resisting crops. Farmers learned to plow and till their lands in ways that prevented the evaporation of precious moisture. By 1910 the eastern plains, particularly the high prairie between the South Platte and Arkansas rivers, had became a successful dryland farming area, with wheat one of the principal crops.

The need to feed the miners, and the merchants and railroaders who came close behind them, led to relatively rapid agricultural development in Colorado. The rise of the cattle industry, irrigated agriculture, and dryland farming in Colorado was not as spectacular and well publicized as the gold and silver strikes. Still, agriculture developed steadily in the state. Yet the rural-agrarian lifestyle on the eastern plains generally developed after, not before, the development of an urban-industrial lifestyle in the mining areas in the mountains and the supply towns on the Front Range.

EARLY TWENTIETH CENTURY

The situation quieted down in Colorado as the twentieth century began. In the 1890s the U.S. government refused to set an official price for silver, with the result that the price fell dramatically and silver mining ceased to be a highly profitable enterprise. Major gold discoveries at Cripple Creek and Victor, two mining towns located on the south slopes of Pike's Peak, brought a gigantic mining boom to that area. The millionaires created by this great gold strike lavished their civic affections on Colorado Springs, the neighboring supply town located at the eastern foot of Pike's Peak. As the federal government moved away from gold money and began to emphasize paper currency in the twentieth century, however, even the boom and glory of Cripple Creek and Victor began to fade.

Like many states, Colorado experienced a period of progressive political reform in the years between 1900 and 1920. In 1907 the legislature adopted the state's first civil service statute for state employees. The legislature also created a state railroad commission to regulate railroads in Colorado. Other major reforms of the period included the adoption of the initiative and the referendum, a primary election law, child labor laws, and laws requiring state safety inspections of factories. A state soil conservation commission also was created. Plainly the moralistic political culture was in the ascendancy in Colorado between 1900 and 1920, as so many progressive reforms were adopted.

Prohibition of the sale and use of alcoholic beverages was an issue in early twentieth-century Colorado. Statewide prohibition of alcoholic beverages was defeated at the polls in 1912, but two years later statewide prohibition was adopted by the voters.

Colorado did its part when the United States entered World War I. The state sent its share of young men to fight in the trenches in Europe, but no major war industries or military bases were located in the Centennial State during that war. Similar to the rest of the nation, Colorado experienced an upsurge in anti-German feelings that evolved into antiforeignism during the post–World War I period.

THE TWENTIES AND THIRTIES

A flood roared down the Arkansas River in 1921 and devastated the Front Range city of Pueblo. In order to get state funds to rebuild the city and construct large flood-control dikes along the Arkansas River to prevent a similar disaster in the future, Pueblo political leaders agreed to support the use of state money to build a railroad tunnel west of Denver.

Up to this time, there had been no direct rail route running west out of Denver to Utah and beyond. Passengers and freight bound west from Denver had to travel north to Cheyenne or south to Pueblo in order to make a rail passage through the Rocky Mountains to Salt Lake City and the West Coast. The new railroad tunnel, the Moffat Tunnel, brought Denver the direct western transcontinental rail connection the city had long desired. It meant there was now a direct transcontinental rail route through Denver that could compete for transcontinental freight and passenger traffic with the earlier transcontinental rail routes constructed across southern Wyoming (Union Pacific Railroad) and New Mexico and Arizona (Santa Fe Railroad).

By the end of the 1920s the mining era was about over. Agriculture had become important, and so had the manufacturing industry, particularly in Denver and Pueblo. With the rise of the automobile and the development of national and state highway systems, tourists began coming to the mountains of Colorado in their automobiles rather than on the train. As automobiles became more dependable and the state highway system improved, auto tourism would become a vital part of the Colorado economy.

The 1920s were the years in which Colorado, and the Colorado lifestyle, became similar to the rest of the United States. The gold and silver mines had played out, most of the booming mining towns were ghost towns, and the "roaring and bawdy" life of the mining era was mainly a treasured memory. Most Coloradans now worked on the farm or in the factory or in the office building. The only mining towns with a future were those few, such as Central City and Aspen, that would become either tourist attractions or ski resorts in the latter part of the twentieth century.

Along with the rest of the United States, Colorado suffered economically during the Great Depression of the 1930s. There was little change, however, in the character of the state. The years from 1919 to 1939 thus were relatively quiet ones. Population growth was slow, and both mining and agriculture had fallen upon hard times. "Observers might understandably predict that the glorious days of the Centennial State had passed; and never again would excitement like that generated by a Leadville or a Cripple Creek lure the fortune-seekers and fortune-makers."[13] Colorado was in one of its bust periods, and as always happened at such times, people wondered if it would ever boom again.

WORLD WAR II

World War II witnessed a major turning point in Colorado history, almost as great a turning point as the discovery of gold on the banks of Dry Creek near Denver in 1858. The Japanese attack on Pearl Harbor plunged the nation into a major war. In the all-out effort to win, the U.S. government sought to expand both military and industrial capacity. Colorado benefitted greatly from this process, more so than most states. The war brought military installations and industrial expansion that completely changed the state, not only during the war itself but long after it ended.

In 1941 the federal government built the Denver Arms Plant, a large arsenal and ammunition works manufacturing cartridges, shells, and fuses. In 1942, on open land just to the northeast of Denver, the Rocky Mountain Arsenal, a chemical warfare plant, was constructed. A Medical Depot was built in northeast Denver and an Ordnance Depot at Pueblo.

The Army Air Forces operated an instruction center for pilots at Lowry Air Base just east of downtown Denver. In Colorado Springs, Peterson Air Field trained bomber crews. Also in Colorado Springs, Camp Carson, now Fort Carson, became a major army training center, particularly for tank warfare. Wounded soldiers recuperated at the army's Fitzsimons General Hospital in Denver.

One effect of the large number of military production and training facilities in Colorado was to expose hundreds of thousands of war workers and service personnel and their families to the attractive climate and recreational potential of the Centennial State. People stationed in Colorado during the war found they liked the sunny, dry climate and the hiking and skiing in the nearby Rocky Mountains. Consequently, after the war was over, many of the wartime visitors moved to Colorado and expanded the state's postwar population.

Along with these many military installations came a budding scientific and defense research industry. Military technology advanced rapidly during World War II, and there was money to be made by firms that specialized in carrying out military research and technological development. Wishing to locate close to the military installations they served, many of these research and development firms chose to locate in Colorado.

The development of the Cold War between the United States and the Soviet Union immediately following the war sustained the military-industrial boom in Colorado. Fort Carson remained a large and active army training center, thereby continuing the population boom in Colorado Springs. The North American Aerospace Defense Command (NORAD), the U.S. Air Force facility charged with defending the United States and Canada from attacking bombers and guided missiles, was located in Colorado Springs, as was the new U.S. Air Force Academy, a military college for training air force officers. West of Denver the U.S. government built Rocky Flats, a major nuclear weapons facility.

Most of the military-industrial expansion in Colorado during and after World War II was centered along the Front Range, particularly in Denver and

Colorado Springs. In the Denver area, many of the new facilities were located in the Denver suburbs rather than in the city itself, thus contributing to rapid suburban growth in the Denver metropolitan area. World War II not only led to increasing population growth in Colorado; it centered that population growth along the Front Range.

In the years following the war, therefore, Colorado rapidly changed from an urban-industrial society into a metropolitan-technological society. In the sprawling suburbs of Denver and the quiet residential neighborhoods of small cities such as Boulder and Colorado Springs (Colorado Springs is sometimes called a suburb without a city), Coloradans were able to have the pleasures of small-town life combined with the convenience and economic opportunity of being close to a major city. The typical Coloradan no longer was a miner or an industrial worker in Denver or Pueblo. The typical Coloradan now was a Denver suburbanite, living in a ranch house and working either in an office building in downtown Denver or in one of the many office parks being built in the Denver suburbs or along what would become interstate highways 25, 70, 76, or 225.

Because World War II was a global conflict, the U.S. Army built Camp Hale high in the Rocky Mountains in the Holy Cross National Forest. Here ski troops were trained in the deep powder snow of the Colorado winter. After the war, a number of these ski soldiers returned to Colorado and played a leading role in the development of major ski facilities and ski communities at such places as Aspen and Vail.

Like the gold and silver boom in the late nineteenth century, the World War II military boom attracted new residents with an individualistic political culture. As hundreds of thousands of service personnel and war-plant workers poured into Colorado, enterprising investors found considerable wealth to be made in real estate, shopping center construction, and other consumer-related enterprises. Business boomed along with the military bases and the military-industrial plants, drawing to Colorado thousands of new residents who were committed to the individualistic philosophy of rapid economic development and free-market profit making. Colorado was once again attracting prospectors, but these new prospectors were coming with blueprints for housing developments and shopping centers rather than picks and shovels.

ENVIRONMENTALISM

As the Front Range continued to boom in the years following the Second World War, so did recreational developments in the nearby mountains. Well-to-do Coloradans, and people from other states as well, began buying second homes in the Colorado mountains. Some were condominiums or chalets in ski areas. Others were "hideaway" homes in more remote areas of the state. In addition to urban sprawl on the Front Range, Colorado was experiencing "resort sprawl" in the mountains.

By the late 1960s and early 1970s, the idea began to grow among a number of Colorado citizens that the concept of "Sell Colorado" had been oversold. People who had moved to Colorado for blue skies, bright sunshine, and exhilarating clear air began to notice that many days of the year certain Colorado cities were covered by a brown cloud of air pollution. Except where national parks and national forests protected them, the formerly pristine mountainsides of Colorado were being cluttered up with vacation homes. Traffic congestion was making Denver almost as unpleasant to drive in as major cities in the Midwest and on the coasts. People began talking about "quality of life" in Colorado as well as "economic opportunity."

The rise of environmentalism as a political issue in Colorado was sharply posed in 1972 when the electorate voted against holding the 1976 Winter Olympic Games in the state. Both the business community and the political leadership had worked hard to get Denver selected over a host of competing cities as the site of the 1976 winter games. Critics, including a young state representative named Richard Lamm, charged the Winter Olympics would overdevelop mountain recreation areas, cause mammoth traffic problems, and increase air pollution. Opponents petitioned the question of holding the 1976 Winter Olympics in Colorado onto the 1972 general election ballot, and hosting the Olympic Games was defeated statewide by more than 180,000 votes. The actual ballot question was a constitutional amendment that prohibited the expenditure of state funds. There also was a Denver city charter amendment that prohibited the expenditure of city funds. "This was the only way we could get a handle on the issue that would actually 'stop' the Olympics," said John Parr, a key organizer of this pro-environment drive.[14]

Concern for the environment represented the rebirth of moralistic political culture in Colorado. Environmentalists were willing to limit the right of individuals to develop their land in any manner they saw fit.[15] Environmentalists emphasized the unique natural beauty of Colorado and called for the preservation of this natural beauty for the common good. In the moralistic-culture tradition, environmentalists turned to government and urged better planning, government-designated wilderness areas, and more national parks and forests as ways to keep Colorado in a more natural state.

The history of Colorado is the history of boom and bust. The discovery of gold in the Denver area ignited a mineral boom that was truly spectacular in the later decades of the nineteenth century and lasted for several years into the twentieth century. In most cases, however, boom towns became ghost towns, and during the 1920s and the 1930s Colorado became a quiet place.

World War II launched Colorado's second great boom. This boom was based on the military needs of the United States during the war and the Cold War that followed. Military research and development became a major part of the Colorado economy in the post–World War II years. Skiing and tourism also flourished in the 1950s and 1960s.

The failure of the Spanish attempt to found a village for the Comanches at San Carlos near Pueblo in 1787 was an important event in Colorado history. If San Carlos had succeeded, the Spaniards probably would have founded more villages in Colorado, and Spanish culture and architecture might have spread widely. As it was, San Carlos failed, and the possibility of a dominant Spanish influence in Colorado was lost.

Following the discovery of gold and silver in Colorado, both the individualistic and the moralistic political cultures gained influence in the state. Prospectors, miners, and farmers were strong representatives of individualistic culture. Yet founders of the colony towns, with their emphasis on community values and cooperation, symbolized the moralistic culture.

These two political cultures continue today to battle for the political mind of Colorado. The individualistic political culture calls for developing the state's economy and attracting new businesses and more people. The moralistic political culture shows more concern for environmental and quality-of-life issues, calling on government to adopt programs that will preserve the natural beauty and enjoyable ambiance of the state, for newcomers as well as old-timers. These clashing political approaches have battled throughout the history of Colorado. They battle still.

CHAPTER THREE

Colorado in the Federal System

When Zebulon Montgomery Pike was exploring eastern Colorado in the early 1800s, he built a small fortification, a breastwork of logs, for defense against hostile Native Americans or Spaniards. He located this minor military project on the north bank of the Arkansas River at the site of the present-day city of Pueblo. The Pueblo telephone directory identifies the location of Pike's log fort as an historic site. If you take the time to visit the location, however, you will find a thriving automobile dealership.

Pike's breastwork of logs in Pueblo represents an important aspect, perhaps the most important aspect, of Colorado governmental history. Modest though it doubtless was, the little log fortification represented the first U.S. government project undertaken and successfully completed in Colorado. It was a harbinger of projects to come. The federal government has played a major role, in many ways *the* major role, in the growth and development of the Centennial State.

There are several reasons for the important role of the federal government. Colorado was not one of the original thirteen colonies. It began as a territory in 1861 rather than as an independent state. The first official government in Colorado—the territorial government—was created by the Congress in Washington, D.C., and not by the people of Colorado themselves. Colorado won its statehood and its own state government later.

Another reason why the federal government is so important in Colorado is its enormous land holdings. About 37 percent of the land in Colorado is federally owned, most of it in national forests and national parks. Four percent is designated as wilderness areas. As the principal landowner, the federal government has a major voice in what happens in Colorado.

An additional factor adding to the influence of the U.S. government is the harsh mountain and desert climate in Colorado. Large federal public works projects, particularly water projects, have been undertaken to make the state more suitable for agricultural and urban development. Colorado lacked the resources to build large water-diversion and electrical-generation projects itself. The U.S. government provided much of the capital for Colorado's internal development, thereby helping the state to overcome its challenging semiarid climate.

Last, and anything but least, since the end of World War II, U.S. government civilian and military installations and related private industries have become a major component of the Colorado economy. Decisions made in Washington, D.C., to locate major federal facilities in Colorado have been indispensable to the development of the state. Lobbying the federal government to locate military installations and governmental offices in Colorado has been a regular part of the state's effort to better itself.

Thus, more than in most states, Colorado's relationship to the federal government has been a critical part of the state's history. Ironically, although Colorado is dependent on the U.S. government for much of its economic success, the state's citizens often have little good to say about the national government and its politicians and administrators.

THE CIVIL WAR

Because Denver is approximately 1,600 miles from Washington, D.C., government officials back in Washington often do not see things the way people in Colorado see them. Colorado is a vastly different place from the nation's capital. Its dry climate and forbidding mountains create problems that are unfamiliar to people in Washington, most of whom are from states with large amounts of annual rainfall and much less challenging geography.

Colorado was designated a United States territory on February 28, 1861. Within a year the newly appointed territorial governor, William Gilpin, became embroiled in a strenuous argument with Washington over how the Civil War should be handled in Colorado.

Gilpin arrived in Denver in May of 1861. He found Denver and Colorado solidly in the Union camp, yet there were pockets of Confederate activity in the territory, particularly near Pueblo and Leadville. Denver's first mayor, John C. Moore, left the territory to join the Confederate army. Another Southern sympathizer, A. B. Miller, openly recruited volunteers to join him in going back to the South to fight for secession.[1]

The U.S. government did have a military presence in the region. The army had two garrison forts, Fort Garland in the San Luis Valley and Fort Wise (later renamed Fort Lyon) in eastern Colorado on the Arkansas River. Governor Gilpin worried, however, that the intensity of the Civil War in the East would cause the U.S. Army to ignore frontier areas such as Colorado. He was particularly concerned Confederate troops from Texas or Oklahoma might invade the territory in an attempt to capture Colorado's newly discovered gold mines and thereby help to finance the Southern war effort.

Gilpin decided to act. He appointed a military staff, began to raise a volunteer infantry regiment, and started collecting guns, rifles, and other necessary instruments of warfare. To finance this essentially unilateral and in effect unauthorized territorial militia, he issued $375,000 in draft notes and guaranteed that the drafts would be paid by the U.S. Treasury. Colorado merchants and tradespeople honored the drafts, and soon the territory had a well-trained and well-equipped infantry regiment composed of ten companies of soldiers.

U.S. government officials in Washington did not share Governor Gilpin's fears of a Confederate invasion. They announced that the U.S. Treasury would not honor Gilpin's drafts, which made him very unpopular with the merchants and others who had put up money for his venture. Gilpin then had to do what many Colorado officials have often done in more recent years. He returned to Washington, D.C., to explain the situation and plead the case for Colorado to unsympathetic federal officials.

In the meantime, Gilpin's view of the military situation in the Mountain West turned out to be more accurate than the view prevailing in the national capital. A Confederate army unit moved across the southwestern desert from Texas up the Rio Grande into northern New Mexico. Led by West Point–educated General John Sibley, the Confederates captured Santa Fe and then marched north toward Colorado and its mineral riches.

The Battle of Glorieta Pass

Gilpin's regiment of infantry, known as the First Colorado Volunteers, headed south out of Denver in February of 1862. Word had come from the Union regulars in New Mexico that help was indeed needed. North met South, or Coloradans plus other Union regulars met Texans, in battle about sixteen miles east of Santa Fe at Glorieta Pass. Located at the southernmost tip of the Sangre de Cristo range, this pass has an altitude of at least 7,500 feet and is marked by rugged piñon and other scrub pine trees and reddish soil.

The Battle of Glorieta Pass took place in late March of 1862. Texans outnumbered Union forces and made initial advances. On March 27, however, Major John P. Chivington of the Colorado forces took a group of soldiers and, with the help of local guides, marched in a twelve-mile sweep through unmarked trails around and behind the Texan forces.

This maneuver succeeded brilliantly. Once Chivington's men had wiped out a small rear guard of Confederates, they destroyed wagonloads of food, ammunition, and supplies. They killed a dozen or so mules and disabled a cannon or two as well. Too undermanned to attack the rebel forces from the rear, they slipped back through the forests around the fighting to rejoin the Union troops.[2]

General Sibley, the Confederate leader, was soon informed his supplies had been destroyed. He had no choice but to retreat. He led his troops back down the Rio Grande to Texas. The heroic Coloradans had helped to deal the Texas Confederates a fatal blow in this "Gettysburg of the West." The Civil War was over for Colorado.[3]

Governor Gilpin's decisive actions in preparing Colorado for war were vindicated. The Treasury Department eventually honored the $375,000 in drafts. Gilpin had become so controversial, however, that President Abraham Lincoln had to remove him as territorial governor. In this first conflict between the "Colorado view" and the "Washington view," however, the "Colorado view" had proven to be the correct one.

REMOVAL OF NATIVE AMERICANS

Prior to the discovery of gold in what is now Colorado, the United States government had negotiated a treaty with local Native Americans designating large stretches of land between the South Platte River and the Arkansas River as Native American hunting lands. As soon as gold was discovered, however, miners and tradespeople raced across eastern Colorado toward the gold fields, trespassing on Native American lands and demanding that the federal government extinguish the Native American claims and make the land available for settlement and ranching.

Federal agents tried to solve the problem by restricting the Native Americans, mainly Arapahoes and Cheyennes, to a triangular-shaped reservation on the banks of Sand Creek, a tributary of the Arkansas River in southeastern Colorado. The U.S. government provided neither fences nor soldiers to mark the boundaries of the reservation, however, and the younger and more aggressive braves began raiding ranches and settlements nearby. On June 11, 1864, Native American raiders savagely attacked a ranch about twenty-five miles southeast of Denver, killing a rancher, his wife, and two daughters. Their mutilated bodies were publicly displayed at the post office in Denver.[4]

Native Americans were considered to come under the jurisdiction of the federal government, but the people of Colorado Territory demanded instant action. Colonel John Chivington, the experienced military leader who had distinguished himself and his command at the Battle of Glorieta Pass, and a regiment of volunteer soldiers, authorized by the War Department in Washington, set out to retaliate against the Native Americans, who were camped at Sand Creek. As the sun rose on the morning of November 29, 1864, Colonel Chivington ordered his men to attack the unsuspecting Native Americans. The troops went out of control, killing and mutilating braves, squaws, and children. Later estimates of the number of Native Americans killed ranged from one hundred to five hundred.

The Sand Creek engagement was one of the most controversial events in Colorado history. Supporters of the Native Americans, and there were many, pointed out that the Native Americans were camped on a federally designated reservation and were sleeping peacefully at the time they were attacked. Supporters of Chivington noted that a number of settlers had lost their lives in Native American attacks and that fresh white scalps were found in the camp when the conflict was over.

The U.S. government ended up as ambivalent about the events at Sand Creek as the people in Colorado. An investigation by a joint committee of Congress described Sand Creek as "a foul and dastardly massacre." Despite that finding, the federal government continued to remove the Native Americans from Colorado and locate them in other states or in far southwestern Colorado. In 1879, following the massacre of Nathan Meeker and eleven other men in northwestern Colorado, the Utes, the last group of Native Americans to roam free in Colorado, were removed to distant reservations.

THE HOMESTEAD ACT

The U.S. government carried out the wishes of many Coloradans where removal of the Native Americans was concerned. In the case of the Homestead Act, however, the national government failed to comprehend the situation in Colorado completely. Passed by Congress in 1862, the Homestead Act permitted the head of a family to gain title to 160 acres of government land by settling on the land and paying a small fee.

The members of Congress who voted for the Homestead Act assumed that the size of the average family farm in the United States should be 160 acres. A farm that size made perfect sense in the well-watered East and Midwest. In high and dry Colorado, however, 160 acres was much too small for a farm to be a viable economic operation. Low rainfall meant low crop yields, thus a successful farm in dryland areas needed to be considerably larger. The same logic applied to cattle ranching. In a state where a rancher needed 50 acres of land for each cow, a ranch of 160 acres made little sense.

Congress failed to respond to the cries from Colorado to permit larger homesteads in low rainfall areas. Homesteading was such a popular concept, however, that farmers from the East and the Midwest continued to come and attempt to operate a dryland farm on only 160 acres. As might be expected, the result was frequent failure. The abandoned cabins and houses of these unfortunate homesteaders, who had the cards stacked against them before they ever began, still dot the Colorado countryside.

Early in the twentieth century Congress began to raise the acreages for homesteading, yet it never raised them enough to make homesteading on the dry plains a successful venture. In 1909 the basic homestead size was raised from 160 to 320 acres, and in 1916 the size for homesteads used for raising cattle and sheep was raised from 320 to 640 acres. These actions were too little and too late, however. Only where irrigation was available, mainly in the Arkansas and South Platte river valleys, were the 160-acre farms mandated by the Homestead Act generally successful in Colorado.

In the 1870s Colorado cattle growers strongly lobbied Congress to preserve the "open range" style of cattle raising by creating 3,000-acre homesteads for ranching in dry areas. Congress failed to act on this proposal, however, and the opportunity to preserve the giant cattle herds of Colorado's early frontier history was lost.

To be fair, the U.S. government did a few things right. As noted, water-scarce Colorado adopted the concept of "prior appropriation," the idea that water in a stream or river belonged to the first person who found and used it. Congress recognized the unique water situation in Colorado and the Rocky Mountain West when, in 1866, it enacted legislation endorsing the doctrine of "prior appropriation" for scarce western water resources.

The federal government also joined Colorado in experimenting with and developing improved techniques for dryland farming. The U.S. Department of Agriculture, for example, opened a dryland experiment station at Akron, Colorado, in 1907, thus enhancing the efforts of the state dryland experiment station at Cheyenne Wells, which had been in operation since 1893.

SUGAR BEETS

The high altitude, cool weather, and controlled irrigation of farmlands made Colorado an ideal state for the sugar beet industry. Following the opening in Grand Junction in 1899 of Colorado's first factory for processing sugar beets into table sugar, the industry grew in the state, particularly in the Arkansas and South Platte river valleys.

The sugar beet industry is dependent, however, on U.S. tariff policies. Because of the expensive industrial processing required to turn sugar beets into marketable sugar, sugar made from beets cannot compete in the domestic marketplace with cane sugar from the Caribbean unless there are high import duties on cane sugar. Thus, as much as any other agricultural industry in the state, the sugar beet industry depends for its success on policymakers in the nation's capital.

THE SILVER STRUGGLE

The greatest conflict between the U.S. government and the state of Colorado was over the issue of silver coinage in the 1890s.

The silver mines in Colorado were so productive that by 1874 the value of the silver being mined in the state exceeded the value of the gold being mined. By 1881 Colorado was the leading silver-producing state in the nation. As silver production increased, however, the price of silver fell. Silver was such a large part of the Colorado economy that almost everyone in the state believed a way must be found to maintain a high price for silver.

As so often happens when the free market fails to produce results, Coloradans turned to the U.S. government to support the price of silver. The most popular suggestion was that Congress purchase silver for coinage at a fixed rate of sixteen ounces of silver for the same price as one ounce of gold. This sixteen-to-one ratio, advocates contended, would increase the price paid for silver and, at the same time, enlarge the money supply, thereby inflating the national economy.

Throughout the 1880s the citizens of Colorado organized to build public support for the free and unlimited coinage of silver. A national Silver Convention, held in Denver in 1885, created the Silver Alliance, which organized silver supporters throughout the state. In 1889 Colorado sent forty-three delegates to the second national Silver Convention, held in St. Louis. In 1892, when a third national Silver Convention met in Washington, D.C., Colorado sent representatives from 220 silver clubs with more than 40,000 members. "The foundation had been laid; the silver banner raised."[5]

Congress responded to the clamor for free silver with the Sherman Silver Purchase Act of 1890. This law doubled the amount of silver being purchased by the United States government to 4,500,000 ounces a month. Instead of purchasing the silver at a ratio of sixteen to one with gold, however, the new law provided for the national government to purchase the silver at the market price.

At first the Sherman Silver Purchase Act increased the market value of silver. As hoped, increased federal purchases reduced the supply of silver. The effect on Colorado was entirely beneficial because by 1890 the state was producing almost 60 percent of all the silver mined in the United States. The higher prices did not last, however, as production quickly increased to meet the government-stimulated demand. By 1892 the price of silver was falling again, and the economic health of the state of Colorado was falling with it.

In terms of national politics, neither the Republican nor the Democratic parties wanted to offend their eastern supporters, most of whom believed in a noninflationary currency based on gold. The result was disillusionment with both national political parties on the part of many Colorado voters. The situation improved for Coloradans in 1892 when a third political party, the Populists, endorsed the free coinage of silver. The Populists believed that increasing the supply of silver coins would have an inflationary effect on the national economy, thereby improving financial conditions for the common people.

In 1892 the Populists nominated James B. Weaver of Iowa as the party's candidate for president. Within Colorado, a full slate of Populist candidates was nominated for all major state offices and the state legislature. Democrat Grover Cleveland won the national presidential election in 1892, but Colorado cast its electoral votes for Weaver. The free silver–Populist political revolution did not stop there, however. The Populists elected the governor and the state's two members of the U.S. House of Representatives, and they gained a majority in the Colorado Senate. Thus even though the silver crusade in Colorado did not win much of a response in Washington, it had an extensive impact on politics in the Centennial State.

The price of silver continued to fall, and Colorado went into an economic depression. Silver mines closed, businesses that supplied them went bankrupt, and Denver banks failed. Instead of coming to Colorado's rescue, however, the national government marched in the opposite direction. President Cleveland called for the repeal of the Sherman Silver Purchase Act, blaming it for the economic depression that was gripping the entire nation at the time. Despite the heroic efforts of Colorado's Senators and Representatives in

Congress to save it, the Sherman Silver Purchase Act was repealed, and almost all hope of the U.S. government supporting the price of silver was lost.

Silver made its last political stand in the presidential election of 1896. Although there were many Republican elected officials in Colorado in the late nineteenth century, the Republican national convention of 1896 refused to help Colorado in any way. William McKinley received the Republican nomination for president and vowed to run on a platform supporting a single monetary standard for the United States—gold. Colorado's best-known Republican, U.S. Senator Henry Teller, walked out of the 1896 Republican national convention in protest.

At the Democratic national convention, however, the free-silver supporters were in control. William Jennings Bryan received the Democratic nomination for president. The party platform called for free and unlimited coinage of silver at the sixteen-to-one ratio. In one of the most famous political speeches in U.S. history, Democrat Bryan pledged to save the nation from crucifixion upon "the cross of gold." The election of 1896 became known as "The Battle of the Standards" because the Republicans were completely committed to the gold standard and the Democrats were completely committed to bimetallism, basing the currency on both a gold and a silver standard.

The election of 1896 thoroughly disrupted normal political party voting patterns in Colorado. U.S. Senator Henry Teller and the "Silver Republicans" threw their support to Bryan and the Democratic candidate for governor, Alva Adams. Colorado Republicans who supported the national ticket ended up in the difficult position of arguing for both William McKinley and the free silver that McKinley so vociferously opposed.

On election day of 1896, William Jennings Bryan and the Democratic ticket swept the state. Bryan defeated McKinley, 161,269 votes to 26,279. Democrat Alva Adams was elected governor, and the Democratic–Silver Republican coalition swept all the major state offices.

For all the hue and cry, however, the great silver crusade failed to change national politics. Republican William McKinley won the 1896 presidential election, and in doing so he defeated once and for all the idea of free coinage of silver. His victory made it plain that the U.S. government was not going to subsidize the silver industry. The great boom days of the silver mines were now definitely over.

Gold mining in Colorado met the same fate. The federal government set the price of gold so low that it was soon no longer profitable to mine gold. Most of the gold camps gradually turned into near ghost towns. Unlike silver, however, the gold mines shut down quietly, and there was no major political effort in the state to save them. The failure of the silver crusade of the 1890s probably convinced most Coloradans that efforts to save gold mining with federal government purchases and price supports would prove fruitless.

More than any other event in the state's history, the silver controversy illustrated the extent to which Colorado's fortunes were tied to national politics and policies. Although silver never came back, the idea of the federal government playing a leading role in what happens in Colorado certainly did.

NATIONAL FORESTS

One of the most controversial federal policies in Colorado has been conservation. Many of the state's citizens strongly support the idea that the United States should pursue policies that preserve Colorado's mountain forests, prairie grasslands, and wild rivers and streams. Other Coloradans become anxious when the federal government implements conservationist policies, fearing lumber companies will be prevented from cutting timber, cement companies will not be allowed to operate gravel quarries, and scenic lands will not be available for real estate development and sale.

By the mid 1880s conservation-minded citizens had become concerned about the overcutting of forests in the state, particularly those forests which surrounded the headwaters of major rivers. If these areas were logged and used for agriculture, the denuding of the mountainsides would greatly reduce stream flow into the rivers, disturbing the irrigation systems and city water supply systems located further down the river valley. Because virtually all of the high mountain forest areas were on public lands belonging to the federal government, Colorado's early conservationists began lobbying Congress to preserve and regulate the use of these critical forest lands.

In 1891 President Benjamin Harrison placed more than one million acres in northwestern Colorado in the White River Plateau forest reserve. It was the first forest reserve designated in Colorado, the second one designated in the nation. By placing the White River Plateau in the forest reserve, President Harrison was, in effect, halting unregulated use of these lands by private citizens. Over the next two years Harrison designated four more forest reserves in Colorado, one of which included Pike's Peak and its surrounding foothills immediately west of Colorado Springs.

At first the forest reserves stirred little controversy in Colorado, mainly because the federal government did not patrol them and enforce the forest laws. In 1897, however, the national government tightened its procedures for administering the forest reserves, putting an end to unregulated timber cutting and stock grazing. In some instances fences and corrals built by stock grazers were physically destroyed by federal government personnel. Immediate protests arose, with critics of the forest reserves charging that Colorado's "states' rights" were being callously overridden by the national government.

Under President Theodore Roosevelt, whose "stewardship" concept called for active federal involvement in preserving the natural beauty of the nation, fourteen new forest reserves were created in Colorado between 1902 and 1907. By 1908 almost 16 million acres of Colorado fields and forests had been withdrawn from the public domain and placed in forest reserves.

In June of 1907 a Public Lands Convention was held in Denver to oppose the expansion of the forest reserves. Speakers at the convention condemned both government interference in individual activity and the extension of national power into matters which, they said, should only be of state concern. These speakers were assuming, perhaps rightly, that Colorado would not be as aggressive as the federal government in adding large acreages to the forest reserves. The Public Lands Convention gave western opponents of the forest reserves an opportunity to express their antagonism toward national forest policies, yet the forest reserve program was not reversed.

There were some minor adjustments, however. Congress combined and consolidated the forest reserves into a system of national forests. A greater emphasis was placed on wise use of national forest lands, with scientific timbering and private stock grazing permitted on a fee basis under watchful government regulation. Later on, portions of the national forests would be developed into major ski areas in Colorado. Hiking trails and camping facilities also were located on national forest lands. As the national forests came to serve agricultural and recreational uses as well as conservation goals, they became increasingly popular.

NATIONAL PARKS AND MONUMENTS

Throughout the 1880s and 1890s, professional and amateur archaeologists unearthed and carried away the Native American artifacts found in the cliff dwellings and mesa-top villages at Mesa Verde. Hundreds of bowls, baskets, tools, and other items of archaeological value were removed, some of them ending up in museums as far away as Helsinki, Finland. In 1906 preservationist groups in Colorado convinced the federal government to create Mesa Verde National Park, both to prevent the "ruining of the ruins" and to make this ancient Native American dwelling place accessible to the public.

In 1911, southwest of Grand Junction, the national government created Colorado National Monument. This action preserved a valley filled with giant red and yellow rock formations, many of them carved by the elements into fascinating shapes.

In 1915 Colorado was granted its second national park. Rocky Mountain National Park consists of more than four-hundred square miles of mountain scenery atop the Continental Divide northwest of Denver.

In 1932 Great Sand Dunes National Monument was created on the west slopes of the Sangre de Cristo mountains northeast of Alamosa. In 1933 a breathtakingly beautiful deep canyon lined with black rock, located east of Montrose in western Colorado, was designated Black Canyon of the Gunnison National Monument.

Similar to national forests, national parks and national monuments had their critics. Once designated, these lands were removed from state and local tax rolls, thereby increasing the taxes that had to be paid by private landholders in the area. Unlike national forests, where timbering and stock grazing could be carried out on a fee basis, national parks and national monuments were closed to logging and animal raising.

With the rapid development of the automobile in the early twentieth century, the national parks and national monuments began to attract large numbers of tourists to the Centennial State. The citizens of Colorado not only enjoyed the national parks and monuments themselves; they benefitted from the considerable income generated by the large influx of out-of-state visitors.

Plainly, the major natural and scenic attractions in Colorado have been protected and developed by the national government rather than by the state. Colorado has a state park system and a small number of state forests, but they pale to insignificance when compared with the national parks, monuments, and forests. The pattern is now firmly established in Colorado that those citizens wishing to preserve natural and scenic areas in the state almost automatically turn to the federal government for action and financing rather than to the state government.

There are two reasons for this. First, the federal government has greater financial resources. Second, most of the lands that now comprise Colorado's national parks, monuments, and forests were originally the property of the U.S. government, so it did not have to raise large sums of money to buy them. The federal government could create national parks, monuments, and forests simply by implementing such uses on land it already owned.

Even before Colorado became a state in 1876, Coloradans were looking to the federal government for aid in building water projects. James Belford, Colorado Territory's nonvoting member of the House of Representatives, beseeched Congress for $50,000 for aid in building dams, reservoirs, and canals in order to irrigate lands along the Arkansas, South Platte, and Cache La Poudre rivers. Although Belford's pleas went unheeded, the precedent was set for Colorado to look to the national government for help in planning and financing major water diversion projects.

By the early twentieth century it had become obvious that large water projects in the arid and semiarid West could be financed only by the federal government, particularly projects that involved large dams and expensive tunnels carrying water from one river valley to another. Private investors would not fund such projects because of the long waiting period before original capital was paid back. State governments lacked both the financial resources and the political will to plan and complete such gigantic public ventures.

In 1902 Congress passed the Newlands Act, the first major legislation providing for the surveying, construction, and maintenance of large water projects in sixteen western states. The new law created a Reclamation Fund to be financed by the sale of public lands. Once water projects were constructed and operating, water users would pay user fees that would replenish the Reclamation Fund and thereby provide new capital for additional projects.

Coloradans moved quickly to make use of the Newlands Act and the federal agency it created, the Bureau of Reclamation. The Uncompahgre River valley in western Colorado was bordered by good agricultural land, but contained little water. Nearby, the Gunnison River had plenty of water, but surrounding lands were unfit for agricultural development. In 1904 the Bureau of Reclamation undertook the first federally sponsored reclamation project in Colorado. It built a dam and reservoir on the Gunnison River, dug a six-mile tunnel over to the Uncompahgre River, and thereby diverted water for irrigation from the Gunnison valley to the Uncompahgre valley.

Colorado's second major reclamation project was built on the Grand River, now known as the Colorado River, near Grand Junction. By 1917, when the project was completed, the Bureau of Reclamation had constructed a dam and major canal stretching sixty-two miles down the Colorado River valley.

The most spectacular water projects were those that diverted water from the western slope of the Continental Divide to the eastern slope. Such projects consisted of building dams on rivers on the western slope, collecting the rain and melted snow in reservoirs, and then digging water tunnels from west to east under the Continental Divide so the water could be piped into rivers on the eastern slope. Once on the eastern slope, the water could be used to irrigate farmlands in eastern Colorado and western Kansas and Nebraska. Some of the water also could be used to add to the municipal water supplies of fast-growing cities on the Front Range.

During the Great Depression of the 1930s, the national government took the lead in financing transmountain water-diversion projects in Colorado. The federal Reconstruction Finance Corporation provided a loan of $1.2 million to help finance the Twin Lakes tunnel under the Continental Divide at Independence Pass, east of Aspen. This project took water from the Roaring Fork River on the western slope and put it in the Arkansas River on the eastern slope. The water then flowed down the Arkansas, eventually to be taken from the river and used to help grow melons and sugar beets in Rocky Ford and Ordway in eastern Colorado.

The most spectacular of all the federal water projects in Colorado was the Colorado River–Big Thompson River Water Diversion Project.[6] This ambitious plan, enacted by Congress in 1937, provided for the construction of two dams high in the Rocky Mountains near the headwaters of the Colorado River. The reservoirs created, Lake Granby and Shadow Mountain Reservoir, became two of the most scenic and most popular recreational bodies of water in the state. Water from these two reservoirs, along with water from the already existing Grand Lake, flows through a tunnel under the Continental Divide in Rocky Mountain National Park. At Estes Park the falling water is used to generate electric power before flowing into the Big Thompson River on the eastern slope. The Big Thompson carries the diverted water to the South Platte River, where it is used to irrigate more than 600,000 acres of farmland.

Like other large federal projects, the Colorado–Big Thompson Project had its critics. A nation with food surpluses should not spend millions of dollars for irrigation projects that will increase food production, said the critics. Construction of a long water tunnel and a major electrical generating plant should not be permitted in the pristine natural beauty of Rocky Mountain National Park, they complained. Initially western Coloradans opposed diversion of waters from the western slope over to the eastern slope, but Congress shrewdly gained their support by including water for western Colorado irrigation projects in the total Colorado–Big Thompson package.

Federal planning and financing of water projects has become a permanent part of Colorado politics. In the 1960s and 1970s the Bureau of Reclamation undertook the Upper Colorado River Project and the Frying Pan–Arkansas Project. The Upper Colorado River Project resulted in the construction of a series of dams, reservoirs, and power plants on the Colorado River and its tributaries in western Colorado. The largest reservoir created, Blue Mesa on the Gunnison River, immediately became a popular boating and camping destination for tourists and state residents alike.

The Frying Pan–Arkansas Project diverted water from the Frying Pan River on the western slope to the Arkansas River in southeastern Colorado. Pueblo Reservoir, located on the Arkansas River just west of Pueblo, stored the diverted water and became the largest body of water in the state. It was close enough to Denver and Colorado Springs that it rapidly became Colorado's most popular recreational lake. In addition to irrigating farmlands in eastern Colorado and western Kansas, the "Fry-Ark" project provides substantial amounts of water for the Pueblo and Colorado Springs municipal water supply systems.

In the late 1970s President Jimmy Carter moved to reduce funding for and thereby slow down the development of a number of federally financed water projects in southwestern Colorado. As might be expected, this action produced a storm of protests from area farmers and water sports enthusiasts. Carter's plan was popular, however, with some environmentalists, who in recent years had become critical of dams and reservoirs because of their destructive effect on the natural character of river valleys and the plants and animals that inhabit them. Clearly, federally financed water projects will continue to be a controversial, but important, part of governmental affairs in Colorado.

THE DEPRESSION AND THE NEW DEAL

The 1929 stock market crash in New York inaugurated a period of extended economic depression in the United States. Although not as hard hit as the more industrialized states, Colorado had its share of economic problems during the depression decade of the 1930s.

One reason Colorado was somewhat less affected by the Great Depression was that the state's principal industry, gold and silver mining, had become depressed long before the stock market crash. As previously noted, the refusal of the federal government to subsidize silver and gold production had reduced those two Colorado industries to mere shadows of their former selves by the early 1920s.

Mother Nature decided to add to the distress of Colorado during the depression years. The early 1930s were years of extended drought, resulting in the great dust storms of the period. Particularly on the dry plains of eastern Colorado, winds picked up the top soil from failed attempts at dryland farming and blew it for miles in swirling clouds of stifling dirt. The Dust Bowl was the final destruction of lands which might better have remained stock-grazing lands with their natural plant cover intact.

What industry there was in Colorado felt the effects of the Great Depression. In 1933 the Colorado Fuel and Iron Company, owner and operator of the large steel mills in Pueblo, went into receivership. Denver's hometown railroad, the Denver and Rio Grande Western, went bankrupt in 1935. As industry failed, so did the banks that financed it. More than one third of the banks in Colorado went out of business as the depression spread.

When Franklin Delano Roosevelt, a Democrat, was elected president in 1932, he immediately inaugurated a series of federal programs to end the Great Depression. Known collectively as the New Deal, Roosevelt's programs pumped millions of dollars into state and local welfare and construction programs.

At the time the depression began, Colorado had neither a state sales tax nor income tax. Anxious to avoid raising state taxes, the Colorado legislature said county and city governments should operate welfare and relief programs and get whatever additional help they needed from federal aid programs. The state legislature was saying, in effect, that it wanted no part of helping to pay the bills for mitigating the effects of the depression in Colorado.

Federal authorities made it clear, however, that they would not continue to fund welfare programs in Colorado without a state contribution. Word came from Washington that if the legislature would not raise some revenue and make a contribution to local welfare programs, federal funds would be cut off.

With many a grumble about unfair pressure from the national government, the Colorado legislature met in special session in August of 1933 and enacted a tax on motor vehicles, with the revenues earmarked for relief. When this law was declared unconstitutional by the Colorado Supreme Court, the legislature held another special session in December of 1933 and imposed a tax on gasoline, with a portion of the revenues set aside for public relief. It was not much of a contribution, but it was enough to keep the federal welfare monies coming into Colorado.

Despite the obvious and overt lack of cooperation from the state legislature, Colorado benefitted greatly from New Deal programs. The Civilian Conservation Corps, the ccc, had been organized to employ jobless youth to build roads and bridges and other facilities on federal property. With its two national parks and its many national forests, Colorado became the scene of much ccc activity. The ccc did not just create outdoor "leaf-raking" jobs. By building roads, bridges, hiking trails, and picnic grounds, the ccc made the national parks and forests more accessible to Colorado citizens and out-of-state tourists.

Another important federal program during the Great Depression was the Works Progress Administration, the wpa. With federal help, a large number of public improvement projects were undertaken throughout Colorado, including building mountain highways, erecting dams and embankments for flood control, and constructing playgrounds.

The state of Colorado benefitted greatly from the New Deal, yet Coloradans continued to express mixed feelings about the federal government. Colorado ranked tenth of the forty-eight states in terms of per capita expenditures from New Deal programs. As in most states, Colorado voted heavily Democratic during the depression and New Deal periods. However, the two men who won the governorship during the 1930s for the Democratic party, Alva B. Adams and Ed Johnson, positioned themselves as anti-Roosevelt and anti–New Deal. They criticized Roosevelt's policies, repeatedly warning that U.S. government aid meant U.S. government control of state and local matters. In 1940, when Roosevelt ran for a third term, Colorado Democrats Adams and Johnson opposed him and threw their support to the Republican candidate, Wendell Willkie. Willkie won Colorado, but Roosevelt was reelected president of the United States.

From a liberal and progressive point of view, the New Deal period represented a lost opportunity for progressive reform at the state level in Colorado. With large Democratic majorities in both houses of the state legislature, and a reform- and progress-oriented Democratic administration in power in Washington, pro–New Deal Democratic governors probably could have initiated and passed into law widespread reform programs for the state. As it was, however, the two Democratic governors during the New Deal period were conservative, anti-Roosevelt, and opposed to liberal reform in Colorado.

Yet liberal and progressive voices were heard in Colorado during the New Deal period. U.S. Senator Edward P. Costigan, a former Teddy Roosevelt Republican and Progressive, served as a pro–F.D.R., pro–New Deal Democrat from 1931 to 1937.[7]

In 1938 a Republican, Ralph Carr, won the governorship. When the U.S. government removed Americans of Japanese ancestry from California during World War II, a large group was interned in the Arkansas Valley in southeastern Colorado. Acting in the best tradition of fairness and social justice, Governor Carr vigorously supported fair treatment for the displaced Japanese-Americans and worked to make their stay in Colorado as comfortable as possible under difficult conditions. Governor Carr later was defeated in a bid for the U.S. Senate, and his sympathetic treatment of Japanese-Americans was an issue in the election campaign.

HIGHWAYS AND AIRPORTS

Transportation has always been a critical problem in Colorado. While the great mountain barrier that runs through the state from north to south is a splendid scenic asset, the mountains are also a mammoth challenge when it comes to building roads and highways. As automobiles became more widely used in the early twentieth century, it became more important for Colorado to find the money to build smooth and safe highways through its mountain and desert wilderness. Although most of the state's population lived on the Front Range, the remainder was widely dispersed. To build and maintain the many miles of roads needed across the state would be a huge expense for a relatively small population to pay.

In the 1920s the federal government began matching state expenditures for highway construction with federal funds. As a result, the U.S. highways in Colorado, principally U.S. 40, 50, 85, and 87, rapidly became the principal tourist routes into the state.

In 1929 the federal government constructed Trail Ridge Road through Rocky Mountain National Park. The highest continuous highway in the United States, it contains more than five miles that are above 12,000 feet in altitude. From the moment it opened, Trail Ridge Road has been one of the major automobile tourist attractions in Colorado.

Trail Ridge Road illustrates, however, both the positive and the negative side of such federal projects. The National Park Service refuses to keep Trail Ridge Road open in the late fall, winter, and early spring. The first heavy snows in October or November mark the closing of the road until the spring thaw. Local business interests would like to keep Trail Ridge Road open all year, pointing out that there are many sunny winter days in the high Rockies when a drive down such a spectacular mountain highway would be a once-in-a-lifetime experience. In addition, tourism boosters note, the Colorado

State Highway Department, through regular plowing and sanding, is able to keep nearby state highways at high altitudes open during the winter months. However, the National Park Service and Congress adamantly contend Trail Ridge Road should be closed during the heavy snow season. Thus the road is a definite asset to the Colorado tourism industry, yet it is an asset which belongs to the federal government and which the state cannot use exactly as it pleases.

The inauguration of the national interstate highway program in the 1950s made a tremendous contribution to highway construction in Colorado. It meant that 90 percent of the cost of building interstate highways through the mountains, deserts, foothills, and high plains of the state would be paid by the U.S. government.

Interstate 25, the major interstate highway running north to south through Colorado, provides a high-speed automobile connection between the major cities of the Front Range and connects them to Cheyenne and Santa Fe.

Interstate 70 runs east to west through Colorado. The eastern portion of the expressway links Denver to Kansas City and St. Louis. Originally the federal government did not plan to build Interstate 70 west of Denver since once again it appeared wiser to go around Colorado's mountain barrier rather than face the engineering challenge and financial expense of building an expressway through the mountains. Heavy lobbying by Colorado's senators and representatives, however, convinced Congress to authorize building I-70 west from Denver to Glenwood Springs and Grand Junction in Colorado and on into central Utah.

This decision has had a major impact on the development of tourism and the skiing industry in Colorado. As construction progressed on I-70 into the Rocky Mountains, major ski resorts were constructed along its route. Not only could Denver-area skiers rapidly access the newly developed ski areas via I-70, but out-of-state skiers could fly into Denver and either take a bus or rent a car to their chosen destination. During the summertime I-70 gives Denver-area residents and out-of-state tourists rapid automobile access to Colorado's hiking trails and scenic mountain vistas.

In 1973 the Eisenhower Tunnel was completed as part of I-70. More than one mile long, the tunnel carries interstate motorists under the Continental Divide, eliminating a tortuous and dangerous drive over a high mountain pass and greatly shortening the driving time between Denver and many major Rocky Mountain ski resorts by up to one hour.

At the same time the U.S. government was subsidizing expensive highway and expressway building, federal dollars were also provided to help with airport construction and air-traffic control. The rising popularity of air travel provided a unique opportunity to Colorado. Unlike the wagon, the railroad, and the automobile, the airplane was not stopped or slowed down by the high Rocky Mountains. Commercial airliners could fly over the mountains almost as cheaply as they could fly over plains and prairies.

The rise of air travel, one of the most heavily subsidized industries in the country, greatly benefitted Colorado. Travelers could now get to Denver and Colorado Springs almost as easily as to any other city in the United States. Further, because of its closeness to the geographical center of the forty-eight contiguous states, Denver began to develop as a major regional hub airport where transcontinental travelers could conveniently change from one airplane to another.

Many Coloradans, and a majority of Denverites, wanted to enhance Denver's role as a major transcontinental air travel hub. In the 1980s, with some financial help from the state of Colorado, Denver began the process of planning a major new airport to replace Stapleton Airport. The first step, successfully accomplished in 1989, was to get a major appropriation from the federal government to help with the planning and design. The resulting financial package called for the federal government to pay a major share of the construction costs, with the new airport scheduled to open in late 1993.

MILITARY SPENDING

It has already been noted how Colorado was changed by World War II. The United States government located so many facilities in the state during the war and the post–World War II period that Colorado's economy and character were changed forever. Because the vast majority of these government projects were military installations, the U.S. military budget became a major determinant of economic well-being in Colorado.

In the late 1980s military spending slowed down in Colorado, which contributed to a minor economic depression in Colorado Springs, a city with many military facilities in its immediate vicinity. It was a reminder that states and cities that thrive when military spending is increasing also must recognize that their economies will suffer when military expenditures are decreasing.

UNDERGROUND NUCLEAR TESTING

In the late 1960s and early 1970s the U.S. government began a series of experiments to see if underground nuclear explosions could be used to release large amounts of trapped natural gas. The Rulison Project (1969–70) and the Rio Blanco Project (1973) were both undertaken on government lands in remote areas of western Colorado. Both projects stirred up a storm of protests from environmentalists and antinuclear groups.

In each case a nuclear bomb was exploded deep in the earth. The tests were a success in that there was virtually no nuclear radiation released into the atmosphere. Also, despite critics' predictions, the nuclear explosions did not cause damaging earthquakes in Colorado. The tests were disappointing, however, because relatively small amounts of natural gas were released by the two underground nuclear explosions.

Following all the publicity and controversy over the Rulison and Rio Blanco projects, citizen groups petitioned onto the 1974 general election ballot an initiative requiring future experimental nuclear blasts to be approved by a statewide vote of the people. Opponents of the proposition contended that even if passed by the voters, the proposed law would have no effect because the citizens of Colorado do not have the legal right to stop federal testing of nuclear bombs on federal property.

Such legal details did not deter Colorado voters, who approved in 1974 the law that no future nuclear bombs could be detonated without a favorable vote of the people. Due to the failure of the Rulison and Rio Blanco projects to release large amounts of natural gas, however, the federal government canceled its plans for further underground nuclear blasting in Colorado, which made moot the question of whether Colorado voters could require a statewide vote on any future federal testing of nuclear bombs in the state.

OIL SHALE POLITICS

Colorado contains virtually all of the nation's usable oil shale, most of it on federally owned land. In the aftermath of the national energy crisis of the mid 1970s, the oil in the oil shale became a natural resource that appeared to be in great demand.

The U.S. government, in partnership with Exxon and a number of smaller entrepreneurs, launched a major effort to begin extracting oil from oil shale. It built large processing plants and brought large numbers of people into western Colorado communities in and around Rifle and Grand Junction. Governor Richard Lamm well understood that this new mineral boom raised several legal and moral problems about the role of the state and its responsibilities. Lamm and other state officials fought against having local communities finance the new schools and public works facilities that would be needed to service the large populations moving into the oil shale areas. Lamm demanded that either the oil companies or the federal government pay for the infrastructure improvements. He also insisted these energy industries "pay their own way." The Colorado legislature passed a severance tax that would help compensate for the impact oil shale would have on the state.

Eventually the oil shale boom busted. On "Black Sunday," May 2, 1982, Exxon and other producers stopped trying to get oil from oil shale and left the state. Their departure resulted in severe hardship in terms of jobs and out-migration in the central western slope area. But the impact was not as great as it might have been had state officials not anticipated the now-predictable boom and bust cycle.

The strains between Coloradans and federal officials were great before, during, and even after this recent oil shale boom. Congress had created the Synthetic Fuels Corporation to encourage oil shale development, and government and corporate economists and others had assumed technological breakthroughs could occur that would make oil shale a major part of the nation's campaign for energy self-sufficiency. But they erred. The price of oil came down, and the oil shale boom never arrived. Yet the dislocations and human costs of this boomlet were substantial.[8]

RELATIONS WITH OTHER STATES

Colorado also must deal with the other forty-nine states. In particular, Colorado must coexist with its immediate neighbors, many of which have the same semiarid climate or are more arid. As might be expected, most of Colorado's relations with other states have to do with water.

In 1907, in the landmark case of *Kansas v. Colorado,* the United States Supreme Court ruled that it had the authority to determine the equitable appropriation of river water among the various states located along a river. In the particular case, the Court ruled Colorado would have to allow a portion of the water in the Arkansas River to flow into western Kansas. The significance of the Supreme Court's decision was that Colorado would not be allowed to keep all the water that arose in its major rivers for its own use. Although the major source of the water was rain and snow that fell in the high Rocky Mountains of Colorado, the water would have to be shared with states downstream.

Rather than allow the Supreme Court to make all the decisions concerning the allocation of river water between states, Colorado began negotiating interstate compacts dividing up water supplies in interstate rivers with its neighboring states. A Colorado River compact was negotiated in 1922 with the six other states bordering the Colorado River. Shortly thereafter, Colorado and New Mexico negotiated an agreement on water flowing in the La Plata River, and Colorado and Nebraska negotiated an agreement for the South Platte River. In 1948 the division of Colorado River waters was further clarified with the negotiation and adoption of the Upper Colorado River Compact.

The interstate water compacts had an effect on water use within Colorado because they required that states either use their allocations of river water or else give them to other states needing the water. This "use it or lose it" philosophy put pressure on Colorado to divert its allocation of Colorado River water from the western slope, where it was not needed, to the eastern slope, where it could be used for farming and city water supply.

THE TWO FORKS DAM DEBATE

In the late 1980s Colorado encountered a water problem with both the U.S. government and the neighboring state of Nebraska. The city of Denver and its surrounding suburbs, anticipating major population growth in the Denver metropolitan region in the future and wishing to guarantee an adequate water supply for this expected growth, planned a major water-supply dam and reservoir to be built at a place named Two Forks on the South Platte River. The project was opposed in Colorado by environmentalists, who claimed the dam and reservoir would destroy a long and scenic stretch of the South Platte River. Nebraskan interests also opposed the Two Forks project, claiming it would significantly reduce the amount of water flowing in the South Platte River in Nebraska, thereby killing the fish, birds, and other wildlife that needed the water to survive. The arguments for and against the proposed Two Forks Dam, often debated in passionate terms, are given below.

The Case for Two Forks

To the extent that Colorado is strong and vital, it is because Coloradans have taken control of their natural surroundings and forged from them a state capable of flourishing during good times, yet able to persevere through times of difficulty. A chief barrier to economic development and prosperous times had always been the scarcity of water. Water is a key, if not the key, to growing cities, expanding suburbs, business expansion, and growth in jobs. The very economic health of the region depends upon available water. Advocates of Two Forks said their proposal was a rare opportunity to plan for the future, rather than be surprised by it.

Two Forks, as proposed, would be an entirely new dam thirty miles southwest of Denver, flooding thirty miles of the South Platte River and creating a reservoir with 11,000 surface acres of water. More than forty suburban cities and water districts concluded, after initial studies, that the most cost-effective way to plan for continued growth in their region was this 1.1-million-acre-foot reservoir at Two Forks.

The 1980 U.S. Census had tallied over a million and a half residents in the six-county Denver region. Projected estimates for 2010 and 2035 went as high as three to four million people.

The city of Denver, because of decades of planning and water-source acquisition, had plenty of water. Denver was not growing much, but it did provide water to many of its fast-growing suburbs. Two Forks was proposed as a regionwide solution. The suburbs agreed to pay 80 percent of all the costs of Two Forks, and they were prepared to pay hefty additional fees to Denver for planning and management.

The ingenious aspect of Two Forks was that it united the various local governments in the state's largest metropolitan center and encouraged them to cooperate in planning for their mutual future.

Advocates of Two Forks predicted the project would cost $500 million and, in the long run, be worth every cent. It would protect against the dry years which might bring economic growth to a halt. It also would begin to store more of Colorado's share of its own water, water that otherwise would be lost to downstream states.

Thus the case for Two Forks was that it would give Colorado both flexibility and sensible planning for the future. Advocates of Two Forks included the Denver Water Board, most city and suburban officials, many business leaders, most developers, labor unions, and most of Colorado's congressional delegation. Investments in major public works or infrastructure projects are always costly, supporters argued, but they always pay rich dividends in terms of spurring new jobs, creating new recreation facilities, and providing new economic opportunities. That's why Two Forks was viewed as essential public policy.

The Case against Two Forks

It is difficult in Colorado to speak against the virtues of economic development, reasonable growth, and cheap water for the vast majority of the citizens. Opponents of Two Forks tried to avoid being cast as antigrowth and merely the zealous friends of rare fish and beautiful streams.

Those arguing against the building of Two Forks disputed the population growth forecasts and pointed out that in the late 1980s the Front Range and Greater Denver hardly grew at all. They claimed proponents of Two Forks greatly exaggerated the growth projections and projected water needs.

Second, opponents said water conservation efforts in the Denver metropolitan area had never been seriously attempted except for token lawn-watering rationing a few year ago. A $200 million investment in water conservation hardware for homes and businesses, such as low-flow shower heads and low-flush toilets, might save as much as two-thirds of the water the Two Forks Dam could provide, opponents claimed.

Then there were the environmental impact arguments. Two Forks, it was said, would inundate over thirty miles of one of the most popular stretches of free-flowing river in the region, an area that attracted over 300,000 visitors for fishing and other recreation each year. That part of the South Platte River has been designated by the U.S. Fish and Wildlife Service as a "unique and irreplaceable resource of national significance." Two Forks thus would reduce a whole range of recreational opportunities for Colorado residents, it was argued.

Opponents claimed that Two Forks would eliminate 10,000 acres of high-quality wildlife habitat, destroy hundreds of acres of valued wetlands, and disrupt the ecological balance of the Colorado River and some of its key tributaries (the Blue, Fraser, and Williams Fork rivers).

Because it would lessen water flow along the South Platte in Nebraska, environmentalists in Colorado and Nebraska said Two Forks would jeopardize critical habitat for several threatened and endangered species, including the whooping crane.[9] Opponents also said the project's cost overruns likely would bring the real estimate to nearly $1 billion, all for a project whose need was unjustified. Yes, it would put people to work, they admitted. Yes, it would provide water for long-term growth. But there were other ways to achieve the same general goals.

There were also economic reasons to oppose Two Forks. One was that tourism and recreation, Colorado's second largest industry, needed to be encouraged. That meant keeping waters in mountain streams and rivers in their original form and not damming them into huge reservoirs. "Most of the water needed for recreation must be kept in our streams and lakes to sustain fish and wildlife, to provide for rafting and boating, and to maintain the beauty and ecology that attract so many visitors here," said former Governor Richard Lamm. "Why should we encumber taxpayers with the staggering expense of water projects that may impinge on lucrative recreational uses?"[10]

Thus certain segments of the tourist industry opposed Two Forks along with environmentalists, water conservationists, residents of the western slope, Nebraskans, recreationists, and antigrowth supporters.

The Decision

In terms of public opinion, the public in 1988 and 1989, when the issue was most debated, was never in favor of the dam. For a time popular opinion was divided, with about 45 percent opposed, nearly the same in favor, and about 10 percent unsure or holding no opinion.

Still, Denver and its neighboring communities had spent nearly eight years and about $40 million on environmental impact planning. According to most indications in 1989, the relevant federal agencies were about ready to approve the project, and the Environmental Protection Agency's regional administrator in Denver appeared ready to sign off favorably on Two Forks.

Both Governor Roy Romer and the *Denver Post* tried to straddle the issue, although they generally favored obtaining national government approval of a permit that would allow for construction of Two Forks anytime in the next twenty-five years. They viewed construction, however, as a last resort, to take place only after rigorous water conservation measures were put in place and after less expensive dams and reservoir structures were developed for future water sources. The *Denver Post,* recognizing that the real question was the price of water, not its availability, pointedly recommended "the dam not be constructed until all homes in the city of Denver are equipped with water meters, to encourage conservation and allow a pricing structure to discourage water waste."[11]

Pressure on the governor and on the U.S. Army Corps of Engineers and the Environmental Protection Agency intensified throughout 1988 and early 1989. The EPA was required by federal law to evaluate the permit to construct Two Forks (and the conditions proposed by the favorable Army Corps of Engineers) and to determine whether the proposed Two Forks project was consistent with the provisions of the National Clean Water Act.

An announcement by President George Bush's EPA director, William Reilly, in March of 1989 shocked water developers and other supporters of Two Forks, and it greatly pleased conservationists. Reilly initiated veto proceedings that would halt the dam project, saying in effect that the proposed Two Forks Dam could result in serious adverse environmental impacts. He also appeared to side with those who believed the huge project was unnecessary to meet the demand for water in the Denver metropolitan region. Other sources and water conservation should be tried first.

Reilly's sudden intervention was legal, yet unusual and perhaps unprecedented in EPA history. Further, Reilly acted after he received a letter signed by about nine heads of national environmental organizations who opposed Two Forks. In addition, Reilly took the unusual step of bringing in the EPA regional administrator from Atlanta to review the project prior to issuing his veto.

When the Environmental Protection Agency said "No!" to Two Forks, it essentially meant Two Forks would not be built. The politics of Two Forks points out again how the state is so often in an awkward embrace with the federal government. In this case, differing from many other occasions, the U.S. government was seen as halting the development of the state and urging the state to be more environmentally conscious of its natural resources. In essence, federal officials were telling Colorado officials to cherish the animals, fish, and natural habitat and try to provide for water needs through conservation and less drastic projects than the proposed Two Forks Dam.

Proponents of Two Forks criticized what they felt was federal intrusion and federal preemption of water project developments. Clearly, new federal regulations and environmental standards were altering how Colorado would make its water policy.[12] To many observers, Two Forks symbolized the very complex intergovernmental decision-making processes now required for any major project affecting the environment. Some also felt that Two Forks set an example that would encourage opponents of state and local government projects (in this case over forty local governments in the Denver metropolitan area were supporting Two Forks) to make end runs around state and local officials and head directly to Washington to block or modify such projects.

Water policy fights will continue as long as there is a Colorado. This episode of the late 1980s, in the longer run, will be viewed as merely one zig, albeit one of considerable significance, in the patchwork of incremental zigs and zags that characterize the evolution of U.S. policy toward Colorado water development.[13]

MEDICAID

Similar to other states, Colorado faced the problem in the late 1980s and early 1990s of the U.S. government providing funds for specific programs but mandating that federal funds be matched with state funds. An example of such a program was Medicaid, which financed health care for low-income persons and families. From 1986 to 1991, the proportion of the Colorado state budget devoted to the Medicaid program increased from 9 percent to 15 percent, mainly because Colorado was forced to match federal expansions of the program enacted in Washington by Congress. In only one year, the 1991–92 fiscal year, the cost of Colorado's mandated share of the Medicaid program increased by over $100 million.

State Senator Mike Bird, a Republican from Colorado Springs, believes the long-term effect of programs like Medicaid is to have Congress, rather than the Colorado state legislature, determine the size of the Colorado state budget. To put control of the state budget back in the state legislature, Senator Bird introduced a bill, SB 92–65, in the 1992 session of the legislature that called for Colorado to withdraw from the Medicaid program unless Congress removed the detailed and specific requirements for matching funds. Once the matching-fund requirements were removed, Bird argued, Colorado could take the federal funds and devise its own alternative to the Medicaid program, one in which Colorado, rather than the federal government, would determine the cost to Colorado taxpayers.

No one expected Senator Bird's proposal to be enacted into law. Colorado needed to supply medical care for its low-income inhabitants, and the state could not provide sufficient care without federal funding. However, Bird hoped his bill would draw attention to the fact that mandated programs such as Medicaid allowed the U.S. government, and not the state legislature, to determine the details of a number of major taxing and spending programs in Colorado.[14]

CONCLUSION

A constant theme in the history of federal-state relations in Colorado has been the unending struggle by Colorado politicians and promoters to involve the U.S. government in financing the development of the state. Particularly in terms of national parks, national forests, water diversion projects, and military installations, the federal government has responded favorably to calls for help and is very much a presence in Colorado.

Statistics in the late 1980s illustrated the magnitude of the U.S. government's role in Colorado. Federal spending in the state totaled $13 billion, or $3,942 per capita, in 1988. That placed Colorado eleventh among the fifty states in per capita distribution of federal funds.[15]

There appears to be no significant slowing of federal spending in Colorado over the long term. From 1981 to 1988 federal expenditures at the national level increased by 51.5 percent, but in Colorado they increased by 73.4 percent. Thirty-six percent of federal expenditures in the state were for defense in 1988, compared to only 25.8 percent throughout the nation.

When preserving Colorado's natural beauty with national parks, national monuments, and national forests, the U.S. government has played the role of curtailing individual interests in order to further the public good. The same moralistic influence can be found in the many water diversion projects planned and financed by the federal government in Colorado. These projects represent organized community action to build public facilities which add to the common wealth and well-being of the overall society.

By and large, the critics of federal involvement in and control over Colorado affairs have spoken from the perspective of the individualistic political culture. They object to government control over vast amounts of public land which, in their opinion, would be better used if placed in private hands and private control. When calling for more state control and less national control, critics of the federal government usually are asserting state rights because they believe the state will be more responsive to individual needs and ambitions than the federal government often is.[16]

Colorado has a love-hate relationship with the U.S. government. Coloradans love to have federal projects, yet they hate the controls, requirements for state matching funds, and limits on individual ambitions that so often come with the federal dollars. For the most part, however, the conflict has been resolved in favor of having the federal government play as active a role in Colorado as possible coupled with grudging acceptance of the resulting controls and restrictions. Colorado politicians ritualistically criticize the U.S. government when campaigning for office. Once elected to office, however, they spend much, if not most, of their time lobbying for more federal projects in the state, even as they seek to minimize various federal restrictions and regulations.

CHAPTER FOUR

The Colorado Constitution and Its Politics

Colorado, like every state, has a constitution. It represents, at least in theory, the basic agreement of the citizens about the shape of state government and the distribution of power between citizens and state government. The Colorado constitution is a political compact that structures state government and specifies how government power is to be divided and constrained.

Colorado's constitution, in common with other state constitutions, is a product of its politics and political culture. It is a set of "rules of the game" that attempts to shape politics and political processes. It is both fundamental law and a highly political document that has major consequences for who gets what political opportunities. Through the amendment process, Colorado's constitution is periodically questioned, challenged, and changed in an effort to redefine basic political rights, values, and opportunities or to rearrange the relationship of citizens and their state.

A major purpose of the state constitution is to establish the basic organization of government and to assign various powers and responsibilities to the three branches of government. Equally important, however, and very much in the American political tradition, the framers of the Colorado constitution used their written constitution to limit and restrict the power of public officials and to prevent the abuse of public power.

State constitutions contain more detail and more restraints than the U.S. Constitution. They are longer and less flexible; as a result, they require more amendment. The national Constitution grants powers in broad and sweeping terms, allowing each generation to write in the details and to adapt the basic charter of government to new conditions. Colorado's constitution, like those in many states, was written by people who distrusted government, or at least feared its potential abuses. Thus the Colorado constitution contains a detailed bill of rights and greater restrictions on government officials than does the national Constitution.

The Colorado constitution was drawn up at a state constitutional convention that met in Denver in early 1876. In many ways, that Colorado constitutional convention is still in session. Back then it was the issues of women's suffrage and railroad regulation; today it might be environmental issues or the legality of abortion. Then and now, Coloradans have found ways of amending their fundamental law with regularity. Moreover, state courts, the legislature, and most governors have also implicitly amended the state constitution on various occasions as they interpret or reinterpret anew what they believe the Colorado constitution means or should mean.

Colorado's constitution does much more than establish a democratic form of government. It calls upon the state to build prisons and reformatories and to provide a uniform system of free public schools. It specifies that Colorado will have colleges and universities, to be located in Boulder, Colorado Springs, Denver, Fort Collins, Golden, and other cities as provided by law. The constitution defines how the state shall collect taxes and borrow money. It establishes how counties, cities, and towns will be created and how mining and irrigation projects shall be protected and regulated. The result is that most of the basic institutions of Colorado state government are required by and provided for in the state constitution.

Most Coloradans know little about the constitution of their state and have only a vague grasp of the importance of the constitutional principles contained within it. Yet to understand a state's politics and government, it is crucial to understand its constitution as well as its political culture. In Colorado's case this requires going back to the 1850s.

COLORADO'S FIRST CONSTITUTIONAL CONVENTION

At the time gold was discovered on the banks of Dry Creek in 1858, the land area that is now Colorado was part of four different United States territories—Kansas Territory, Nebraska Territory, New Mexico Territory, and Utah Territory. The immediate area where the gold was first found, the Pike's Peak area, was technically a part of Kansas Territory, but no formal governmental authority had been established or was being exercised there. As more gold seekers poured into the area with each passing day, support began to grow for the idea that this rapidly populating and developing area should become a territory and a state in its own right, rather than being governed as part of Kansas.

In the summer of 1859, only a year after gold was first discovered, a constitutional convention was held at what is now Denver. Fifty men were present representing thirteen different districts. Unable to decide between territorial status or statehood, the convention sent a message to Congress requesting territorial status, but it also drafted a state constitution. The question was submitted to a vote of the people, and Colorado's first popular referendum election resulted in 2,007 votes for territorial status and only 1,649 votes for statehood.

Unwilling to wait for congressional action, and armed with a popular vote of the people for territorial government, the convention leaders set up their own creation—the Territory of Jefferson. A territorial governor was elected along with a two-house legislature. The new government failed to survive, however, because many of the early settlers, particularly the miners, refused to pay taxes to a government that had not been officially sanctioned by the U.S. Congress. Still, the unsuccessful experiment with the Territory of Jefferson had given early settlers some initial experience at writing a state constitution, conducting a referendum election, and setting up and attempting to operate a democratic form of government.

Congress failed to approve the Territory of Jefferson because of the political situation in Washington, D.C. The conflict between the northern and southern states over slavery, and tension concerning the approaching presidential election of 1860, made territorial status controversial, mainly because it was assumed the new territory would strongly favor the North.

TERRITORIAL STATUS

The situation changed when Abraham Lincoln, the Republican candidate, was elected president in 1860. The southern Senators and Representatives departed Congress as the South seceded from the Union, thereby removing the opposition to both statehood for Kansas and territorial status for Colorado.

The name *Colorado* was adopted in place of Jefferson for two reasons. Many people believed George Washington should be the only president to have a state named for him. Others, mainly members of the Republican party, argued that Thomas Jefferson was too closely identified with the Democratic party. *Colorado,* the Spanish word for "ruddy colored," was the name finally agreed upon, and Colorado became a territory on February 28, 1861.

Colorado remained a territory until 1876. During that interval the governor, the justices of the territorial Supreme Court, and most other territorial officers were appointed by the national government. Territorial posts thus were considered partronage positions, and they often were given to close associates of the president or other important national government officials. As a result, territorial officials changed mainly because of events in Washington rather than events in Colorado. Statehood remained a political issue throughout this period. Groups in both Colorado and Washington favored or opposed statehood depending on how it would advantage or disadvantage their particular position or private interest.

COLORADO'S SECOND CONSTITUTIONAL CONVENTION

In early 1864 the Republicans in Congress passed statehood-enabling acts for Colorado, Nebraska, and Nevada in hopes of getting extra electoral votes for Abraham Lincoln in the 1864 presidential election. A proposed state constitution was hastily drawn up for Colorado at a convention which completed its work at Denver in the summer of 1864. To save time, a slate of candidates for the various elected offices of the proposed new state, including the governor and the member of the House of Representatives, was adopted along with the proposed constitution.

The latter act doomed this first attempt at statehood and a state constitution for Colorado. Many voters found the nomination of candidates along with the proposed new constitution to be politically high-handed and self-serving. The voters rejected statehood, and with it Colorado's second proposed state constitution, by a lopsided vote of 4,676 opposed to 1,520 in favor.

COLORADO'S THIRD CONSTITUTIONAL CONVENTION

Less than a year later, in 1865, there was another drive for statehood and a third convention to write a state constitution. This time, however, voters in Colorado Territory narrowly approved statehood and the proposed constitution. Then, without waiting for President Andrew Johnson to proclaim Colorado a state, statehood advocates put the new constitution into operation by electing a governor, a member of Congress, and a legislature. When this "state" legislature convened, it elected two United States Senators.

Back in Washington, however, President Johnson was beginning his post–Civil War battle with the radical Republicans in Congress. Because the Republican party had elected all of the officials for the new "state" government, including the member of the House of Representatives and the two Senators, Johnson saw no reason to increase his hostile opposition in Congress. He refused to proclaim Colorado a state, contending the enabling legislation passed by Congress in 1864 had expired. Once again the handiwork of a Colorado constitutional convention came to naught.

One year later, in 1866, the Republicans in Congress again were anticipating that Colorado would send a Republican Congressman and two Republican Senators to Washington if granted statehood. Once again an enabling act for Colorado statehood was passed, but President Johnson, still hoping to minimize his Republican opposition in Congress, vetoed it. There were insufficient votes in Congress to override the veto.

COLORADO'S FOURTH CONSTITUTIONAL CONVENTION

By this time it was obvious that if Colorado was going to gain statehood and have its own constitution, political conditions would have to be favorable in both Washington and Colorado. The conditions for success finally came about in 1875, when the Republicans in Congress again went looking for additional electoral votes in an upcoming presidential election. They saw a new state of Colorado as three guaranteed Republican electoral votes in 1876. Congress passed an enabling act for Colorado statehood (the third in Colorado Territory's brief fifteen-year history) on March 3, 1875.[1]

The constitutional convention with thirty-nine delegates gathered in Denver's Odd Fellows Hall beginning in December of 1875. They met for eighty-six days. Twenty-four of the delegates were Republicans and fifteen were Democrats, thus giving the Republicans partisan control. The debating and voting at the Colorado constitutional convention did not break down on Republican-Democratic lines, however. Most of the arguments were tied to political controversies of the time rather than disagreements over established principles of government.

By 1875 there was general agreement throughout the United States on what a state constitution should include and how a state government should be structured. As a result, there was little debate and rapid agreement at the Colorado constitutional convention on the basic structure of the proposed state government.

COLORADO CONSTITUTION

Boundaries and Bill of Rights

Article I of the Colorado constitution established the boundaries of the proposed state. By mandate of Congress in the enabling act for Colorado statehood, the boundaries were the same as those for Colorado Territory.

Article II provided for the state's bill of rights, which was listed near the beginning of the proposed state constitution, rather than as amendments at the end, as is the case with the U.S. Constitution. The state bill of rights was placed in a prominent position, immediately after the preamble and the boundaries, and was given a preamble of its own, which states the purpose of the bill of rights is "to assert our rights, acknowledge our duties, and proclaim the principles upon which our government is founded."

The Colorado bill of rights is much longer than the U.S. Bill of Rights, consisting of twenty-eight sections, compared to the federal Constitution's ten amendments. In essence, it is a statement of timeless doctrines that transcend government but that the government is obliged to guarantee and protect.

This bill of rights clearly states that Colorado will be governed by the people. Section 1 asserts "all political power is vested in and derived from the people . . . is founded upon their will only, and is instituted for the good of the whole." Section 2 further elaborates this idea with specific reference to the proposed state constitution. It declares "the people of this State have the sole and exclusive right of governing themselves, as a free, sovereign and independent State; and to alter and abolish their Constitution and form of government . . ."

The drafters of the Colorado constitution drew upon the Declaration of Independence and various provisions from other states' declarations of rights as well as the U.S. Bill of Rights. They made explicit the property rights that are only indirectly referred to in the Declaration of Independence. Section 3 of the Colorado bill of rights declares: "All persons have certain natural, essential and inalienable rights, among which may be reckoned . . . acquiring, possessing and protecting property . . ."

The Colorado constitution deals with freedom of speech more explicitly than the U.S. Constitution, but an effort was made to protect those who might be harmed by abuse of freedom of speech. Section 10 of the bill of rights states: "Every person shall be free to speak, write or publish whatever he will on any subject, being responsible for all abuse of that liberty . . ."

The remaining sections of the Colorado bill of rights closely parallel the protections found in the U.S. Constitution. Ex poste facto laws, self-incrimination, double jeopardy, and unreasonable searches and seizures are forbidden. A fair trial, religious freedom, free and open elections, due process of law, and freedom of conscience are all expressly guaranteed.[2]

Separation of powers, a concept only indirectly referred to in the U.S. Constitution, is explicitly provided for in most state constitutions. Colorado directly proclaims separation of powers as a principle of government in Article III. The powers of the state are allocated among executive, legislative, and judicial departments, and "no persons, or collection of persons, charged with the exercise of powers properly belonging to one of these departments shall exercise any power properly belonging to either of the others" except as the constitution expressly permits.

The next article establishes the office and powers of an elected governor, thereby placing the gubernatorial article ahead of the state legislative article. This is the reverse of the U.S. Constitution, where the legislative article is placed in the prior position, and probably indicated that distrust of the executive power, which was so strong at the time the U.S. Constitution was written in 1787, had faded somewhat by the time the Colorado constitution was being written, almost ninety years later.

In addition to the governor, six other executive officials were to be elected by the people: the lieutenant governor, attorney general, treasurer, secretary of state, auditor, and superintendent of public instruction. Similar to most state constitutions at the time, the Colorado constitution weakened the power of the governor by having other principal executive officers elected by the people rather than appointed by the governor.

The Colorado legislature is called the General Assembly and, similar to the national Congress, has two chambers. The Colorado Senate is roughly one-half the size of the Colorado House of Representatives. Members of the house are elected every two years for a two-year term of office. One-half of the members of the senate are elected every two years to a four-year term, the other half being elected two years later, also to a four-year term.

The constitution established a third branch of state government, the judiciary. Unlike the judicial article in the U.S. Constitution, which is short and general, the Colorado judicial article carefully structures the entire state judiciary. State constitutions as a rule are more detailed about courts because they have to establish a wide variety of courts and because, even today, state courts handle at least 95 percent of all judicial business in America.

Thus a county court was provided for each county, and a district court system was established to try major offenses against state law. Final appeal was to a state supreme court of three members elected for nine-year terms.

The terms were staggered, and the justice with the least amount of time left to serve automatically would be the chief justice.

One other difference from the U.S. Constitution is that the Colorado Supreme Court can give "advisory" opinions when requested to do so by the state legislature or state executive officials. Several other states also provide for such advisory opinions. Unlike the U.S. Supreme Court, which only renders decisions on actual court cases, Colorado's highest court does not have to wait for a trial and an appeal before being able to render its judgment on important state issues of jurisprudence.

CONTROVERSY AT THE CONVENTION

The basic structure of state government, so familiar and well tested in the other states of the 1870s, was readily agreed upon. Major debates and disagreements at the Colorado constitutional convention of 1875–76 erupted, however, over four hotly debated political issues of the day—economic regulation, the vote for women, state aid to parochial schools, and whether to mention God in the preamble.

Economic Regulation

Government regulation of railroads and other private business corporations presented a major dilemma to the convention delegates. Nearby midwestern states were combating monopoly abuses by railroads and grain storage elevators by passing laws limiting railroad rates and grain storage charges. On the other hand, Colorado was at the frontier and badly needed the capital investment which major railroads and similar large corporate enterprises could bring to the area. Convention delegates sought to provide a measure of state regulation of private business, yet not so much that it would stop private corporations from wanting to invest in the state.

The proposed constitution required a general incorporation law, thereby reducing the prospect of private corporations receiving special privileges from the state legislature. Irrevocable corporation charters were prohibited, and railroads were forbidden to merge competing railroad lines or to discriminate unjustly or unreasonably between customers. Government regulation went no further than these general principles, however. No state agencies were created to regulate railroads or other public utilities, and no provision was included to give the state specific powers to set corporate charges and prices.

Votes for Women

The women's suffrage movement was well underway at the time of the Colorado constitutional convention. Those who supported giving women the vote collected thousands of signatures and presented them to the delegates convened in Denver. Pressure was exerted to make Colorado the first state in the United States to grant the vote to females. It was noted pointedly that women in nearby Wyoming Territory (not yet a state) had enjoyed voting rights since 1869. Several delegates, including Judge Henry Bromwell of Denver and Agipeta Vigil representing Huerfano and Las Animas counties, wanted to take this historic step, but most delegates were not ready. By a twenty-four to eight vote the convention denied suffrage to women.

After considerable discussion, a compromise was fashioned. Women would not get the right to vote, except in school elections, but delegates agreed to put the question of full suffrage for women to a vote of those then eligible to vote. All eligible voters at the time were, of course, male.

The promised referendum was duly held two years later. Colorado's first governor, John Routt, endorsed women's suffrage. Noted suffragists Susan B. Anthony and Lucy Stone campaigned actively in Colorado for a positive vote, but the state's male electorate rejected full voting rights for women. It would take until 1893, another fifteen years, for Colorado's male voters to approve women's suffrage. The winning vote for women's suffrage was 35,798 in favor and 29,451 opposed.

Colorado would, at that later date, become the second state to grant full suffrage to women, but it was the first state in which women's suffrage was established by a separate vote by an all-male electorate. Wyoming women, as noted earlier, were given the right to vote by the Wyoming territorial constitution of 1868, and that right carried over when Wyoming became a state in 1890.[3]

State Aid to Parochial Schools

In the enabling legislation for Colorado statehood, Congress provided for two sections of land in each township to be reserved to finance schools. The land was to be sold and the proceeds used to build and maintain school facilities. The Colorado constitutional convention debated heatedly the question of whether church-related private schools could receive a portion of these school land monies. While many Roman Catholics wanted parochial schools to receive school land funds, Protestants tended to argue that such funds should be for public schools only. The Protestant viewpoint prevailed as the proposed constitution denied state aid, other than exemption from taxation, to "any sectarian institution."

Mention of God

The U.S. Constitution makes no reference to God, but by the 1870s a number of states had included some mention of the deity in their constitutions. Convention delegates discussed at length whether to put God in the proposed Colorado constitution. Once again controversy was settled with something of a compromise. The preamble refers to "the Supreme Ruler of the Universe."[4]

THE FINAL DOCUMENT

The Colorado constitutional convention of 1875–76 lasted eighty-six days. The 23,000-word final product was five times as long as the 4,543 words of the unamended U.S. Constitution. It included considerable detail not found in the federal Constitution, yet it was not substantially longer nor more detailed than other state constitutions written close to the same time. As would be expected, the Colorado framers borrowed extensively from the recently written state constitutions for Illinois, Missouri, Nebraska, and Pennsylvania.[5]

The delegates mainly were interested in achieving statehood. Plainly they were not trying to invent new, or more innovative, forms of state government. Nor were they trying to institute a more egalitarian or progressive "new state." These were practical people primarily motivated to win statehood and clearly guided by the widely accepted models of the existing states and relatively proven constitutional principles. They willingly compromised when this was necessary, as on women's suffrage, but theirs was basically an act of imitation rather than one of political innovation or constitutional creativity.

The convention adjourned on March 14, 1876. The delegates apparently had written a popular constitution, for July 1, 1876, the voters of Colorado Territory overwhelmingly voted for statehood and the proposed constitution by a vote of 15,443 to 4,062. On August 1, 1876, a date now celebrated as Colorado Day, President Ulysses S. Grant proclaimed Colorado a state. The constitutional convention's handiwork became the Colorado constitution. Although considerably amended over the years, this same constitution is still in effect.

Because Colorado voted for statehood and was proclaimed a state almost exactly one-hundred years after the U.S. Declaration of Independence on July 4, 1776, the new state was nicknamed the Centennial State.

The plan by the Republicans in Congress to admit Colorado to the Union and thereby garner three Republican electoral votes in the 1876 presidential election was a success. The new state constitution provided that the new state legislature would choose Colorado's three presidential electors for the 1876 election, and that the voters would chose the electors in succeeding presidential elections. In the early fall of 1876 the Colorado legislature gave its three electoral votes to the Republican candidate for president, Rutherford B. Hayes. In one of the closest and most contested presidential elections in U.S. history, Hayes defeated his Democratic opponent, Samuel Tilden, by only one electoral vote. Thus Colorado's unusual legislative vote for president was a critical part of Hayes's narrow victory.

AMENDING THE COLORADO CONSTITUTION

The original Colorado constitution has been amended many times over the years. The first amendment was adopted in 1878, only two years after the constitution itself was adopted. Between 1876 and 1992, 122 amendments were added, doubling the length of the document and causing the present-day constitution to be even more detailed than the 1876 original.[6]

By the mid-1990s there were twice as many sections of the Colorado constitution as there were in 1876. Technically, Colorado is still operating under the 1876 constitution as revised, yet there are important differences between the constitution adopted in 1876 and the much amended constitution that governs Colorado today.

The 1876 constitution provided only two methods for amending the constitution. Under the first method, which has never been used, a *constitutional convention* is proposed by a two-thirds vote of all the members of both houses of the state legislature. The constitutional convention would actually convene, however, only if approved by a majority vote at the next general election. If approved, the constitutional convention would consist of seventy members, two elected from each of Colorado's thirty-five state Senate districts.

Between 1876 and 1900, Colorado legislators and other political leaders made more than twenty attempts to persuade the state legislature to propose to the voters the question of calling a state constitutional convention. An 1899 proposal failed to gain approval in the state legislature by only one vote. Three times in the early twentieth century, in 1916, 1922, and 1930, the

Colorado legislature submitted proposals for a state constitutional convention to the voters, but the voters rejected all three.[7]

Under the second method of amending the Colorado constitution, which is regularly used, a *referred amendment* must pass both houses of the state legislature by a two-thirds majority (currently forty-four of sixty-five votes in the state House of Representatives and twenty-four of thirty-five votes in the state Senate). The amendment then is referred to the voters at the next general election and must receive a majority vote to be adopted.

In 1910, yet another method of amending the Colorado constitution, *the initiated amendment,* was adopted. The initiative process, first proposed by Populist party leaders and endorsed by Colorado's Populist Governor Davis Waite back in the early 1890s, later was vigorously championed by the Progressives. The initiative allows voters to propose a legislative measure or a constitutional amendment by filing a petition bearing a required number of valid signatures.

Supporters of an initiated amendment circulate petitions and obtain the signatures of registered voters equal to 5 percent of the votes cast in the last general election for Colorado secretary of state.[8] If a sufficient number of signatures are collected, the proposed amendment is placed on the ballot at the next general election and must receive a majority vote to become part of the state constitution. Although not as frequently used as referred amendments, initiated amendments are popular in Colorado and have been used to make significant and important changes in the state constitution.

In Colorado, as in a few other states, the final battles over whether or not to adopt the initiative process pitted Democrats, who had been converted to the cause by Populists and labor interests, against Republicans, who generally held a more traditional view favoring representative government. In supporting the measure, Democratic Governor John F. Shafroth said in 1910 that if he could have only one reform, it would be the initiative.[9] The fact that citizens could initiate laws and constitutional amendments, Shafroth believed, would make state legislators more careful and accountable.

Opponents of the initiative in Colorado, notably the Republican party, claimed direct democracy measures such as the initiative would be alien to representative government and harmful to the financial and social welfare of the state. According to the *Denver Republican:* "The initiative and referendum both conflict directly with the representative principle, and to the extent to which they may be applied, representative government will be overthrown . . . Cannot the people of Colorado do a little sober thinking for themselves and on their own account? Must they adopt every newfangled

notion which may be adopted or experimented with in some other state? . . .
Let Colorado always be sober and sane.''[10]

But Colorado adopted the initiative, and this had a significant effect on opening up the political process. Many initiated constitutional amendments would not have been adopted by the more traditional method of amending the Colorado constitution by referral from the state legislature. Populist groups on the left and right, good-government groups, and occasionally even an impatient legislator or governor have used the initiated amendment to bring about constitutional change in Colorado.

The amendment process, both referred and initiated, has had a major impact on government in Colorado. Significant constitutional amendments *referred by the legislature,* and subsequently adopted by the voters, include establishing the state income tax, reorganizing the governor's office, setting a four-year term of office for the governor, and providing equal rights for women. Initiated amendments that made important changes include establishing procedures for recalling state officials, making judges appointed rather than elected, setting home rule for cities and towns, establishing the state civil service system, repealing state prohibition, creating a reapportionment commission to draw state legislative districts, limiting the power of cities to annex territory without a favorable vote of the people who live in the territory to be annexed, permitting low-stakes gambling in historic mountain mining towns, and setting eight-year-term limits for all state elected officials.

Housecleaning Amendments

The amendment process has generally been used in Colorado to make the state constitution longer and more detailed, but there are some exceptions. A 1974 amendment deleted language that required listing and publishing the number and amount of every warrant paid by the state treasurer.[11] In 1988 an amendment removed or shortened dated provisions concerning suffrage for women, selection of the site for the state capital, and appropriations for the state capitol building.[12] In 1990 a "housecleaning" amendment removed, among other things, an obsolete provision that prevented a person who fights in a duel, or is a second in a duel, or assists in a duel, from holding office in the state.

"Principle" Amendments

Similar to other states, Colorado has had its share of "principle" as well as "programmatic" amendments to the state constitution. Principle amendments establish an idea or concept rather than being directly concerned with the way government is structured and operated. In 1972 Colorado adopted a referred amendment guaranteeing equal rights on the basis of sex (Colorado Equal Rights Amendment).[13] An initiated amendment to repeal this Colorado ERA was defeated in 1976.[14] While people debate whether such principle amendments make any difference in the actual conduct of state and local government, the Colorado ERA was strongly supported by its proponents and adamantly fought by its opponents when it twice appeared on the Colorado ballot.

An equally controversial principle amendment was petitioned to the voters in 1988. It declared that "the English language is the official language of the State of Colorado."[15] Part of a nationwide movement to establish English as the "official" language of the United States, the "Official English" amendment immediately came under fire from Spanish-surnamed political leaders in Colorado who viewed it as hostile to the large number of Spanish-speaking citizens in Colorado. Opponents attempted to rename the amendment "English Only" and launched a major campaign to defeat it.

Of the eight constitutional amendments on the Colorado general election ballot in 1988, the Official English amendment was one of the most controversial. It was frequently pointed out that English was required by statute in all written proceedings in Colorado courts of law and therefore the amendment would have no practical effect.[16] Colorado voters settled the issue by adopting the Official English amendment by a vote of 829,617 in favor of the amendment to 527,053 against.[17]

"Cause" Amendments

As in other states, the linking of the Colorado constitution with the initiative process has encouraged various groups with political "causes" to use the constitutional amendment process to enact their version of social, economic, or political reform. In 1984 antiabortion groups in Colorado petitioned onto the ballot a constitutional amendment forbidding the use of state funds to pay for abortions. The amendment was narrowly adopted. Four years later, in 1988, pro-choice groups initiated a constitutional amendment that would repeal the amendment and permit state-subsidized abortions.[18] Public opinion in Colorado apparently had shifted in the direction of antiabortion supporters, however, because the 1988 attempt to repeal the ban on state-financed abortions failed by the substantial margin of 809,078 votes against the amendment to 534,070 votes in favor.[19]

A recurring event in Colorado in recent years has been the attempt by antitax groups to initiate a constitutional amendment requiring a vote of the people every time the state or a local government proposes to raise taxes. For instance, in 1976 a group of "fiscal conservatives" collected enough signatures to put such a "vote on all tax increases" amendment on the Colorado ballot. The idea did not fare well in the general election, however. A powerful alliance of elected officials, public employee associations, and lobby groups representing city and county governments (such as the Colorado Municipal League and Colorado Counties) strongly opposed the proposed amendment, and the measure was overwhelmingly rejected by the electorate.[20]

The possibility of initiating constitutional amendments onto the ballot in Colorado has resulted in a wide variety of tax-limitation proposals coming before the voters. An initiated amendment in 1978 would have required a vote of the people on any state or local tax increase that exceeded the rate of inflation. It was defeated by the voters by almost a three to two margin.[21] In 1988 an initiated amendment once again called for a public vote on most state and local government tax increases, and once again it was easily defeated, 778,075 votes against the amendment to 567,884 votes in favor.[22] In 1990 a similar, though slightly modified, measure was put before the voters, but this time the vote was much closer. Tax limitation was defeated by a vote of only 515,234 against to 493,456 in favor.[23] But in 1992 a tax-limitation initiated amendment passed by a decisive margin.

Referred versus Initiated Amendments

In the 116 years from 1876 to 1992, constitutional amendments referred to the voters by the Colorado state legislature have had much greater success than initiated amendments in being approved by the electorate. Of the 157 amendments referred to the voters by the legislature during this time period, 92 were adopted, for a 59 percent rate of approval. Since 1910, when the initiative was adopted in Colorado, there have been 99 initiated constitutional amendments, 33 of which were adopted, for a 33 percent rate of approval.[24]

One explanation for the higher rate of voter approval of referred amendments over initiated amendments is that constitutional amendments referred by the legislature must pass each house of the state legislature by a two-thirds vote of all the members, and therefore must have broad geographical and partisan support. It makes sense that a measure that wins such widespread support in the state legislature would have a good chance of receiving a simple majority of the votes cast in a general election. Still, Colorado voters have rejected about 41 percent of the state legislature's efforts to alter the constitution. This rejection rate is not much different, perhaps a slight bit higher, than the experiences in other states.[25]

The necessity of a two-thirds vote in both houses of the Colorado legislature to refer a constitutional amendment probably is one of the reasons the initiative is frequently used. The number of signatures required (five percent of the most recent vote for secretary of state) compares favorably with the number of signatures required in other states that use the constitutional initiative. Many groups, even those formed for no other purpose than to initiate a particular constitutional amendment, have demonstrated that with determination and an appealing cause, the necessary signatures can be gathered. Following through with a successful campaign to win a majority of the statewide vote for a citizen-initiated amendment can be an enormous challenge, however, and this could explain why a lower percentage of initiated amendments are approved by the voters.

How one views the role of citizen-initiated amendments depends on a number of factors, including one's political vantage point and ideological outlook. The initiative process especially appeals to activists on the left and right, to people who do not generally win at their state capitol, and to people who are either outside the mainstream or who grow impatient and frustrated by the incrementalist and brokerage orientation of the state legislature. These activists often wish to stop progress or to push things forward fast. As one longtime aide to the Colorado legislature put it: "The conservatives most often use initiated constitutional amendments to try to stop people and government from doing things. The liberals are more likely to use initiated constitutional amendments to try to get things going."[26]

The number of initiated constitutional amendments increased during the 1970s and the 1980s. In the five general elections from 1950 to 1958, eight initiated amendments were presented to the voters, the same number as were placed on the ballot in the five elections from 1960 to 1968. In the five elections from 1970 to 1978, however, there were twelve initiated constitutional amendments sent to the voters, and in the seven elections from 1980 to 1992 there were 24. Clearly, initiated constitutional amendments are gaining in popularity in Colorado.

The U.S. Supreme Court gave a boost to those who initiate constitutional amendments when it ruled the state of Colorado could not outlaw the use of paid workers to gather signatures for an initiative petition.[27] This decision increased the opportunity for persons and groups with substantial financial resources to be able to get their favorite idea or reform for the state constitution initiated onto the general election ballot. A staff member in the Colorado secretary of state's office speculated that special interests in the state might begin using paid petition circulators in an effort to initiate constitutional amendments that would provide them direct economic benefits.[28]

The initiated constitutional amendment sometimes becomes a not-too-subtle element in the partisan competition between the Democratic and Republican parties in Colorado. For instance, in 1966 an initiated constitutional amendment mandated single-member legislative districts in Colorado, a reform generally acknowledged to have helped the Republicans.

ANOTHER CONSTITUTIONAL CONVENTION FOR COLORADO?

In 1976 and again in 1987, citizen groups sponsored major assemblies at which unelected "delegates" discussed the question of calling a constitutional convention to rewrite the Colorado constitution.

The 1976 group was known as the Citizens' Inquiry into the Colorado Constitution and held a Citizens' Assembly on the State Constitution at Boulder in August of 1976. The meeting was part of Colorado's celebration of both the bicentennial of the Declaration of Independence and the centennial of Colorado statehood. Although calling for a constitutional convention was seriously debated by this group, it recommended instead that a "Constitutional Review Commission should be established to study the Constitution and to make recommendations for change."[29] The proposed commission was given the responsibility of deciding what parts of the constitution to change and the best method of changing them. However, due to lack of support from the governor's office as well as from the state legislature, the Constitutional Review Commission was never authorized.

In the report of its proceedings, the Citizens' Assembly made a series of general recommendations for amending the Colorado constitution, including strengthening the appointive and budget powers of the state governor, eliminating unextendable time limits on sessions of the state legislature, providing for consolidation of city and county governments, and removing or reducing constitutional limitations on the state's ability to borrow money and incur public debt.[30]

In 1987 the Graduate School of Public Affairs of the University of Colorado at Denver sponsored a Model Constitutional Convention on the Colorado constitution. Delegates from throughout the state were invited to Denver to mark the bicentennial of the writing of the U.S. Constitution by reviewing the Colorado constitution and making recommendations for change.

Two of the recommendations of the 1976 Citizens' Assembly were reiterated by the Model Constitutional Convention: strengthening the appointive and budgetary powers of the governor and making it easier for cities and counties to consolidate. The Model Constitutional Convention disagreed with the 1976 Citizens' Assembly by recommending a limit on legislative sessions and by urging that Colorado continue to prohibit deficit spending in the state constitution. "New ideas" that emerged from the 1987 Model Constitutional Convention included prohibiting the majority party in the state legislature from using the binding caucus and making the constitutional amendment process more difficult.[31]

The 1987 Model Constitutional Convention urged its members to "support . . . current legislative initiatives to simplify and clean up the constitution."[32] Two of its recommendations, the limit on legislative sessions and the elimination of the binding caucus in the state legislature (later known as the GAVEL amendment to stand for "Give A Vote to Every Legislator") were placed on the 1988 general election ballot and adopted by the voters.

As a follow-up to this Model Constitutional Convention, a subcommittee was designated to brief the governor and leaders of the state legislature. They did hold such meetings, but legislative leaders showed little interest in the Model Constitutional Convention's recommendations.[33]

Despite these citizens' meetings, there is little sentiment in the state, even among those government officials who work most closely with the state constitution, to undertake any overhaul of the Centennial State constitution. As a researcher for the legislature put it: "There is no certainty that Colorado's long constitution is a real impediment to legislation. The legislative staff periodically is asked what is or is not constitutional, but only occasionally."[34]

Nor is there strong grassroots sentiment for overhauling the constitution. A poll for the *Denver Post* conducted by Talmey and Associates in 1988 found only about a third of their respondents agreed with this statement: "The Colorado state constitution is out of date and needs to be revised."[35] In a political environment where few groups are feeling hampered by a long and detailed state constitution, there are not likely to be any significant or effective movements for a major rewriting.[36]

CONCLUSION

Citizens of Colorado remain largely indifferent to their state constitution. Elected officials, especially state legislators, are apparently satisfied that they can live and work with the constitution as it is.

Many elected officials worry about the process by which citizen groups and groups supporting a particular cause initiate amendments that alter the constitution. Yet these same officials are afraid to take that power away from the people—nor could they, since the voters themselves would have to do so by a positive vote to amend the existing constitution.

Most legislators and most political scientists have long favored relying on elected officials for lawmaking and for amending constitutions, contending there is a difference between public opinion and the public interest. But it is clear that most American voters, and an even higher percentage of Colorado voters, want to have a voice in the shaping of laws and in the reshaping of their constitution.

The Colorado constitution continues to grow. Some would say it is an appropriate living institution adapting to new needs and changing demographic and political values. Others bemoan the large amount of new detail in this ever-lengthening document.[37]

Central participants in the policymaking and lawmaking process not only manage to live with the Colorado constitution, in all its revised and expanded annotations and amendments, but they also plainly prefer to cope with it as it is rather than take any chances on a constitutional convention that might weaken the document or alter the strategic balance of power that it describes. Middle-of-the-roaders and mainstreamers active in political life have pretty much adopted this rule: "If it ain't really broken, you don't have to fix or even tinker much with it." Only a relatively small number of ever-present process-reformers want to overhaul the constitutional system in the Centennial State. And invariably this is because they believe a different set of policies might be produced by a different document, an "improved" and "streamlined" state constitution.

CHAPTER FIVE

Coloradans and Their Political Beliefs

Who are the people of Colorado? What do they believe? What do surveys and poll data tell about the attitudes, values, and political views of Coloradans?[1]

Surveys and poll results are merely a snapshot of what citizens are thinking at a particular time. Specific percentage distributions usually vary in different polls at different times. Yet, it is the patterns that are of interest. Where possible, the views of Coloradans will be compared with the views of Americans throughout the entire nation. One general conclusion is that Coloradans in the early 1990s are more conservative, more Republican, and more favorable to local government as opposed to the federal government than are Americans in general.

Future treatments of Colorado politics may pose many of these same questions to citizens of the Centennial State, thus allowing for comparisons of these political beliefs over time. Doubtless, the general leanings revealed by most of these polls will not change much over time, at least in the near future.

DEMOGRAPHIC PROFILE

One of the profound demographic realities in contemporary Colorado is that roughly seven out of every ten adults were born outside Colorado. Colorado is fifth in the nation of state residents claiming some other state as their birthplace. Thus, Colorado is notably a state of "immigrants," and this has been the case throughout the state's history. It has been a state of steady and sometimes transforming population growth for more than a hundred years.

There were about 100,000 "Coloradans" when the state began in 1876. Sixty-five years later, around the start of World War II, Colorado's population had grown to about 1.2 million. The state's population doubled in the next forty years, and by 1990 Colorado had about 3.3 million residents. State demographers estimate there will be 3.8 million Coloradans around the year 2000 and perhaps as many as 5 million by year 2030.

Where do Coloradans come from? They come from virtually all corners of the United States, although most are from either nearby states or the megastates, such as California. More come from the West, Midwest, and South than from the Northeast. California, Texas, Illinois, and Arizona alone account for about a third of Colorado's newest residents. Florida sends a large number. Neighboring states, such as Wyoming, Oklahoma, Kansas, and Nebraska, also exported a reasonable share of residents to the Centennial State.

U.S. Census data also track the out-migration of Coloradans. Not surprisingly the Sun Belt states of California, Texas, Arizona, and Florida lead the list of where Coloradans go when they leave. Washington, New Mexico, and Kansas are next in line for exiting Coloradans. Overall, census data suggest Coloradans stay in the West, rather than migrating to the Midwest or East. Indeed, more than 40 percent of those leaving Colorado relocate to other states in the Rocky Mountain West or Pacific West.

Colorado has a relatively young population. Young adults, often risktaking adults, come in search of both jobs and the great outdoor attractions the state so amply provides. Its reputation for boom and bust may deter older Americans from coming. And certainly its challenging winters help explain why older Americans probably do not relocate in large numbers to the state.

Doubtless, too, these same factors explain why many older Coloradans move southward and southwestward after retirement. Unlike Florida, Arizona, or similar Sun Belt states, Colorado is not considered a retirement location. The high altitude is hardly an inducement for older people concerned about heart troubles, and Colorado-style skiing, mountain climbing, and hunting generally are not prime senior-citizen diversions. Thus, the elderly population is a small fraction of the state's total—only 9 percent are over age sixty-five, giving Colorado a national rank of forty-seventh in this age category. Accordingly, Colorado ranks forty-seventh in Social Security recipients.

EDUCATION AND ETHNIC CHARACTERISTICS

Colorado in recent years has had one of the highest percentages of residents with a college degree. Yet "half of them earned their degrees in other states, meaning that the good taxpayers of Michigan, Massachusetts, Indiana and

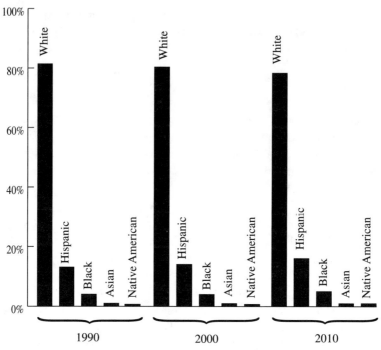

Figure 1. Present and Projected Ethnic and Race Populations for Colorado
(Source: Jim Westkott,"Summary of Ethnic Projections," Colorado Department of Local Affairs, mimeo, April 1990, p.3.)

Ohio paid for that education, after which the recipient took it to Colorado.''[2] One reason Colorado usually bounces back from its cyclical economic busts is this reservoir of well-educated younger workers. Colorado's investment in higher education and its public schools, however, often have been below that of most other states.

Colorado high school students who took the SAT and ACT competitive college entrance exams in recent years have scored above the national averages. However, the graduation rate from high school (about 75 percent) is near the national average (twenty-fourth in 1988). Average teacher salaries ranked seventeenth in the nation, while average expenditures per student ranked sixteenth. Pupil-teacher ratio, however, at about eighteen to one, gave Colorado a rank of thirty-fourth in the nation. Beginning salaries for teachers put Colorado in thirty-sixth place.

Colorado's racial and ethnic makeup is predominately white and European, although the state's minority populations continue to grow. Minorities will comprise about 25 to 30 percent of the state's population in the year 2020. If present trends continue, minorities will be a majority of the population in Denver by the year 2000. Hispanics and Asian-Americans are the fastest growing ethnic populations. The largest numbers of Colorado's blacks, Hispanics, and Asian-Americans are concentrated in or near Denver (see figure 1.)

Women comprise nearly 45 percent of the work force in Colorado, making the state tenth in the nation in this ranking. Ethnic minorities currently comprise over 15 percent of the work force, and this number will rise to about 20 percent or more a generation from now. Colorado's minorities earn higher incomes than their counterparts in most parts of the country, and yet there is still a wide margin between minority and Anglo earning power.

Most Coloradans of all races and ethnic groups believe race relations need to be improved. Significant numbers (between 20 and 40 percent) of African-Americans report feeling discriminated against by the police, in housing, in getting a job, and in job promotion. Over a third of both Latino and African-American populations in Colorado can recall being the object of racial or ethnic slurs. Everyone agrees that schools need to improve the quality of education given to minorities and that everyone should avoid discrimination. Two-thirds of those surveyed in our own September 1990 poll of adult Coloradans agreed with this statement: "If minorities are not receiving fair treatment when it comes to jobs or housing, it is the responsibility of government to step in and make sure they are treated fairly."[3] While this is not the same as saying one would pay more taxes to help ensure and enforce fairness, it does suggest a positive, if general, affirmation of social justice ideals.

Hispanics, in part because of concentrated populations and because of strongly developed roots in Colorado's history, have long enjoyed reasonable representation in the state legislature. They have served in legislative leadership posts, such as president of the state Senate and minority leader in the state House of Representatives. Federico Pena, a Texas-born Hispanic, served two terms as mayor of Denver. Blacks have been underrepresented in the legislature, although George Brown, a black former state legislator, also served as lieutenant governor in the 1970s. Denver's first black mayor, Wellington Webb, was elected in 1991.

OTHER CHARACTERISTICS

The typical Coloradan is thirty years old, lives in the suburbs of Denver, is employed, and owns a home. Studies done at the University of Colorado in

Denver report there were about 3,500 homeless people in Colorado on any given night in 1990 and perhaps as many as 10,000 homeless in any year. Many are homeless for short periods, thus explaining the difference in these figures. Colorado's homeless population is proportionally less than in states along America's two coasts.

Another 8,000 or more persons are in prison or jail in Colorado at any given time. About 55,500 Coloradans work for the state government and nearly 150,000 work for county or local governments. Over 8,000 hold elective office of some kind, ranging from U.S. Senator to library and park district boards. Colorado is ranked ninth in numbers of Hispanics and twenty-eighth in numbers of African-Americans. Fully 82 percent of Coloradans are classified as living in metropolitan areas or cities, somewhat higher than the nation's average.

Coloradans ski, hunt, fish, and enjoy the out-of-doors more than most Americans. Coloradans are first in the nation in subscriptions to outdoor recreation magazines. According to the U.S. Fish and Wildlife Service, Colorado in recent years has led all states in revenue from sales of hunting licenses. In 1989, for example, 731,744 fishing licenses and 340,911 hunting licenses were issued in the state.

One national study concluded that the Denver area "has nearly three times as many skiers than the national average." Denver-area residents also have much higher inclinations toward camping and hiking, bicycling, recreational vehicles, motorcycles, and running and jogging.[4]

Colorado workers in 1990 earned $22,909 a year—slightly below the average in the nation.[5] Coloradans live, on average, more than seventy-five years, putting the state among the nation's top ten in terms of life expectancy. Violent crime occurs less frequently in Colorado than elsewhere in the country. But the state has no lack of lawyers. There is a lawyer for every 284 Coloradans, the fifth highest ratio in the United States. The state ranked fifth in foreclosed mortgages in the late 1980s, and its suicide rate has been among the top ten in the nation in recent years, according to U.S. Census figures. In 1988 Colorado led the nation in business failures.

The wholesale and retail trades employ 25 percent of the labor force in Colorado. The service sector employs another 23 percent. Nineteen percent are employed by governments at one level or another as teachers, civil servants, postal workers, and the like. Thirteen percent are employed in manufacturing. Seven percent of the labor force is engaged in finance, insurance, or real estate. Five to six percent are workers in transportation or public utilities. Finally, only about 3 percent are now employed in two of Colorado's oldest and most noted economic sectors, agriculture and mining.

Colorado is one of the top ten states in the number of federal employees. Over 100,000 civilian or military federal employees made their residence in Colorado as of 1993. It also is in the top ten for federal spending in the state per person. In 1989 this amounted to $4,216 per Coloradan.

Religious beliefs are generally viewed as a personal matter in Colorado, and most residents do not know the religion of their neighbors. Carl Miller, formerly of the *Denver Post,* said the difference at cocktail parties in Colorado, as opposed to such places as Texas, is that instead of asking new acquaintances where they go to church, people in Colorado are more likely to ask, "Where do you and your family ski?"[6] A *Rocky Mountain News* editor, Vincent Carroll, said Coloradans are conservative, "yet not in the Bible Belt sense. People here are tolerant of religious practices and the religious beliefs of others."[7] Abortion, of course, has been a potent political issue in many states, and this is true of Colorado as well. A 1990 Ciruli and Associates poll found that 17 percent of those polled consider abortion the most important issue to consider when voting for a candidate.[8] Still, religious preferences and beliefs have generally been viewed as a private matter. Only 10 percent of a 1984 Talmey and Associates poll disagreed with the statement that "Religion and Faith are Private Matters and do not belong in Partisan Political Debate." In this same survey, only 14 percent of Coloradans affirmed that "Atheists should not be allowed to hold public office."[9]

POLITICAL CONSERVATIVES

In our survey of Coloradans, 44 percent identified themselves as conservatives in political outlook. One-third said they were middle-of-the-roaders, and less than a quarter called themselves liberals. Figure 2 summarizes the way Coloradans characterized themselves in terms of political ideology.

A similar question was posed at about the same time to a nationwide sample of Americans. Virtually the same percent (22 percent) of Americans as Coloradans called themselves liberal. However, there were 12 percent fewer conservatives nationwide than in the Colorado sample. Thus 44 percent of Coloradans, but only 32 percent of Americans, called themselves conservatives in late 1990.[10]

In addition to calling themselves primarily either conservatives or middle-of-the-roaders politically, Coloradans also emphasize the importance of individual responsibility. Sixty-one percent of a statewide sample agreed

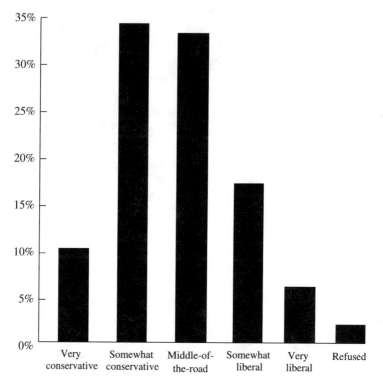

Question: "And in terms of political outlook, do you usually think of yourself as very conservative, somewhat conservative, middle-of-the-road, somewhat liberal, or very liberal?"

Figure 2. Coloradans' Assessment of Their Political Outlook
(*Source:* Colorado College – Colorado Citizens Poll, conducted by Talmey-Drake, September 1990, N = 614.)

that "each individual should take care of him or herself." Only 35 percent favored the idea that "government should work to make people's lives, and community life, better."

The citizens of Colorado, also as expected, said they thought governments closer to them were more efficient than those at a distance, such as the national government. About half of those polled believed their state government was wasteful and inefficient, but they still preferred it over the federal government. As one citizen in Crawford said: "The local and state governments aren't all that bad, but I don't like the government in Washington—they really know how to waste money."[11] Data in figure 3 suggest three times

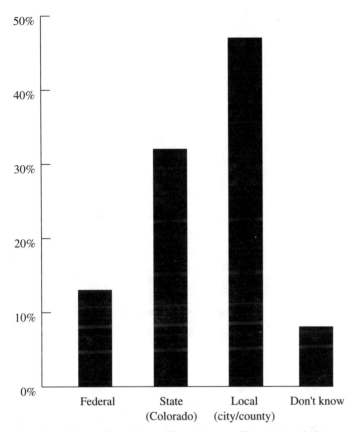

Question: "Regardless of how efficiently or inefficiently you feel state government operates, which of the three levels of government – federal, state, or local –
do you think is the most efficient?"

Figure 3. Coloradans' Ranking of Efficiency of Levels of Government
(Source: Colorado College – Colorado Citizens Poll, conducted by
Talmey-Drake, September 1990, N = 614.)

as many Coloradans believe local governments are less wasteful of their taxpayer dollars than is the federal government.

A nationwide survey conducted by the Advisory Commission on Intergovernmental Relations (ACIR) found twice the number of Americans as Coloradans who held positive views of the federal government. The question the
ACIR posed was worded slightly differently, yet essentially asked for the
same response: "From which level of government do you feel you get the
most for your money—federal, state or local?" This 1991 poll found 26 per-

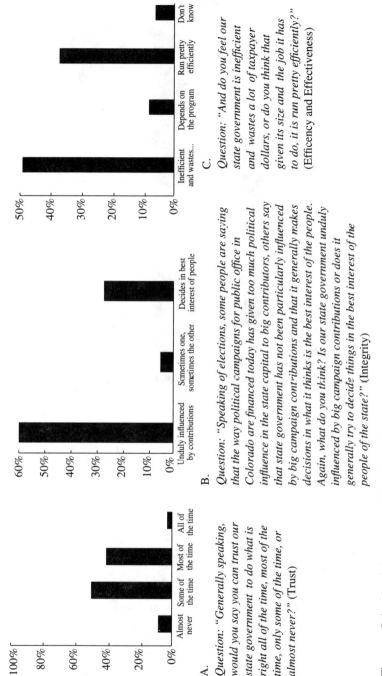

Figure 4. Coloradans' Assessment of Integrity of State Government

(*Source:* Colorado College – Colorado Citizens Poll, conducted by Talmey-Drake, September 1990, N = 614.)

A.

Question: "Generally speaking, would you say you can trust our state government to do what is right all of the time, most of the time, only some of the time, or almost never?" (Trust)

B.

Question: "Speaking of elections, some people are saying that the way political campaigns for public office in Colorado are financed today has given too much political influence in the state capital to big contributors, others say that state government has not been particularly influenced by big campaign contributions and that it generally makes decisions in what it thinks is the best interest of the people. Again, what do you think? Is our state government unduly influenced by big campaign contributions or does it generally try to decide things in the best interest of the people of the state?" (Integrity)

C.

Question: "And do you feel our state government is inefficient and wastes a lot of taxpayer dollars, or do you think that given its size and the job it has to do, it is run pretty efficiently?" (Efficency and Effectiveness)

cent saying federal, 22 percent saying state, and 31 percent saying local (22 percent failed to answer).[12] Overall, in this comparison, Coloradans were much less favorable to the federal government and considerably more respectful (by a 47 to 31 percent differential) of the efficiency of their local governments.

Coloradans who called themselves conservatives were at least three times more likely to be Republicans than Democrats and tended to be somewhat older than those who called themselves liberals. Conservatives were more likely to be married than single, separated, or divorced, and were somewhat more likely to own their own homes and have higher incomes than did liberals. But aside from the partisan differences, these other correlations were not statistically strong. Moreover, gender, urban or rural residence, level of education, or having children at home made no perceptible difference in predicting a liberal, as opposed to a conservative political outlook.

SKEPTICISM TOWARD STATE GOVERNMENT

Most Coloradans, according to a random sample, said their state government is inefficient and wasteful. They also thought "fat cats," or big contributors, have undue influence and that state officials often do not decide in the best interests of the people. Further, Coloradans were not convinced their government does what is right all of the time. On the contrary, at least three-fifths of the citizenry said the state does what is right only some of the time, or "almost never." These findings, presented in figure 4, suggest a strong skepticism toward state government and may explain why voters in 1992 voted in favor of limiting state government spending and requiring statewide votes on major new taxes. Voters in that same election voted against Governor Roy Romer's plan to raise the 3 percent state sales tax to 4 percent.

On balance, the responses to these questions suggest the majority of Coloradans are skeptical, if not hostile, to state government. However, this sample of Coloradans was decidedly less harsh or critical toward their elected and appointed public officials than they were to government in the abstract. Indeed, nearly three-quarters of those polled (72 percent) approved of the job Roy Romer was doing as governor in late 1990. A mere 18 percent disapproved of his performance. (Two years later in late 1992 the governor still enjoyed a better than 60 percent approval rating.) Colorado citizens also gave their assessment of the state legislature, the state courts, and the thousands of state employees who help run the state bureaucracy. Figure 5 indicates that more than 50 percent approved of the general performance of the state legis-

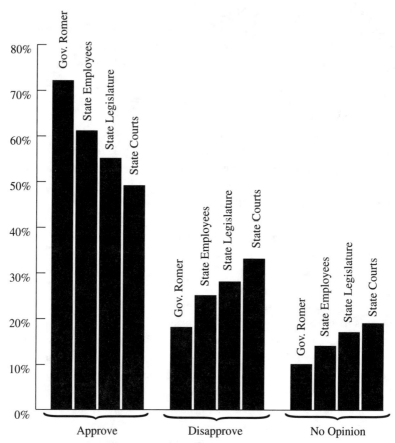

Question: "Do you approve or disapprove of the job . . . is/are doing . . . ?"

Figure 5. Coloradans' Assessment of Branches of State Government
(*Source:* Colorado College – Colorado Citizens Poll, conducted by Talmey-Drake,
September 1990, N = 614.)

lature and state employees, and nearly 50 percent approved the general way
in which the state courts were working.

This approval of state employees should not be construed as anything but
a general sentiment. A January 1989 Talmey Research and Strategy poll for
the *Denver Post* asked whether Coloradans would favor passage of a law to
"increase the salaries of state employees." By a vote of 51 percent to 27 percent, a random sample of Coloradans rejected this idea.[13] Coloradans can
think state employees are working efficiently without wanting to pay them

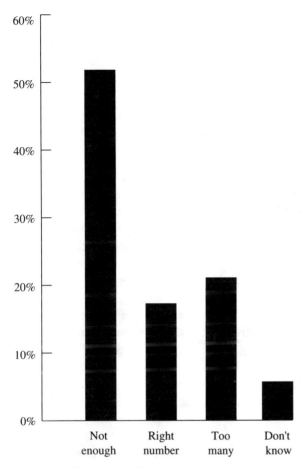

Question: "As you probably know, in almost every election, voters in Colorado are asked to vote directly on various ballot issues or questions. Some people say there are too many of these direct votes or referendums; others say they should have the opportunity to vote on even more issues. How do you feel? Are there too many referendums in Colorado or not enough?"

Figure 6. Coloradans' Preference for the Initiative Process
(*Source:* Colorado College – Colorado Citizens Poll, conducted by Talmey-Drake, September 1990, N = 614.)

more. No doubt this is due to their perceptions of their own salaries and of the general economic situation. Thus there is no contradiction in their views.

The approval rating of 55 percent favorable for the state legislature is up fourteen percentage points from the response to the same question asked of Coloradans in 1986 and reported in the *Denver Post*.[14] Approval of then Governor Lamm was 69 percent.

PREFERENCE FOR VOTING ON ISSUES

Governor Roy Romer and several state legislators have complained about the number of citizen-initiated referendum issues that have been put on the ballot in recent elections. They suggested lawmaking should be left to the lawmakers and that too frequent use of the initiative and referendum process weakens and undermines representative government. Americans have, these officials liked to emphasize, a "representative democracy, not a direct democracy."[15]

Pollster Paul Talmey said he thought that Coloradans might be getting tired of having so many legislative and constitutional issues on the ballot every election. But he was wrong. Centennial State citizens believe, if anything, there should be more such opportunities to vote directly on various state issues. Coloradans doubtless admire and respect the virtues of representative government, but as figure 6 suggests, most citizens in the Centennial State want a greater voice in approving or disapproving state laws and constitutional amendments. That Coloradans like voting on issues may be a sign of basic moralistic commitments or just another illustration of general populism. Fifty-four percent said there are not enough questions on the ballot, and only 22 percent complained there are too many referendum issues on election day.

This commitment to direct democracy was put to the test in November of 1992. At that election there were thirteen general ballot issues amending the state constitution or enacting laws, three referred by the legislature and ten initiated by citizen-signature campaigns. But by the time election day had arrived, most voters had prepared themselves for the task of selective lawmaking—and, as usual, voters voted to defeat most of the citizen-initiated proposed laws.

MORE SERVICES FOR LESS MONEY

Coloradans are like citizens everywhere in the United States. They believe taxes are too high, yet they also believe state government should be provid-

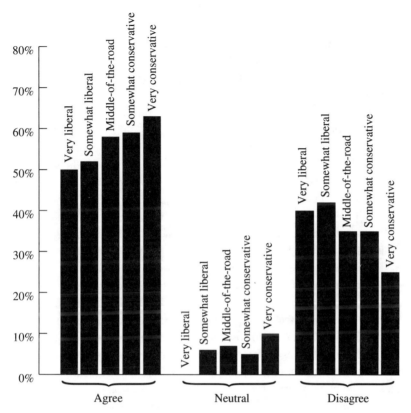

Question: "Taxes are too high and the state legislature needs to do something about it . . . "

Figure 7. Coloradans' Attitudes toward Taxes Correlated with Political Outlook (*Source:* Colorado College – Colorado Citizens Poll, conducted by Talmey-Drake, September 1990, N = 614.)

ing more and better services. This sounds contradictory, and it is. But such ambivalence is nothing new in America or elsewhere. Humans are full of contradictions. Also, few people really understand the cost of public services, or see clearly that there is a direct connection between the amount of government services provided and the amount of taxes paid.

What makes these beliefs noteworthy is that taxes are not unusually high in Colorado. Various state economic development booklets frequently boast: "Doing business in Colorado is anything but taxing." Colorado's 3 percent state sales tax is among the lowest of the forty-five states that impose sales taxes. Corporate income tax rates are the lowest among the forty-four states that have them. Personal income tax rates are twenty-fourth out of the forty-two states with income taxes. Even when state and local tax rates are combined, including property and sales taxes, Colorado ranks about in the middle of the fifty states. In short, Colorado is not what anyone could justifiably consider a heavily taxed state.

Polling revealed, however, that Coloradans consider themselves heavily taxed and want taxes lowered. Sixty-nine percent of those interviewed said state government is doing only a fair or poor job of "keeping state taxes down." Fifty-seven percent in this same survey agreed with the statement that "taxes in Colorado are too high, and the state legislature has got to do something about cutting the state's tax burden." Even those who call themselves liberals say taxes are too high. Figure 7 compares liberals and conservatives and their views about taxes. Those who call themselves very conservative are most strongly against the taxes they pay in Colorado, but there is a widespread antitax sentiment across all ideological outlooks.

Although most of those surveyed said Colorado government is doing a good or even excellent job providing parks and recreation facilities, they are otherwise critical of the job the state is doing on most other programs. Thus 60 percent of those surveyed complain that the state is doing only a poor or fair job of maintaining the state's roads and highways; 55 percent say the state does only a poor or fair job in protecting the environment; 57 percent feel it is doing only a poor or fair job of providing social services for Colorado's low-income residents; and nearly half say Colorado government is doing only a poor or fair job of promoting economic development.

All of this is a painfully familiar refrain for legislators and governors: "Do more, yet tax us less!" Most citizens genuinely believe better and more services and benefits can be rendered and, at the same time, taxes can go down. Their simple solution is to cut all the waste and inefficiency in government. One little problem often arises, however—one person's waste is usually another's vital service or indispensable benefit. Thus, while a majority of Coloradans concur that the state highway system needs to be improved and expanded, only 29 percent of the citizenry supported the idea of a $150 million increase in state taxes for highway construction and maintenance.[16]

This is not to say, however, that Coloradans are unwilling to pay more taxes if they can be assured the funds are well spent on some desired service or protection. For instance, in 1986 two-thirds of Coloradans favored a 25 percent increase in the state sales tax to build a new medium-security prison.

And voters in and around Denver have voted to tax themselves to support the zoo, the symphony, and the library system and to build a stadium to help bring a major-league baseball team to Denver. Most Coloradans also said that they would pay slightly more in taxes for better schools and for increases in teacher salaries.

EMPHASIS ON ECONOMY AND ENVIRONMENT

The economy and the environment, although not always in that order, head the list of major public worries in Colorado. In the boom economic years of 1986–87, most Coloradans saw the environment as the most important problem, with the economy in second position. In 1989 and 1990, however, when Colorado was in one of its periodic economic slumps, the economy and unemployment came first and the environment was in the runner-up spot.

KNOWLEDGE OF POLITICS

Polls reveal that most adult Coloradans subscribe to and at least casually read a newspaper. More than half subscribe to cable television. But few can name their state legislators or U.S. representative. A *Denver Post* poll in May of 1986 found that more than 85 percent of a random sample of Coloradans drew a blank when asked to name their state senator or state representative. Only 36 percent could name one of the state's six-member delegation to the House of Representatives.

"The lack of public awareness indicated by the poll most likely will work in favor of incumbents at election time," observed a *Denver Post* columnist. "If people don't know who their representatives are, they can't have much of an opinion of their job performance. And that means they will have a tendency to vote for the current officeholder."[17]

While only a small percentage (12 percent) of a random sample of Coloradans say they follow politics "all of the time," about 60 percent say they follow political matters at least "most of the time." Doubtless this is a little inflated, for people are inclined to tell telephone interviewers that they follow civic affairs somewhat more than they probably do. More revealing is that 57 percent of Coloradans in 1990 could not identify correctly the party holding a majority of the seats in the Colorado state legislature—despite the fact that Republicans have controlled both houses of the state General Assembly since the mid 1970s.

Voters with college degrees and an income over $50,000 are almost twice

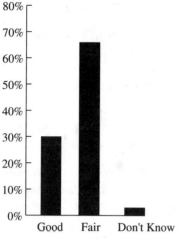

A. *Task: "Getting things done"*

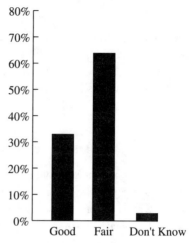

B. *Task: "Keeping citizens informed about what goes on in state government*

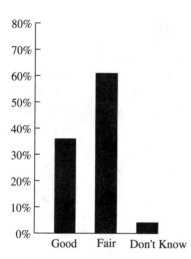

C. *Task: "Representing people like me"*

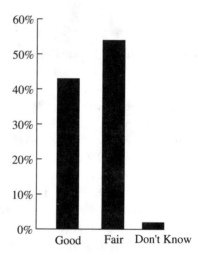

D. *Task: "Knowing the issues and problems that are important to the people of Colorado"*

Figure 8. Coloradans' Rating of State Government
(*Source:* Colorado College – Colorado Citizens' Poll, conducted by Talmey-Drake, September 1990, N=614.)

as likely to follow politics as people who have a high school education or less or who earn less than $20,000 a year. Males are somewhat more likely to follow public issues than females. And those who identify themselves as very liberal are much more likely to stay informed than those who are middle-of-the-roaders or conservatives.

There was no significant difference between Republicans and Democrats in terms of awareness of civic affairs. In general, people between the ages of forty-five and sixty-five were most apt to say they followed the news on a regular basis. Citizens who stay best informed tend to be well-educated, high-income males who are liberal and regularly read newspapers.

RESPONSIVENESS OF GOVERNMENT

Coloradans were asked how they felt about the performance of state officials and state government at such general tasks as "getting things done" and "representing people like me." Figure 8 shows that for these kinds of tasks, the citizens of Colorado basically registered a vote of no confidence in state government. This rating of the state government as "fair" rather than "good" implies that Coloradans do not think their state government listens to them or represents them adequately, and that they think state government should have more integrity. In effect, Coloradans were giving state government a grade of C or C- for awareness of citizen needs.

CIVIL RIGHTS, CIVIL LIBERTIES, AND FEAR

As noted earlier in the chapter, a clear majority of Coloradans said the government should ensure that minorities receive fair treatment when it comes to housing and job hiring. But when responding to questions on civil liberties, large numbers indicated they would sacrifice many of the safeguards specified in the Bill of Rights. At least a third of Coloradans interviewed in recent statewide polls did not believe drug dealers should be accorded the rights of other accused criminals. Similarly, many Coloradans would ban books that advocate racial hatred or racial violence. Censorship of pornography was also advocated by many. Pollster Paul Talmey found that Coloradans are not particularly supportive of several aspects of the Bill of Rights. Indeed, he said the whole document "would be in trouble if we had to put it to a vote of the people these days."[18]

Coloradans generally side with the right of individuals to do what they want with their own lives. Thus 82 percent said that "the government has no business controlling or regulating private sexual practices between consenting adults.'' Eighty-seven percent indicated that "the family of a person who is in a coma should have the right to disconnect all life-support equipment, including a feeding tube, if medical experts say there is no hope of recovery." Fifty-three percent of Coloradans favored an amendment to the state constitution to allow a woman to have an abortion, for any reason, during the first trimester of pregnancy. Thirty-one percent oppose abortion, and 16 percent are undecided. [19]

Chauvinism, however, is still alive in Colorado. When Japanese companies bought two major Colorado ski resorts and several golf courses, a majority of Coloradans apparently opposed these purchases. State officials, however, actively court Japanese investments and downplay any notion of Japanese "control" or undue influence in the Colorado economy. Fifty-two percent of respondents to a statewide survey in February 1990 said the Colorado legislature should do something to stop the Japanese from buying up Colorado's ski areas, while only a third of those surveyed said they disagreed with that idea.

This should not be interpreted as suggesting Coloradans are anti-Japanese, but rather that they fear ownership of one of the state's most symbolic industries is slipping away from American control. It is doubtless also a matter of pride. In fact, most major industries in Colorado are owned by out-of-state interests, and British, German, Australian, and Canadian investors have a higher, or at least as great, economic interest in Colorado as do the Japanese. Yet perhaps there is at work a little lingering racism combined with resentment that a defeated foe in World War II is succeeding so well.

As is now well known, Coloradans in late 1992 voted (53.4%) to prohibit cities from passing laws preventing discrimination against homosexuals. The measure, which was pushed by the "religious right," won majority approval in a controversial election. Critics of the ban called it a "hate measure," and minority, gay rights, and many progressive groups launched a major counter-offensive in the courts. Some groups inside as well as outside of Colorado mounted a "Boycott Colorado" campaign that led to the cancellation of many conventions scheduled for Colorado in the mid and late 1990s.

Polls taken after the election indicate that most Coloradans were not so much opposed to gays as they were opposed to granting special rights to gays. Most Coloradans told pollsters that they were strongly opposed to discrimination against gays and that they also rejected the "hate state" label. Proponents of the now famous (or infamous) Amendment 2 successfully sold their constitutional initiative as a measure preventing "special" protection when in fact the laws passed by Denver, Boulder, and Aspen had not granted special rights. A December 1992 poll by the Talmey-Drake Research Company of Boulder found that 13 percent of Coloradans polled believed that homosexual behavior should be against the law, and 18 percent believed that gays should not be allowed to teach in public schools. Nearly 60 percent said they thought gays should be allowed to serve in the armed services. In short, although some Coloradans are intolerant, the majority claimed not to be.[20]

However, many prejudiced Coloradans may not be sharing their true views when they talk to pollsters. Indeed, most of the polls taken in the state prior to the 1992 elections did not indicate that Amendment 2 was likely to win voter approval. Election analysts have had to infer that certain kinds of values, such as anti-gay views, are not only more prevalent in modern-day Colorado than state opinion leaders wish to acknowledge but are difficult to study through typical public-opinion survey instruments.

Thus, while attitudes toward homosexuals in Colorado are probably about the same as they are elsewhere in most other states, Colorado earned widespread criticism and, at least in some quarters, a national reputation for bigotry because of the passage of Amendment 2. The measure could be overturned by state and federal courts, or perhaps at the 1994 elections. Still, its passage alone will ensure that Coloradans will have to defend or explain themselves for some time to come.

Pollster Paul Talmey suggests there also may be a touch of paranoia among Coloradans. Thus 69 percent of Coloradans agree with this statement: "Even though you almost never hear much about them, there are a few really powerful people in the country who pretty much make all the important decisions about how the country is run." An impressive 40 percent of those polled strongly agree with that view, and only 25 percent disagree. "Political paranoia has been stereotypically associated with the right, and while there is no shortage of right wing paranoids in Colorado," says Talmey, "Coloradans who consider themselves politically liberal are actually more likely to accept the notion of a secretive cabal running the country than are those with a conservative bent . . ."[21] The Talmey-Drake Report in September of 1992 went on to suggest that this notion of people feeling that they are losing control of their lives and that the American dream is no longer available to most people is backed up by a number of other sentiments of powerlessness and disappointment. Such people, the report suggests, may be more receptive to unorthodox and extremist solutions to state and national problems.[22]

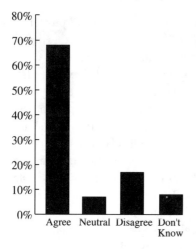

A. *"State government should be doing more to plan and regulate land use in Colorado."*

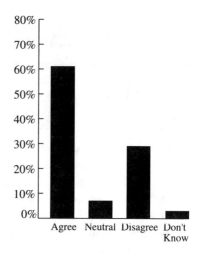

B. *"We have to protect the environment no matter what the costs."*

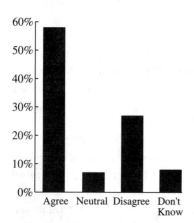

C. *"Colorado needs stronger laws to protect the natural environment even if those laws endanger jobs and economic growth in the state."*

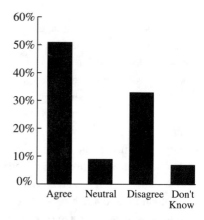

D. *"The state of Colorado should be spending more of its tax dollars on buying open spaces and developing parks and recreation areas."*

Figure 9. Coloradans' Views on the Environment
(*Source:* Statewide poll conducted by Talmey Research and Strategy, reported in the *Denver Post*, January 8, 1990, p.83, N = 506.)

Most polls in 1990 found that between 60 and 70 percent of Coloradans called themselves environmentalists. Of those, nearly a quarter belonged to an organization that works to promote or lobby on behalf of the environment, such as the Sierra Club.

As noted, most Coloradans do not believe their state government is doing enough to protect the environment. The majority of Coloradans surveyed told pollsters that they are "very concerned" about contaminated drinking water, toxic chemicals and hazardous waste in the workplace, air pollution in greater Denver, and radioactivity from nuclear plants and waste in Colorado.

About 80 percent of Coloradans responded favorably to the idea of designating large tracts in the state as wilderness areas. Polls found that about 70 percent of Coloradans said society should be restructured to be more in harmony with nature.

Figure 9 summarizes a January 1990 survey of Coloradans that indicated state officials need to be even more aggressive in environmental protection efforts. Whether those same proponents would be willing to pay more taxes for these often-costly efforts is, of course, a different matter, although some of the statements in the survey do imply these policies may cost more and may restrict certain kinds of economic growth.

PARTY LOYALISTS

In recent years about 30 to 33 percent of Coloradans who register to vote register as Democrats. An even larger number, typically about 33 to 36 percent, register as Republicans. The remainder, and occasionally the largest number of all, between 30 and 40 percent, register as "unaffiliated." Pollsters and political scientists have long believed that about two-thirds of these so-called independents or unaffiliateds regularly vote for one party or the other. Indeed, they may be even moderately or strongly tied to that party.[23]

For a variety of professional, personal, or even idiosyncratic reasons, these voters registered as unaffiliated. In late 1990 a random sample of Coloradans was asked: "Regardless of how you are registered to vote, do you think of yourself as a Republican or do you think of yourself as a Democrat?" Notice this question did not offer the interviewed individual the option of selecting independent or unaffiliated. The posed question deliberately tried to get people to indicate their true party loyalties. Three-quarters of the respondents did indicate a preferred party. Quite a number of others, however, specified, even though unprompted, that they were independents. The poll results indicated that 41 percent of the respondents considered themselves Republicans, 35 percent considered themselves Democrats, and 21 percent considered themselves Independents (unprompted); nearly 4 percent did not know or perhaps had loyalties to some minor party. (The same question asked in late 1992 found that 38 percent of Coloradans considered themselves Republicans and 33 percent said they were Democrats.)

In the fall of 1990 results of a nationwide survey of Americans indicated that they were more Democratic and less Republican than Coloradans, in response to this question: "Generally speaking, do you consider yourself a Republican, a Democrat, an independent, or what?" Only 30 percent in this *New York Times–CBS News Poll* replied they were Republicans; 34 percent said they were Democrats; and another 32 percent identified themselves as independents. But 47 percent of the so-called independents thought of themselves as closer to the Democratic party. Thus the nationwide breakdown was about 49 percent leaning Democratic and only 42 percent leaning Republican, while in Colorado at that time 41 percent of respondents were leaning Republican and 35 percent were leaning Democratic.

Nationwide, Republicans and Democrats were asked whether they considered themselves strongly or only moderately Republican or Democratic. Thirty-one percent of these partisans affirmed strongly loyalties, while 69 percent said their ties to the party of their choice were merely moderate.[24]

Who are the Republicans in Colorado and how do they differ from the Democrats? There are few pronounced demographic differences. Surveys of Colorado's partisans permit only these rather confirming generalizations. The Republican party attracts few minority members. Republicans are twice as likely to attract party recruits from the upper-income levels, just as they are twice as unlikely to win supporters from those at the bottom of the income ladder. But there is no real difference in party ties in the lower-middle to upper-middle income bracket in Colorado. Republicans enjoy a slight edge among male registered voters and also among older Coloradans.

Colorado Republicans also were predictably much more likely to call themselves conservative in their political outlook and less likely to consider themselves as environmentalists. Republicans also were more prone than Democrats to embrace an individual/self-reliance political philosophy as opposed to an affirmative view of the positive role of government. Such attitudes as well as differences about the role of government in the area of civil rights are summarized in figure 10.

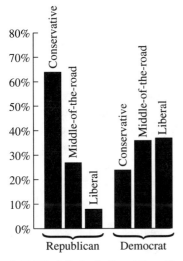

A. Political Outlook, Republican/Democrat

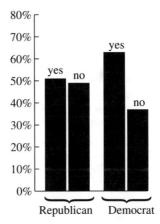

B. Considers Himself/Herself Environmentalist

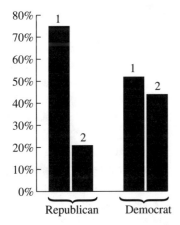

C. Attitudes about Government

1. *"Each individual should take care of him- or herself."*
2. *"Government should work to make people's lives – and community life – better."*

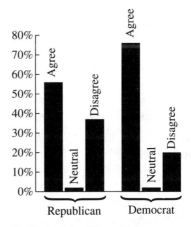

D. Civil Rights Disposition

"It's a responsibility of government to step in and make sure minorities are treated fairly."

Figure 10. Coloradans' Party Ties and Philosophical Differences
(*Source:* Colorado College – Colorado Citizens Poll, conducted by Talmey-Drake, September 1990, N = 614.)

While there are general differences between Republicans and Democrats in Colorado, one has to be careful in making sweeping generalizations. For example, even half of the Republicans liked to think of themselves as environmentalists, and a majority of registered Republican voters affirm a positive role for government in enforcing fairness and civil rights laws. And only a third or so of Colorado Democrats admitted to being liberals. Indeed, a fourth of registered Democrats viewed themselves as conservatives. Further, most Democrats placed a hearty emphasis on personal self-reliance over and above the role of government as a prime protector in everyone's lives.

Partisan differences are sharpest on election day, when most Republicans vote for Republicans and most Democrats vote for Democrats. As a rule, Colorado Republicans turn out to vote in higher numbers and are more loyal to their fellow partisans. That is, they are more likely to stick to voting for their party's nominee than are Colorado Democrats.

Republicans tend to be less favorably disposed toward government regulation of business and to worry more than Democrats about the negative impact that environmental measures might have on jobs and economic growth. One issue that set Republicans apart from Democrats is the proposal that nurses and physicians be required to donate forty hours each year for health services to indigents. Two-thirds of the Democrats favored this idea, which was actually introduced as a legislative bill in a recent session of the Colorado state legislature. Republicans, however, were far less receptive to this compulsory measure. Figure 11 illustrates the broad policy cleavages that help to define the two major parties in Colorado.

Democrats and Republicans did not differ about the crucial issue of baseball, as recorded in polls immediately before a 1990 referendum on a slight increase in the sales tax in the Greater Denver area to build a new baseball stadium in an attempt to lure a National League expansion team to Denver. If anything, Republicans supported the baseball referendum in slightly higher percentages than Democrats, as did, in more pronounced numbers, the suburbanites in Arapahoe and Jefferson counties. Nor was there a gender gap in the support of this baseball policy referendum.[25]

CONCLUSION

The demographic statistics and surveys summarized in this chapter confirm an image of Colorado as somewhat conservative, populist, and leaning Republican. Coloradans are tough critics of government at all levels but espe-

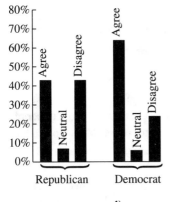

A. *"The government should be doing more to regulate and control the economy and big business."*

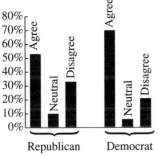

B. *"Colorado should be spending more tax dollars on open spaces, parks and recreational areas."*

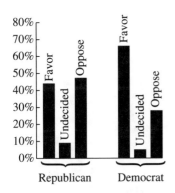

C. *"We should require health-care professionals to give 40 hours a year uncompensated care to the poor."*

Figure 11. Coloradans' Party Ties and Policy Differences
(*Source:* Various surveys conducted by Talmey Research and Strategy and reported in the *Denver Post* or on file in the *Denver Post* files late 1989 and early 1990.)

cially of the state and federal levels. Coloradans, more than most Americans, favor local governments over the state and federal governments and favor the Republican party over the Democratic party.

Coloradans express disappointment with many of the services and programs of state government, and would also like to see a far higher standard of integrity in government. They want their legislators to listen more to people like themselves and less to the "fat cat" big contributors. Most Coloradans like voting on issues at election time—they want to have a voice in the governing of the state.

Like citizens everywhere, Coloradans want economic growth and a safe environment, but they do not relish the idea of new or higher taxes to accomplish these objectives. The old perennial "more services but less taxes" and a skepticism about the integrity and efficiency of the governmental process are part of the enduring political makeup of Colorado.

CHAPTER SIX

Political Parties and Elections

The Centennial State is a Republican state and has been for most of its history, yet Democrats compete successfully for a number of statewide and congressional offices and, especially, for governor. As would be expected in a state where both parties win major statewide offices, there is an enormous amount of ticket splitting.

There also is something of a pattern of officeholders' switching parties. "It's very simple," said former U.S. Senator Floyd Haskell, who switched from Republican to Democrat in 1970. "Once you win an office and have to vote regularly on issues, you discover your true policy views. In my case, I found myself voting more and more with the Democrats and also found them supporting my bills."[1] Haskell became a Democrat in 1970 and, remarkably, won his new party's nomination for the U.S. Senate in 1972. He went on to win an upset victory in the general election over Republican Gordon Allott.

In 1987 Republican state Senator Martha Ezzard, who represented the affluent south Denver suburbs, announced her resignation from the legislature and her switch to Democrat. Though fiscally conservative, Ezzard's views on many social and environmental issues differed from GOP conservatives in the legislature. She was pro-choice on the abortion issue and in favor of the Equal Rights Amendment to the U.S. Constitution. "I changed parties because I couldn't change my philosophy, not because I changed my philosophy," she said. "I was very discouraged that the Republican Party wasn't being responsible on the issues. I became tired of always being on the defensive about them. I wanted a chance to play on the offense."[2]

Later that same year, Republican Attorney General Duane Woodard switched to Democrat. He said he was tired of being "beaten down" by GOP-sponsored budget cuts and other political backstabbing by fellow Republicans. "There comes a point in time when you realize that maybe representative government in the state of Colorado is a myth," Woodard said. "I'm tired of being a voice in the wilderness in the Colorado Republican Party."[3] Woodard was defeated by a relatively unknown Republican, Gale Norton, when he ran for reelection as a Democrat in 1990.

But there have been at least as many, and probably more, switches in recent years that have seen Democrats become Republicans. This has been especially true of a handful of state legislators, including Bob Kirscht from Pueblo and Faye Fleming from Thornton. Both switched as they grew somewhat more conservative and, more important, as they perceived the Democratic party becoming too liberal and politically ineffective in the state legislature.

For example, Representative Kirscht changed his affiliation to Republican in early 1981 right after his Democratic colleagues failed to reelect him as minority floor leader. Kirscht stated that "the Democrats had drifted away from the mainstream" of Colorado political life and were too unwilling to compromise some of their more liberal stands on certain issues.[4] Another possible factor was that in Colorado's Republican-dominated legislature, Kirscht could chair committees and get more bills passed as a Republican than as a Democrat.

Former Lakewood Mayor Linda Shaw was another Democrat-turned-Republican in the late 1980s. Shaw, who was a full-time elementary school teacher as well as mayor, said it was not so much a matter of issues as that she felt she could be more effective as a member of her city's majority party. "When I was in the minority party I was always a bit suspect," she said. "A lot of people were not inclined to help me, perhaps thinking I might run for higher office [against a Republican] someday. Also, the more I worked with many of the legislators and county commissioners in my area, the more I discovered many moderate and thoughtful Republicans whom I respected. I got tired of Democrats who constantly criticized all the Republicans as terrible. That just wasn't my experience. So I switched, and I know it has helped me to be far more effective in my job as mayor."[5]

What does all this party switching mean? It suggests, among other things, that Coloradans can sometimes be mavericks and independents. It also is a reflection of the basically weak parties in the state. Parties count, and often count more than anything else, in determining elections in the counties and for the state legislature. Yet working politicians and political observers must always be aware there is a streak of unpredictability in the party loyalty of Coloradans.

State law carefully spells out how the two major political parties in the state will be organized and will nominate candidates for office. Except in a number of cities and towns that have the option of holding nonpartisan municipal elections, almost all elected offices in Colorado are held by either a Democrat or a Republican. In most cases, those who wish to function effectively in Colorado politics and government must first learn how to function effectively in one of the two major political parties.

REGISTERING TO VOTE

In order to vote, citizens must register to vote. In rural areas voter registration takes place at the county courthouse, while in the more populated counties there is usually a county election office located near the courthouse in the county seat. Coloradans may register in one of the two major parties, Republican or Democratic, or as unaffiliated. Unaffiliated voters are not allowed to participate in the party nominating process in Colorado. Despite this, at least one-third of all registered voters in Colorado are registered as unaffiliated.

In the 1980s Colorado adopted "motor-voter" registration. Coloradans are asked if they want to register to vote whenever they obtain or renew their driver's license. "Motor-voter" has proven to be a convenient way to get newcomers and younger citizens registered to vote.

Although historically Colorado has always been regarded as a Republican state, throughout the late 1960s, the 1970s, and the early 1980s there were more registered Democrats than Republicans. In 1986, 1988, and 1990 the number of registered Republicans exceeded the number of registered Democrats. In 1992, however, the number of Democrats once again exceeded the number of Republicans. Throughout much of recent Colorado political history there were more voters registered as unaffiliated than as either Democrats or Republicans (see Table 1).

THE NOMINATING PROCESS

Colorado has an ingenious and detailed system for nominating party candidates. There are party primary elections, one in the Republican party and one in the Democratic, and these primary elections are held in August prior to the November general election. To qualify for the primary election ballot, however, would-be party candidates must receive 30 percent or more of the dele-

Table 1. Colorado Voter Registration, 1966–92

Year	Democratic	Republican	Unaffiliated	Total
1966	335,779	252,096	336,972	924,968
1968	338,907	280,193	351,475	970,575
1970	344,156	291,433	333,393	968,982
1972	413,529	343,193	462,859	1,219,591
1974	448,535	345,156	433,801	1,227,492
1976	—	—	—	—
1978	470,858	373,270	500,876	1,345,004
1980	455,825	439,610	538,822	1,434,257
1982	463,047	460,240	532,447	1,455,734
1984	514,715	514,383	592,208	1,621,306
1986	560,942	599,214	650,842	1,810,998
1988	621,624	671,160	744,711	2,037,435
1990	601,738	657,212	672,504	1,931,454
1992	682,412	670,282	648,058	2,000,752

Source: Registration data provided by the office of the Colorado Secretary of State and compiled by M. Trevithick. Registration data for 1976 is inexplicably unavailable.

gate votes at a party convention held the previous May or June. Delegates to party conventions are initially selected in party precinct caucuses.

The Precinct Caucus

Political and electoral activity in Colorado begins at the precinct level. The precinct is the smallest-sized voting unit in the state, consisting of approximately a thousand registered voters who live in the same neighborhood. On election day, the registered voters in a precinct vote at the precinct polling place, usually a public school, public library, or other public building located in or near the precinct.

Statewide elections are held every two years. On the first Monday in April of each election year, precinct caucuses are held in every precinct to begin the party nominating process. There are two separate caucuses in each precinct, one for Republicans and one for Democrats. The caucuses customarily are held in the home of a loyal party worker, but on occasion they are held in a meeting room at a local elementary school or some other public or semipublic place. Only registered Democrats can vote at the Democratic precinct caucus, and only registered Republicans can vote at the Republican precinct caucus. Colorado thus has a "closed" caucus system in which only registered party members can actively participate.

One suggestion for increasing voter participation in Colorado party politics is to allow unaffiliated voters to attend either the Republican or the Democratic precinct caucus. This would give unaffiliated voters a say in which candidates receive a particular party's nomination for office. It also would bring unaffiliated voters into the party process, perhaps encouraging them to join one of the major political parties. Critics of this suggestion, however, claim that only loyal party members, those who care enough about the party and its policies to register in the party, should participate in something as important to the party as nominating candidates for office.

In each party precinct caucus, two precinct committee members are selected to organize the precinct and to turn out the party vote on election day. In the past, one committee member was a man and one was a woman, and in many precincts in Colorado it is still customary to select a man and a woman to handle party chores. The two committee members are selected every two years at the precinct caucus.

The major event that takes place at the precinct caucus is the election of delegates from the precinct to the party county convention.[6] This is important because the county convention will begin the process of nominating party candidates for county offices, including county commissioner, county clerk, and county assessor. The county convention also will select delegates to the party's state convention, where the first steps will be taken in nominating party candidates for statewide elected offices, including governor, attorney general, U.S. Senator, and state treasurer. In presidential election years, a party's state convention also will select those party members who will serve as delegates to the party's national convention.

Thus the party precinct caucus is important in Colorado because it is the first step in a lengthy nominating process that eventually decides the party nominees for local and statewide offices. In many cases, candidates for major office in Colorado begin campaigning at the precinct level, urging their supporters to go to the caucus and to elect delegates who support the candidate to the various party conventions. When a candidate does a good job of turning out supporters to a precinct caucus, he or she is said to have "stacked the caucus."

There is great variety in the way party precinct caucuses are conducted in Colorado. Some are well attended, with much discussion of the various party candidates and the positions they have taken on various issues. In some of these lively caucuses, elections may be required to determine the precinct's delegates to the county convention. The various candidates for delegate to the county convention may or may not identify themselves with the various candidates running for county, state, or national nominations for office.

Many other party precinct caucuses are poorly attended, however, and there is little or no discussion of party politics or the various candidates for party nominations. Occasionally every person who attends the party precinct caucus will be offered the opportunity to go as a delegate to the county convention, since there are often more delegate spots at the county convention for the precinct than people in the precinct who want to go. In many precincts, committee members must recruit party members to serve as delegates to the county convention, using arguments about "good citizenship" and "party loyalty" to get people to undertake the task.

Some critics say the party precinct caucus is a poor way to begin the party nominating process in Colorado. Every registered member of a political party can attend his or her party precinct caucus, yet relatively few bother. There can be lively discussion and competition between candidates for the county convention at precinct caucuses, but that is a rare occurrence. In many of the precincts, probably a majority, the same party stalwarts dutifully attend the precinct caucus, vote themselves and their friends a trip to the county convention, and adjourn, often without even discussing which of the various candidates might make the better nominees for office.

A possible reform in Colorado precinct caucuses would be to require candidates for delegate to the county party convention to state which of the various candidates for office they intend to support at the county convention. Such a requirement would give caucus-goers an idea of the differences between the various candidates for convention delegate.

Those who like the current precinct caucus system point out that it places power right where it belongs—in the hands of faithful party members who are sufficiently committed to the party to take the time to attend precinct caucuses, county conventions, and, periodically, state conventions. Moreover, it is said, people should vote for county convention delegates because they trust the delegate's judgment, not because they are committed to one candidate or another.

Candidates for political office have learned how to win with the precinct caucus system. It is known that in many precincts the same people go to the precinct caucus year after year and, frequently, are elected delegates to the county convention. Candidates for office get lists of these party "regulars" and contact them—by mail, by telephone, or, occasionally, in person—in an effort to get their votes at the county and state party conventions. In most cases it is easier and more productive for candidates to campaign for the votes of these party regulars than it is to try to elect their own people to the county and state conventions. Working the party regulars tends to be a more fruitful endeavor than attempting the considerably more difficult task of turning out supporters at the precinct caucuses.

The candidates who are most likely to work to bring new people to precinct caucuses are party newcomers who are challenging an incumbent party officeholder for the party nomination. It is well known that the party "loyalists" who regularly attend precinct caucuses are most likely to support party incumbents. "Upstart" candidates challenging an incumbent thus will work to get large numbers of new party members to the precinct caucuses in an effort to outvote the party regulars.

The County Convention

In each of the sixty-three counties in Colorado, usually on a Saturday in May, the delegates elected at the precinct caucuses meet and hold the county convention. Customarily the convention is held in the auditorium of a high school in or near the county seat, but in larger counties the convention may be held in a hotel, a convention center, or other large public facility. The number of persons eligible to attend the county convention varies with the population of the county, with roughly three to eight delegates and three to eight alternates for each precinct in the county. Alternate delegates qualify to vote at the county convention when one of the regular delegates fails to attend or leaves before voting is completed.

The county convention is an important party event. Ample time is provided before the convention begins for party members to socialize and renew political acquaintances. Candidates for nomination greet convention delegates, hand out campaign buttons and bumper stickers, and sign up supporters. Also present will be incumbent officeholders, even those who are not currently up for reelection. The county convention is a perfect opportunity for party officeholders to shake hands with the party faithful, hear about the concerns of their constituents, and demonstrate that they, too, are loyal, hardworking party members.

Two important items of business are carried out at each party's county convention. First, delegates are elected to the party state convention. In certain cases, as delegates to the county convention check in, they are asked if they want to be delegates to the state convention. The names of those who indicate interest are put on a list, and a group of county party leaders will meet and examine the list, deciding on those who will be nominated as delegates and alternates to the state convention. In other cases would-be delegates to the state convention put their names in a hat and are chosen by lot. The list of names is then presented to the county convention and, in most cases, readily approved.

In some instances candidates for important statewide offices will be competing for delegates to the state convention. Often county party leaders will work to resolve disputes by balancing the recommended list of state convention delegates among competing candidates. If things cannot be worked out in that manner, delegates at the county convention may have to choose between competing lists of state convention delegates, with each list committed to a different candidate.

The second order of business at the county convention will be the nomination of party candidates for county offices. Following brief speeches by the candidates for a particular office, a secret ballot will be conducted. All candidates who receive 30 percent or more of the delegate votes will be eligible for the August party primary election. The candidate with the highest number of votes will be listed first on the primary election ballot, the candidate with the second highest number of votes will be listed second, and so forth.

Candidates for party nominations work hard to get the most delegate votes and to qualify for "top line" designation on the primary ballot, but that does not necessarily mean they are going to win the primary election. No one knows exactly what "top line" designation is worth in added votes, but it is often said that it is worth "10 percent of the vote."

Colorado election laws provide one last option to those would-be candidates who fail to get at least 30 percent of the delegate vote at the county convention. If they wish, after the county convention adjourns, such candidates can go door-to-door and collect the signatures of registered party members on a petition supporting their candidacy. Once they have gathered a minimum number of authenticated signatures, they will have "petitioned" their way on to the primary election ballot. In most instances, however, candidates who fail to get 30 percent or more of the vote at the county convention accept the judgment of their fellow party loyalists and do not attempt to petition their way onto the primary ballot.

In addition to electing delegates to the state convention, the county convention also will elect delegates to the congressional district convention, where the party's nominees for the U.S. House of Representatives will be voted on. Delegates will also be elected to the judicial district convention, where the party's nominees for district attorney will be selected. These conventions are similar to the county convention in that any candidate who receives 30 percent or more of the convention vote is automatically placed on the primary election ballot.

For party members who want to be actively involved in party affairs, it is relatively easy to become a delegate to the county convention. Once there, delegates can get involved in the democratic process, mingling with officeholders and party leaders, listening to speeches by prospective party candidates, and voting for one's choices among the various candidates for nomination to a number of important local offices. County conventions are usually successful in building party "spirit" as well as beginning the process of nominating candidates.

The State Convention

Each of the two major parties holds a state convention, customarily in June in election years.[7] Historically, state conventions have been held in one of the larger cities on the Front Range, including Denver, Boulder, Colorado Springs, and Pueblo. In recent years, both the Republican and Democratic state conventions have become such large gatherings that they are usually held in Denver, either at a big downtown hotel, the McNichols sports arena, or the convention center. Democrats, however, occasionally meet in the large Colorado University Events Center in Boulder.

The state convention is primarily an enlarged version of the party's county convention. There is much talking and socializing, as well as a great deal of speechmaking by statewide officeholders and party candidates for statewide offices. As at the county convention, those candidates whose names will appear on the party ballot in the August primary election must receive at least 30 percent of the delegate vote at the state convention, and the person who receives the most votes gets the valued "top line" designation. Those who fail to get 30 percent have the option of petitioning their way on to the statewide primary ballot.

State Party Platforms

Few aspects of politics so openly invite skepticism and cynicism as do the party platforms of the major parties. The program of either party, most close observers agree, actually lies in the pragmatic vision of the key candidates a party chooses to lead it. Still, fights over the platform reveal the character of the political coalitions the two parties present to the public.

Platforms can be divisive or integrating. Most candidates in Colorado and their campaign managers want platforms that are vague and generally allow the candidates to specify precise policy stands. Thus platforms are generally less meaningful than the fall campaign statements and pledges of the state-wide candidates. Yet platforms are useful guides to the major concerns of the state parties. They are, to be sure, often inclusive, "something for everyone" reports. These platforms invariably illustrate compromises of sectional and factional views.

The authors would include here a few sections from recent Democratic and Republican state platforms, but we know too well that most readers would let their eyes glance ever so quickly over such platform examples, even though merely excerpts! It goes without saying that platforms gather more dust than readers. Newspaper reporters may pick out a controversial item or two. Research teams for the opposition parties read one another's platforms to try to discover embarrassing planks. But few voters in Colorado, or any other state, ever read state party platforms.

Then why go to the bother of preparing them? In a democracy, people want to have choices. People take pride in a democratic system that has built into it several opportunities for people to have their say. With all its imperfections, the party platform process remains reasonably open, porous, and democratic. For those who care enough to request and read them, platforms are available and do reveal the broad outlines of the political and philosophical principles of the two major parties.

The Primary Election

The nominating process in Colorado concludes with the August primary election. Colorado has a "semiclosed" primary. Only registered Democrats can vote in the Democratic primary. Only registered Republicans can vote in the Republican primary. However, on primary election day, unaffiliated voters can go to their polling place, announce they want to join one political party or the other, and vote in that party's primary election.

Relatively few unaffiliated voters exercise this right to declare a partisan affiliation on primary election day and then vote in the appropriate primary. It happens occasionally, however, particularly when there is a hotly contested and well-publicized primary. Those unaffiliated voters who declare a partisan affiliation on primary election day remain registered in that political party. If they wish to be unaffiliated again, they must go to the county election office and formally change their registration back to unaffiliated.

As previously noted, over the past several years the two major political parties in Colorado have been fairly evenly balanced in terms of party registration, one party leading during one period and the other party during another period. Because of this relatively even party balance among registered voters and the high proportion of unaffiliated voters, party primary elections do not attract great attention in Colorado.

There are local areas in the Centennial State, of course, where one political party wins the general elections so regularly that winning that party's primary *is* tantamount to winning the general election. The Democratic party tends to be so dominant in Denver and Pueblo that winning the Democratic primary is a bigger challenge for those seeking political office than winning the general election. In heavily Republican areas, such as the southern and western Denver suburbs and the Colorado Springs area, the Republican primary usually determines the eventual officeholder.

In recent years both political parties in Colorado have had some hard-fought primary elections. Often these bruising contests have helped the opposition party, particularly when the party in office did not have a tough primary fight. For example, in 1980 the Republicans had a lively four-way race for the party nomination for U.S. senator. Ironically, the candidate who finished last in the balloting at the party state convention, then Secretary of State Mary Estill Buchanan, won the August primary.[8] She was narrowly defeated in the general election by Democrat Gary Hart, the incumbent senator, who used many of the same arguments against her in the general election campaign that were used against her in the Republican primary.

Another highly competitive statewide Republican primary occurred in the 1986 election for governor. Three well-known candidates—state Representative Bob Kirscht from Pueblo, businessman Steve Schuck from Colorado Springs, and state Senator Ted Strickland—battled for the Republican nomination. Strickland narrowly defeated Schuck to win the primary, and Kirscht ran a strong third. The charges and countercharges in the Republican primary provided plenty of campaign ammunition for the Democratic candidate, state treasurer and businessman Roy Romer, who was unopposed in the Democratic primary and who easily won the general election.

The Democrats have had their share of hotly contested statewide primary elections. In 1974 the Watergate scandal in Washington and the resignation of Republican President Richard Nixon indicated it would be a good election year for the Democrats. As a result, there was a bruising contest for the Democratic nomination for governor between state Senator Tom Farley and state Representative Dick Lamm. Lamm won the Democratic primary and, despite the heavily contested primary election, went on to defeat his Republican opponent in the general election.

Another hard-fought Democratic primary, this one for the right to be the Democratic nominee for U.S. senator, took place in Colorado in 1990. Josie Heath, a county commissioner from Boulder County, locked horns with Carlos Lucero, an attorney from southern Colorado. Although Heath won the Democratic primary, she lost the general election to the Republican candidate, U.S. Representative Hank Brown of Greeley.

Two years later, in 1992, the Democrats had another three-way shootout for a U.S. Senate nomination. A Native American, Ben Nighthorse Campbell, defeated both Josie Heath and former Governor Richard Lamm. This tough primary fight did not hurt Campbell, who easily defeated Republican Terry Considine in the general election.

Similar to most other states, voter turnout in primary elections in Colorado is approximately 30 percent of the total number of voters registered in the particular political party. In those primary elections where a race is hotly contested and well-publicized, however, the percentage increases.

The Nominating Process Evaluated

The nominating process in Colorado is a combination of both party conventions and the primary election. In effect, a system of caucuses and conventions is used to narrow the field of candidates that eventually run against each other in the primary election. Under this system, party regulars—people dedicated enough to the party to attend caucuses and conventions—make the "first cut" in the pool of candidates available for party nomination to elected office. The "final cut" to a single party nominee is made by the rank and file—those persons registered in the party who take the trouble to vote in the primary election.

The nominating process thus retains the strengths of both the convention and the primary election. The party convention provides the opportunity for face-to-face politics, bringing party members together both to socialize and to begin the nominating process. The primary election, however, provides the opportunity for less-committed party members to participate by voting for their first choice from a final list of candidates selected by the caucus-convention process.

The party nominating system used in Colorado is the *reverse* of the system used to nominate party candidates for president of the United States. At the national level, primary elections are held *before* the national conventions, not *after* them. In the spring of each presidential election year, a series of presidential primaries in nearly 40 states is used to weed the few strong finalists from the many initial contenders. At the national conventions, delegates supposedly make the final choice between the one or two candidates who remain after the winnowing process of the state primaries. In recent decades, however, the national conventions have had little to do because one candidate has already "sewn up" the nomination by winning most of the presidential primaries.

A few scholars have been looking at the nominating system used in the Centennial State as a possible model for reforming the national presidential nominating process.[9] If the "Colorado plan" were adopted at the national level, precinct caucuses, county conventions, and state conventions would be held in the spring of presidential election years in each of the fifty states. Instead of campaigning for primary election votes, as they do now, presidential candidates would campaign for delegate votes at county and state conventions. The state conventions would elect delegates to the national conventions.

At the national conventions, both of which would be held in July, each delegate would vote for his or her choice for the presidential nomination, and any candidate who received 30 percent or more of the vote would appear on the ballot in a national presidential primary election. The Republican presidential primary and the Democratic presidential primary would be held on the same day, probably a Tuesday in early September. The winners of the two national party primaries would run against each other in the November general election.

There are two major arguments in favor of the "Colorado plan" for nominating presidential candidates. First, national party conventions, which now have little to do, would gain the meaningful task of narrowing the field of presidential candidates. Second, every U.S. citizen registered in one of the two major political parties would get to vote in a national presidential primary and choose between the party's top two or three candidates for president.

Although the "Colorado plan" is an interesting alternative to the present presidential nominating system in use in the United States, its adoption is improbable.

A PRESIDENTIAL PRIMARY FOR COLORADO

Prior to the 1992 presidential election, Colorado did not have either a Democratic or a Republican presidential primary election. Delegates to national party conventions were selected at state party conventions and congressional district conventions, and the delegates were permitted to vote as they pleased when they attended the national convention.

By the late 1980s, however, nearly forty states had adopted some form of presidential primary election for choosing and/or instructing delegates to the national party conventions. In an age when so many other states were turning to presidential primaries, the presidential nominating process in Colorado had become increasingly irrelevant. By the time the Colorado delegates arrived at the Democratic or Republican national convention, the party nominee had already been determined in presidential primary elections in other states.

In November of 1990 voters approved by popular referendum the idea of holding presidential primary elections in Colorado. Early in 1991 the state legislature passed enabling legislation setting the first Tuesday in March as presidential primary day. Although Colorado's delegates to national party conventions are still selected by state party conventions and congressional district conventions, delegates are required to cast their votes at the national convention in accordance with the outcome of the Colorado presidential primary. Thus, if a Republican candidate for president receives 40 percent of the vote in the Colorado presidential primary, he or she receives the support of 40 percent of Colorado delegates to the Republican national convention.

Colorado held the first presidential primary in its history on Tuesday, March 3, 1992. In the Democratic primary, former California Governor Jerry Brown narrowly defeated Arkansas Governor Bill Clinton and former U.S. Senator Paul Tsongas of Massachusetts. In the Republican primary, President George Bush defeated challenger Patrick Buchanan, who did not campaign in Colorado, by more than a two to one margin.

GENERAL ELECTIONS

Colorado has been a two-party competitive state since the time of its founding as a territory in 1861. Over the years Republicans have won more offices than the Democrats, doing particularly well at winning presidential elections and controlling both houses of the state legislature for long periods of time. Still, there have been many periods in the state's political history when Democrats have won the governorship and have had working majorities in both houses of the state legislature.

Presidential Elections

In the nine presidential elections from 1960 to 1992, the Republican percentage of the vote for the entire United States averaged over 51 percent. During

Table 2. Two-Party Voting Results in Colorado Presidential
Elections, 1960–92

Year	Total Vote	Margin	Rep. %	Dem. %
1960	732,871	71,613 R	54.9	45.1
1964	772,791	179,257 D	38.4	61.6
1968	744,519	74,171 R	55.0	45.0
1972	927,169	267,209 R	64.4	35.6
1976	1,044,720	124,014 R	55.9	44.1
1980	1,020,237	284,291 R	63.9	36.1
1984	1,276,792	366,842 R	64.4	35.6
1988	1,349,630	106,724 R	54.0	46.0
1992	1,189,636	66,762 D	47.2	52.8

Average Republican % 55.3
Average Democratic % 44.7

this same period in Colorado, however, Republicans averaged over 55 percent of the votes, 4 percentage points higher for Republicans than the nation as a whole. Of the fifty states, Colorado was the nineteenth most Republican in terms of the vote for president from 1960 to 1992.

Colorado's population, and therefore the size of its electorate, grew somewhat faster than the United States as a whole in the 1960s, 1970s, and 1980s. These population gains relative to the remainder of the country also are reflected in the fact that Colorado had four members of the U.S. House of Representatives (and six electoral votes for U.S. president) in the 1960s, but had six members of the House (and eight electoral votes) by the 1980s.

Colorado is *not* a "bellwether" state that votes for the winner in every presidential election. It is too Republican to be a "predictor" state. In the nine presidential elections from 1960 to 1992, Colorado voted for the national winner only seven times. In both 1960 and 1976, it voted for the Republican candidates for president (Richard M. Nixon in 1960 and Gerald R. Ford in 1976), but the Democratic candidates (John F. Kennedy in 1960 and Jimmy Carter in 1976) were elected by the nation as a whole (see table 2).

Presidential elections can have a major impact on state elections in Colorado. A big vote for one party or the other in the presidential race will have a "coattail" effect that will help the winning party's candidates in Colorado's statewide and local elections. The best example of this was in 1964, when Democratic presidential incumbent Lyndon B. Johnson scored a landslide victory over his Republican challenger, Arizona Senator Barry Goldwater.

Table 3. Two-Party Voting Results in Colorado Gubernatorial Elections, 1958–90

Year	Total Vote	Margin	Rep. %	Dem. %
1958	549,808	92,522 D	41.6	58.4
1962	612,232	86,452 R	57.1	42.9
1966	643,862	69,598 R	55.4	44.6
1970	653,122	48,258 R	53.7	46.3
1974	820,106	62,292 D	46.2	53.8
1978	801,277	166,693 D	39.6	60.4
1982	930,700	325,220 D	32.5	67.5
1986	1,050,745	181,905 D	41.3	58.7
1990	984,435	267,629 D	36.4	63.6

Average Republican % 44.9
Average Democratic % 55.1

In Colorado, thanks to the Johnson landslide, the Democrats gained control of the lower house of the state legislature. In the 1966 election two years later, however, without a popular Democratic presidential candidate at the top of the party ticket, the Democrats lost control of the lower house back to the Republicans.

Gubernatorial Elections

In the 114 years from the state's birth in 1876 through 1990, Colorado has had twenty-one Democrats and seventeen Republicans serve as governor. Democrats have done remarkably well at winning the governorship in the past generation. In the nine gubernatorial races from 1958 to 1990, Democrats won six times and Republicans won only three times. The Democrats averaged 55.1 percent of the vote in these nine governorship races, compared to only 44.9 percent for the Republicans (see table 3).

Conventional wisdom in Colorado is that the Republicans always win the governorship, except when the party makes political mistakes and gets in trouble with the voters. If this conventional wisdom is true, then clearly the Republican party has made many political mistakes in recent years.

Democrat Richard Lamm captured the Colorado governorship in 1974 in the national "Watergate sweep." Voters were outraged by the criminal activity and abuse of executive authority that Watergate symbolized, and they expressed their outrage by voting solidly Democratic in the 1974 gubernatorial election. In that election, the conventional wisdom about the Colorado governorship had proven true. The national Republican party had antagonized and infuriated the voters with the Watergate scandal, and as a result, a Democrat was elected governor of the Centennial State.

The Democrats not only took the governorship in the Watergate sweep of 1974 but also gained control of the lower house of the state legislature. By 1976, however, voter anger over Watergate had cooled in Colorado, and the Republicans regained majority control of the lower house.

The Democrats controlled the Colorado governorship for the twenty years from 1974 to 1994. Richard Lamm was elected three times, in 1974, 1978, and 1982. In 1986 Lamm voluntarily retired from the office and was succeeded by the state treasurer, Democrat Roy Romer. Lamm was so popular with the voters that he probably would have been reelected in 1986 if he had decided to run for governor again. Romer appeared to be following in Lamm's popular footsteps, easily winning reelection over his Republican opponent in 1990.

Since 1976, Democratic governors Lamm and Romer have been faced with a Republican-controlled state legislature. It thus appears that Coloradans like having one political party control the governorship and the other political party control both houses of the state legislature.

State Legislative Elections

In the sixty-six years from 1928 to 1994, the Republicans controlled both houses of the Colorado legislature for forty-two years, the Democrats controlled both houses for twelve years, and the parties split control of the houses for twelve years. In the eighteen years from 1976 to 1994, the Republicans continuously controlled both houses of the Colorado legislature, often by substantial majorities. As of 1993, in only eight other states (Utah, Arizona, Idaho, New Hampshire, New Jersey, Kansas, and Wyoming) did the Republicans control both chambers of the legislature.

It is the Republican party's ability to dominate state legislative elections (as well as presidential elections) that leads political observers to conclude Colorado is a predominantly Republican state. From 1958 through the early 1990s the Republicans won an average of 56 percent of the seats in both houses of the Colorado legislature. Democrats have not controlled both houses since 1962.

One of the major questions asked in Colorado is, Why, in recent years, have the Republicans lost so many statewide races for governor yet had little problem maintaining solid control of the state legislature? There is no simple explanation for this, other than the obvious fact the Democrats have suc-

Table 4. Two-Party Voting Results in Colorado Senatorial Elections,
1968–92

Year	Total Vote	Margin	Rep. %	Dem. %
1968	785,536	134,368 R	58.6	41.4
1972	905,502	9,588 D	49.5	50.5
1974	797,199	146,183 D	40.8	59.2
1978	810,843	150,349 R	59.3	40.7
1980	1,161,796	19,206 D	49.2	50.8
1984	1,283,148	384,494 R	65.0	35.0
1986	1,042,443	16,455 D	49.2	50.8
1990	994,794	143,302 R	57.2	42.8
1992	1,455,450	142,374 D	45.1	54.9

Average Republican % 52.6
Average Democratic % 47.4

ceeded in nominating attractive candidates for governor. On the other hand, the Democrats have tried hard but have not been able to find either the candidates or the political issues that will enable them to win control of the legislature.

U.S. Senate Elections

Since Colorado became a state in 1876, eighteen Republicans and thirteen Democrats have served the state in the United States Senate. An additional Senator from Colorado, Henry Teller, first served as a Republican (starting in 1884) but subsequently switched his party affiliation to Democratic over the free-silver issue.

In the nine U.S. Senate elections held in the state from 1968 to 1992, the Republicans won four elections and the Democrats won five. Colorado Republicans averaged 52.7 percent of the vote in Senate elections during that twenty-four-year period (see table 4). The high Republican average percentage of the vote is deceiving, however, because Republicans have tended to win a number of the races by high percentages. Democrats, on the other hand, have won three recent U.S. Senate elections by razor-thin margins, thus electing a senator but only slightly raising the Democratic percentage.

Throughout most of the 1960s, the state had two Republican U.S. Senators, Gordon Allott and Peter Dominick. In 1972, however, Allott was defeated by Republican-turned-Democrat Floyd Haskell, who attacked Allott during the campaign for his lack of concern on environmental issues. Haskell was also an anti–Vietnam War candidate just when the antiwar movement was gaining some support in Colorado. Two years later, in the 1974 anti-Republican "Watergate sweep," Republican incumbent Peter Dominick was defeated by Democrat Gary Hart.

In 1978, when Democratic incumbent Haskell came up for reelection, he was challenged by a popular Republican congressman, William Armstrong. In a race that was mainly a personal popularity contest, Republican Armstrong easily defeated Democrat Haskell, and Colorado had one Republican senator (Armstrong) and one Democratic senator (Hart).

Hart came up for reelection in 1980. His Republican opponent, Mary Estill Buchanan, won the nomination in a hard-fought Republican primary election against three other candidates. Despite the fact that the Republican candidate for president in 1980, former California Governor Ronald Reagan, won Colorado by a large margin, Democrat Hart was able to stem the Republican tide and, by the narrowest of margins, keep his seat in the U.S. Senate. Colorado continued its newly established pattern of having one Senator from one party and one from the other.

Republican Senator Armstrong came up for reelection in 1984. Not only was he a popular incumbent, but he was running as a Republican in a year when the incumbent Republican president, Ronald Reagan, was sweeping to a giant reelection victory throughout the United States. Armstrong was reelected to the Senate in 1984 by one of the largest majorities in the state's history.

In 1986 Democratic Senator Hart declined to run for reelection, choosing instead to concentrate his efforts on running for the Democratic nomination for president in 1988. Two members of the U.S. House of Representatives, Republican Ken Kramer and Democrat Tim Wirth, ran for Hart's seat. In a closely contested election filled with negative campaigning, Wirth edged out Kramer.

In 1990 Republican Senator Armstrong declined to run for reelection to the U.S. Senate. Popular U.S. Representative Hank Brown, a Republican, defeated Boulder County commissioner and issue activist Josie Heath in a spirited contest for Armstrong's seat. Two years after that, in 1992, Democratic Senator Wirth decided not to run for a second term. Ben Nighthorse Campbell, a Democrat from the western slope, won the right to succeed Wirth with a comfortable victory over Republican Terry Considine.

House of Representatives Elections

From 1876 to 1994, twenty-nine Republicans and twenty-five Democrats served Colorado in the United States House of Representatives. In 1986,

1988, and 1990, Colorado elected three Republicans and three Democrats to the House. In 1992 four Republicans were elected and only two Democrats. Throughout most of the state's political history, the Colorado delegation to the House has been more or less evenly split between the two major political parties. Republicans typically win House seats in the more affluent Denver suburbs or the heavily Republican cities of Colorado Springs and Fort Collins. Democrats generally win House seats in the downtown Denver area and the Boulder area.

Every ten years, following the U.S. Census, new district lines must be drawn for Colorado's six U.S. House of Representatives districts. The state legislature establishes new district lines by legislative act, but the redistricting bill, as it is called, must be approved and signed by the governor. Because Colorado has had a Republican legislature and a Democratic governor in recent years, it often has been difficult to get the two branches of government to agree on new congressional district boundary lines. The Republicans in the state legislature try to draw district lines that will elect more Republicans to the House, and the Democratic governor, quite naturally, maneuvers to get district lines that will help elect more Democrats.

A number of observers believe that congressional redistricting in Colorado should be carried out by an appointed commission rather than the legislature and the governor. Such a commission, it is argued, would be less partisan in its deliberations and its line drawing than are the state legislature and the governor. A bipartisan commission is already used in Colorado to draw district lines for the state legislature, and it would be a simple matter to have this commission draw district lines for the U.S. House of Representatives as well.[10]

VOTING PATTERNS

Because most of the population in Colorado is concentrated in the megalopolis that extends along the eastern foot of the Front Range of the Rocky Mountains, most of the voting power in the state is also concentrated there. In fact, at least 80 percent of the vote statewide is cast in the heavily populated Front Range area extending from Fort Collins and Greeley on the north to Pueblo on the south. Within the Front Range corridor, the Denver metropolitan area is the most significant voting group. In the average statewide election, Denver and its surrounding suburbs cast 60 percent of the statewide vote.

Table 5 lists Colorado's sixty-three counties from most Republican to most Democratic in terms of *average vote margins* in presidential elections

Table 5. County Presidential Election Returns in Colorado
Ranked by Average Vote Margins, 1960–92

Rank	Name	Margin	Rep. %	Dem. %
1	EL PASO	29,801R	65.1	34.9
2	JEFFERSON	28,978R	60.8	39.2
3	ARAPAHOE	26,629R	63.0	37.0
4	LARIMER	10,705R	61.3	38.7
5	WELD	7,110R	59.4	40.6
6	MESA	6,613R	61.3	38.7
7	DOUGLAS	4,326R	69.2	30.8
8	LA PLATA	2,040R	60.1	39.9
9	DELTA	1,949R	62.1	37.9
10	MONTROSE	1,946R	61.6	38.4
11	FREMONT	1,936R	59.0	41.0
12	BOULDER	1,860R	52.8	47.2
13	MORGAN	1,757R	61.4	38.6
14	LOGAN	1,647R	60.8	39.2
15	GARFIELD	1,439R	58.8	41.2
16	MONTEZUMA	1,430R	63.2	36.8
17	YUMA	1,171R	64.3	35.7
18	MOFFAT	1,061R	64.6	35.4
19	RIO GRANDE	1,003R	62.3	37.7
20	KIT CARSON	1,000R	65.2	34.8
21	TELLER	999R	64.3	35.7
22	RIO BLANCO	876R	69.5	30.5
23	ELBERT	864R	66.1	33.9
24	WASHINGTON	856R	66.9	33.1
25	OTERO	850R	54.9	45.1
26	GRAND	780R	64.3	35.7
27	BACA	758R	65.9	34.1
28	CHAFFEE	702R	57.1	42.9
29	EAGLE	651R	55.6	44.4
30	PROWERS	643R	56.7	43.3
31	GUNNISON	618R	58.0	42.0
32	ROUTT	562R	55.3	44.7
33	LINCOLN	552R	62.5	37.5
34	PARK	489R	62.5	37.5
35	PHILLIPS	478R	61.1	38.9
36	ALAMOSA	458R	55.0	45.0

Table 5.
(Continued)

Rank	Name	Margin	Rep. %	Dem. %
37	SEDGWICK	382R	61.9	38.1
38	CLEAR CREEK	339R	56.5	43.5
39	ARCHULETA	327R	58.5	41.5
40	SUMMIT	317R	55.7	44.3
41	CUSTER	304R	67.4	32.6
42	CHEYENNE	292R	63.0	37.0
43	OURAY	291R	64.0	36.0
44	KIOWA	277R	62.5	37.5
45	JACKSON	272R	66.8	33.2
46	CROWLEY	263R	58.8	41.2
47	DOLORES	186R	62.8	37.2
48	HINSDALE	108R	68.8	31.2
49	BENT	75R	51.3	48.7
50	MINERAL	53R	55.9	44.1
51	SAGUACHE	37R	51.0	49.0
52	GILPIN	35R	52.1	47.9
53	SAN JUAN	27R	53.0	47.0
54	SAN MIGUEL	67D	47.9	52.1
55	PITKIN	118D	49.5	50.5
56	ADAMS	191D	49.1	50.9
57	CONEJOS	273D	45.8	54.2
58	LAKE	438D	41.6	58.4
59	COSTILLA	593D	31.1	68.9
60	HUERFANO	677D	39.4	60.6
61	LAS ANIMAS	1,987D	36.7	63.3
62	PUEBLO	7,887D	41.7	58.3
63	DENVER	20,566D	44.8	55.2

from 1960 to 1992. Map 4 is based on table 5 and shows the ten most Republican counties and the ten most Democratic counties in terms of presidential *vote margins*.[11]

Note in table 5 that fifty-three of Colorado's sixty-three counties cast a positive vote margin for the Republicans in presidential elections from 1960 to 1992. In those nine elections over thirty-two years in those fifty-three counties, the Republicans received more votes, on the average, than the

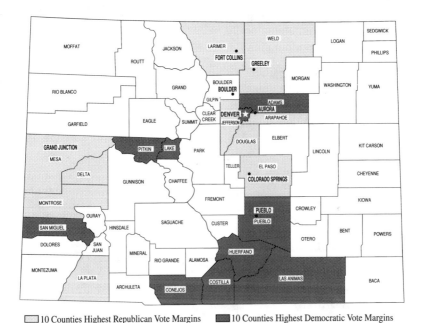

☐ 10 Counties Highest Republican Vote Margins   ■ 10 Counties Highest Democratic Vote Margins

Map 4.   Voting Patterns in Colorado Presidential Elections by County, 1960–92

Democrats. In only ten of the state's sixty-three counties did Democrats receive more votes, on the average, than Republicans.

Table 5 and map 4 indicate that the traditional areas of Democratic
strength in Colorado elections are Denver and Pueblo counties. Because
they contain large numbers of industrial working-class people and large
numbers of minority voters, primarily African-Americans and Hispanics,
Denver and Pueblo counties would be expected to vote heavily Democratic—and they do.

Other areas of Democratic strength include Lake County (Leadville),
which once had a large population of molybdenum miners, and four counties
in southern Colorado that have a high percentage of Spanish-surnamed residents (Conejos, Costilla, Huerfano, and Las Animas counties). Democrats
also do well in Adams County, an industrial suburb located to the northeast
of Denver. In recent years the city of Boulder, which is northwest of Denver
and the home of the University of Colorado, has tended to vote more Democratic in presidential elections.

Table 5 and map 4 suggest the major areas of Republican voting strength
in Colorado are the southern and western Denver suburbs concentrated in

Table 6. County Presidential Election Returns Ranked
by Percentage of Total Colorado Vote, 1960–92

Rank	Name	1992	1960	Change
1	JEFFERSON	14.4	7.8	+ 6.6
2	DENVER	13.9	30.0	-16.1
3	ARAPAHOE	11.7	6.0	+ 5.7
4	EL PASO	10.8	6.6	+ 4.2
5	BOULDER	8.1	4.4	+ 3.7
6	ADAMS	6.6	5.4	+ 1.2
7	LARIMER	6.4	3.2	+ 3.2
8	PUEBLO	3.6	6.6	- 3.0
9	WELD	3.5	3.9	- .4
10	MESA	2.8	3.0	- .2
11	DOUGLAS	2.0	.3	+ 1.7
12	FREMONT	1.0	1.3	- .3
13	LA PLATA	1.0	1.1	- .1
14	GARFIELD	.9	.8	+ .1
15	DELTA	.7	1.0	- .3
16	EAGLE	.7	.3	+ .4
17	MONTROSE	.7	.9	- .2
18	MORGAN	.6	1.1	- .5
19	LOGAN	.5	1.1	- .6
20	MONTEZUMA	.5	.7	- .2
21	OTERO	.5	1.4	- .9
22	PITKIN	.5	.2	+ .3
23	ROUTT	.5	.4	+ .1
24	SUMMIT	.5	.1	+ .4
25	ALAMOSA	.4	.6	- .2
26	CHAFFEE	.4	.5	- .1
27	GUNNISON	.4	.3	+ .1
28	LAS ANIMAS	.4	1.3	- .9
29	TELLER	.4	.2	+ .2
30	CLEAR CREEK	.3	.2	+ .1
31	ELBERT	.3	.3	0
32	GRAND	.3	.2	+ .1
33	MOFFAT	.3	.4	- .1
34	PARK	.3	.1	+ .2
35	PROWERS	.3	.8	- .5

Table 6.
(Continued)

Rank	Name	1992	1960	Change
36	RIO GRANDE	.3	.6	- .3
37	YUMA	.3	.6	- .3
38	ARCHULETA	.2	.1	+ .1
39	BACA	.2	.4	- .2
40	CONEJOS	.2	.5	- .3
41	HUERFANO	.2	.6	- .4
42	KIT CARSON	.2	.5	- .3
43	LAKE	.2	.4	- .2
44	RIO BLANCO	.2	.3	- .1
45	WASHINGTON	.2	.4	- .2
46	BENT	.1	.4	- .3
47	CHEYENNE	.1	.2	- .1
48	COSTILLA	.1	.3	- .2
49	CROWLEY	.1	.2	- .1
50	CUSTER	.1	.1	0
51	DOLORES	.1	.1	0
52	GILPIN	.1	.1	0
53	JACKSON	.1	.1	0
54	KIOWA	.1	.2	- .1
55	LINCOLN	.1	.3	- .2
56	OURAY	.1	.1	0
57	PHILLIPS	.1	.3	- .2
58	SAGUACHE	.1	.3	- .2
59	SAN MIGUEL	.1	.2	- .1
60	SEDGWICK	.1	.3	- .2
61	HINSDALE	.0	.0	0
62	MINERAL	.0	.0	0
63	SAN JUAN	.0	.1	- .1

Arapahoe and Jefferson counties. In recent elections an even more Republican area has been El Paso County, which contains the city of Colorado Springs and its surrounding communities.

Other areas of Republican strength are some major counties and cities on the Front Range, including Larimer County (Fort Collins), Weld County (Greeley), and Douglas County (Castle Rock). Outside the Front Range area, the Republicans do well in Mesa County (Grand Junction), La Plata County (Durango), and Delta and Montrose counties on the western slope.

Partisan elections in Colorado tend to be battles to win votes on the Front Range. Republicans work to get out as large a vote as possible in El Paso County (Colorado Springs) and also hope to turn out a large vote in Arapahoe and Jefferson counties. Democrats, on the other hand, work to turn out as large a vote as possible in Denver and Pueblo counties and also hope to pick up support in Boulder and Adams counties. The central arena of competition between the two major political parties, therefore, is the Denver suburbs.

POPULATION CHANGES

The major change occurring in Colorado is the declining influence of the city of Denver and the increasing influence of the Denver suburbs. At the time of the 1960 presidential election, Denver cast more than 30 percent of the statewide vote. By the mid 1990s, however, Denver cast less than fourteen percent of the state's vote (see table 6).

At the same time, Denver suburban counties were growing in importance. In the 1992 presidential election these four Denver suburban counties—Adams, Arapahoe, Boulder, and Jefferson counties—cast a combined total of more than 40 percent of the total vote cast in Colorado.

The decline in Denver's percentage of the vote has *not* significantly reduced Denver's role as the principal source of Democratic votes in Colorado. As its size relative to the remainder of the state has declined, Denver has become increasingly Democratic in voting behavior. It continues to produce large Democratic vote margins (some in the 50,000-vote range), although it is growing much more slowly than the rest of the state.

The considerable growth in the population and the voting influence of the Republican Denver suburbs should help ensure Republican statewide victories. However, the increasing tendency of Boulder County to vote Democratic rather than Republican undermines the idea of any guaranteed Republican victories because of the suburban vote.

With each passing year the rural areas of Colorado—both the eastern plains and the western slope—continue to decline in voting power in comparison with the thickly populated counties on the Front Range. Only the fashionable winter skiing and summer hiking resorts, such as Eagle County (Vail), Pitkin County (Aspen), Summit County (Breckinridge), and Routt County (Steamboat Springs) are increasing in population faster than the rest of the state.

Because over 80 percent of the voting population of Colorado is concentrated on the Front Range, candidates for statewide political office spend most of their time campaigning up and down Interstate 25, the major expressway that runs down the middle of the Front Range from north to south. Denver and the Denver suburbs get the major attention, but frequent trips are made also to Fort Collins, Castle Rock, Colorado Springs, and Pueblo. Candidates will wander a little way off I-25 (only a half-hour's drive) to campaign in Greeley and Boulder.

Early in the campaign, candidates for statewide office will make major campaign trips out to the eastern plains and into the more remote areas in the Colorado mountains. Such trips often are designed mainly to get media coverage rather than win votes in the sparsely populated parts of the state. As election day nears, however, candidates concentrate on the major population centers on the Front Range.

There is one aspect of campaigning for statewide office in Colorado that makes things easier than it is in a number of other states. There are only two major television markets—the Denver metropolitan area and the Colorado Springs–Pueblo area. With the rise of cable television, even the rural areas of Colorado mainly watch Denver television. Candidates for statewide office can map out just two television campaigns—one for Denver and one for Colorado Springs–Pueblo—and be assured they are in a position to have their message seen by 90 percent of the voting population of the state.

CONCLUSION

Because of the Republican party's demonstrated strength in presidential and state legislative elections, Colorado deserves its reputation as a "Republican-leaning" state. But the Democrats do win a share of elections in Colorado. In the 1970s and 1980s, they completely dominated gubernatorial elections in the state. Another way to describe Colorado might be as a two-party state that has been "characterized by a slow drift toward the [Republicans] over the past thirty years."[12]

As has happened increasingly throughout the United States, current Colorado voters often split their tickets. Although Republicans get most of the votes, an attractive and hard-working Democratic candidate has a good shot at winning statewide office. "It's a Republican-leaning state, yet appealing, pro-business, and pro-Colorado Democrats can win there," will continue to be an apt one-sentence description of statewide elections in the Centennial State.

CHAPTER SEVEN

Electing the Legislature

Former Democratic state Representative Jerry Kopel of Denver was a veteran door-to-door campaigner. He invariably asked constituents if he could help them in any way. In one campaign, one woman told him, "Yeah, you can water my petunias." Kopel said, "Sure," went outside, turned on the hose, and watered the petunias.[1]

Coloradans have, as Kopel found out, a pragmatic approach to their state legislators. They want them to be honest and responsive. They also want them to keep taxes down. Yet most Coloradans do not know their legislators' names, few attend "meet the candidate" forums, and few write or otherwise contact their legislators.

The Colorado state legislature has been dominated by the Republican party for more than a generation. At times the legislature has operated in a highly partisan manner, with the majority party working to exclude the minority party from the legislative process. At other times the two parties function in a more cooperative manner, although the majority party is always clearly in control.

Colorado has had a two-house state legislature since its inception. While only Nebraska has a one-house legislature, occasionally a legislator or a citizens group proposes a unicameral legislature for Colorado. For example, state Representative John Carroll urged this in 1974. He said having a senate and a house of representatives at the state level was "expensive duplication, an unneeded luxury."[2] His resolution produced discussion in the press yet failed to win support in Colorado's two legislative chambers.

STAGGERED SENATE TERMS

General elections for the Colorado legislature are held on the first Tuesday in November of even-numbered years. Ever since the state constitution was adopted, state representatives have been elected every two years to a two-year term of office. One half of the state senators are elected every two years to a four-year term of office, and the other half are elected two years later, also to a four-year term of office. In Colorado's first general election, in 1876, half of the state Senate was elected for a two-year term and half for a four-year term, thereby instituting the "staggered" system of state Senate terms.

This staggered system has had a definite effect on the partisan composition of the Colorado legislature in the past generation. With only one-half of the Colorado Senate up for reelection at any one time, it is difficult for the minority party in the state Senate to gain a majority of Senate seats in one election. Usually the party out of power in the Senate will have to make gains in two or three consecutive elections before it can become the majority party in the upper chamber.

This contrasts with the situation in the Colorado House of Representatives, where every seat is up for reelection every two years. If the party out of power is popular at the time of a particular election, it has the opportunity to win a large number of seats in the House.

During the 1962–1994 period, for example, Democrats in Colorado enjoyed two winning election years, yet they were only able to gain control of the Colorado House of Representatives. The first time was in the general election of 1964, when a controversial Republican presidential candidate, Senator Barry Goldwater of Arizona, enabled the Democratic presidential candidate, incumbent President Lyndon B. Johnson, to carry Colorado by a large majority. Johnson's popularity produced a "coattail effect." People who were voting Democratic for president decided also to vote Democratic for state legislative seats. In the resulting Democratic victory, Democrats easily won control of the Colorado House of Representatives. But because only one-half of the seats in the state Senate were up for election, the Republicans were able to keep control, albeit narrowly, of the Senate. The end result was that Democratic bills that easily passed the Democrat-controlled state House of Representatives often were defeated in the Republican-controlled state Senate.

If the Democrats could have won additional legislative seats in the 1966 general election, they might have taken control of the state Senate and retained their control of the state House of Representatives. As it turned out, however, without a popular Democratic presidential candidate leading the ticket in Colorado, the Democrats suffered losses in the 1966 general election. The Republicans not only maintained control of the state Senate in the

1966 balloting, but they also won enough Democratic seats to regain control of the state House of Representatives.

The same situation was repeated in Colorado in the 1974 general elections. This time it was the Watergate scandal, in which Republican campaign workers had authorized an illegal burglary of the offices of the Democratic National Committee at the Watergate building in Washington, D.C., that produced a Democratic landslide at all electoral levels in Colorado. The Democrats easily won a majority of the seats in the Colorado House of Representatives. But because only one-half of the seats in the Senate were up for reelection, the Republicans retained a thin majority in the state Senate. Once again majority Democrats passed bills in the state House of Representatives, only to see much of their legislative handiwork killed or weakened in the Republican-controlled Senate.

Two years later, the 1976 general election offered the Democrats the opportunity to gain control of both houses of the Colorado legislature. The other half of the Senate seats were up for reelection, and more Democratic gains easily could have given the Democrats control of the state Senate. By this time, however, irate voter reaction to the Watergate scandal had diminished. Colorado reverted to its normally Republican voting behavior in legislative elections. Republicans strengthened their control over the Colorado Senate and regained a majority of the seats in the House of Representatives.

The major effect of the staggered election of seats in the Colorado Senate, therefore, has been to make it difficult for the Democratic party to gain control of both houses of the legislature at the same time. The Democrats have not been able to gain large numbers of legislative seats in consecutive elections. Thus, Republicans have maintained firm control over the state Senate for thirty years, despite Democratic victories in legislative elections in 1964 and 1974.

REQUIREMENTS AND TERM LIMITS

A candidate for either house of the Colorado legislature must be a U.S. citizen and at least twenty-five years old. Candidates must have been a resident of their district for at least twelve months prior to the general election.

Until 1990 there was no limit on the number of times a person could be reelected to the Colorado legislature. A citizen-initiated constitutional amendment, adopted by the voters at the 1990 general election, limited Colorado elected officials to eight years in office. The amendment, known as "term limitation," passed by a wide margin—71 percent in favor to 29 percent against.

A citizen-initiated constitutional amendment approved in 1966 set the total membership of the Colorado legislature at 100. There are thirty-five state senators and sixty-five state representatives. The same constitutional amendment required that state legislators be elected from single-member districts.

REDISTRICTING AND REAPPORTIONMENT POLITICS

Every ten years the U.S. government conducts a census. The Colorado constitution requires that Colorado Senate and House of Representatives district lines be redrawn every ten years to conform to the latest census figures, a process known as *redistricting*.

As a result of a series of U.S. Supreme Court decisions in the early 1960s, the population of state Senate districts must be "substantially equal," as must the population of state House of Representatives districts. This process of apportioning voters to state legislative districts, in an effort to put equal numbers of voters in each Senate district and equal numbers in each House district, is known as *reapportionment*. Obviously, reapportionment of legislative districts takes place at the same time that district lines are redrawn.

Prior to 1980, redistricting and reapportionment in Colorado were carried out by passing a bill through the legislature and obtaining the governor's signature. Under that system, if a political party had a majority in both houses of the legislature, the district lines usually were drawn in such a way that the majority party had a better chance of winning legislative elections. If the governor at the time was a member of a different political party from the one that enjoyed a majority in both houses of the legislature, the governor could veto the redistricting and reapportionment bill, thereby forcing the legislature to come up with a plan that created less partisan legislative districts.

In 1974 Colorado voters approved an initiated constitutional amendment establishing a new procedure for redistricting and reapportioning state legislative districts. Instead of the legislature and the governor drawing legislative district boundary lines, the eleven-member Colorado Reapportionment Commission is appointed to do the job. In an effort to reduce the partisan character of the reapportionment process, not more than six of the eleven members of the commission can belong to the same political party.

An important part of this new reapportionment system is that members of the commission are appointed by all three branches of Colorado state government. Four members of the commission are appointed by party leaders in the state legislature, three members are appointed by the governor, and four members are appointed by the chief justice of the state Supreme Court.

The four members of the commission appointed by party leaders in the state legislature are named in the following fashion. Two commission members are from the majority party, one selected by the Speaker of the state House of Representatives and one selected by the president of the state Senate. Because they are the elected leaders of their respective houses, the Speaker of the House and the president of the Senate are always members of the majority party. The other two members of the reapportionment commission are from the minority party, one selected by the Senate minority leader and the other selected by the House minority leader. If they wish, the legislative leaders can appoint themselves to serve on the commission.

Once appointed, the Colorado Reapportionment Commission operates under a tight time schedule. Using census materials, maps, voting returns, and special computer programs, the commission has ninety days to draw up a preliminary redistricting and reapportionment plan for the state.[3] The commission then holds forty-five days of public hearings on its preliminary plan, after which it has another forty-five days to draw up a final plan. This final plan is then submitted to the Colorado Supreme Court, which carefully reviews it to make certain the new legislative districts meet constitutional requirements concerning equal population of districts, compactness of districts, and preservation of traditional communities of interest in the state.

The Colorado Reapportionment Commission operated for the first time following the 1980 census. As expected, the Republican leadership in the legislature appointed two Republicans to the commission, and the Democratic leadership appointed two Democrats. Also as expected, the Democratic governor, Richard Lamm, appointed three commission members favorable to the Democrats. The chief justice of the Supreme Court, Paul Hodges, was a staunch Republican and appointed four Republican party activists to the Reapportionment Commission. The result was that the Republicans had six of the eleven votes on the commission and the Democrats only five.

The Republican majority on the 1980 Reapportionment Commission, it is said, drew up legislative district lines that strongly favored the Republican party.[4] Republicans apparently persuaded Democrats on the commission to support a large number of fairly secure Republican seats in exchange for a somewhat smaller number of relatively strong Democratic seats. According to the *Denver Post,* "[the Republicans] proceeded to outfox the Democrats on the panel, who were more interested in feathering their own political nests than looking out for their party statewide." As a result, the Republicans were able to redistrict the legislature in a way that "gave the Republican party a tremendous—but inequitable—advantage."[5]

Both the Democrats and the Republicans expected the 1991 redistricting and reapportionment, based on the 1990 census, to be favorable to the Democrats.[6] Unlike 1981, when the chief justice of the Colorado Supreme Court was a loyal Republican, the chief justice in 1991 was merely a nominal Republican, Luis Rovira, who was appointed by Democratic Governor Richard Lamm. The *Denver Post* and many others described Chief Justice Rovira as an excellent choice for chief justice and predicted he would be evenhanded in redistricting and reapportionment matters.

Prominent Colorado Democrats were looking forward to the work of the Colorado Reapportionment Commission in 1991. Dick Freese, chair of the Colorado Democratic party, said he expected a fair-minded commission that "will lay out the state senate and state house districts in such a way that each district reflects the state proportions of Democrats and Republicans." According to Freese, "this will produce more evenly balanced and competitive legislative districts. The result of this higher level of party competition for legislative seats will be higher-quality legislators."[7]

A Republican party worker dismissed the idea, however, that the Democrats could become the majority party in the Colorado legislature by means of the redistricting and reapportionment process. The rural areas and the Denver suburbs are so strongly Republican, he said, that there is no way that anyone could draw district lines that would produce Democratic victories. Only by creating elongated districts that started in downtown Denver, which is heavily Democratic, and came out to the suburbs, which are heavily Republican, could anyone hope to produce a large number of competitive legislative districts in Colorado. The Republican party worker concluded that "it is doubtful they could get away with such [unusual] political district drawing."[8]

As it turned out, the 1991 Colorado Reapportionment Commission did not draw legislative districts that were evenly balanced along partisan lines. In a repeat of the 1981 reapportionment, the commission drew up legislative districts that gave the Republicans a number of safe seats, gave the Democrats a somewhat smaller number of safe seats, and left only a few seats that were evenly balanced between the two major political parties. When the new legislative districts were announced early in 1992, veteran political observers predicted the Republicans would maintain control of both houses of the Colorado legislature.[9] The November 1992 election results proved them right, but by very narrow margins.

Despite its tendency to preserve the partisan status quo, the Colorado Reapportionment Commission is generally admired by political commentators. The commission only reapportions the state legislature. Colorado's congressional districts, from which are elected Colorado's members of the U.S. House of Representatives, still are drawn by the state legislature and signed into law by the governor. This process is highly political and often results in heated arguments between a legislature dominated by one political party and a governor from the other party. Many observers of Colorado politics argue that congressional district lines as well as legislative district lines should be drawn by the Colorado Reapportionment Commission.[10]

ELECTION CAMPAIGNS

In terms of general elections, seats in the Colorado legislature are usually classified into three categories—safe Democratic seats, safe Republican seats, and swing seats.

Safe Democratic seats are those easily won by the Democratic candidate. Often Republicans cannot find a challenger or do not even bother to recruit an opposition candidate. Safe Democratic districts in Colorado are located in center-city Denver, Adams County (an industrialized area northeast of Denver), the city of Pueblo, the city of Boulder, and in the San Luis Valley in southern Colorado. One Democratic member of the state House of Representatives, Wayne Knox of south central Denver, has such a safe seat that he has served in the legislature for thirty years.

Safe Republican seats are those that are easily won by the Republican candidate. Just as Republicans have trouble finding candidates to run in safe Democratic districts, Democrats often have trouble recruiting candidates to run in safe Republican districts. Most of the safe Republican seats in the Colorado legislature are found in the upscale Denver suburbs in Jefferson and Arapahoe counties, as well as in El Paso County (Colorado Springs) and many of the rural areas of the state. Chuck Berry, the speaker of the Colorado House of Representatives, sits in a seat so safe that no Democratic candidate could be found to oppose him even the first time he ran for the legislature, nor has any Democrat opposed him since.[11]

Swing seats are legislative districts which, based on their voting records and demographic characteristics (such as average income, average educational levels, percentages of minorities), can vote either Democratic or Republican in the next election. As expected, both political parties put forth their greatest electoral efforts to win and retain the swing seats in the state Senate and state House of Representatives.

A swing seat is most likely to switch from one political party to the other when it is an "open" seat, that is, when neither party has an incumbent legislator running for reelection. Because the average voter does not pay much attention to legislative elections, and because name familiarity is one of the biggest factors in winning elections, incumbent members of the state legislature generally have an easy time getting reelected. When an incumbent is not running for reelection in a swing seat, however, each party will have the opportunity to win the seat in the next general election, and each party will "target" the seat and make an extra effort to win it.

In late 1989 John Britz was serving as director of the House Democratic Majority Fund, a special group created by the Colorado Democratic party to help its candidates running for the state House of Representatives in the 1990 general election. The Democrats apparently decided to concentrate all their electoral efforts on the Colorado House in 1990, mainly because few swing seats were up for election in the state Senate and, as already noted, only one-half of the state senators come up for reelection in any one election. In 1992, when a larger number of swing seats were up for election in the state Senate, the Democrats planned a major effort to win swing seats in the state Senate.[12]

According to Britz, there are three steps in the process of establishing which swing seats the Democratic party will target for extra campaign efforts. First the party will study the *voting history* of the various legislative districts, studying how Democratic and Republican candidates for U.S. president, U.S. senator, governor, and so on have done in each district. If Democratic candidates for national and statewide offices have done well in a particular district, it becomes a possible target district.

The second factor, Britz indicated, is the *demographics* of the various districts. Generally speaking, the lower the educational levels and income levels in a legislative district, the more likely it is to vote Democratic. Precincts with high percentages of black voters and Spanish-surnamed voters also are more likely to vote Democratic. Other demographic factors that can help Democratic candidates are high percentages of older voters and large numbers of labor union members in the district.

The third factor in establishing target districts, Britz said, is *candidate strength*. The Democratic party will pay particular attention to those legislative races in which the Democratic candidate appears to be particularly popular with the voters and is proving a strong and energetic campaigner. At the same time, the Democrats look for legislative races in which the Republican candidate appears to be a weak candidate with little voter appeal and few campaign skills. Candidate strength is rapidly becoming the most important factor in determining target legislative districts, Britz said. "The voters are looking more closely at the individuals running for the state legislature and paying less attention to party affiliation."[13]

John Britz's opposite number at Republican headquarters in 1990 was Hank Hahne, political coordinator for the Colorado Republican Committee. Similar to Britz, Hahne used computerized voting returns, demographic data, and candidate strengths and weaknesses in determining which legislative seats the Republican party would target in the 1990 general election. As for demographics, the Republicans tend to do best in legislative districts that have high income and educational levels, low percentages of black and Spanish-surnamed voters, and large numbers of young suburban families with small children.

Hahne emphasized the importance of party leaders, in both the legislature and the legislative districts, for help in selecting target legislative races. Party chairs and other knowledgeable political observers are particularly valuable in identifying strong candidates for the Republican party and weak candidates for the Democratic party, Hahne said. Legislative leaders, familiar with how legislators from both parties work and vote on a day-to-day basis, can offer invaluable tips on a candidate's character, particularly on how members of the opposition party may have cast votes that will make them unpopular if and when they run for reelection.

Both parties in Colorado concentrate their efforts on target seats. As a result, in any given general election, a mere twelve to fifteen of the total eighty-two or eighty-three legislative races are regarded as important by the two political parties. Hahne argued that both political parties in Colorado target the same way and pour all their money into the same legislative races. Both parties start with a long list of thirty or so swing seats that have potential for being targeted, but the list narrows as it gets closer to election day. In some of the races, a candidate gets way ahead and the party no longer feels the need to target the race. In other cases, the opposition candidate develops a big lead and the party decides it would be wasted effort to emphasize that district. In the end, Hahne concluded, "the two parties have targeted the same twelve to fifteen legislative seats and fight it out for those twelve to fifteen seats.[14]

Once they have decided which legislative races to target, the two major political parties in Colorado provide essentially the same kind of campaign help for their respective candidates. Voting data are provided that can be used to identify voting precincts in which there are large numbers of voters favoring the political party. The assumption is party candidates will campaign heavily in these precincts, working hard to turn out known party supporters to the polls on election day. The two parties not only will provide campaign funds to party legislative candidates but will also offer advice on how best to spend the money. In recent years, both parties have been encouraging their legislative candidates to make extensive use of direct mail, sending their campaign materials to computerized mailing lists of frequent voters.

Because most legislative elections have low visibility and attract little voter interest, candidates for the state legislature tend to concentrate their campaigns in the last two or three weeks before election day. They send out their direct mail and run almost all of their political advertising during this brief period before the election, although weeks of preparation are required to produce direct mail and political advertising.

Challengers who seek to unseat an incumbent or legislators who reside in districts with a registration ratio favoring the opposite party have to campaign much harder. Indeed, their campaign often begins a half-year or more in advance of election time. And it very often involves weeks and months of door-to-door canvassing. Candidates with sufficient campaign funds can purchase street listings with information as to whether residents are registered to vote and how they are registered. Armed with this information, candidates for election or reelection can make better use of their time—concentrating on meeting and winning the support of their own partisans and also trying to win over the unaffiliated voters to their cause.

UNCOMPETITIVE CHARACTER OF LEGISLATIVE ELECTIONS

A study of election results for the years 1972 through 1988 concluded that legislative elections in Colorado tend to be noncompetitive. The study found that legislative campaigns are characterized by little party turnover, large margins of victory, large numbers of unopposed candidates, and low percentages of defeated incumbents.[15]

The low level of party turnover—Democratic to Republican or Republican to Democratic—in Colorado legislative races was even more pronounced in the 1980s than it was in the 1970s. In the 1970s an average of only 12 percent of all state House seats and 8.5 percent of all Senate seats changed parties in general election contests. In the 1980s, however, an average of only 9 percent of House seats and 3 percent of Senate seats changed from one political party to the other. The actual percentages are even smaller because a number of the changes were the result of incumbent legislators changing parties rather than an incumbent being defeated by a candidate from the opposition party.

As would be expected in a state legislature where few seats change hands from one party to the other, most winners, Democrats and Republicans alike, are elected by large margins of the vote. This trend also became more pronounced in the 1980s. In House races in the 1970s the average percentage of the two-party vote earned by the winning candidates was 64.8 percent, while Senate winners averaged 66.2 percent of the vote. In the 1980s House winners averaged 70.6 percent of the vote and Senate victors averaged 72.8 percent.

In addition to low party turnover and high margins of victory, Colorado legislative races are characterized by large numbers of unopposed candidates. In the 1970s 18.5 percent of state House candidates and 23 percent of state Senate candidates ran unopposed in the average general election contest. In the 1980s 35 percent of House candidates and 40 percent of Senate candidates had no opposition.

The low level of two-party competition in Colorado legislative contests also is reflected by an unusually high percentage of incumbent victories. Incumbents are not present in every House and Senate race; yet when they are present, they almost always win. Again this trend was stronger in the 1980s than it was in the 1970s. In the 1970s incumbents won 89 percent of all House races and 97 percent of all Senate races in which an incumbent was running for reelection. In the 1980s incumbents won in 91 percent of all House races and 100 percent of all Senate races in which an incumbent was involved.

In general, races for seats in the Colorado legislature are generally noncompetitive. Most incumbents who run for reelection win. Many candidates run unopposed. The winning candidate usually wins easily. Most districts do not experience party turnover. For those who believe the electoral process works best when there is healthy two-party competition for elective offices, the statistical picture presented by general elections for the Colorado legislature is, to say the least, sobering.

In terms of the success of the two major political parties in Colorado legislative elections, the Republicans do appear to have a decided advantage over the Democrats. During the 1980s, the Colorado House of Representatives had thirty-seven safe Republican seats, eighteen safe Democratic seats, and ten swing seats. In the Senate during that decade there were twenty-three safe Republican seats, nine safe Democratic seats, and only three marginal seats.[16]

Because Colorado election laws provide for party primaries, incumbent state legislators in both political parties occasionally are defeated in their party primary rather than in the general election. Primary elections are held in early August, three months before the November general election.

Legislative primary elections frequently occur when there is an open seat and two or more party members want to try for the party nomination. Because the voter turnout is much lower in primary elections than in general elections, candidates running in a legislative party primary will emphasize highly "personal" campaign techniques, such as personally telephoning registered party members with a record for voting in primary elections. Another popular technique is to "walk the precinct," getting a list of voters registered in the particular political party and knocking on their doors in hopes of getting to chat with them about the upcoming primary election.

The primary election process has its greatest effect on state legislators who represent safe Democratic or safe Republican seats. Such legislators probably will not face a serious reelection challenge from the other party in the general election, yet they may be challenged in their own party primary. As a result, legislators from safe seats often become more concerned about the voters who vote in their party primary, a relatively small number of people, rather than the much larger group of voters who vote in the general election.

This phenomenon of legislators from safe seats caring more about the primary election than the general election has philosophical effects. The people who vote in Republican primaries tend to be more conservative than the general electorate. A Republican legislator sitting in a safe Republican seat thus will have relatively more conservatives voting in the Republican primary than vote in the general election. The result is to encourage the Republican legislator to be more conservative than he or she might otherwise be. The philosophical effects are the opposite in the Democratic party. A Democratic legislator from a safe Democratic seat will have relatively more liberals voting in the Democratic primary than vote in the general election. A safe-seat Democrat thus will often be more liberal than he or she might otherwise be.

Are safe Republican and safe Democratic seats good or bad for the Colorado legislature? In one sense they are good, because they provide a solid base for each of the two political parties. No matter how badly a party might lose any particular general election, it will still have its safe seats, and thus some representation, in the state legislature.

On the other hand, safe party legislative seats can be viewed as bad for the legislature. Because safe-seat Republicans tend to be very conservative, and safe-seat Democrats tend to be very liberal, one effect of safe seats is to polarize the legislature and create core groups in each of the two political parties that tend toward philosophical extremes.

WHY REPUBLICANS DOMINATE

As noted, Republicans have dominated elections for the Colorado General Assembly for over thirty years. Knowledgeable observers give one or more of the following reasons for this recent Republican domination of the legislature.

Single-Member Districts

As previously noted, the voters of Colorado in 1966 approved an initiated constitutional amendment providing for single-member districts in both the state Senate and House of Representatives. Prior to the 1960s, state legislators were elected countywide, with the more populous counties being apportioned multiple numbers of legislators. Thus Denver at one time had more than ten state representatives, all of them elected by the entire city.

Veteran state Representative Wayne Knox, of south central Denver, explained how this multimember electoral system worked: "If Denver had seventeen state representatives, that meant that seventeen Democrats would run against seventeen Republicans, and every Denver voter cast seventeen votes for the seventeen spots in the lower house of the state legislature."[17] What this meant was that, in big Democratic years, the Democrats would sweep all seventeen seats. The same thing would happen in Adams County (northeast Denver suburbs) and Pueblo County. There would be a multiple number of state representative seats up for election in the county, and the Democrats would sweep all of them in years when the Democrats were popular.

The last big Democratic landslide in Colorado under the multimember district system was in 1958, when a national economic recession crippled the Republicans.[18] The Democrats won the governorship and swept both houses of the legislature. Representative Knox concluded: "The shift to single-member districts in the 1960s really did hurt the Democrats. The Republicans now are able to hold onto seats they used to automatically lose in big Democratic election years.''[19]

Another supporter of the idea that the shift from multimember to single-member legislative districts hurt the Democrats in Colorado is Lyle Kyle, director of research for the state legislature from 1958 to 1985. He noted that the move for single-member districts in the legislature was always a Republican issue. The Democrats wanted to stick with at-large elections countywide, because at-large helped the Democrats to win control of the legislature when they were sweeping in legislative elections.

According to Kyle, the business community joined the Republicans in backing single-member districts because they believed single-member districts would make the legislature more conservative. Kyle concluded: ''The general public in Colorado was never aware of the partisan angle, which is why single-member districts passed as an initiated constitutional amendment.[20]

Another negative effect of single-member districts on the Democrats in the Colorado legislature was that it sometimes attracted Democratic candidates with lower educational levels and less experience. Many able Democrats who could get elected under the at-large system lived in highly educated upper-income neighborhoods that were likely to choose Republicans in single-member district elections. A number of observers pointed out that those Democrats who would be skillful and effective at working for liberal legislation were not necessarily those living in the poorly educated lower-income districts that would be most likely to elect Democrats to the legislature.[21]

Court-Ordered Reapportionment

In 1962 the United States Supreme Court ruled in *Baker v. Carr* that legislative districts in the fifty states must henceforth be "substantially equal" in population. Two years later, in *Reynolds v. Simms,* the Court ruled that the equal population requirement applied to the upper houses of state legislatures as well as the lower houses.

The most immediate effect of court-ordered reapportionment in Colorado was a great increase in the number of state representatives and state senators from the Denver suburbs. This occurred because the Denver suburbs were the fastest growing areas in Colorado in the years following World War II. Unfortunately for the Democrats, the middle-class voters moving to the Denver suburbs tended to favor the Republican party.

At the same time that rapid population growth was occurring in the Denver suburbs, the traditionally Democratic cities of Denver and Pueblo were either growing slowly or declining in population. The result was that the number of state senators and representatives apportioned to these strongly Democratic cities decreased.

In addition to the growth of the Denver suburbs, rapid population growth was also occurring in the cities of Colorado Springs and Fort Collins. Similar to the Denver suburbs, these predominantly middle-class cities (and the counties in which they are located) have a decided preference for the Republican party on election day.

Population growth in the Denver suburbs, the tendency of these new suburban residents to vote Republican, and court-ordered reapportionment that increased the number of suburban state legislators—these three factors combined to preserve the Republican party's electoral domination of the Colorado state legislature from 1962 to 1990.

Coattail Effect

The strong Republican "coattail effect" in presidential elections compared to the weaker Democratic "coattails" in gubernatorial elections helped Republicans continue their domination of the legislature. During the 1970s and 1980s, it was one of the famous clichés of Colorado politics that the Republicans did well in the state in presidential election years and the Democrats did well in gubernatorial election years. Many more Coloradans vote in presidential elections than vote in gubernatorial elections. Republicans won Colorado in every presidential election from 1968 to 1988. When large numbers of voters were going to the polls to vote Republican for president, a substantial number decided to vote Republican for the state legislature as well.

This "coattail effect" from Republican victories in presidential elections in the 1970s and 1980s was particularly pronounced when the Republican presidential candidate was winning in Colorado by a landslide. This happened three times between 1968 and 1988—in 1972, 1980, and 1984. In each instance Republicans scored big gains in both the Colorado Senate and the Colorado House of Representatives. In 1984, when a popular incumbent Republican president, Ronald Reagan, was sweeping Colorado, Republicans won so many legislative seats that both houses of the state legislature had more than a two-thirds Republican majority.

From 1974 through 1990, the Democrats won every gubernatorial election. Democrats always take some state legislative seats away from Republicans at the same time they win the state governorship, yet they customarily do not win enough seats to gain control of either house of the legislature.

Only in 1974, when the Watergate scandal weakened the Republican party, were the Democrats able to win control of the Colorado House of Representatives.

The decade of the 1990s started out strongly for the Democrats in Colorado. The 1992 Democratic candidate for president, Arkansas Governor Bill Clinton, won a comfortable victory in Colorado over his Republican opponent, incumbent President George Bush. Exactly as victorious Republican presidential candidates had coattails in Colorado in the 1970s and 1980s, Democrat Clinton had coattails in 1992. The Democrats gained four seats in the state Senate and four seats in the state House of Representatives. Despite these solid Democratic gains in the 1992 elections, the Republicans retained narrow three-vote majorities in both houses of the Colorado General Assembly.

Incumbency Advantage

One of the major characteristics of American politics during the 1970s and 1980s has been the increase in importance of incumbency advantage, the ability of most officeholders who run for reelection to get reelected. This phenomenon has been most pronounced in the case of the U.S. House of Representatives, yet it has also been the case at the state legislative level in Colorado. The ability of incumbent state legislators to generate publicity and build a record of service for their constituents gives them a decided advantage over challengers who try to unseat them at reelection time.

In Colorado state legislative races, the phenomenon of incumbency advantage has favored the Republicans, mainly because the great majority of the incumbents during the 1970s and 1980s have been Republicans. Incumbency advantage, obviously, favors the party that already holds a majority of the legislative seats, and this in recent decades has been the Republicans in the Colorado legislature.

Incumbency advantage results in *sophomore surge* and *retirement slump*. Sophomore surge is the tendency of newcomers to the state legislature to obtain a greatly increased percentage of the vote the first time they run for reelection. The surge is caused by the fact that the newcomers are no longer newcomers and, for the first time, are running for office with incumbency advantage.

Retirement slump occurs when an incumbent state senator or state representative retires from office and does not run for reelection. His or her political party's percentage of the vote "slumps" in the next general election for that particular legislative seat because that political party will have to recruit a new candidate and thus will not have the customary advantages of incumbency. Because of the phenomenon of retirement slump, both the Democrats and the Republicans in Colorado pay close attention when an incumbent dies, retires, or decides to run for higher political office.

A major factor contributing to incumbency advantage in Colorado legislative races is the rise in the importance of political action committees (PACS). Customarily representing either business groups or labor organizations, PACS are permitted to raise campaign funds and contribute them to candidates running for political office. Under Colorado law, there is no limit on the amount of money which political action committees can contribute to political candidates.

By 1986 political action committees had become the primary sources of funding for candidates for the state legislature. According to a study by Colorado Common Cause, "special interest PACS accounted for 59 percent of contributions to state House candidates and 62 percent of contributions to state Senate candidates."[22] The study revealed that PAC contributions slightly tend to favor winning Republican legislators over winning Democratic legislators. Winning Republicans in both the House and the Senate received an average of 67.9 percent of their contributions from PACS, while winning Democrats received an average of 60.3 percent.[23]

The system of PAC campaign financing in Colorado, Common Cause continued, heavily favors incumbents. In the 1986 Colorado legislative elections, "PACS contributed 61 percent of their funds to incumbents, 29 percent to open seats and only 10 percent to challengers." Common Cause concluded that "PACS tend to provide financial support for the candidates they expect to win, regardless of party or philosophy. This is a major reason why more than 88 percent of incumbents were successful in retaining their seats.[24]

Because PACS mainly, and understandably, contribute to incumbents, PAC contributions heavily favor the current majority party in both houses of the Colorado legislature—the Republicans. Also, because PACS give so much money to Republican incumbents, Republican candidates for the legislature depend much more heavily on PAC contributions than Democratic candidates do. Common Cause found Republicans received 69 percent of their campaign funds from PACS, while Democrats received only 31 percent from these organizations.[25]

FUTURE PROSPECTS FOR DEMOCRATS

As for the future, Colorado Democrats believe, or perhaps hope, they will be able, sooner or later, to break the Republican grip on both houses of the state legislature. Renny Fagan, formerly a Democratic member of the Colorado House of Representatives from El Paso County, acknowledged that the Democrats did poorly in the 1984 legislative elections and ended up with less than one-third of the members of each house. But he noted that the Democrats have been doing better since then, gaining seats in the 1986, 1988, and 1990 elections. (The Democrats continued to gain in the 1992 elections.) More important, Fagan argued, Democrats have been gaining seats in the traditional Republican strongholds of Jefferson and Arapahoe counties (southwest suburban Denver) and El Paso County (Colorado Springs). Perhaps most important, Fagan concluded, Democrats are winning seats occupied by moderate Republicans. That means the Republicans remaining in the state legislature are very conservative and are pursuing policies that are too conservative for most Colorado citizens. Looked at from former Representative Fagan's point of view, Democratic prospects for winning the state legislature are more positive than many observers believe.[26]

Republican strategists agree with this view that control of the Colorado legislature will go to the political party which does the best job of winning suburban Denver legislative seats. According to one Republican political operator, however, the Democrats will have to change their party philosophy if they want to be big winners in Colorado's fast-growing suburban areas. "The problem is," he explained, "the Democrats do not want to become a carbon copy of the Republican party in Colorado in order to win some suburban seats. Whether they can accomplish such a goal—win in the Denver suburbs without becoming more like the Republicans—is an interesting question.[27]

LIMITING LEGISLATIVE TERMS

At least a dozen efforts have been made in recent years to impose limits on legislative terms of office in Colorado. None have won support in the Colorado legislature. In 1990 state Senator Terry Considine, a Republican from the wealthy suburbs south of Denver, proposed another such measure to the legislature. It failed once more. This time, however, Considine and a group of political allies started an organization called Coloradans Back in Charge, or CBIC, and launched a campaign to collect the needed number of citizen signatures to qualify their term-limitation measure for the November 1990 ballot.

Considine and his organization succeeded in putting on the ballot a constitutional amendment limiting legislative terms. On November 6, 1990, term limits were overwhelmingly approved by Colorado voters, 707,114 to 289,046. Seventy-one percent of those voting voted for the measure.

There were many theories as to why term limits were adopted so overwhelmingly in Colorado. Some believed it was the result of the general antigovernment attitude found among voters in the state. Others argued that Coloradans liked the idea of a "citizen" legislature rather than a "professional" legislature. There was also the point that although some members of the state legislature made statements to the news media questioning the wisdom of term limits, there was no organized campaign against their adoption.

The Considine Term Limitation Initiated Amendment was one of the most sweeping measures of its kind. It limited all elected state officials to eight years in the same office (two four-year terms or four two-year terms). Further, U.S. senators and representatives from Colorado in the U.S. Congress are prohibited from serving more than twelve consecutive years in the same office.

TERM LIMITS—A DEBATE

Proponents of term limitation point out that 90 percent or more of Colorado's legislators who run for reelection are routinely returned to office by their constituents. The only way to get large numbers of newer and younger members into the legislature, they argue, is to limit incumbents to only eight years in office.

Another advantage of term limitation is its effect on electoral competition. A variety of studies show that party turnover and close races are more likely when the contested seat is an open one. The absence of an incumbent allows the election to focus more on policy questions and on leadership qualities rather than on "years of service" to the people of the district. Term limitation means more seats will be open more often, and thus voters, it is argued, are more likely to have a meaningful choice when they go to the polls.

Finally, term-limitation backers argue that democracy is in trouble and that not enough citizens care enough to bother to register and vote. Term limits, they imply, will create more competition and motivate more people to vote. It also will change the way lawmakers view their responsibilities. "Someone who views holding public office as a short term opportunity to do something good acts differently than a career politician. He or she is more likely to take stands on principle, and less likely to kowtow to the bureaucracy and the special interests."[28]

Opponents say term limitation imprudently and undemocratically narrows the choices available to voters. Voters ought to be able to elect whomever they choose, even if the person is a twenty- or thirty-year incumbent. Moreover, experience in legislative service should be viewed as a positive qualification. People do not stop going to a favorite dentist or auto mechanic just because eight years have gone by. On the contrary, people value the service of that dentist or auto mechanic precisely because he or she has served them well over a long period of time.

Term limitation attacks the symptoms but not the real problems, opponents argue. The problems of safe seats, incumbency advantage, and "insider" influence are likely to persist even with term limits. If the aim is to have more competitive elections and to limit the advantages of the incumbent, those goals can be achieved with direct reforms, such as drawing more competitive legislative districts and limiting PAC contributions.

Opponents acknowledge that regular and more rapid turnover in the state legislature would probably mean some of the more junior members would gain more influence. But it also is likely to mean that the already powerful legislative staff would become even more influential as the legislators become "fresher" and less experienced.

Another unforeseen consequence of this well-intentioned "reform" would be to weaken the legislature vis-à-vis state bureaucrats. Experienced civil servants with long years on the public payroll are more likely to be held to account by veteran rather than novice legislators.

Good points were raised on both sides of the term-limitation debate in Colorado. Its supporters probably promised more than their amendment can deliver. It is doubtful that increased voter turnout and truly competitive seats will result from this term-limitation "reform." Strengthening the parties, drawing more competitive legislative districts, and regulating campaign spending also will be needed.

CONCLUSION

For three decades, ever since 1962, the Republicans have dominated state legislative elections in Colorado. One reason for this has been the growing size and voting strength of Denver's pro-Republican suburbs. Another has been the powerful coattails of Republican presidential candidates during the 1970s and 1980s. Structural factors, such as the requirement of single-member legislative districts and the rise of incumbency advantage, also are said to help explain why the Republicans win most of the state legislative races in Colorado.

The challenge of encouraging party competition, voter turnout, and voter interest in state legislative elections is a continuing one. Many Coloradans are too laid-back or preoccupied with their jobs, families, and leisure-time pursuits to take an interest in which party dominates the state legislature and why. This is not much different from the situation in other states, yet it remains a challenge.

There is an enduring paradox about the Colorado General Assembly, a paradox found in other states and the national Congress. Colorado's state legislators are regularly returned to office by the same voters who constantly complain about high state taxes and who express frustration with the overall performance of the legislature.

Chapters 8, 9, and 10 examine, in detail, the politics of the legislative, executive, and judicial branches of the state government of Colorado.

CHAPTER EIGHT

Legislative Politics and Procedures

Colorado's legislature, officially called the General Assembly, is popularly referred to as the state legislature. While every state has a legislature, few states have as influential a legislature as Colorado. As one scholar put it: "The fifty American states vary in the relative power of their legislative and executive branches, but in Colorado, the relationship is clear: Ours is a system of legislative dominance."[1]

There are several reasons for this. One reason is that the Colorado legislature, through an unusual institution known as the Joint Budget Committee (JBC), exercises considerable influence over state budgeting and spending decisions. Second, the Colorado constitution limits the power of the governor in several ways, particularly the governor's ability to appoint and control administrative offices and personnel. Third, the legislature has been a partisan and feisty institution, jealously guarding its prerogatives and regularly portraying itself as a guardian of the taxpayers against the encroachments of the governor and the state bureaucracy.

What do Colorado legislators do? They enact laws that help finance public education, build state parks and highways, specify salaries for state officials, fix state tax rates, determine the number and quality of state prisons, and much more. State legislators oversee the administration of state programs. Although they do not administer programs directly, legislators influence the way programs are carried out through hearings, investigations, audits, and direct involvement in the budgetary process.

State legislators have the twin responsibilities of lawmaking and representation. While they do most of their lawmaking at the statehouse, they spend even more time acting as representatives of their local constituencies, a year-round job. A good state legislator is constantly listening, learning, and trying to find out what people like and dislike about state programs. State legislators try to make themselves accessible, often holding "open house" or "town meeting" gatherings in their home communities. "A good legislator will 'bond' with the voters in his or her district, learning their interests and concerns and letting them know he or she will look out for those interests and concerns up at the state capital."[2]

WHO ARE THE COLORADO STATE LEGISLATORS?

The typical American state legislator is a forty-two-year-old white male Protestant lawyer or businessperson of Anglo-Saxon origin who has had previous political or volunteer service at the community level. This is pretty much the case in the Centennial State as well. Colorado, however, has one of the highest percentages of women in the state legislature, around 30 percent. For instance, in the 1987–88 session, twenty-five of the sixty-five seats in the House of Representatives were held by women. Perhaps more important, eighteen of the forty Republicans, the majority party in the House at that session, were women. "It was stamped on the consciousness of everybody doing business in the Colorado House that women were not that many votes away from a majority."[3]

The location of the state capitol in the central population region of the state makes it relatively easy for people to commute to the legislature. Over 60 percent of the legislators can easily commute to the statehouse from their homes in Denver, the Denver suburbs, and other nearby cities. This may help to explain why there is such a large number of women in the Colorado legislature. There is less disruption of family life and no need to maintain a second home near the state capitol, which is a necessity for most legislators in many other states.

Serving in the Colorado legislature is a "part-time" job. The legislature meets in formal session only four months of the year, which gives most members time during the other eight months to work in other professions. One out of every three members of the Colorado legislature is either an attorney or a teacher. During recent sessions, 20 percent of the legislators were lawyers and 15 percent were teachers. Two other well-represented occupational groups are businesspeople (12 percent of the legislators in 1987–88) and farmers and ranchers (10 percent). Despite the fact that the Colorado legislature is considered a part-time institution, twelve members in a recent session listed their profession as full-time legislator.[4] Eleven of these twelve self-proclaimed full-time legislators were women.

Members of the Colorado House and Senate received a salary of $17,500 a year in 1992, and this was regarded as a part-time salary. The low pay is another reason that is often given for the high percentage of women in the Colorado legislature. At $17,500 for half a year's work, one woman legislator pointed out, "most men aren't interested in the job."[5]

Colorado state legislators also receive funds to help meet living and travel expenses while the legislature is in session. In addition, they are reimbursed for expenses when they attend to legislative business when the legislature is not in session. According to one state senator, "the combination of salary plus expenses, with expenses being tax-free, means that Colorado legislators are satisfactorily remunerated for their part-time jobs."[6]

RULES AND REGULATIONS

Once elected to the Colorado legislature, senators and representatives enter a highly regulated and regimented world. Because the legislature meets for only a limited amount of time each calendar year (120 days), bills must be introduced and advanced according to a detailed legislative deadline schedule. Enforced with reasonable strictness in both houses, the deadline schedule is designed to provide for an orderly flow of work under tight time constraints. Colorado's carefully scheduled legislature is far more "tidy" than the "freewheeling" processes in the U.S. Congress.

The deadline schedule used in recent years requires that requests for drafting bills be submitted to the Legislative Legal Services Office by the tenth day of the legislative session. The deadline for senators and representatives to introduce a bill is the twenty-fifth day of the session. By the forty-fifth day a bill has to be reported out of committee in the house in which the bill originates, and by the fifty-fifth day a bill has to pass the house of origin and thus be available for consideration in the second house. By the seventieth day a bill has to be reported out of committee in the second house and by the eightieth day a bill has to have passed the second house. This schedule leaves sufficient time for further consideration of a bill in both houses. Often bills need to be sent to a conference committee to iron out differences between the bill that passes in the house of origin and the bill that passes the second house.

It is customary procedure in the Colorado legislature for a bill to be introduced in only one house and then, after consideration and passage in that house, to move to the second house. Occasionally identical bills are introduced in both chambers and start moving through both houses simultaneously, but this method is the exception rather than the rule.

In addition to having to conform to a strict set of legislative deadlines, Centennial State lawmakers are limited as to the number of bills they can introduce at any one session of the legislature. Each legislator can introduce no more than five bills.

The legislative deadline schedule and five-bill limit have a definite effect on the behavior of Colorado state legislators. They are encouraged to choose carefully the bills they introduce. They are required to introduce those bills early in the session, and, whenever possible, are encouraged to get requests for bill drafting to Legislative Legal Services before the session begins.[7] The atmosphere created by all the rules and schedules is one that encourages legislators to plan carefully and move their bills along systematically. Spontaneous actions, such as introducing large numbers of bills and rushing new bills through late in the session, are discouraged.

LEADERSHIP

Speaker of the House

Every two years, shortly after the November general elections, the two major political parties in the Colorado legislature hold their respective organizational caucuses. In the House of Representatives, the majority party selects its candidate to be the speaker of the House. In addition, the majority party elects the House majority leader, the assistant House majority leader, and the chair of the House majority caucus. The minority party, meeting separately, elects the House minority leader, the assistant House minority leader, and the House minority caucus chair. Since the mid 1970s the Republicans have been the majority party in the Colorado House and the Democrats have been in the minority.

The speaker of the House, described as "the power center in the Colorado House of Representatives,"[8] is elected by majority vote of all the members of the House, but the candidate chosen by the majority party caucus invariably wins the office. The speaker presides over meetings of the House, preserving order and recognizing state representatives who wish to address the House. The speaker can designate another member of the House, by custom always a member of the majority party, to preside over House meetings in his or her absence. This person is frequently referred to as the speaker pro tempore.

The speaker appoints the chairpersons and majority party members of the major House committees. The speaker also decides the number of members on each committee and the number from each political party, carefully seeing to it that there are always more members of the majority party on a committee. The speaker also decides which bills will be considered by which committees.

The minority leader in the House of Representatives appoints members of the minority party to committees, but even these minority party appointments are subject to the final approval of the speaker of the House. If the speaker does not want a certain minority party legislator on a particular committee, he or she can override the minority leader and prevent assigning the minority party member to that committee.

Members of the majority party in the Colorado House of Representatives may submit their preferences for committee assignments to the speaker, but he or she is not bound to honor those requests. In the same manner, the speaker may or may not consult with veteran members of his or her political party when deciding on majority party committee appointments.

It is the power to appoint committees and to route bills to particular committees that makes the speaker of the House so important. Speakers generally appoint a number of their close friends or political allies in the majority party to three or four major committees, thereby creating a majority in these committees that will, within reason, do what the speaker desires. Speakers then route major or controversial bills to one of these three or four committees, confident that the bills will be processed with the speaker's views in mind.

If the speaker especially wants a bill voted down in committee, he or she sends it to one of these three or four committees, which thus become a convenient instrument for eliminating bills that the speaker considers frivolous, inappropriate, or untimely. Because of the utility of these committees for voting down bills opposed by the leadership of the House majority party, they are often referred to as the "killer committees" or "death committees."[9]

From 1981 to 1991 the speaker of the Colorado House of Representatives was Carl "Bev" Bledsoe. A resident of Hugo, a small agricultural town on the eastern plains, Bledsoe represented a district that was decidedly conservative and Republican. When he retired from the legislature in 1991, Bledsoe had served as House speaker longer than anyone in Colorado history.

To many observers, Speaker Bledsoe was the last remnant of the "cowboy caucus," a powerful group of rural legislators who, prior to court-ordered reapportionment in the 1960s, dominated the Colorado legislature. As one member of the Legislative Council staff put it: "Bev Bledsoe has kept the cowboy caucus alive beyond its time." Bledsoe, in effect, used his powers as speaker to further rural conservative policies and programs that were less relevant in a mainly urban and suburban state.

Moreover, Democratic members of the Colorado House accused Bledsoe of using the speakership to further the interests of the Republican party as well as rural conservative points of view. According to veteran Democratic Representative Wayne Knox of Denver, "there is no question that the Republican leadership in the House is oppressing the Democrats. Under Speaker Bledsoe there has been a steady accumulation of tactics and decisions limiting the role of the minority." [10]

Democrats charged that some of the things done to them by Speaker Bledsoe and the majority Republicans in the Colorado House of Representatives were just plain petty. At one point House Democrats were informed they could no longer bring their brown-bag lunches into committee rooms and eat them during their noon party caucuses. The Democrats had to start holding their brown-bag lunches in the Democratic governor's office. Another time the Democrats were told that any memorandums or reports on bills and committee hearings that they had printed or photocopied at state expense would have to be shared with the Republicans and the general public. [11]

As might be expected, Republican members of the state House of Representatives were quick to defend Speaker Bledsoe and Republican domination of the House. They saw Bledsoe as having the strong support of the majority of his fellow Republicans, most of whom were from suburban Denver and not the rural areas of the state. As for the charge that Bledsoe was oppressing the Democrats in the House, the Republicans claimed that Bledsoe was only using the traditional techniques speakers have always used to maintain party control, and some sort of order, in the House. Also, Republicans liked to point out, the majority Republicans oppressed the minority Democrats in the Colorado legislature much *less* that the majority Democrats oppress the minority Republicans in the U.S. House of Representatives.

Following Bledsoe's retirement, Representative Chuck Berry of Colorado Springs became speaker of the Colorado House. A young man in his forties with a small-city constituency rather than a rural one, Speaker Berry took a less hostile and exclusionary attitude toward House Democrats and the bills they sponsored. Democrats in the House talked about a complete change in atmosphere, almost as if they had been "set free from years in solitary confinement." Instead of shutting the Democrats out, as Bledsoe had done, Berry was described by one Democrat in the House as "allowing other people to grow and become leaders."[12]

Berry acknowledged that he conducted the House so that "every legislator, Democrat or Republican alike, was able to participate in the process." He felt the result of this action was that for the first time in years, the press concentrated on the laws being passed by the legislature rather than on what the Republicans were doing to the Democrats. Berry concluded: "I think we helped restore the public's faith in the legislature."[13]

The contrasting styles of speakers Bledsoe and Berry illustrated one very important point about the Colorado House of Representatives. The speaker of the House has the power to run things, or not run them, as he or she sees fit. The speaker of the House has the power to exclude the minority party from much of the legislative process in the House, or the speaker can give the minority an expanded role to play. The choice clearly is the speaker's, and that makes the speaker, whether ruling with a tight hand or a loose one, the most powerful member of the Colorado House of Representatives.

Other House Leaders

The majority leader and the minority leader in the House work to develop the positions of their respective parties on the various bills that are under consideration by the legislature. They are aided by the assistant leaders, who are often referred to as "party whips" because of their task of "whipping party members into line" to support bills the party leadership wants passed and to oppose bills the party leadership wants defeated.

The majority leader and the minority leader also direct floor debate for their respective political parties. The two leaders are often called upon to serve as spokespersons for their parties, explaining to the public what bills and positions the party is backing and why. Because the majority leader and the minority leader play the roles of partisan disciplinarians, the speaker of the House, if he or she wishes, can stay above the open partisan fight and attempt to play a mediator role.

Senate Leadership

Although a number of the positions and functions of the Senate leadership are similar to the House leadership, there are differences. The Senate is a smaller body, with only thirty-five members, rather than sixty-five. This smaller size permits the Colorado Senate to operate somewhat more infor-mally than the House, and with less discipline and less centralized control.

The top officer in the Senate is the president of the Senate. Similar to the procedure used to select the speaker of the House, the members of the major-ity party in the Senate caucus and choose their party candidate for Senate president. This candidate then is generally elected on the first day of the ses-sion.

The major difference between the president of the Senate and the speaker of the House is that the Senate president does *not* have the sole power to ap-point majority party members to Senate committees. This task is given to the Committee on Committees, a small committee composed of the key leaders of the majority party in the Senate. The Committee on Committees also de-termines the number of members on each Senate committee (except where the number is set by law) and the number of members from each political party. The minority leader appoints the minority party members to Senate committees.

The Senate president does have the power, however, to assign bills to committee. The only exceptions to this are bills which increase salaries and appropriations bills, which are automatically referred to the Senate Finance Committee.

The Senate elects a president pro tempore to preside over Senate sessions when the president is absent. Similar to the president of the Senate, the presi-dent pro tempore is nominated in the majority party caucus and elected in a partisan vote. The Republicans have been the majority party in the Colorado Senate for over a generation and hence during this period the president and the president pro tempore were always Republicans.

For several years in the 1980s and early 1990s Senator Ted Strickland from Westminster, a northern Denver suburb, served as president of the Col-orado Senate. Viewed by most people as a moderate conservative, Strick-land operated the Senate in a manner that provided opportunities for minor-ity Democrats to participate in the legislative process.

According to Jana Mendez, a Democratic member of the Senate, the Re-publicans assert their position over the Democrats in the Senate, but "it is not really something you can put your finger on." Senator Mendez said the partisan discrimination mainly takes the form that Democrats with talent do not get to introduce and work on bills they might otherwise get to introduce and work on. "If a Democrat works hard in the Senate and develops a special area of knowledge and expertise," Mendez concluded, "the Republicans will let that Democrat introduce and work for major bills. Now, the Republicans in the Senate do not hand the Democrats anything on a silver platter. You really have to earn your stripes when you are in the minority."[14]

One reason the Senate Republican leadership is friendlier to Democrats is doubtless the smaller size of the Senate. With fewer people available, Republican senators perhaps are thankful that Democratic senators are willing to help do some of the work. Also, there is more of a "club" atmosphere in the state Senate. Senators get to know one another better, and that makes the majority Republicans somewhat more cooperative with the minority Democrats.

Other Senate Leaders

The other Senate leaders are the majority leader, the assistant majority leader, the minority leader, and the assistant minority leader. Elected at party caucuses, these leaders play the same role in the Colorado Senate that their counterparts play in the Colorado House. They work to establish party positions on bills and then line up party members to support those positions. As in the House, the assistant party leaders often are referred to as whips.

HOUSE AND SENATE COMMITTEES

Committees that meet and work during regular sessions of the Colorado legislature are known as *committees of reference*. All bills are referred to committee shortly after they are introduced in a house (the house of origin) or after they move from one house to the other (the second house).

The real work of the Colorado legislature takes place when bills are in committee. The details of bills and the advisability of enacting them are carefully considered by the various committees. Committee meetings are open to the public, and interested citizens have the opportunity to express their views on proposed legislation.

After studying a bill and hearing public comment on it, a committee can recommend the bill for passage, amend the bill and then recommend it for passage, refer the bill to another committee, postpone consideration indefinitely, table the bill for consideration at a later date, or kill it outright by voting it down. Because of the careful scrutiny given to bills by committees of reference, the debate on bills when they reach the House or Senate floor is often brief.[15]

Each house of the legislature has ten committees of reference. For the most part, House and Senate committees have the same names and cover the same areas of concern (see table 7). Thus, the House has a Local Govern-

Table 7. Colorado Legislative Committees of Reference

HOUSE	SENATE
Agriculture, Livestock, and Natural Resources	Agriculture, Natural Resources, and Energy
Appropriations	Appropriations
Business Affairs and Labor	Business Affairs and Labor
Education	Education
Finance	Finance
Health, Environment, Welfare, and Institutions	Health, Environment, Welfare, and Institutions
Judiciary	Judiciary
Local Government	Local Government
State Affairs	State, Military, and Veterans Affairs
Transportation and Energy	Transportation

ment Committee, the Senate has a Local Government Committee, and both committees review and vote on bills concerning towns, cities, special districts, and so on, in Colorado.[16]

Partisanship is a factor in committee work in the Colorado legislature, yet apparently not a big factor. Although Republicans have a majority of the members on each committee, all committee members from both political parties share in the work load and participate in discussions. Most important, amendments proposed by Democratic members of committees are frequently adopted in committee.

The committee chairperson is a member of the majority party, which means that in recent years all chairs in both the House and the Senate have been Republicans. The most important formal functions of the committee chairs are calling meetings, determining the order in which bills are reviewed, and scheduling votes on bills.

Prior to the adoption of the GAVEL ("Give A Vote to Every Legislator") Amendment to the state constitution in the 1988 general election, committee chairs in the Colorado legislature had the power to "pocket-veto" bills. This meant that a chairperson could single-handedly kill a bill sent to the committee by "putting it in his or her pocket," that is, by refusing to schedule a hearing or a committee discussion of the bill.[17] Democratic members of the legislature contended the pocket veto had mainly been used in recent years as a way for Republican committee chairs to kill Democratic bills summarily. Adoption of the GAVEL Amendment made it a constitutional requirement that every bill sent to a legislative committee be voted upon in committee.

Democratic legislators contended that requiring a hearing and vote on every bill that comes to a committee helped the Democrats have a greater voice in the legislative process.[18] Republican legislators argued the GAVEL Amendment had little effect on how committee business is handled. "GAVEL modestly reduced the power of committee chairmen, but not much," a Republican state senator explained. "All the chairpersons had to do was find other ways to kill insignificant and unimportant bills."[19] The most popular way was to have the committee majority vote down large numbers of bills at marathon bill-killing sessions. Two committees which did a great deal of bill killing were the appropriations committees in each house.

The GAVEL Amendment also eliminated another tool of majority party control in the legislature—the House of Representatives Rules Committee. Prior to the adoption of GAVEL, the House Rules Committee could refuse to send to the House floor the bills that had been reported out by committees of reference. The Republican leadership in the House controlled the House Rules Committee and often used it to prevent unwanted bills (usually Democratic bills) from reaching the House floor. Once the GAVEL Amendment removed the ability of the House Rules Committee to kill bills, the Republican majority in the House abolished the Rules Committee.

THE MAJORITY PARTY CAUCUS

An important part of the legislative process in both houses of the Colorado legislature is the party caucus, particularly the majority party caucus. Periodically all the legislators in the majority party in a particular house meet together to debate and discuss the major bills that have been reported out of committee and that are ready for debate and final adoption on the House or Senate floor. The meeting is run by the chair of the majority party caucus, who is considered an important member of the majority party leadership in the particular house.

The Republican party caucus has been the Senate majority party caucus since 1962 and the House majority party caucus since 1976. During the 1980s, the Republicans often used the majority party caucus in both houses to get enough Republican votes to be able to pass key bills the party supported on the House or Senate floor. The majority party caucus thus was also a "majority vote" caucus, where the Republican leadership lined up the Republican votes needed to guarantee a majority vote on the House or Senate floor for those bills the leadership supported. One bill that was always first approved by the majority party caucus was the budget bill.

As might be expected, the Democrats in the legislature were critical and resentful of the majority party caucus as it was used in the 1980s. They claimed that bills were "locked in" in the majority party caucus and that Democrats thus were not allowed to participate fully in the legislative process. Instead of major bills, such as the budget and tax bills, being adopted by the entire House of Representatives or the entire Senate, such bills were essentially adopted in the Republican party's majority party caucus. As a result, Democrats were left out of major decisions and could only "ratify" on the House or Senate floor those major bills that emerged from the Republican caucus.

Most galling to the Democrats, however, was the "conservatizing" effect of the majority party caucus on the legislation that was finally adopted by the Republican-dominated legislature. Conservative Republicans went into the majority party caucus, Democrats contended, and "held out" their support for the bill in question until their conservative demands were met. In the interest of "party harmony," the moderate Republicans "gave in" to the conservatives. Particularly bothersome to the Democrats, most of whom were not conservatives, was the fact that if the moderate Republicans and the Democrats voted together in regular legislative sessions, they could easily outvote the Republican conservatives.[20]

IMPACT OF THE GAVEL AMENDMENT

Prior to 1989 Democrats contended that under the Republicans the majority party caucuses in the House and the Senate had become "binding caucuses" in the sense that the majority party was requiring its legislators to vote the same way on the House or Senate floor as they voted in the party caucus. To prevent this practice, a section on caucuses was included in the GAVEL Amendment, which was petitioned on to the general election ballot and adopted by the voters in 1988. GAVEL thus put in the Colorado constitution that legislators cannot "commit themselves . . . through a vote in a party caucus . . . to vote in favor or against any bill. . . ."

Adoption of the GAVEL Amendment did not end Republican and Democratic bickering in the legislature over the role of the majority party caucus. In April of 1989 an employee of the Colorado Democratic party began videotaping House Republicans as they conducted their majority party caucus on the state budget bill. The Democrats charged the Republicans were violating the GAVEL Amendment by assigning six or seven Republican House members to gather "commitments" on major budget proposals during frequent caucus breaks. When the Democratic videotaping continued during a caucus recess, a Republican House member, Dick Mutzebaugh of Conifer (southwest suburban Denver), jumped in front of the Democratic video camera. When asked why he was disrupting Democratic efforts to videotape the caucus break, Mutzebaugh stated: "Just to harass him, that's all. Just like he's doing."[21]

Chris Paulson, the House Republican leader at the time, said getting vote commitments did not violate the GAVEL Amendment because the commitment gathering occurred while the caucus was in recess. "We're talking about colleagues asking each other how they're going to vote," Paulson said. "That goes on all the time. There could not possibly be a prohibition against that in the [state] constitution."[22]

In a similar incident in the Colorado Senate, the Republican caucus reviewed the state budget and insisted on favorable "straw votes" of eighteen Republican members, the number required for passage in the Senate, before ending discussion on each section of the budget. One Republican state senator, Sandy Hume of Boulder, considered the straw votes to be a violation of the GAVEL Amendment and refused to vote. Despite Senator Hume's refusal to participate, Senate Republican leaders were able to get eighteen Republican straw votes for almost every section of the state budget before it moved to the Senate floor for a final vote.[23]

After the 1989 session of the Colorado legislature adjourned, Common Cause, the citizens' organization that led the fight for the adoption of the GAVEL Amendment, filed a lawsuit against all thirty-nine Republican members of the Colorado House of Representatives. The suit charged that the gathering of vote commitments during breaks while the state budget was before the House majority party caucus violated GAVEL's prohibition against binding vote commitments. Common Cause decided not to sue the Senate Republicans because the group felt the straw votes in the Senate majority party caucus were not as clearly a violation of GAVEL as the vote commitments lined up by Republicans in the House.

House Republicans moved quickly to defend themselves against the Common Cause lawsuit. Speaker Bledsoe explained the Republican position: "I feel that we lived up to the letter of the law and went to great efforts to do so. We analyzed the amendment very carefully and spent a number of hours trying to devise a procedure."[24]

The dispute ended, at least temporarily, when a Denver district court judge ruled that under the centuries-old doctrine of legislative immunity, the Republican majority in the House of Representatives could not be sued. However, a higher court reversed the lower-court decision and said a trial on the issue could take place.

Before the new trial could get underway, Chuck Berry replaced Bev Bledsoe as the speaker of the House. Berry publicly acknowledged that there were "objections to the budget [and a number of other major bills] being 'locked up' in the Republican caucus."[25] Starting with the 1991 session, Berry had the state budget adopted on the floor of the House with the Democrats fully participating in the process.

Because of the GAVEL Amendment and Speaker Berry's cooperative attitude toward the minority Democrats, it was clear by the early 1990s that at least for the time being, binding votes in the majority party caucus were a thing of the past in the Colorado legislature. This did not mean the Republicans did not control both the House and the Senate in Colorado—they enjoyed majorities in both houses. What it did mean was that the minority Democrats and the voters they represented were no longer partially excluded from the legislative process in Colorado.

THE MINORITY PARTY CAUCUS

Similar to the majority party, minority party members in both the Colorado House and Senate caucus periodically to review major bills, particularly budget and finance bills. As might be expected, nowhere near as much attention is paid to amendments proposed by the minority party caucus as is paid to amendments proposed by the majority party caucus. Periodically, however, minority caucus amendments are adopted on the House or Senate floor, although this appears to happen more frequently in the Senate than in the House. The minority party caucus is not a complete waste of time, however. Democrats grumblingly point out that good ideas that emerge from the minority party caucus have a way of subsequently appearing in the Colorado House and Senate—in Republican-sponsored bills.

THE HOUSE AND SENATE IN SESSION

When the Colorado legislature is in session, the majority leader and the minority leader in each house occupy the two front-row center seats, making it easier for them to confer on such routine questions as the schedule for the day, the time of adjournment, and related matters. Unlike the U.S. Congress, in which Democrats sit on the left side of the aisle and Republicans on the right, there is no partisan pattern for assigning seats in the Colorado House and Senate. In the Senate, seats are chosen by the senators on the basis of seniority.

The regular time for the House and Senate to begin meeting is 10 A.M., but the speaker of the House or the president of the Senate can schedule different starting times. Both houses begin each meeting by calling the roll to make certain a quorum—a majority of all members of the particular house—is present. If a quorum is not present, no legislative business can be transacted until enough members are present to constitute a quorum.

Debate is limited in both houses of the legislature. Unless consent is given to speak longer, members of the House must limit their speeches to ten minutes. Senators' speeches are limited to one hour. As a result, legislators cannot filibuster—attempt to kill a bill by giving never-ending speeches against it.

Upon being introduced in either house of the Colorado legislature, a bill is given its *first reading*. Actually, only its title gets read—the term *reading* is a carry-over from English parliamentary procedure. Then the bill is referred by the House speaker or the Senate president to committee. If the bill is reported favorably, that is, approved by the committee, it is given a *second reading,* at which time it is debated and possibly amended on the House or Senate floor. The bill is then given a *third reading* and either passed or rejected by the particular house.

When taking up a bill for second reading, the Colorado House of Representatives resolves itself into the Committee of the Whole. This means the entire membership of the House becomes a committee instead of remaining in regular session. Organizing as a committee permits the House to operate in a more informal manner and to do away with some of the cumbersome requirements of being in regular session, particularly the requirement that a quorum needs to be present at all times.

When the Committee of the Whole has finished debating and amending a bill on second reading, it reports the results of its work to the full House membership. The House, when meeting in regular session, subsequently will pass or defeat the bill on third reading.[26]

A voting machine is used to record votes on bills and amendments in the Colorado House of Representatives. In the Senate, however, a voting machine is not used, and the roll is called to record each senator's yea or nay.

CONFERENCE COMMITTEES

When there are differences between the text of a bill passed by the House and that passed by the Senate, a conference committee is appointed. Each house sends three members, two from the majority party and one from the minority party, as its delegation to the conference committee. Because the Republicans have controlled both houses since the mid 1970s, conference committees in recent years have always consisted of four Republicans and two Democrats. The six legislators, called conferees, meet and work to resolve the differences in the two versions of the bill. If the conference committee succeeds in writing a compromise version of the bill, it is sent back to each house for a vote on final passage without amendment.

JOINT SESSIONS

Periodically both houses of the legislature meet for a joint session. These sessions are held in the House chamber with the Senate president presiding and House rules in effect. The most widely publicized joint session occurs at the beginning of each annual meeting of the legislature when the governor presents a "State of the State" address. Customarily the governor comments on the condition of the state's economy and presents the highlights of the proposed budget and related new initiatives. The legislature also meets in joint session to receive a report from the chief justice of the Colorado Supreme Court on conditions in and needs of the state court system.

CARRYING A BILL

At the time a bill is introduced in either house of the legislature, it is assigned a bill number. In the Senate bills start with number 1. In the House they start with number 1001. A bill has both a House and a Senate sponsor, and it is these two legislators who shoulder the major responsibility for steering the bill through their respective houses of the legislature. The sponsor of a bill in a particular house is said to be "carrying the bill" in that house.

Legislators are most anxious to carry important bills before their house. It represents their best opportunity to show how effective they are and to have their names and accomplishments reported in the news media. A legislator carrying a bill will line up favorable testimony before the committee of reference, lead the debate in favor of the bill on the House or Senate floor, and, if necessary, work to see that a compromise version of the bill is agreed upon in conference committee.

INTERIM COMMITTEES

Starting in 1989, annual sessions of the Colorado legislature have been limited to 120 days. Even before that limitation took effect, however, the legislature was having trouble getting all necessary work, particularly research and bill writing, completed during the regular session. In order to proceed with work while the legislature is not in session, special committees of legislators are appointed to work during the "interim," the eight-month period between the adjournment of one session and the beginning of the next. Two of these interim committees are described below.

Legislative Council

An important interim committee is the Legislative Council. It is composed of six members of the House appointed by the speaker and six members of the Senate appointed by the president, the appointments subject to the approval of the respective houses. The speaker of the House and the president of the Senate serve as *ex officio* (automatic) members of the Legislative Council.

During the interim the Legislative Council collects data, reviews major issues of public policy in Colorado, studies possible amendments to the state constitution, and holds hearings on proposed bills to be considered by the legislature during the next regular session. The Legislative Council organizes itself into committees so that detailed attention can be given to the various proposals which it considers.

The information-gathering and data-collecting functions of the Legislative Council require that a full-time research staff work year round for the legislature. The Legislative Council staff, although essentially hired by the majority party, is considered nonpartisan and serves all the members of the Legislative Council, regardless of party affiliation. During regular sessions of the House and Senate, the Legislative Council staff researches proposed bills and constitutional amendments for all the members of the legislature.

Joint Budget Committee

Perhaps the most important of all the interim committees is the Joint Budget Committee, a group of six legislators who do the major work in preparing the annual state budget.

Few state legislatures use their "power of the purse" as much as the Colorado legislature does. In most states the governor and the executive branch prepare the annual state budget and make major spending recommendations. The legislature merely reviews the governor's budget and, for the most part, follows the executive department's lead on questions of state spending.

In Colorado, however, the budget process is centered in the legislative branch. It is the legislature's Joint Budget Committee and its staff, not the governor's budget director, that make the major recommendations as to how much money will be spent and for what purposes. According to a respected student of state legislatures, Colorado is third on the list of states where the legislature exerts "enormous control through the budget." Only the Texas and South Carolina legislatures are viewed as having stronger budgetary powers than the Colorado legislature.[27]

Organization. The Joint Budget Committee of the Colorado legislature is noted for its small size and its two-to-one partisan character. There are three members from the House of Representatives (appointed by the speaker) and three members from the Senate (elected in party caucuses). The delegation from each house consists of the chair of the Appropriations Committee (always a member of the majority party), one majority party member, and one minority party member. As a result, when one political party controls both houses of the legislature, four members of the Joint Budget Committee are from the majority party and two members are from the minority party.[28] Since the Republicans have been the majority in both houses of the Colorado legislature in recent years, they have controlled the Joint Budget Committee by a margin of four votes to two votes.

The chair of the Joint Budget Committee alternates back and forth between a House member and a Senate member. When a Senate member is chair, a House member serves as vice-chair, and vice versa.

The Joint Budget Committee, commonly referred to as the JBC, works year round and has a full-time staff of about twelve persons. Committee members work three days a month from June to October, but then work almost every day during November and December and during the January to May session of the legislature. The committee occupies a suite of offices in the Legislative Services Building (located immediately south of the state capitol building) and has its own private hearing room.

On the wall behind the chairs of the JBC, in full view of those requesting funds, is a photograph of a turn-of-the-century fire department, fire axes at the ready. The symbolism, that this is the room where budget requests get "chopped," is not overlooked. One day JBC members were surprised to discover that someone had taken red ink and painted "blood" dripping from the firemen's fire axes. After an appropriate amount of time for this act of humorous vandalism to be properly appreciated, the red ink was removed. The axes remained, however, both in the photograph and in the Joint Budget Committee.

The JBC, created in 1959 when Democrats controlled both the legislature and the governorship, is powerful for several reasons. Over the years it has been led by strong personalities, such as former Senator Joe Shoemaker, who worked hard to expand the committee's influence.[29] It also is the only committee of the Colorado legislature that has a staff of its own.

Role in the Budget Process. The budget cycle in Colorado begins in the executive branch, yet it does not stay there long. Budget proposals from state departments and agencies are reviewed by the Office of State Planning and Budgeting (OSPB) and then sent to the governor, who puts top limits on the budget amounts to be requested by the various departments. Department budget requests then are submitted to the Joint Budget Committee.

There is much discussion (and a number of jokes) about exactly how much attention the Joint Budget Committee pays to the budget requests that come from the governor and executive departments. Most observers agree that the JBC gives the governor's budget more than just a casual glance, yet plainly the JBC always reserves the right to prepare its own budget rather than merely "review" the governor's recommendations.

Although no one seems certain whether the story is true or not, it is often said that one time the chair of the Joint Budget Committee actually picked up the book of gubernatorial budget requests and publicly threw it in the wastebasket.[30] One expert on state politics wrote: "The executive budget prepared by the governor in Colorado is said to have as much status as a child's letter to Santa Claus."[31]

Each year during the months of November and December, the JBC and its staff carefully review departmental budget requests, and staff members prepare a recommended series of issues to be discussed by the JBC. Spokespersons for the departments of state government, often department heads and top budget officers, attend these meetings and defend their requests before the JBC. Once the legislative session begins in January, the Joint Budget Committee begins writing the long appropriations bill, customarily referred to as the long bill. This giant piece of legislation contains the entire budget for the state of Colorado for the following fiscal year.

The Colorado constitution prohibits deficit spending and thereby requires a balanced annual state budget. Hence, before the JBC can write the long bill of expenditures, it must know how much money the state is going to collect in taxes and fees during the fiscal year. Revenue estimates are presented to the committee by both the Office of State Planning and Budgeting and the Legislative Council staff. The JBC begins its work by adopting the revenue estimates for the coming fiscal year, which become an integral part of the final budget the JBC recommends to the legislature.

Over the years, members of the JBC have noticed that the executive branch's revenue estimates are almost always higher than those presented by the Legislative Council staff. A recent chair of the JBC theorized that the governor influences staff members to increase the revenue estimates so that the governor can include more programs and projects in the administration budget request. "The governor knows the JBC will lower the revenue estimates and eliminate some programs and projects," the JBC chair pointed out, "but it is a good way for the governor to call attention to things he thinks the state needs and ought to be spending money on."[32]

Although the majority party in the legislature dominates the membership of the Joint Budget Committee, the committee usually does not go about its fiscal chores in a partisan manner. Members of the committee, Democrats and Republicans alike, are given a portion of the state budget in which to specialize. Although the Republicans have controlled both houses of the legislature since the mid 1970s, Democratic members of the JBC are allowed to lead the meeting when their assigned portion of the budget is undergoing public hearings or is up for review. Because of all the extra work, and because they spend so much time together, members of the JBC develop an esprit de corps and loyalty to the committee that usually is more significant than political party membership.[33]

In early February the Joint Budget Committee begins the most important part of its work, "figure setting." Line item by line item, the committee goes through the budget and "sets" the actual amounts of money that will be spent during the next fiscal year. These meetings are open to the public. Early in the morning, from 7:30 to 9:00 A.M., any citizen can come in and address the JBC concerning budget matters. Persons directly affected by the budget, such as department heads and lobbyists for key interest groups (or their personal representatives), often are sitting in the audience and watching closely as pet programs are voted up or down.

The long bill then moves to the majority party caucus and the minority party caucus in both the House and the Senate. The budget is discussed and debated at length in the various caucuses. Amendments proposed in the majority and minority party caucuses may or may not be adopted on the House or Senate floor. Once the party caucuses are finished with it, the long bill moves simultaneously to the House and Senate Appropriations committees. Approval by these two committees is typically a mere formality since the chairs of both Appropriations committees are both on the Joint Budget Committee.

If different versions of the long bill are adopted in the House and Senate, as almost always happens, the JBC serves as the conference committee for ironing out the differences between the two houses. During this process the majority party caucuses meet and approve the settling of differences. Similar to any bill emerging from a House-Senate conference, the long bill cannot be amended when it returns to each house for final passage. Notice that the Joint Budget Committee, sitting as the conference committee, gets to "dot the final i" and "cross the final t" in the writing of the Colorado state budget.

Evaluation. Criticism, as well as praise, surrounds the Joint Budget Committee and its activities. The JBC is criticized for arbitrarily "axing" the funding requests of governors and executive branch agencies and for its monopoly over the state budget. "They're neanderthals over there," said one executive branch official. "They're unrepresentative, unresponsive and irresponsible . . . I just don't know how it happens, yet the most conservative members of both political parties usually get on the JBC."

Another criticism is that the JBC staff is too powerful. The elected legislators on the committee, it is argued, become dependent on the information, homework, and suggestions offered by the unelected staff. And, say some executive branch officials, these staff members are often "clueless" about what is important. In the final analysis, according to this view, it is the JBC employees, and not the legislature, who become the state's most powerful budgeteers.

The JBC also has been faulted for enlarging its budget staff (more than twenty times larger in 1992 than it was in 1962) while the governor's staff is treated much less generously.

It also is charged that Republicans on the JBC use their budgetary powers to harrass Democratic governors. "More often than not," writes *Denver Post* reporter Fred Brown, "the legislature . . . [is] looking for picky little ways to get under the Governor's skin, nagging him for not cutting spending enough, trying to ride herd on every line of the budget—in short, acting as if everyone is an employee of the legislative branch."[34]

Finally, many governors and their aides believe that the JBC's inflexibility undermines good management practices in state government. "Because of the JBC's practices, the governor does not have the ability to transfer monies from one program to another, and not even within an agency, and this hinders good management decisions," says former gubernatorial Chief of Staff Stewart Bliss.[35]

Former Governor Dick Lamm attributes the great strength of the JBC to the campaign state Senator Joe Shoemaker waged to make the JBC a rival to the governor's office. "You have to know Shoemaker," says Lamm. "He is very bright, very able and does everything in a zealous . . . way." Lamm added, "It is hard to recapture power when it has flowed away to a power center like the JBC."[36]

Some Democratic critics of the JBC acknowledge, however, that it is the JBC "system," more than the Republican majority on the JBC, that stymies their efforts to give Colorado a more adventurous and dynamic government. "The most limiting part of the system is the constitutional prohibition on deficit spending," a Democratic state senator explained. "It really is tough to find money for a new program when you have to take it from an existing program. Instead of setting goals and solving state problems, the JBC just starts with last year's budget and makes minor adjustments."[37]

For every critic, there is a defender of the Joint Budget Committee and the disciplined way in which it reviews the state budget. A memorandum from the Legislative Council staff gave succinct and positive defense of the JBC as it presently exists: "Colorado's legislative budget review procedure, directed by the Joint Budget Committee, provides the kind of strong adversarial confrontation with the executive branch that the General Assembly believes is necessary to foster efficiencies and uphold the separation of powers."[38]

As for the frequent efforts to enlarge the Joint Budget Committee, former JBC chair Joe Shoemaker wrote a strong defense of the committee's small size: "Over the years, six proved to be a good number for the JBC's elective membership. . . . It left us with a lean, streamlined force that didn't discuss itself to death with all the verbiage a larger group would have produced."[39]

State Senator Mike Bird, who served as chairman of the JBC during the 1989, 1991, and 1993 sessions of the Colorado legislature, lauded the JBC system for the comprehensive review it gives of the entire state government: "The Joint Budget committee is at the epicenter of information flow in the state legislature. It is the only group that sees the overall financial picture of Colorado state government in a nonfragmented way." Bird emphasized that "the careful questioning of state programs and state government bureaucrats by the legislators on the JBC really does produce more efficient and cost-effective state government."[40]

One notable reality of the JBC process is that politically shrewd executive branch division heads realize their programs and funding are dependent on the JBC far more than on the governor's office. They act accordingly, forging alliances with appropriate legislators and JBC staff. Understandably, governors and their central review staffs are left frustrated by this process.

The general effectiveness of the JBC in providing cost-effectiveness and accountability for the taxpayer's money has earned the JBC significant credibility. The survival and continuation of the Joint Budget Committee is not in doubt. Its success will depend on both the personal character of its ranking members and its overall performance. For the foreseeable future, the JBC will be a major political and philosophical force to be reckoned with in Colorado.

LEGISLATIVE EFFECTIVENESS

How effective is the state legislature at providing policy leadership for the state of Colorado? Most observers agree the legislature does a good job of keeping taxes low and checking the expansion of state programs and services. Those who criticize state lawmakers are most likely to point out that the legislature has failed to raise the money and provide the services that Colorado needs to solve its problems effectively.

By the early 1990s state finances in Colorado appeared to be in particularly poor shape. The gap between the cost of programs authorized by the legislature and the money being collected through taxes and service charges became large, at one point totaling more than $100 million. The legislature struggled to close this budget shortfall, reluctant either to raise taxes significantly or to make major cuts in promised state services.

Bob Kirscht, a lobbyist and former state legislator from Pueblo, blamed the legislature for Colorado's fiscal woes in the early 1990s. He noted that in the mid 1970s Colorado had a large budget surplus and a progressive state income tax that produced income for the state in good economic times and bad. In the late 1970s, however, the legislature became embarrassed over running such a large surplus and began looking for ways to win votes by returning some of the money to state voters in the form of tax cuts. Kirscht explained: "What followed in 1978, 1979, 1980 and 1981 was a deluge of tax-cutting legislation that swept billions of dollars from collections and obliterated the progressive tax system that had been devised more than a decade earlier to produce the reserves Colorado had accumulated by the late '70s."[41] In addition, Kirscht noted, the legislature began exempting more and more goods from the state sales tax and passed a number of property tax rebates. The final result was a state government with greatly reduced fiscal resources that was repeatedly cutting or delaying necessary state programs or resorting to nuisance taxes to close budget shortfalls temporarily.

One result of the mammoth fiscal problems facing Colorado in the early 1990s was declining public approval of the state legislature. *Denver Post* political editor Fred Brown summed up the situation this way: "The really sad thing is that all this pandering after public approval hasn't helped the legislature at all. Even though Governor Roy Romer talks constantly about tax increases, his popularity still ranks far ahead of the legislature's in any public opinion poll."[42]

Defamation of Vegetables Bill

Although it was having great difficulty wrestling with the state's fiscal problems in the early 1990s, the Colorado legislature was more than equal to the task of introducing and passing bills of such an unusual character that they received comment from the national press. Steve Acquafresca, a member of the state House of Representatives from the western slope, became concerned over the way medical warnings about food products could wreak economic havoc on farmers. He was reacting to the Alar scare, where reports warning that apples treated with Alar might be dangerous to human health had reduced apple sales and proven costly to apple growers.

Acquafresca introduced a bill, entitled the Disparagement of Perishable Agricultural Food Products Act, that allowed farmers to sue for triple damages wherever there was "dissemination to the public . . . of false information . . . on the safety of any perishable agricultural food product." The bill passed both houses of the legislature and immediately became the butt of jokes in the national press. The *Washington Post* speculated that there would now be such crimes as "lettuce libel" and "salmon slander."[43] Colorado was saved from any further embarassment when Governor Roy Romer vetoed the defamation of vegetables bill and the legislature failed to override the veto.

LOBBYISTS AS UNELECTED LEGISLATORS

Colorado has more than 250 registered lobbyists,[44] many of whom perform several of the same functions as state legislators. They represent citizens and interest groups. They research and prepare legislative bills and amendments to bills. They fight to enlarge or to cut various parts of the state budget. They care a great deal about who wins and who loses elections.

One respected Colorado lobbyist is Roger Alan Walton, who studied political science at the University of Colorado at Boulder and worked on the gubernatorial campaign of John Love in 1962. When Love won, Walton joined his staff in the governor's office. There he learned firsthand about how things get done inside state government and inside the legislature. A few years later he left to serve on the government relations staff of an airline. Later still he became a full-time lobbyist, contracting with a number of banks, airlines, and other business interests to handle their legislative business at the statehouse.

Walton, who lives in the Denver suburb of Lakewood, works out of an office in his home and a table that is perpetually reserved for him at the Profile Restaurant, which is conveniently located just one block north of the capitol building. ''The Walton table'' is part of his mystique as a regular and visible working lobbyist. ''The key to effective lobbying around here is doing your homework,'' Walton said. ''Also important is the integrity of your word and your reputation. You have to be able to provide accurate and useful information. And you have to win the trust of the legislators, and especially the leaders. That's essential.''[45]

There are two to three times as many lobbyists at the state capitol as there are members of the two houses of the General Assembly. Is lobbying necessary and valuable? ''Definitely,'' writes Walton. ''Members of the legislature cannot possibly have the depth of information they need to make sound decisions on all pending legislation. Lobbyists can readily provide information on certain issues and also represent the views of specific segments of the electorate.''[46]

Lobbyists seek to influence the legislature with campaign contributions at election time. Many people are understandably suspicious of these contributions, but campaign contributions are a form of free speech and thus are a protected right of every citizen under the U.S. Bill of Rights.

Lobbyists must register with the Colorado secretary of state, but there are relatively few state restrictions on lobbyists. During the 1992 session of the state legislature, Senate President Ted Strickland introduced legislation requiring lobbyists to report the name of any legislator on whom they spent more than $5. In addition, the bill prohibited lobbyists from making campaign contributions to state legislators while the legislature is in session, and it barred from the legislature any lobbyist who tried to influence a state lawmaker through deceit, threats of violence or economic reprisal, or providing false information. Another bill, introduced by Representative Steve Arveschoug of Pueblo, required lobbyists to disclose their exact sources of income and mandated a cooling-off period of two years before a former legislator could become a lobbyist.[47] This flurry of bills, none of which were passed, indicated there was growing concern in Colorado about the power and influence of lobbyists.

CONCLUSION

Three major conclusions can be drawn about the Colorado legislature: It is powerful relative to the governor, and in several ways its power is growing. Power is centralized in the hands of the majority party leadership. The legislature is partisan, which for nearly a generation has meant control by the Republicans.

The most conspicuous example of the recent centralization of power in the legislature is the increasing influence of the Joint Budget Committee, both over the state budget and within the legislature. Much of state politics is about who controls the budget, and in Colorado the response is the legislature in general and the JBC in particular.

The Governor

Colorado governors play a central role in the politics and governing of the state. In recent years, however, governors and their advisers continually complain about the power struggles between their office and the state legislature. Here is how three recent governors put it:

Governor Stephen McNichols (Democrat, 1957–63):

> I think one of the most tragic things that's happened to this state is the loss and the abdication of the governor's responsibility in the state. Today the Joint Budget Committee [of the legislature] runs the whole show. . . . They can completely frustrate a governor in the administration of the government. Governors are expendable.

Governor John A. Love (Republican, 1963–73):

> From the beginning Colorado has been . . . cursed with a weak-governor kind of system. . . . It has been weakened further in recent years, and I share part of the blame in that I was not able to overcome the Joint Budget Committee. . . . That needs to be changed.

Governor Richard D. Lamm (Democrat, 1975–87):

> Then along came Watergate, and almost every legislator seems to feel that it is his or her sworn duty to watch the governor and to take power back. . . . Every institution needs a leader. I think a state needs a governor, and it needs a strong governor.[1]

As these views suggest, there is a built-in antagonism between governors and the legislature. This tension is partly written into the state constitution and partly exacerbated by the reality that both legislators and governors see themselves as the chief policymakers for Colorado. And although they often are in conflict, these two branches of government actually cooperate far more than is generally appreciated.

The office of governor in American states has been an evolutionary one, and this has also been the case in Colorado. In recent years the Colorado governor has grown in stature and importance, in part because the term has been lengthened from two to four years, in part because of the growth in the state's population and problems, and in part because the governorship has been occupied by able people. The job of any governor in the late twentieth century is plainly one of the most exacting challenges in American politics. Both the Reagan and Bush administrations succeeded in decentralizing to states many of the responsibilities previously considered national policy priorities.

Governors in Colorado, as in all the states, are expected to be more than effective managers. They also are expected to be leaders, asking the right questions, considering long-term implications and side effects of their policies, and involving large numbers of expert advisers to help point the state in the right direction.

Coloradans want their governors to be excellent judges of people and, in working with legislative and departmental leaders, to be able to make tough decisions and assume responsibility—especially in crisis situations. A governor is expected, among other things, to be the state's chief policymaker, the chief initiator of the state budget recommendations, a savvy political leader, the chief recruiter of departmental administrators, and a builder of confidence in state programs.

Governors must also enforce the laws of the state, even, as is occasionally the case, when they disagree with the law. Thus, in 1993, Governor Romer had to enforce Amendment 1 and Amendment 2, passed by the voters in the tumultuous election of 1992, even though he had been an outspoken opponent of both measures. Colorado governors, like their counterparts in other states, also champion the state's interests against the encroachments of the federal government. Governors are expected to act as the state's chief booster to attract tourism and business investment. Effective governors now also have to formulate and implement their own "foreign policy," making trips to foreign nations to encourage foreign investment as well as to promote the state's products abroad. Governors are expected to lead by suggesting initiatives in education, economic development, highway construction, environmental protection, and much more. An effective governor is also expected to perform countless symbolic and ceremonial functions and thereby win the respect of the people.

Governors have many formal powers, yet often their most important re-source is their informal or personal power to persuade, celebrate, and pro-mote. Thus a governor's formal power means little if he or she is not a per-suasive communicator with good judgment and the capacity to think clearly. Colorado governors in the recent past have generally been male, lawyers, and in their forties or fifties. Their rate of reelection has been very high, but their chances for accomplishing what they set out to do are nearly always overestimated by everyone, including themselves.

TERM, TERM LIMITS, SALARY, HOUSING

Until 1958 Colorado governors served a two-year term of office. Since 1958 the gubernatorial term has been four years, as it is in nearly all states. Until 1990 there was no limit on the number of times the Colorado governor could be reelected. A constitutional amendment adopted by the voters in 1990 now limits the Colorado governor to eight years (two terms) in office.

Putting an eight-year limit on serving as governor may not change things much. Prior to the 1920s, no Colorado governor had ever served more than four years in office. Only two Colorado governors, John A. Love in the 1960s and 1970s and Richard D. Lamm in the 1970s and 1980s, served more than six years in office. Love occupied the governor's chair for ten years, and Lamm, the longest-serving governor in Colorado history, held office for three full four-year terms for a total of twelve years.

Before gubernatorial term limits were adopted in Colorado, the governor was never a "lame duck," an incumbent office holder who was prohibited from running for another term. The eight-year term limit changes that. The Colorado governor will automatically be a lame duck as soon as his or her second four-year term begins.

The governor's salary has increased steadily over the years, yet it has al-ways been modest compared to what successful persons in other fields are paid. Colorado's first governor in 1877 earned $3,000 a year. By 1930 the gubernatorial salary had increased to only $5,000 a year. The 1960 yearly salary was $20,000, and in the early 1990s it was $76,000 a year.

In addition to salary, the Colorado governor receives the customary fringe benefits associated with being the chief executive of one of the fifty states. Principal among these is the privilege of living in the elegant Gover-nor's Mansion, formerly the home of a millionaire and located in Denver's Capitol Hill neighborhood, six blocks south of the capitol building. This lav-ish home was built by an important early resident of Denver, Walter Cheesman, and was later occupied by Claude Boettcher, owner of a prosperous Denver stock brokerage and investment firm, and a "mover and shaker" in Colorado politics.

Colorado has had a governor's mansion only since 1960. Prior to this time, governors who were not from the Denver area were expected to live in hotels or apartments near the capitol during their term in office. Perhaps that helps to explain why no Colorado governor before the 1960s ever served more than six years in office. William "Billy" Adams, who was governor from 1927 to 1933, lived and took his meals at the Brown Palace, the most prominent hotel in Denver.

Because it was one of the later states to be settled and granted statehood, Colorado did not have a native-born governor until Teller Ammons, a Democrat, was elected in 1936. All of the state's governors have been white males, although women have been elected lieutenant governor, attorney general, secretary of state, and state treasurer, and an African-American served as lieutenant governor in the mid 1970s. Before being elected to the state's highest office, Colorado's governors have worked in a wide variety of occupations reflecting the state's history—miners, smeltermen, farmers, ranchers, and newspapermen. Recent governors, however, have been attorneys or business executives.

Does Colorado have a strong or weak governorship? This question is frequently asked and extensively debated. A simple answer is that the Colorado governorship is strong in theory yet weak in practice. Governors have the constitutional and legal powers they need to be strong chief executives, but traditional practices and political party competition have reduced their influence over the day-to-day operations of state government.[2]

STRENGTHS OF THE GOVERNORSHIP

One of the important strengths of the Colorado governor is the power to appoint judges to state courts and justices to the state Supreme Court. Since 1967, the Colorado constitution has required the governor to select his choices for the judiciary from three persons who have been nominated by judicial selection panels. Yet governors who are politically savvy can have much to say about who serves on these judicial panels. As one former governor's aide said: "Governors in effect control the judiciary through their appointment power and their influences over those panels."

The Colorado governor has more control over the judicial selection process than the governors of most other states. In about half the states, judges are still elected by the public. In a handful of states, such as New York and Massachusetts, the governors appoint judges, yet the state Senate has the right to confirm or reject such nominees. The state legislature in Colorado has no role in confirming gubernatorial appointees to the bench in Colorado. Because Democrats occupied the Colorado governorship from 1975 through the mid-1990s, the Colorado judiciary currently is filled with Democrats.

The Colorado governor also has the power to appoint a large number of volunteer boards and commissions which help shape policy and help oversee the operation of various branches of state government. For instance, the governor appoints the state Board of Agriculture, which supervises the operation of three public colleges—Colorado State University in Fort Collins, Fort Lewis College in Durango, and the University of Southern Colorado in Pueblo. The governor's appointments to the Board of Agriculture (similar to most state boards and commissions) must be confirmed by the state Senate, yet in most cases the governor's nominees are carefully considered and then approved by the Senate.

Another important power of the Colorado governor is the veto power. When a governor disapproves of a bill passed by the legislature, he or she can veto the bill, and the legislature will need to achieve a two-thirds vote in both houses in order to override the veto. In most instances governors will have enough members of their own party in at least one house of the state legislature to prevent a legislative override of their vetoes.

The Colorado governor also possesses the "item veto" on appropriation bills. Thus a governor can strike individual appropriation items out of spending bills without killing the entire bill. Governors can use the item veto to eliminate state programs and projects to which they are opposed. Similar to any vetoed bill, however, an appropriation item that has been vetoed by the governor can be reinstated by a two-thirds vote in both houses of the state legislature.

Another formal power of the governor, at least on paper, is to initiate the budget process in Colorado. The governor appoints an executive budget director whose main duty is to gather and critique state budget requests for the following fiscal year. The governor can put a cap, or upper limit, on the amount of money that any particular department of state government can request from the legislature. (Of course, most governors would prefer to set the minimum figure for spending rather than the cap.) When the Joint Budget Committee of the state legislature begins its work, it starts with the executive budget prepared by the governor and the governor's budget staff, although the JBC rarely feels constrained by the governor's budget plans.[3]

Colorado governors have some informal powers that strengthen their hand in state politics. They can generate almost unlimited publicity about their proposals and policy ideas, especially since the state capitol is in Denver, the major media and population center of the state. Governors receive many invitations to give speeches around the state, each of which provides an opportunity for the governor to describe and "talk up" his or her plans and programs.

This list of gubernatorial powers, many of them constitutional powers, suggests that the governor of Colorado is a strong chief executive. A 1963 study of gubernatorial power throughout the United States ranked Colorado just above the middle of the fifty states. On an elaborate rating system used by the study, Colorado's governor scored a fourteen on the gubernatorial power scale, with the median score of all the state governors being thirteen.[4]

A more recent study, conducted for the National Governors' Association, compared the institutional powers of the fifty state governors over the twenty-five-year period from 1965 to 1990. The study ranked the governors according to appointive powers, veto power, budget-making powers, political party opposition in the state legislature, and the legislature's budget-changing authority. This study classified the power of the Colorado governor as "moderate." Other states in the "moderate" category included California, Georgia, Washington, and Wyoming. At least half of the states, according to this study, had governors with more power than Colorado's. The study also compared the powers of the Colorado governor in 1965 to the powers of the Colorado governor in 1990 and found there had been little change in the power score over the twenty-five years.[5]

Despite such studies, one hears repeatedly that the Colorado governorship is weak, that executive power has been eroded by the state legislature, and that the situation has grown particularly acute in the past generation. The constitutional and legal powers that make the Colorado governor appear moderate to strong in state-by-state comparisons apparently do not give governors the power they, and their advisers, wish they had to control state government effectively.

WEAKNESSES OF THE GOVERNORSHIP

The greatest constitutional weakness of the Colorado governor is limited appointment powers. The administrative branch of state government is organized into twenty major departments and is restricted by the state constitution to only that number. A governor can appoint fifteen of these department

Table 8. Departments of Colorado State Government

1. Education **	11. Administration
2. Higher Education **	12. Revenue
3. Social Services	13. Military Affairs
4. Highways	14. Regulatory Agencies
5. Institutions	15. Agriculture
6. Health	16. Law *
7. Natural Resources	17. Personnel
8. Corrections	18. State *
9. Labor and Employment	19. Planning and Budgeting
10. Local Affairs	20. Treasury *

heads, known as executive directors, *and these are the only administrative appointments he or she can make in state government.*

Listed above are the twenty departments of Colorado state government, arranged according to annual expenditures in the late 1980s, the department with the highest expenditures being at the top of the list. Departments with one asterisk (*) have an executive director elected by the voters—the attorney general for the Department of Law, the state treasurer for the Department of Treasury, and the secretary of state for the Department of State. Departments with two asterisks (**) have an executive director apppointed by a board (Education) and a commission (Higher Education)—independent of the governor's influence.[6]

Below the level of executive director or department head, the governor has no appointive powers at all. There are approximately 120 agencies within the twenty major departments, and each one is presided over by an agency head, or division director, who is a civil service employee in the state bureaucracy. All the agency heads are thus appointed to office on the basis of civil service tests and job performance evaluations. Their selection as agency head is not under the direct control of the governor. As one state legislator said of this heavy bias toward the civil service system, "Rather than get rid of the spoils system, it created another kind of spoils."[7]

Even in those major departments where the department head is appointed by the governor, there will be agencies over which the governor's department head has no effective control. These agencies, called Type 1 agencies, report to an appointed board or commission. Although the current governor, and previous governors, may have had a hand in appointing the board or commission, the governor will not have direct control over the Type 1 agencies. Of the 120 agencies in the Colorado bureaucracy, about 70 are Type 1 and report to a board or commission. The remaining 50 agencies are Type 2 agencies, where the civil servant in charge of the agency reports to a department head. The particular department head may or may not be one of the fifteen out of the total twenty department heads appointed by the governor.

Governors do, of course, appoint their immediate executive staff, including a chief of staff, press assistant, policy research director, legislative lobbyist, and appointment secretary. In addition, the governor appoints the state planners and financial analysts who work at the Office of State Planning and Budgeting.

Eugene Petrone, a former executive director of the Office of State Planning and Budgeting, says the limited number of direct gubernatorial appointments erodes executive authority in Colorado: "The way things are now in Colorado, classified civil service employees are driving policy rather than appointees of the governor. The result is a very rigidified system under which the governor cannot have the personnel he wants running the various agencies."

Because the governor has no control over them, Petrone pointed out, the agency heads learn to go directly to the legislature for what they want and bypass the governor. "Often, the only real control there is of the civil servants who run the individual agencies is the legislature's control of their appropriations [the amount of money they will have to spend each year]."[8]

This view of how the lack of appointive powers weakens the governor was confirmed by Larry Kallenberger, executive director of the Colorado Department of Local Affairs. People assume the Colorado governor has powers that he or she really does not have, Kallenberger said. "Putting so many agency heads under the merit system [civil service] creates a bureaucracy that is responsible to the legislature, not the governor." Kallenberger concluded: "Even the governor's own department heads get savvy and start playing ball with the legislature and pay less attention to the governor."

Kallenberger argues that having such a powerful civil service bureaucracy greatly weakens control of state government by the voters. Too much power is given to people who are not elected, he said, or who are not directly responsible to people who are elected. "A person can be governor for many years and never get the reins of bureaucratic control firmly in hand."[9]

There have been periodic attempts in Colorado to have the 120 agency heads (division directors) appointed by the governor rather than remain under civil service. Proposals for this kind of personnel reform were on the general election ballot in 1976 and 1986, but a well-organized opposition, led by the Colorado state employees' labor unions, succeeded in defeating both proposals at the polls.

Several people who worked for recent governors said that good management practices as well as an effective governorship required greater control over personnel. Gene Petrone, who worked as budget director for Governor John Love as well as Governor Roy Romer, said it made sense to allow the governor the authority to appoint every agency head. That would give the governor some real clout.[10]

Governor Romer's chief of staff, Stewart Bliss, generally agreeing, said governors need the flexibility to move people around at the agency-head level. "We really ought to be able to move the best talent to where it is needed. I wouldn't want a return to the spoils system, yet there is no real system that allows for effective management of the executive branch bureaucracy."[11]

Former Governor Richard Lamm also noted this was a chief weakness of the governorship. He said he would settle for just being able to replace a handful or so of agency heads. "I'd wait until they proved to be deliberately undermining a program and then I'd fire them or transfer them out. Heck, you'd only need to do that in a limited number of cases to gain better influence over the sprawling bureaucracy."[12]

Another weakness of the governor's office in Colorado is its lack of control over state education programs, a particularly notable weakness because two-thirds of the state's annual budget is devoted to education (kindergarten through twelfth grade plus state colleges and universities). Most of the control over public education rests with two boards that are elected by the voters—the state Board of Education and the regents of the University of Colorado. Governors regularly lament that they have minimal influence over how education funds are spent.

The Colorado governor also has minimal control over the state highway program. Governors appoint the state Highway Commission, but they must appoint commission members from specified regions of the state. The state constitution requires that neither the governor nor the state legislature can make major changes in the amounts of money the Highway Commission specifies for various highway projects in Colorado.

PLANNING AND BUDGET POWERS

The extensive control of the Colorado state budget by the legislature is described in chapter 8. The Joint Budget Committee (JBC) and its staff have gradually taken over what is elsewhere considered an executive responsibility—that of budgeting for the state. As a result, a small group of people, the six members who constitute the legislature's JBC, are often, in effect, managing the administrative branch of government, a job many people believe should be given to the governor and his or her direct political appointees.

As the legislature has increased the staff of the JBC over the years, it has simultaneously cut the number of planners and budget officials working in the governor's Office of State Planning and Budgeting (OSPB). Between 1974 and 1992, the JBC staff was raised from 10 to 14.5 employees, a gain of 4.5 employees. At the same time, however, the OSPB staff was reduced from 47.8 to 20.5 employees, a loss of 27.3 employees. As previously noted, the legislature is plainly concentrating more planning and budgeting power in its own hands, particularly at the staff level.

The much-mentioned item-veto power rarely provides much real power to Colorado governors. If the legislature was a notoriously big spender, often adding more funds to programs than the governors wished to have spent, then the governors would obviously find the item veto an especially helpful weapon in their arsenal. But, as earlier discussions explained, the Colorado legislature is known more for its cutting than its spending habits. "I never found a way to imaginatively use the item-veto authority," former Governor Lamm said. "If you have a tight-fisted, penny-pinching legislature, as we have, then the item veto power isn't really much of a power. In my case, when we differed, I usually wanted to spend or invest a bit more, not a bit less."[13]

POLITICAL PARTY COMPETITION

Under normal circumstances, the two-party system in Colorado should periodically strengthen the position of the governor vis-à-vis the state legislature. From time to time, the same political party that elected the governor should have comfortable working majorities in both houses of the state legislature. The governor could then use party loyalty and a spirit of party cooperation to get the legislative majority to support his or her programs for the state.

Since 1975 the governor always has been a Democrat. Since 1977 both houses of the legislature have been under the solid control of the Republicans. From 1977 through the mid 1990s, therefore, the two-party system has exacerbated gubernatorial-legislative relations in Colorado rather than improved them. In recent years Democrats have charged that the Republican majority in the legislature opposes the governor's programs, not because they are bad programs, but because the Republicans do not want to enhance the political image and influence of a Democratic chief executive.

One effect of Colorado's two-party deadlock, where Democrats win the governorship but the Republicans keep control of both houses of the legislature, is that the governor usually is cautious about sending bold proposals to the legislature. Wade Buchanan, a top aide to Governor Roy Romer, said that when there are sharp partisan differences between the governor and the legislature, the governor has to work at being less confrontational with the legislature. "He tries to make less use of the veto," Buchanan explained. The governor has to keep a clear mental picture of what he can and cannot do. After a while, the governor learns to be general rather than specific about issues and legislative proposals. Buchanan added: "This keeps him or her from looking like a loser when specific issues or legislative bills fail in the legislature."

In fact, Buchanan concluded, sometimes the governor will not endorse legislation he supports for fear the endorsement will inspire the legislature to kill the legislation for partisan reasons. "There is no question that the strong partisanship in Colorado is beginning to effect the relationship between the executive and the legislative branch."[14]

A second Romer aide and department head, Larry Kallenberger, contends that although the Republicans in the state legislature would never admit it, they actually prefer having Democratic governors. Republican legislators, according to this theory, can kill and cripple a Democratic governor's programs without feeling guilty about it. They can quietly reduce the power of the governor without being in the position of reducing the power of a fellow Republican.

Republican legislators are happier with a Democratic governor, Kallenberger says, because it permits them to be totally in charge themselves. They would have to respond to a Republican governor and advance his or her programs and bills in the legislature. "Worst of all for the Republican state legislators, they would feel real pressure to give more power and authority to a Republican governor."[15]

EFFECTS OF A WEAK GOVERNORSHIP

As would be expected, close friends and political appointees of the Colorado governor criticize the effects of reduced gubernatorial power. Here again, former legislative lobbyist and department head Larry Kallenberger has a strong opinion. "The real result of a weakened governorship," he said, "is that the governor is not able to move state government." Bureaucrats and legislators tend to resist change, he explained, so giving them so much power means that issues do not get addressed, problems do not get resolved, and people who want things to happen get frustrated and alienated. In the end, Kallenberger notes, "the state loses the ability to react to public concerns with good public programs."

With the governor so weak, Kallenberger continued, state government does not change very much. The bureaucrats and legislators only add a little here and subtract a little there. "The public ends up with little confidence that state government can solve problems. The final conclusion is that the system is not functioning in the best interests of democracy."

At the end of his interview, Kallenberger compared the Colorado state bureaucracy to a headless snake. "It moves. It winds around. When you first look at it, you see motion. Due to the weak governorship, however, the Colorado state bureaucracy has no head and thus never goes anywhere."[16]

LIEUTENANT GOVERNOR

Colorado has a lieutenant governor whose major function is to succeed the governor if he or she should die in office or resign. As a result of a 1974 amendment to the state constitution, the lieutenant governor runs for office teamed with the governor, and thus they are always members of the same political party. At the political party state nominating convention, however, the lieutenant governor is nominated separately from the governor and thus may not always represent the same wing of the political party as the governor.

A debate arises from time to time over whether Colorado really needs a lieutenant governor. Eight states have done without the office and seem to get along just fine. Although the position works out well in several other states, a view persists that lieutenant governors are often in search of both a definition of their job and assignments that will help advance their political careers. The lieutenant governor in Colorado often carries out a number of ceremonial and representational functions, but only when the governor assigns him or her such functions.

Former Colorado state Senate President Ted Strickland, who himself served as lieutenant governor in 1973 and 1974, calls it "a useless office" that costs taxpayers money yet fulfills little purpose except at ceremonial functions. He repeatedly called for abolishing the office, but he failed to garner the necessary two-thirds votes in the state legislature that would be needed to refer the proposal to the voters as an amendment to the state constitution.

A 1990 statewide poll conducted for this book indicated plurality support for doing away with the lieutenant governorship in Colorado. Forty-four percent favored eliminating the office, 8 percent were neutral, and only 31 percent wanted to keep it.[17] In short, the value of this obscure statewide political office in Colorado is debatable.

MAKING THE MOST OF THE GOVERNOR'S ROLE

Given this perceived or apparent lack of power, how does a governor conduct business in Colorado? Governors make use of the "bully pulpit" and thereby help frame the policy agenda for the state. The statements and speeches given by a governor are by definition "news" and are well covered by the Colorado news media. A governor can identify problems, propose general solutions to those problems, and thereby work to mold public opinion and build public support for new ideas and programs. By operating in this manner, the governor sets a "tone" or creates an "atmosphere" that calls for action—or inaction.

Governor Roy Romer often made effective use of this bully pulpit. A senior aide, Deputy Chief of Staff B. J. Thornberry, described Romer's techniques for getting the most influence available out of a weak governorship. "This governor is an activist and a populist," she said. "He effectively uses the publicity powers of the governorship to set a vision for the future of the state." Thornberry noted that Romer likes to get out of the Denver area periodically in order to learn what people all over the state are thinking. She concluded: "He listens to the people. Then he articulates what they tell him as goals for the future. When you mobilize your constituents behind ideas and programs in this way, eventually the changes you want will be implemented."[18]

As a spokesperson for change, the governor works to influence more than just the legislature. The governor will also endeavor to provide leadership on local government issues to the cities and counties in the state. For instance, when the public schools in Denver were about to be closed by a teachers' strike in the spring of 1991, Governor Romer personally intervened, mediated the dispute, and eventually produced an agreement that was acceptable to both the teachers and the school board.

Colorado governors provide leadership and vision to the wide variety of boards and commissions that govern so many of the activities of state government. Often a governor will meet with a board or commission, making his or her views clear to the members and urging various plans of action—or inaction—on them. As former OSPB Executive Director Gene Petrone commented, "If the governor keeps after the various boards and commissions he appoints, his policies will likely be implemented by them."[19]

Some observers point out, however, that the bully pulpit used so effectively by Colorado governors has severe limitations. It has become the *only* way governors can influence things over which they have no direct control—an opposition-party legislature and a highly independent bureaucracy. "Drumming up public support for ideas and legislation is a technique that only works occasionally," said a Romer aide. "The daily verbal hammering the governor has to do on issues and programs takes a long time to take effect."[20]

Romer himself appeared to be well aware that the Colorado governor's powers have been eroding and that getting public opinion behind him is his only way, as a Democrat, to have an impact on a Republican legislature. "And it is unfortunate," notes Romer. "You'd have better government if you had more governor's involvement in the budget and the education process. . . . [Mobilizing public opinion] is a very tough way to organize power. That's what causes me to work 16-hour days instead of 8-hour days."[21]

On balance, Colorado governors are effective only to the extent they are able to persuade others to join them voluntarily in various state programs and projects. The role of the governor is, above all, that of a persuader. To get the job done, the governor must influence administrators, state legislators, federal officials, local officials, party leaders, business leaders, the press, and the public. If governors are successful persuaders, they create power and influence that can result in an effective administration.

RECENT COLORADO GOVERNORS

One of the best ways to understand the Colorado governorship is to review the careers and accomplishments of recent governors. Stephen McNichols,

John Love, Richard Lamm, and Roy Romer all brought their own approach and style to the job. As a result, the four governorships were different in terms of tone and accomplishments.

Stephen McNichols

Stephen McNichols was the lieutenant governor of Colorado when he was elected to the governorship in 1956. Only forty-two years old at the time, McNichols was a native of Denver and had grown up a few blocks from the state capitol. An activist Democrat, McNichols was a World War II veteran and, before being elected lieutenant governor and governor, served six years in the state Senate. He was the first Catholic to be elected governor.

McNichols based his first campaign for the governorship on a well-thought-out program for state government reform and program expansion. He pledged to work for fair legislative reapportionment, a statewide watershed survey, the establishment of a state planning agency, and more equitable apportionment of state taxes.

Unlike many previous governors, Steve McNichols was willing to lobby the legislature openly in order to achieve his legislative goals. He sometimes would walk up from the governor's office, which is on the first floor of the capitol, to the second floor, where the House and Senate chambers are located. He would work the halls and legislative lobbies just outside the House and Senate, buttonholing hesitant legislators and trying to win their votes. When he could not get his fellow Democrats to support what he wanted to do, he was more than willing to try and talk Republicans into supporting his programs, and he was often successful.

McNichols pressed the state legislature to spend more money for education, particularly to increase faculty salaries at the state's public colleges and universities. He supported decreasing the number of school districts in Colorado, hoping to create larger, better-financed districts that could provide a higher-quality public school education. He also was able to create a state planning department with sufficient financing to operate successfully.

McNichols strengthened the powers of the governor's budget office and, as a result, presented a rigorously analyzed and carefully pruned budget to the state legislature each year he was in office. It was not until the later years of his governorship that the legislature's Joint Budget Committee (JBC) came into existence. In addition, McNichols expanded the state highway system, established the University of Colorado Medical Center in Denver, improved state mental hospitals, and undertook a program of state prison reform. As might be expected of a boy who grew up on Denver's Capitol Hill, it was Stephen McNichols who accepted, on behalf of the state, the gift of a splendid town mansion and turned it into the Colorado Governor's Mansion.

Longtime statehouse reporter Charles Roos recalls the McNichols era as "almost a golden age," when the governor and the legislature worked and cooperated together to produce major legislative victories. "It was a rare and exciting period in Colorado politics," said Roos of those years in the late 1950s and early 1960s. Why was McNichols successful? Doubtless he was able to pass so many of his programs because his political party had large majorities in both houses of the legislature. Reporter Roos believes, too, that McNichols accomplished much because so little had been done by governors or the legislature in the previous decade. "But it is also clear," added Roos, "that Steve McNichols was a political leader. He sold the legislature on his programs, and he also sold the people to some extent."[22]

Stephen McNichols was the last Colorado governor to serve a two-year term of office (1957–59) and the first to serve a four-year term (1959–1963). He was defeated for reelection in 1962 by Republican John Love, a popular newcomer on the Colorado political scene who simply pledged to cut taxes. McNichols's activist reforms and successful government innovations caused opponents to charge that he had become "power hungry" and had raised taxes too high.

Many Coloradans were more conservative than McNichols and did not sense the need for his programs of reform as strongly as he did. In the end, however, it was reform and change that were the main characteristics of his tenure as governor. "If one takes the position that government can play a positive role in the lives of people, few, if any, Colorado governors have accomplished as much as Stephen McNichols."[23]

John Love

At the time he was elected governor in November of 1962, Colorado Springs attorney John Love had no previous political or governmental experience. His only attempt at electoral office had been an unsuccessful race for El Paso County Republican chair, a race which he lost by one vote. In the early days of his campaign for governor, Love proved such an inept candidate that his managers hired a speech coach to teach him how to give an effective political talk.

But Love quickly became an attractive campaigner. The state Republican party united behind his candidacy. Because he had never been in political office, Love had no political record to defend and no political enemies. He thus was able to exploit the opposition that had developed toward Stephen McNichols during the Democrat's activist and reformist six years in office.

John Love was governor of Colorado during the turbulent 1960s—a period of urban unrest, minority demands, and violent protests against United States military involvement in Vietnam. Governor Love brought the state through this difficult period with a minimum of public strife, working hard to maintain an equilibrium between the need for a stable society and various protests. He was proud of his friendly relations with the various minority communities in Colorado.

When a group of protesters camped in shacks and tents on the Denver University campus, university officials asked the governor for help in getting them to leave. Love sent in the state's National Guard, but without bullets in their guns. The Colorado governor did not want a repeat of the situation at Kent State University in Ohio where, in May of 1970, four protesting students were shot and killed by National Guard soldiers. As it turned out, by the time the Colorado Guard arrived on the Denver University campus, the protesters had already left of their own volition. "Woodstock West," as the Denver newspapers called it, had a happy ending.

Governor Love had his share of problems with the newly emerging Joint Budget Committee in the state legislature. "[My] biggest problems were always budgetary," Love said.[24] In spite of the fact he was a Republican, Love frequently squared off with the Republican majority on the JBC, striving to preserve the budgetary prerogatives of the Colorado governorship from legislative usurpation.

John Love's major achievement was the steady expansion and improvement of education in Colorado. During his tenure in the governor's chair, the World War II "baby boom" generation hit the college campuses, requiring the building of new facilities and enlarged teaching staffs.

In his 1970 and 1972 State of the State messages, Love was the first Colorado governor to urge his constituents to devote more time and attention to preserving Colorado's unique and beautiful natural environment. He failed to realize, however, that emerging environmentalist sentiment in Colorado would lead the state's voters to oppose, strenuously, holding the 1976 Winter Olympic Games in Colorado. Love had backed the Olympics enthusiastically and was personally disappointed when a majority of Coloradans, in a 1972 referendum, failed to share his enthusiasm and voted down hosting the Olympics.

In July of 1973, after more than ten years in office, John Love resigned the

Colorado governorship in midterm and went to Washington, D.C., to become director of the Office of Energy Policy under Republican President Richard M. Nixon. Love's ideas clashed with higher-up officials in the Nixon administration, however, and he resigned his new post after only a few months on the job. He and his wife came back to Denver, where he returned to private life as an attorney and businessman.

Unlike Stephen McNichols, who is remembered as a programmatic leader, John Love is remembered more for the way he presided over a difficult period in Colorado history. His evenhanded manner and quiet ability to persuade gave stature to the office. Associating himself with the moderate or progressive wing of the Republican party, Love became known nationally as a qualified and respected western Republican governor.

When John Love resigned the Colorado governorship in 1973, Lieutenant Governor John Vanderhoof became governor. Vanderhoof, a Republican, ran for election to a full term in the 1974 general election, but he was defeated by his Democratic opponent, Richard Lamm.

Richard Lamm

Richard Lamm first attracted attention in 1969 when, as a state legislator, he challenged then Governor John Love's efforts to "sell" Colorado and bring new industry and new people into the state. He suggested Colorado might do better to limit population growth, thereby preserving the state's great natural beauty and avoiding the problems of overcrowding and overbuilding that afflicted many other parts of the United States. If attracting new industry and new people produced the good life, Lamm said, then "Los Angeles must truly be one of America's most liveable cities."[25]

Lamm gained statewide attention by leading the fight to prevent the 1976 Winter Olympic Games from being held in Colorado. When the state's voters rejected state financing for the Olympics at the 1972 general election, Lamm emerged as the principal Colorado spokesperson for environmentalism. He ran for governor in 1974 on environmental issues and was easily elected.

Lamm served three full four-year terms. His twelve years of service were the longest time in office of any Colorado governor to date. The entire time he was governor, however, either one or both houses of the state legislature were in firm control of the Republican party. As Lamm came more and more to symbolize environmentalism and controlling population growth in Colorado, the Republican-dominated state legislature became more and more committed to strengthening the business community and stimulating economic growth. The result was constant conflict and wrangling between Democratic Governor Lamm and a Republican state legislature.

Throughout the late 1970s and early 1980s, Governor Lamm became particularly concerned about the effects of the energy crisis on Colorado. As the U.S. government inaugurated a major program to extract large amounts of oil from vast deposits of oil shale in the western part of the state, Lamm gave increasingly dire warnings about how such large-scale energy projects would threaten the natural beauty of Colorado. "We are going to have to be a region with synfuel plants and wilderness areas side by side. Our streams must support fish and wildlife, agriculture and industry. It's going to require a good deal of creative planning to bring about that balance and harmony."[26]

But Lamm's repeated calls for better state planning and control of population growth usually fell on deaf legislative ears. Colorado's population and industrial base expanded rapidly throughout the late 1970s. Cities on the Front Range, such as Denver and Colorado Springs, became larger and more crowded. The ski resort areas near Breckenridge, Aspen, and Vail also expanded rapidly. Throughout it all, Lamm bickered with the state legislature about the state's future. In the end, little was accomplished in the way of state programs for controlling population growth and protecting the environment.

One of Lamm's few environmental "victories" later came back to haunt him. He opposed the construction of an Interstate highway, to be built with federal funds, that would have formed a beltway around southern and eastern Denver. The environmentalist governor believed the new beltway would encourage further population growth and commercial development in a portion of the Denver suburbs that was already overdeveloped and overcrowded. Lamm stated he would drive "a silver stake" in the heart of the giant suburban highway project, and he used his appointive powers on the state Highway Commission to accomplish his purpose. Lamm never heard the end of this, especially from real estate developers and residents of that part of suburban Denver. Ironically, the beltway around southern and eastern Denver (Colorado 470) was subsequently constructed, using, at least in part, state rather than federal funds.

Lamm was credited by many for recruiting scores of talented young professionals to his cabinet and to his state capitol office. He often said that whatever else historians may say, he believed his most significant accomplishment was having surrounded himself with gifted and talented people. Lamm also opened up state government to large numbers of women and minorities, appointing the first woman and first Hispanic justices to the Colorado Supreme Court and hiring the first black and Hispanic department heads.

In 1975 Lamm called for and later signed into law the nation's first sunset law, which helped eliminate fifteen agencies and countless unneeded regulations. Lamm also appointed consumer advocates to all regulatory boards and commissions and initiated the creation of the Office of Consumer Counsel. That office, first funded by federal funds and subsequently funded by the legislature, helps represent consumers in utility rate proceedings.[27]

By the time Richard Lamm was serving his third term as governor, population growth and rapid economic development were no longer problems in Colorado. As the energy crisis eased, the federal government abandoned its expensive attempts to produce oil from western Colorado oil shale. An economic downturn in the electronics industry and cuts in military spending by the federal government further weakened the Colorado economy. Controlling growth and preserving the environment receded somewhat as major issues in Colorado politics.

At the end of his tenure as governor, Lamm began using the bully pulpit of the Colorado governorship to draw attention to what he believed were major problems facing both the state and the nation. He began publishing books and giving out-of-state speeches on such subjects as the environmental destruction of the West, the welfare problems being created by immigration of foreign nationals into the United States, and the rapidly increasing cost of public health care.[28] In one particularly famous 1984 speech, Lamm sparked a national controversy by appearing to say that terminally ill medical patients had a "duty to die" and thereby save the government the high medical cost of prolonging their lives: "We've got a duty to die and get out of the way with all of our machines and artificial hearts and everything else like that and let our society, our kids, build a better life." Because of the pessimistic tone of his books and speeches, Lamm's critics labeled him "Governor Gloom."

Richard Lamm decided not to run for reelection as governor in 1986, even though most political observers thought he could have easily been elected to a fourth term in office. Lamm gave his support to Roy Romer, a longtime political ally in the Democratic party who was serving as state treasurer. Romer easily defeated his Republican opponent in the 1986 general election, thereby continuing Democratic control of the Colorado governor's office.

Lamm's career as governor was controversial. He often was criticized for being confrontational with the Republican leadership in the state legislature. Some observers suggested he might have done better by working with the legislators and being more willing to compromise. His lengthy tenure as governor illustrated the point that if a Colorado governor cannot persuade the Colorado legislature to adopt his programs and policies, most of those programs and policies are never going to be implemented.

But even those who disagreed with Richard Lamm admired his strength of conviction, his intelligence and integrity, and his celebration of the beauty and majesty of Colorado. On balance, Lamm felt the need to "save" and not to "sell" Colorado. He wound up doing some of both.

Roy Romer

When Democrat Roy Romer was inaugurated governor of Colorado, he faced a much different situation from that faced by Richard Lamm when he was inaugurated twelve years earlier. Instead of rapid population growth and an economic boom, the state was in a major economic slump. Unemployment rates were rising, more people were moving out of the state than were moving into it, and "overbuilt" Denver and Colorado Springs had large numbers of vacant offices, apartments, houses, and shopping centers.

Romer made economic development the major theme of his governorship. He appointed a Colorado Springs business executive, Stewart Bliss, as his chief of staff. Romer also put Bliss, a Republican, in direct charge of the state's economic development efforts. Romer himself began touring the United States and foreign countries, carrying the message to all who would listen that Colorado was "open for business." Once again, a Colorado governor had felt the need to "sell" Colorado.

Democratic Governor Romer took a less abrasive stand with the Republican state legislature. He tended to highlight general areas that needed action rather than sending specific bills to the House or the Senate. In something of a contrast with his predecessor, Romer let it be known that he was available to work with and compromise with the legislature. Instead of making Republican legislative leaders come down to the governor's office, as Governor Lamm had done, Romer would sometimes climb the stairs in the capitol building and meet with legislative leaders in their offices.

Romer won praise from many legislators and lobbyists for his willingness to work with them. One lobbyist said Romer was his own best lobbyist because he was never timid about meeting with legislators and coming to them and asking for their help. The fact that he had been around state government for nearly thirty years was obviously an asset. "I can be the point man and political leader on some issues," said Romer, "but not on every issue. . . .

[This] particular office doesn't have a lot of constitutional power, but it has a lot of power if you know how to use it. You need to pick your issues and pick good people. I pay a lot of attention to appointments. . . . Finally, my philosophy is that popularity is not something you put in the bank. You use it. . . ."[29]

Perhaps no governor in Colorado history has made better use of the bully pulpit of the governorship than Roy Romer. He earned a reputation for being willing to travel the state and attend almost any event that would be enhanced by the presence of the governor. He gave countless speeches at county fairs, local parades, and annual dinners. Under his "Dome on the Range" program, he and key members of his staff would travel to outlying parts of the state and visit with those citizens who had problems to discuss with the governor.

Governor Romer also associated himself with major projects that would enhance the economic climate in Colorado. He strongly supported the construction of the new Denver Convention Center and a new Denver regional airport. After a long struggle with the legislature, he succeeded in implementing a major portion of his plan for improving the state highway system. He also took the lead in the successful effort to bring major-league baseball, the National League Colorado Rockies, to Denver.

Not every project Romer supported was a success. In cooperation with Denver officials, he worked to get United Airlines to locate a major airplane maintenance facility near the new Denver airport, but United eventually decided to locate the new facility in Indianapolis.

Backed by a surprising number of business leaders and Republicans, Roy Romer was easily reelected in 1990 by 63 percent of the vote. In his second term, Romer became increasingly involved in the National Governors' Association as a spokesperson for educational reform in the states. By 1991 he was cochairing a national panel on educational goals and won recognition from fellow governors as one of the top governors in the nation. In 1993 he was chairman of the National Governors' Association.

CONCLUSION

Colorado has a governorship of mixed power, yet the problem does not lie in the Colorado constitution. It is more a matter of tradition. Over the years, the tendency has been to put many executive functions under the control of appointed boards and commissions rather than under the direct control of the governor. At the same time, budgetary power in the Centennial State has moved from the executive branch to the legislative branch.

The Colorado constitution vests the governor with the "supreme executive power of the state." Most observers carefully point out, however, that the powers of the Colorado governor might better be described as "illusory" rather than "supreme." As former governor John Love suggested, "Colorado governors have the responsibility but not the authority to run the state."[30]

Yet effective governors in Colorado learn to stretch or maximize the power of the governorship. They do this by personal leadership, effective bargaining, negotiation, and persuasion. They pyramid their resources, form alliances with interest groups and lobbyists and legislators, and infuse vision into the enterprise of state government.

Many Colorado citizens, however, are inherently skeptical of government. Governors have to demonstrate that government can work and that state government has affirmative responsibilities. This is no small challenge. To a large degree, the effectiveness of governors is often dependent on the support citizens give them. Governors can be creative or effective leaders only to the extent citizens recruit and elect good leaders in the first place, insist on their integrity in office, and support them when they make the right decisions.[31]

CHAPTER TEN

Judges and Justice

There are those who have called the judiciary in American government the branch most removed from politics or the least political branch. Yet judges and courts at all levels of government play a vital role in determining who gets what, where, when, and how. Thus judges play a crucial role in making public policy. State and municipal judges preside over most criminal trials, settle most lawsuits between individuals and companies, and administer most estates. If anything, state courts have become even more prominent in the political life of the nation in recent years. State judges apply the state bill of rights to more and more matters. And there have been significant developments in state law dealing with damages to compensate people for legal wrongs done to them. Many of these changes have opened state courts to more people to sue more often about more things.

"As state courts have become more active, state judges have become embroiled in visible controversial issues and have antagonized various interests. And as the public has grown more sophisticated about the importance of judges as policy makers, judicial politics has become a significant feature of the political landscape."[1] This has certainly been the case in Colorado, where both the legislature and recent governors have occasionally been irritated with opinions from both the state Supreme Court and lower courts. One such feud arose in 1991 when the Colorado Supreme Court declared the state's death penalty unconstitutional on grounds that legislative revisions to the law in 1988 made the death penalty too "automatic."

These kinds of decisions prompt Colorado citizens to complain about "soft" or overly lenient judges. Also, attorneys regularly complain about court delays and the uneven quality of the people serving on the bench. Controversy also continues as to how justices and judges should be appointed to the courts. In short, the judiciary in Colorado has its own politics. Although judges are generally removed from overt electioneering and day-to-day political pulling and tugging, they are important public figures who are shaped by and help shape the political life of the state.

Prior to the gold rush of 1858–59, law-and-order matters in the Pike's Peak area were essentially an "everyone for themselves" situation. Mountain trappers and prairie buffalo hunters, the first non–Native Americans to come to the region, relied on pistols and rifles to guarantee their safety and property. A rough sort of frontier order reigned, and once in a while a trial or two took place at the trappers' rendezvous or at the fur trading post. By and large, each person and every party out in the Colorado wilderness were "on their own."

After 1854 the territorial governments of Utah, New Mexico, Nebraska, and Kansas were supposedly maintaining order and dispensing justice in the Colorado region. These governments, however, were too far away to have effective legal and judicial control. Not until gold was discovered at Dry Creek and thousands of people migrated to Colorado did the early mining camps and valley towns begin organizing "miners' courts," "claim clubs," and "people's courts" to dispense something approaching orderly justice. Finally, in 1861, when Colorado Territory was created, vigilante justice gradually gave way to more institutionalized forms of judicial authority.

With Colorado's admission to the Union as a state in 1876, a judiciary largely patterned after that in other states was provided for in the newly adopted constitution. The state was divided into four large judicial districts, each with a district court to hear and try major crimes. Lesser crimes were tried in separate county courts. Each of the then twenty-six counties covered a large land area, and it often was quite a trek to the county seat for a county court trial. It was usually even longer, of course, to get to one of the four districts.

High mountains and vast rolling prairies were formidable barriers, isolating the dispersed communities that collectively constituted Colorado in the late 1870s. Plainly there was a need for local courts that could try criminals and settle disputes quickly and reasonably. Thus justice-of-the peace courts were organized in each community to provide the desired local law enforcement and to settle minor civil matters. Hence, from its earliest development, Colorado's judicial system was highly decentralized, with local justices of the peace playing a leading role.

The number of justice-of-the-peace courts expanded rapidly as the state grew in population. There was little or no coordination between these local courts, however, and the elected justices of the peace often were local residents who had minimal legal training or sometimes none at all. Each justice of the peace set up court the way he liked. Further, the quality of justice varied greatly from one local court to the next, as did the justices' qualifications and, importantly, the extent to which decisions actually corresponded with state law.

THE JUDICIAL REFORM MOVEMENT: THE MISSOURI PLAN

The rapid expansion in Colorado's population during and after World War II highlighted some of the inadequacies of the justice-of-the-peace courts. In 1962, following a number of studies, the state legislature referred to the voters a constitutional amendment that provided for the first major reorganization of the court system since 1876. The amendment was adopted overwhelmingly by a vote of 303,740 to 169,032. It abolished all justice-of-the-peace courts, set higher qualifications for judges, and gave the state Supreme Court the responsibility of setting uniform standards and procedures for the various courts throughout Colorado. This court reorganization plan went into effect in early 1965 and provided an integrated statewide, rather than a localized, focus for the state judicial system.

The judicial reform movement that swept through Colorado in the early 1960s next turned its attention to the way in which judges were selected. At that time Colorado citizens selected judges by means of partisan elections. To be a judge, a person had to be nominated by a political party and then elected, like any other candidate for office, in a partisan general election. Party politics—whether a candidate was a "good Democrat" or a "good Republican"—often was the chief factor in who was or was not elected to the bench. Thus loyal Democrats became judges in Pueblo and Denver, while loyal Republicans won the elections in Colorado Springs and in many of the Denver suburbs and outlying agricultural regions.

Another problem was that the names of the various candidates for judges appeared at the bottom of the general election ballot. Judicial election campaigns received little attention or newspaper coverage, thus making it hard for voters to know the candidates and their qualifications. Still another problem was the concern that judges, facing an upcoming reelection contest, might be tempted to shade or even shape decisions to curry votes rather than impartially administer justice.

Pressure was put on the legislature to change the judicial selection process in Colorado. When such efforts failed, several citizen groups, notably the League of Women Voters, began to collect signatures for an initiated constitutional amendment to be placed before the voters. Their proposal provided for judges to be appointed rather than elected.

The judicial reform amendment recommended a version of what in legal circles is known as the "Missouri Plan." Under this plan the governor has the power to appoint people to state courts when a vacancy occurs, but the prospective judges must come from lists of nominees provided by specially appointed judicial nominating commissions.

Here is how the Missouri Plan works: When a vacancy occurs on a district or county court, a judicial nominating commission already in place for that district or county submits two or three names of potential candidates to the governor's office, presumably names of people who have the proper training and experience. The governor and his or her staff do their own evaluations and telephone checks on the nominees.

Then the governor chooses from this short list. The governor's selection automatically becomes the judge until the next general election, at which time the voters are asked, "Shall Judge X be retained in office?" If a majority agrees, the judge serves a full new term. If the judge fails to win a majority, the judicial nominating commission begins its search all over again.

Judges, according to the Missouri plan, do not run against an opponent— only against their own record. Also, judges running for retention in office are not identified with any political party on the ballot. Once on the court, district judges can serve as long as they are able to earn reelection every six years or until they reach the mandatory retirement age of seventy-two. County judges serve for four years before coming up for reelection.

The proposed Missouri Plan was hotly debated in the mid 1960s. The Colorado Bar Association advocated its adoption, but others opposed this bold judicial reform plan. Arguments for and against the reform plan are summarized below.[2]

The Case for the Missouri Plan

1. The Missouri Plan would encourage more well-qualified persons to be considered as judges since they would have the likely assurance of longer tenure and would not have to participate in partisan election campaigns.
2. The courts would be more removed from partisan and election politics, thereby freeing judges from the pressures of campaign politics and enabling them to devote more of their attention to conducting judicial business.

3. The Missouri Plan nominating process would place emphasis on the legal and philosophical qualifications of a prospective judge, not on political party affiliation and party loyalty. In effect, this would be a peer-review process conducted by a specially designated commission charged with producing highly competent nominees.

4. The Missouri Plan would enable voters to focus on a judge's record and performance, which would facilitate the removal of inept or incompetent judges and the retention of hard-working and responsible judges.

5. Finally, it was claimed, the Missouri Plan, by attracting more qualified judges and increasing the likelihood that they would be reelected, would provide for more continuity in the Colorado court system, thus promoting efficiency and speeding up the administration of justice.

The Case against the Missouri Plan

1. The Missouri Plan's removal of judges from election by the people would take away from the people a basic democratic right and would give this power to the governor and a handful of other elites. Appointing judges under a nonpartisan process would make judges less responsive to the voters and hence less accountable.

2. This plan, its opponents said, would weaken and perhaps even destroy the doctrine of separation of powers, the idea that state government should consist of three separate, independent branches. The Missouri Plan would give the governor so much power over the judiciary that it might destroy the judiciary's independence.

3. The plan would have the additional side effect of weakening political parties. In effect, it would eliminate party participation in the procedures of the judiciary.

4. The plan would make it too difficult for voters to remove unqualified and incompetent judges in office until compulsory retirement at age seventy-two.

5. Finally, skeptics of this plan disputed whether the politics could really be taken out of the process. Leaders in the legal profession, or advisers to the governor, they contended, would get added clout over these critical nominations if the Missouri Plan were adopted.

Adoption of the Missouri Plan

After the debates and the 1966 election were over, the Missouri Plan amendment was approved by state voters 293,771 to 261,558, with nearly 53 percent of the voters in favor of the reform. Today, about three decades later, the Missouri Plan is generally accepted as an improvement over the old system. It attempts to create a neutral appointment process and thereby remove judicial selection from narrow partisan politics. It is also an attempt to enlarge the list of potential judges. In the past, people from the minority parties in one-party areas of the state—not to mention those who disliked campaigning and electioneering for office—were eliminated from being considered as judges.

And who serves on these judicial nominating commissions? Members are selected from the geographical area corresponding to a court's jurisdiction. Thus a commission nominating candidates to the Fourth District Court (El Paso and Teller counties) is selected from those counties. A commission nominating candidates to the state Supreme Court is selected from the entire state.

A district nominating commission is composed of seven members. Three members must be lawyers and are appointed jointly by the governor, the state attorney general, and the chief justice of the state Supreme Court. The other four members must be nonlawyers and are appointed solely by the governor. No more than four of the members of the seven-member commission can belong to the same political party. Judicial nominating commission members serve a six-year term in office and cannot be reappointed.

When a vacancy opens on the Colorado Supreme Court or the Colorado Court of Appeals, a special Supreme Court nominating commission comes into play. This commission is composed of twelve members, two from each of Colorado's six congressional districts. One member from each congressional district must be a lawyer and one must be a nonlawyer. The lawyers are appointed jointly by the governor, the state attorney general, and the chief justice of the state Supreme Court. The governor appoints the nonlawyers.

Commission members, lawyers and nonlawyers alike, are usually civic, professional, and party leaders. They come from the ranks of law firms, banks, small and large businesses, former party officials, college professors, and citizens' groups. The 1966 amendment stipulated that no person serving as a member of a nominating commission could simultaneously hold any elective office or any elective political party office.

How political are Colorado's judicial nominating commissions? Under Republican governors the commissions are more conservative. Under Democratic Governors Lamm and Romer the commissions reflected a more liberal or at least middle-of-the-road cast. Democratic governors did appoint some Republicans, yet they were more likely to appoint moderate or progressive Republicans to the nominating commissions.

Commission members from both parties typically seek out the best candidates, and the party affiliation of the nominees often is never even considered. Commission members say they have been impressed by the nonpartisan, professional character of these deliberations and the overall emphasis on competence of the prospective nominees.

Plainly, while the reform has taken the opposing candidate out of judicial elections, politics cannot be entirely removed from the judicial selection process. In the Colorado version of the Missouri Plan, the governor was given a decisive role in determining who becomes a judge. The governor has a role in naming the lawyers on the commissions and has the sole say in the appointment of the nonlawyers. A determined governor can clearly have a major influence in shaping these commissions. And it is the governor who makes the final appointment from the two or three names the nominating commission submits to the governor's office. In political terms, this plan strengthened the hand of governors and gave them a leading role in shaping the state's judiciary.

Evaluation of the Missouri Plan

Early in 1990 Joseph R. Quinn, chief justice of the Colorado Supreme Court at the time, gave the following evaluation of the judicial nominating process in Colorado: "I practiced law under the prior judicial selection system, which was partisan and political, and the difference between what Colorado had then [elections] and what Colorado has now [appointment] was like night and day. Now we truly have a merit system."

Chief Justice Quinn said that all of Colorado's recent governors, both Republicans and Democrats, have been very responsible in both appointments to judicial nominating commissions and in appointing judges to the bench. Above all, he argued, the judicial nominating commissions have functioned in such a way that they have nominated candidates for judge with no political considerations at all.[3]

Many others echoed the positive view of Justice Quinn. Former Supreme Court Justice Jean E. Dubofsky, the first woman to sit on the high court, agreed that the Missouri Plan and its nominating commissions have worked well. "The quality of judges is definitely higher now than in the past," and judges and justices are clearly more insulated from politics and from party and election pressures. Yet there have been other subtle changes as well, said Dubofsky. On the positive side, most judges decide cases on a case-by-case basis, not according to their campaign platforms or with their eye on their next election opponent. On the negative side, judges these days may not be quite as polite and cordial to those who appear in their courtrooms as in the past. When they do not have to campaign or worry about a serious political challenger at the next election, "judges are less responsive politically to the moods of the day and probably also less courteous to those who show up in their chambers."[4]

Most attorneys and the Colorado Bar Association also indicate satisfaction with the more than two decades of experience with this reform. Yet not everyone is pleased. Several state legislators, led by Senator Ralph A. Cole, a Republican from Littleton, introduced various measures calling for either a return to the old system or modification of the new one in ways that would weaken the power of the governor. Senator Cole, for example, unsuccessfully introduced legislation that would have required that the governor's nominations to the district and state courts be confirmed by a majority vote of the state Senate comparable to the federal requirement that the U.S. Senate approve nominations to the U.S. Supreme Court.

Senator Cole also introduced legislation returning Colorado to a system of electing judges and having judges run against other candidates, but to do so in nonpartisan elections. This legislation also did not win approval. Several states in the West and upper Middle West hold nonpartisan primaries for nominating judicial candidates and electing them on nonpartisan ballots. That a nonpartisan ballot is used does not necessarily mean that political parties are unimportant—in at least half the states that hold nonpartisan elections, parties actively campaign in behalf of particular candidates.

Senator Cole said he thought Governor Richard Lamm abused his appointive powers. Cole claimed Colorado merely substituted one form of politics in the selection of judges for another. "Moreover," he said, "it's more undercover these days . . . and these appointments are for life. . . . You need political pull with the governor to win appointment and you need to politick to get on the bench." Cole also complained that too many liberals have been appointed in recent years.[5]

A top state political analyst said he wished judges were still elected. Colorado lost something in that reform, he said. Judges are, he added, too insulated from the political life of the state.

It is well known, too, that Governor Lamm became frustrated with some of his own appointees after they had been on the bench a while. He thought some of his nominees were or became insensitive to the public's concern about crime and the desire for tougher sentencing. "I made a mistake in being overly impressed by brains and legal talent," Lamm said. In the process, "I unbalanced the Court, which I never meant to do."[6]

After having been in office for nearly two terms, Lamm began appointing more "hard-line" judges who he hoped would rule somewhat differently on criminal issues than several of his earlier appointments. Aides and associates said Lamm began appointing people who almost exclusively had experience as prosecutors and district attorneys—presumably to get judges more sympathetic to the victims and the prosecutors. It was said by his critics, a bit in derision perhaps, "Lamm wants to be governor of all of the people," suggesting Lamm knew where the voters' sentiments were on criminal issues. Whether or not this change in his judicial nominating practices made a political difference is hard to determine, but it is worth noting that Lamm did win a landslide reelection victory in 1982.

Governor Roy Romer spends considerable time interviewing his prospective nominees for judges at all levels, including county judges. He will occasionally travel to a district or county and personally interview the candidates who are finalists, asking about their experience and judicial philosophy.

Another complaint about the quality of judges comes from attorneys who practice before the district courts. They complain, not about the Missouri Plan, but about the uneven or sometimes poor quality of people applying for the bench. This is perhaps because the work loads are heavy and the pay is low. In 1992 prestigious law firms in Denver paid top recruits right out of law school about the same first-year salary as Colorado paid district court judges—$63,000 a year. Colorado presently ranks in the bottom ten of the fifty states in terms of salaries for district judges. As a result, Colorado is not getting the best people to serve. The state judicial system would be improved by doubling judges' salaries and creating more judge positions—ideas the legislature is unlikely to welcome, let alone act upon.

Former District Judge John F. Gallagher was first elected to the bench in 1964 (before Colorado voters had approved the Missouri Plan) and served with distinction for twenty-five years in the Fourth Judicial District (El Paso and Teller counties). Judge Gallagher commented that the increased work load and low salary have badly hurt the quality of the court system in Colorado. "You just do not have time any more to think and read and reflect." Further, Gallagher said, it is difficult to say that judges appointed in recent years are, as a group, better qualified by experience, intellect, and temperament than their elected predecessors, as a group.

Gallagher believed the problems facing the Colorado courts had nothing to do with merit selection as opposed to election, but rather with the fact that the staffing and resources allocated to the court system in the last several years have been worse than niggardly. In addition, he pointed out, judicial salaries have not even been close to being competitive with what judges are paid in other states or in the federal system or with what lawyers in the major metropolitan areas earn in the private sector. The result has been congested dockets, a rising backlog of cases, insufficient time for consideration of motions and briefs, and low morale. "Members of the bar are obviously aware of this situation," Gallagher concluded, "and the number and quality of applicants for district court vacancies have suffered noticeably."[7]

The Missouri Plan reform effort also provided for one additional improvement in the system: creation of the Commission on Judicial Discipline. As amended in 1982, this provision allows for removing or disciplining a judge or justice "for willful misconduct in office, willful or persistent failure to perform his [or her] duties, intemperance or violation of any canon of the Colorado code of judicial conduct, or he [or she] may be retired for disability interfering with the performance of his [or her] duties which is, or likely to become, of a permanent character." Until the adoption of this amendment, there was no practical way of getting rid of a "bad" judge except at a subsequent election (which sometimes did not work) or by impeachment (which is often a most cumbersome process).

FEDERAL COURTS IN COLORADO

Colorado is not the only government operating a court system in the state. The United States government has its own court system for trying those persons accused of breaking federal laws. Generally referred to as federal courts, these U.S. government courts also try cases involving controversies between states, cases in which the United States is a party, controversies between citizens of different states involving large amounts of money, and cases involving a federal offense.

Denver is an important federal court center. Each state of the Union has at least one U.S. District Court within its boundaries, and the District Court for Colorado sits in Denver. Also located in Denver is the tenth Circuit U.S. Court of Appeals. Decisions can be appealed to this court from the District Court for Colorado and other district courts in the surrounding states that compose the tenth circuit.

At the top of the federal court system is the U.S. Supreme Court in Washington, D.C. This court, "the highest court in the land," hears appeals from the various U.S. appeals courts scattered throughout the nation. If a Colorado state court decision is alleged to violate the U.S. Constitution, the decision can be appealed from the Colorado Supreme Court to the U.S. Supreme Court.

For cases that originate in both the U.S. courts and the Colorado courts, the U.S. Supreme Court is "the court of last resort." Its decisions are final— there is no higher court to which its decisions can be appealed. Decisions by the U.S. Supreme Court concerning state powers and state laws have to be recognized and followed by all Colorado courts.

A COLORADO CASE: FROM DISTRICT COURT
TO THE SUPREME COURT

What follows is a Colorado case that went all the way from the District Court for Colorado to the U.S. Supreme Court.

On November 21, 1982, U.S. government drug enforcement officials and local police searched the Lakewood, Colorado, home of Albert and Victoria Levy. The raid was fruitful. The federal agents seized over $1 million in cash and gold bars, the proceeds from a recently completed cocaine deal.

One month later, the Colorado Department of Revenue assessed taxes totaling $194,000 against Albert Levy. Colorado tax officials said Levy owed this amount in state taxes on alleged narcotics sales of almost $3 million in 1982. The state sought to collect Levy's state taxes by taking a portion of the money seized by federal agents in the raid on Levy's home.

The federal officials, however, went into the U.S. District Court in Denver and claimed the total value of the seized property for the U.S. government. They said a 1978 federal law gave the federal government the right to take title to property seized from drug traffickers by U.S. narcotics agents. Federal lawyers argued the federal claim was superior to any claim made on the property for payment of state taxes.

The Colorado attorney general decided to contest the federal government's claim on the money. The initial trial went well for the state. U.S. District Judge John Kane, Jr., ruled that part of the state's tax claim should be paid from the cocaine deal proceeds seized by the federal government.

U.S. Justice Department lawyers appealed the case, however, and a higher federal court overruled Judge Kane and ruled the proceeds of drug transactions are not subject to state taxes if they have been seized by U.S. officials. Colorado officials refused to accept this decision and appealed the case to the U.S. Supreme Court. On February 20, 1990, the high court decided the case in favor of the federal government. It let stand the lower court ruling that drug transaction assets seized by U.S. agents are not subject to state taxes.

The state of Colorado may have lost its case, yet it had its day before the U.S. Supreme Court. Despite the outcome, Colorado Attorney General Duane Woodard hinted the decision was, in the state's opinion, incorrect: "We thought that drug dealers should have to pay taxes just like ordinary working citizens are required to do."[8]

STATE COURTS IN COLORADO

Colorado Supreme Court

The Colorado Supreme Court has seven justices who serve ten-year terms and who are subject to mandatory retirement at age seventy-two, unlike U.S. justices and judges, who serve as long as their health permits or until they wish to step down. Until a woman was named to the Supreme Court in 1979, this body had been entirely male for its first hundred years. The first African-American justice, Gregory K. Scott, joined the Colorado Supreme Court in 1993. The court decides cases appealed to it from lower courts in the state. In addition, the Colorado constitution requires the Colorado Supreme Court to give "advisory opinions" on important questions presented to it by the governor or by either house of the state legislature. In its role of giving advisory opinions, the Colorado Supreme Court possesses a power not possessed by the U.S. Supreme Court, which can only render decisions on actual court cases and cannot give advisory opinions.

The chief justice of the Colorado Supreme Court is elected by colleagues on the court and serves as long as they keep reelecting him or her. This process differs significantly from the U.S. Supreme Court and from many states, where the president or the governor has the power to nominate and, in effect, select the chief justice. This intracourt selection process also leads to some ongoing, if muted, politicking on the court. While not every member would want to serve as the chief justice (who earns just a few thousand dollars more in salary), those who do get selected or who retain their role must display an evenhanded approach, must be skilled listeners, must be willing to fashion necessary compromises, and must work to maintain harmony on the court.

A chief justice in Colorado can voluntarily step down from the leadership position and stay on the court as a regular justice. In 1990 Chief Justice Joseph R. Quinn did that after about five years of service as chief justice. Associate Justice Luis D. Rovira was elected by his colleagues to replace Quinn.

In addition to serving as presiding officer of the state Supreme Court, the chief justice also is the executive head of the entire Colorado court system. This means that in addition to working with colleagues rendering decisions on cases appealed to the Colorado Supreme Court, the chief justice must administer the Supreme Court and the lower courts in the state court system.

A recent chief justice described his job and the job of his fellow justices on the Colorado Supreme Court. He noted that as chief justice, he participates in all Colorado Supreme Court decisions. In addition, he has administrative responsibility for the entire state court system. "I spend about forty hours a week researching cases, presiding over Supreme Court sessions, and writing opinions. I spend another twenty hours a week administering the state court system." Fortunately, his colleagues on the Supreme Court help him with administrative duties by serving on public education committees, grievance committees, long-term court planning committees, and so on.[9]

Similar to the U.S. Supreme Court, the Colorado Supreme Court justices are not always unanimous in their decisions, although the vast majority of decisions (more than 90 percent) are unanimous. When there is a "split decision," different justices prepare a majority opinion and a minority opinion.

Oral arguments before the Supreme Court are open to the public, but the real debate and clash of opinions occurs in the private chamber on the fourth floor of the Judicial Building. Chief Justice Rovira described the scene: "It's only seven of us—nobody else is there. It's just a little conference room, and there's barely room for the seven of us there. And we don't wear our judicial robes."[10]

The justices use a rule of "juniority," making the most recently appointed justice speak first. One by one, the justices state how they stand on the case before the court. The chief justice assigns one of the justices on the majority side to write the opinion. After the majority opinion is written and circulated, an even more heated debate occasionally breaks out. If someone disagrees strongly with the majority opinion, that person prepares a dissent and circulates it among the justices. Occasionally a dissenting opinion is so persuasive that it convinces some of the justices to change sides, with the result that sometimes the dissenting view becomes the majority view.

According to Chief Justice Rovira, "someone may say, if you can change this, then I can join the opinion, but if you leave it this way to say that, then I can't join you." Then the individual justice must think whether he or she can change the wording as asked without destroying the integrity of the opinion. "Maybe yes, maybe no. That's where it's done. In the writing. Change a sentence, change a few words in some cases, and it may make one heck of a lot of difference. . . ." The chief justice said he had anticipated that there would be much arm-twisting between the various members of the court, "but there really isn't."[11]

For a few illustrations of major Colorado Supreme Court rulings in the 1981–91 period, see figure 12.

The Colorado Supreme Court originally occupied the north wing of the state capitol in Denver. Since 1977 it has occupied a modern high-rise building at East 14th Avenue and Broadway specifically constructed for the state courts and called the Colorado Judicial Building. Located about one block southwest of the capitol, the building, according to staffers there, was already too small the year they moved into it. (The ornate chamber formerly used by the Supreme Court in the state capitol has been converted into a large legislative hearing room.) Each justice has two law clerks and a secretary. A handful of administrative assistants complete the Supreme Court's lean staff.

While the U.S. Supreme Court has grown somewhat more conservative in the past generation, the Colorado Supreme Court, has occasionally engaged in a more expansive interpretation of certain provisions of the Colorado constitution. In a number of cases, the Colorado court has taken a broader approach than the U.S. Supreme Court. Colorado Chief Justice Luis D. Rovira said it is not that the Colorado high court is more liberal, but that, "in a few areas, such as equal protection of the laws, due process of law, and double jeopardy, we have been somewhat more expansive in our reading of the Colorado constitution."[12]

For example, in *People v. Sporleder* (Colorado, 1983), the defendant was found to have a constitutionally protected expectation of privacy in telephone numbers dialed on a home telephone. The Colorado Supreme Court found this privacy protection in the state constitutional proscription against unreasonable searches and seizures. This decision differed from a U.S. Supreme Court decision in 1979 which held that any subjective expectation of privacy in dialed telephone numbers, even from a home telephone, is not one society is prepared to recognize as "reasonable."

In another case, *People v. Oates* (Colorado, 1985), the Colorado Supreme Court held that the Colorado proscription against unreasonable searches and seizures protects a greater range of privacy interests than does its U.S. counterpart. Here the Colorado court departed from the U.S. Supreme Court's reasoning, finding that the presence of a beeper placed in a drum of acid used for the manufacture of methamphetamines infringed upon the defendant's constitutionally protected right against warrantless searches.

Figure 12. Major Rulings of the Colorado Supreme Court, 1981–91

- November 30, 1981—Admitting that it was bucking a nationwide trend, the court bans the use of lie-detector tests in criminal trials.

- January 31, 1983—The court rules police did not have probable cause to believe a crime had been committed when they stopped a man on the street with a shirt draped over a TV.

- September 6, 1983—The court overturns conviction of Russell Eugene Freeman, who confessed to killing a man and a woman in order to sell their cars to a police sting, ruling his confession was involuntary.

- July 8, 1984—The court rules that the confession of Francis Connelly, who walked up to a police officer and confessed to murder, could not be used as evidence against him.

- February 25, 1985—The court strikes down major portions of an anti-pornography law as unconstitutionally vague.

- June 23, 1986—In a 4–3 decision, the court says criminal defendants who take the witness stand in their own defense must first understand that they have the right to remain silent and that the right is waived ''voluntarily, knowingly, and intelligently.''

- June 29, 1987—In a unanimous decision, the court declares that minor defects in police search warrants do not necessarily make them invalid and says judges should take a ''common sense'' approach.

- February 8, 1988—Reversing a decision it handed down twelve years earlier, the court rules that military retirement pay is marital property subject to division in a divorce proceeding.

- July 19, 1988—In a unanimous decision, the court rules that Colorado employers who provide group health insurance must include pregnancy care coverage.

- May 15, 1989—The court votes unanimously to uphold a 1986 antipornography law.

- May 14, 1990—In a 4–3 vote, the court upholds the death penalty for convicted murderer Gary Lee Davis.

- May 29, 1990—The court orders the release of child molester Robert Thiret from prison after ruling the almost seven years spent behind bars completes his ten-year sentence when ''good time'' is included.

Figure 12.
(Continued)

• May 29, 1990—In a 4–3 decision, the court upholds the death sentence for Frank D. Rodriguez.

• September 24, 1990—The court rules that drugs sniffed out by a police dog at a pay-and-lock private storage area can be used as evidence.

• October 9, 1990—The court rules that Colorado counties have the authority to restrict all-nude entertainment.

• July 9, 1991—Because of 1988 amendments to Colorado's death penalty, the court rules the new law is unconstitutional.

• July 11, 1991—By a 4–3 vote, the court upholds a $115 million financial incentive to encourage United Airlines to build a $1 billion maintenance plant in Denver. (Despite the favorable ruling from the Colorado high court, United Airlines subsequently located the plant in Indianapolis, Indiana.)

(*Source: Rocky Mountain News,* August 4, 1991, p. 34.)

In 1991, in yet another instance of a more expansive Colorado interpretation, *Bock v. Westminster Mall,* the Colorado Supreme Court addressed the rights of an unincorporated political association to distribute political leaflets in the between-stores areas of a privately owned shopping center. Finding that there was government involvement in the mall and that the open spaces of the mall essentially operate as a public place, the Colorado Supreme Court held that the free-speech provision of the Colorado constitution prevented the shopping mall owner from excluding citizens engaged in nonviolent political "speech." Colorado's justices ruled in effect that the Colorado constitution provides greater protections of freedom of speech than does the First Amendment of the U.S. Constitution.

These rulings, and a number of similar ones, illustrate how the Colorado Supreme Court bases its decisions, especially in rights cases, on the state constitution rather than the U.S. Constitution.

Colorado Court of Appeals

The workload for the Colorado Supreme Court became so great in the late 1960s that in 1970 the Colorado Court of Appeals was created to hear appeals from lower courts. The Court of Appeals consists of sixteen judges who serve eight-year terms. This court was created solely to help ease the civil caseload on the crowded Supreme Court schedule. It is not a trial court. Although the decisions of the Court of Appeals can be appealed to the Colorado Supreme Court, such appeals are not made often. Only about 10 percent of the workload of the Colorado Supreme Court consists of hearing cases that have been appealed from the Colorado Court of Appeals.

The Colorado Court of Appeals has its own courtroom, which is located adjacent to the Supreme Court courtroom in the Judicial Building in Denver. Each judge has one law clerk and one secretary. They also are assisted by a small group of staff attorneys.

District Courts

Colorado is divided into twenty-two judicial districts. Each district must be a compact territory containing one or more counties, and judicial district lines must correspond to county lines. Six of Colorado's twenty-two judicial districts are composed of one county each (Adams, Boulder, Denver, Mesa, Pueblo, and Weld counties). The other sixteen districts contain between two and seven counties each.

Each district court has one or more judges who serve a six-year term. Even if there is only one district court judge, the chief justice of the state Supreme Court will appoint a chief judge to administer the district. The chief judge will supervise the district court as well as preside over his or her appropriate share of district court cases.

District courts in Colorado have original jurisdiction in criminal cases that are felonies (serious crimes for which a sentence of one year or more in the penitentiary may be imposed) and in civil cases involving more than $5,000. All civil cases involving mental health, divorce, child custody, adoption, juvenile delinquency, dependent and neglected children, and probate matters must originate in district courts.

The Colorado constitution endeavors to protect the district courts from undue meddling by the legislature. A change in judicial district boundary lines requires a two-thirds vote in each house of the legislature, as does any increase or decrease in the number of judges assigned to each district.

In each judicial district there is a district attorney elected by the voters of the district. The district attorney, or D.A., has the responsibility of prosecuting all violators of state law. Unlike judges in Colorado, who are insulated from partisan politics by the complex judicial nominating procedure, district attorneys run for office as Republicans or Democrats. In heavily populated judicial districts, the district attorney can appoint an appropriate number of assistant district attorneys, and these assistants are often (though not always) appointed on a partisan basis. The district attorneys are represented at the state capitol by their own lobbying organization, the Colorado District Attorneys' Council.

Is Colorado doing the right thing by electing D.A.'s in partisan elections? Some fear that partisan D.A.'s can become too political and start "throwing the book" at alleged criminals in an effort to boost their reelection chances. "We ought not to elect D.A.'s," observes former Justice Jean Dubofsky. "We ought to have an appointive process just as the U.S. government has for U.S. Attorneys."[13] On the other hand, appointed D.A.'s could turn into faceless bureaucrats unresponsive to the public's concerns.

County Courts

Each of Colorado's sixty-three counties has a county court with at least one judge. County courts try misdemeanors (minor crimes such as traffic offenses, loose dogs, and disturbing the peace) and handle minor civil suits (involving less than $5,000). Prior to 1975, county courts mainly handled traffic cases, but this work load was substantially reduced when the legislature passed a law permitting all but the most serious traffic fines to be paid by mail.

Only ten Colorado counties have more than one county court judge (Adams, Arapahoe, Boulder, Denver, El Paso, Jefferson, Larimer, Mesa, Pueblo, and Weld counties). The state legislature sets the number of county judges in each county except Denver. County court judges serve a four-year term.

In the larger counties in Colorado the county court judges are required to be lawyers, yet in some of the smaller counties only a high school diploma is required. This is because a number of rural counties are so small in population that a lawyer from the county is not always available to serve as county court judge. County judges who are not lawyers are required to attend classes on the duties and functioning of the county court conducted under the supervision of the state Supreme Court.

County court decisions can be appealed to the district court and from there to the Colorado Court of Appeals and the Colorado Supreme Court.

Municipal Courts

Cities and towns in Colorado may create municipal courts to try cases involving municipal ordinances. Similar to county courts, municipal courts try traffic cases, although serious traffic offenses, such as drunk driving or hit-and-run driving, must be tried in county court.

Similar to judges in small rural counties, municipal court judges are not required by state law to be lawyers. In the larger cities, however, city laws have been passed requiring that all municipal court judges have a law degree. State law requires that municipal judges be paid a salary rather than a fee for each case handled. This is to prevent municipal court judges from being tempted to increase their pay by encouraging the police to arrest more citizens and thus bring more cases (and more fees for the judge) into court.

Municipal courts are the lowest courts. Decisions by municipal court judges can be appealed to the county court, and from there to the district court, the Court of Appeals, and the Colorado Supreme Court.

Specialized Courts

There are a number of courts in Colorado that have been created for specialized purposes:

Small Claims Courts. Each county court has a small claims court where trials involving small sums of money (less than $1,000) are held as inexpensively and rapidly as possible. There is no jury, and neither side in the dispute is represented by a lawyer. Evening and Saturday sessions are often held to make the small claims court as convenient and accessible to the public as possible. Parties to a dispute file all their own papers (with the assistance of court clerks) and present their own cases to the judge for decision.

Water Courts. Colorado has had water courts since 1969. The purpose of these courts is to simplify the process of establishing water rights and to keep more accurate water rights records. There are seven water courts in the state, one for each major river drainage basin. Each water court has a "water judge" who is appointed by the Colorado Supreme Court from among the district court judges in the particular area. Water judges and the appropriate water records are located in Alamosa (Rio Grande), Durango (Las Animas River), Glenwood Springs (Colorado River), Greeley (South Platte River), Montrose (Uncompahgre River), Pueblo (Arkansas River), and Steamboat Springs (Yampa River).

Denver Juvenile Court. Because it is the largest city in the state, Denver has three specialized courts that carry out functions that are handled by the district courts elsewhere in the state. One of the most important is the Denver Juvenile Court, which tries all cases in Denver involving juvenile delinquency, adoption, child neglect, and child support. Denver was one of the first cities in the United States to experiment with a juvenile court. Judge Ben Lindsey, who became a legend throughout the country for his progressive values and innovations, instituted the Denver Juvenile Court in 1907 as a creative social experiment. He came up with ways of rehabilitating young offenders other than sending them off to regular jails, which he knew were schools for crime. He set up separate jails for juveniles and spoke out against child labor practices. His ideas spread rapidly throughout Colorado and the remainder of the United States.[14] Unfortunately, the Ku Klux Klan targeted Lindsey, and he was defeated in the 1928 election.

Denver Probate Court. A second specialized court in Denver is the Denver Probate Court, which administers the settling of estates of deceased persons. The court proves wills, appoints and supervises conservators of estates, and provides guardianship for funds inherited by minors.

Denver Superior Court. In cities and counties other than Denver, county court decisions are appealed to the district court. In Denver, however, there is a special court, the Denver Superior Court, to hear appeals from the Denver courts. The Denver Superior Court consists of one judge appointed for a six-year term. Decisions by the Denver Superior Court are appealed directly to the Colorado Court of Appeals and the Colorado Supreme Court, rather than to the Denver District Court.

PUBLIC DEFENDER

One of the most important problems in state court systems is the provision of lawyers to indigent persons accused of crime. An indigent person is someone who cannot provide for his or her own support and thus does not have funds available to hire and pay an attorney. Because the state and local governments pay prosecutors to prosecute criminal cases aggressively, it is not regarded as fair to send a person of limited means into court without a paid attorney who will be as aggressive as the prosecutor in providing a defense. Moreover, the U.S. Supreme Court ruled in the 1962 case of *Gideon v. Wainwright* that virtually every indigent defendant has a basic right to defense counsel.[15]

Prior to 1970, Colorado used court-appointed lawyers to represent defendants who could not afford to hire their own lawyers. Court-appointed lawyers received low payment for their services, and thus young and inexperienced lawyers generally represented indigent defendants. Also, low pay often prevented court-appointed lawyers from devoting sufficient time to individual cases to mount an effective defense.

In 1970 Colorado established the Office of the State Public Defender, an agency of the Judicial Department. The office is headquartered in Denver, but there are a number of assistant public defenders located at regional offices throughout Colorado. Public defenders are paid full-time salaries and thus can spend all their working hours representing indigent defendants. The State Public Defender is appointed by the Colorado Supreme Court to a five-year term of office.

Public defenders are brought into criminal cases either at the request of the defendant or by order of the court. Customarily public defenders handle felony cases, yet they can represent people accused of misdemeanors and also indigent youths in juvenile court. The public defender determines whether a particular defendant is indigent and thus qualified for free representation, but the decision can be appealed to the courts.

Public defenders are generally viewed as doing a fairly good job on behalf of those without the means to hire their own attorneys. One result of this system is that nearly every criminal defendant who wants an appeal gets one, which is another reason why criminal cases take up so much of the judicial system's time.

GENDER BIAS

In 1988 Chief Justice Joseph R. Quinn appointed a volunteer committee of twenty-six persons to study possible sexual discrimination in the Colorado court system. The Colorado Gender Bias Task Force specifically addressed the question of whether women were treated differently from men in court in any of their contemporary roles—as judges, lawyers, employees of the court, defendants in criminal trials, parties to civil suits and domestic relations cases (divorce and child custody), and as victims of crime, particularly domestic violence.

The task force found that much of the information on gender bias in Colorado courts is "conversational" and "anecdotal." Stories of gender bias exist, yet many of them are difficult to document. In those cases where the task force endeavored to measure the extent of gender bias, it was often difficult to verify that the differences in treatment of men and women were really the result of gender bias and not other factors.

Preliminary results of the Gender Bias Task Force study revealed that 19 percent of judges in Colorado are women, a figure that puts Colorado in the forefront of the fifty states. This was considered particularly significant in view of the fact that approximately 20 percent of all lawyers in Colorado are women; thus there is as high a percentage of women judges as there is of women lawyers.

The task force established that the most frequent complaints concerning gender bias in Colorado courts occurred in child custody cases. Ironically, in many instances divorcing fathers and mothers had the same complaint. The fathers complained that courts tend to exclude men as fit parents for young children. The mothers complained that courts tend to give young children to the mother, thus saddling her with the demanding and time-consuming task of raising young children. "The task force had to struggle with the difficult question of whether gender bias was producing custody decisions that put small children with the mother or whether the courts were simply reflecting the parenting values of the larger society."[16]

Another instance of apparent gender bias was the tendency of judges to give lighter sentences to women than those given to men who had committed the same crime. Lighter sentences were particularly given to women who were caring for small children. "When confronted with this fact of lighter sentences for women with children, however, judges defended the practice as the desirable thing to do under the circumstances."[17]

The Gender Bias Task Force found instances where concern for treating the sexes evenly still led to gender bias. Courts assumed that women in divorce cases would have equal earning power with men. In reality, however, the women often have much lower earning power, mainly because women more frequently stay home with children and thus are absent from the work force for a number of years. Courts often gave the former wife and the former husband equal financial responsibility in a divorce case, but the financial burdens would fall more heavily on the former wife due to her lower earning power.

In contrast, courts tended to give more money to men than women if they lost time at work due to an injury. The tacit assumption appeared to be that a man is worth more on the job than a woman. On the other hand, women tended to receive larger damage awards than men if they were disfigured in an accident. In child custody cases, a woman often was seen as an unfit parent if she was living with a man to whom she was not married. There was less of a tendency to see a man as an unfit parent if he was living with a woman to whom he was not married.

The Gender Bias Task Force concluded its report by recommending that all court personnel learn to recognize gender bias—both in themselves and in others—and to work to reduce it whenever possible.

JUDICIAL INNOVATIONS

Because of the rapid population growth in Colorado following World War II, the state's court system has struggled with a heavy caseload in recent decades, resulting in overworked judges and long delays in cases coming to trial. The legislature has increased appropriations for the judicial system and authorized the hiring of additional judges, yet the improvements always seem to run behind the increases in the caseload. "These are chronic problems that will always be there," stated a recent chief justice. "The Colorado court system has no choice but to live with limited resources."[18]

In recent years, by order of the chief justice of the Colorado Supreme Court, criminal cases have been given top priority in the state court system. Civil suits have been given second priority, and domestic relations cases (divorce and child custody) are the third priority. Under this system, state courts are keeping up with criminal caseloads yet are experiencing delays and backup in bringing civil cases and domestic relations cases to trial. Domestic relations cases, being of lowest priority, are particularly liable to being "put off" by the overcrowded state court system.[19]

As a result of the heavy caseload pressure, the Colorado court system has been experimenting with a number of innovations, most of them seeking inventive and judicially sound systems for more rapid and efficient processing of court cases.

Arbitration

One plan for reducing the civil caseload in Colorado is mandatory arbitration. In civil suits of $50,000 or less, the parties involved are required to present their case to a professional arbitrator who listens to both sides and then renders a settlement. If either party is unhappy with the arbitrator's decision, a trial can be requested. There is a possible penalty, however, for appealing an arbitrator's decision. If the trial does not change the amount of the financial settlement by at least 10 percent, the party requesting the trial has to pay all of the expenses involved.

Mandatory arbitration of civil suits under $50,000 has been tried in eight of the twenty-two judicial districts in Colorado. Hundreds of civil cases have been handled by arbitration, and no more than 10 percent of that total have been appealed to a trial. "Mandatory arbitration is an idea that is taking hold and starting to have an effect on reducing the civil caseload," said Justice Joseph R. Quinn. "It has been successful enough that we intend to pursue the system further."[20]

In civil suits over $50,000, the parties can, if they wish, go to voluntary arbitration. There has been a major increase in voluntary arbitration in recent years, especially since the cost of business litigation has skyrocketed. In voluntary arbitrations, disputes are resolved by an adversary hearing, yet without the pretrial and trial trappings and expense of a lawsuit. Arbitrations are usually settled in a few months, and the only prehearing discovery permitted is an exchange of documents. This cuts costs enormously.

There are several ways that voluntary arbitration is different from courtroom litigation. First, the parties involved have some control over who serves as the arbitrator. Instead of selecting a person with legal experience, such as a former judge or attorney, either or both parties may prefer an arbitrator with industry experience or technical knowledge bearing on the dispute. Second, arbitrators do not have to follow technical courtroom rules of evidence and do not have to be strict in applying federal, state, or local law in rendering their decisions. Third, arbitrations are conducted in private. The news media and other members of the public can be excluded, in contrast with courtroom trials, which are public events and subject to close press scrutiny.[21]

But some judicial system watchers are concerned about the increase in arbitrations, both mandatory and voluntary. They worry that as corporate and general business interests shift away from the district courts, this segment of the general public will be less inclined to work on behalf of a quality public court system with the needed pay and personnel to do its job.

Mediation

Mediation is an additional system for expediting court work and reducing delays. Under mediation, both parties voluntarily meet with a mediator and work to solve their differences as amicably—and cheaply—as possible. No testimony is taken, and rather than competing with each other, the parties to the dispute are encouraged to cooperate.[22] Mediation is most likely to be used in divorce cases as a noncombative way of settling alimony, child custody, and property settlement issues. Under mediation, the court abstains from arbitrarily dividing children and property between divorcing couples, encouraging the former husband and wife to work things out on their own.

Mediation customarily involves a neutral third party, often a former judge or a professional facilitator, who meets with the parties, with or without their lawyers, to attempt to find a mutually satisfactory, nonbinding resolution of a dispute. A compromise of both parties' original positions is usually the end result.

Mediation has proven successful in 70 percent of the cases in which it has been tried. When mediation fails, the parties involved take their case to court for settlement. Although the methodology for mediation has been in place in the Colorado court system for some time, the state legislature has refused to provide funds for this important court reform. In view of this fact, the Colorado court system has considered having the costs of mediation paid for by the parties involved rather than by the state.[23]

Prison Overcrowding

Similar to most other states, Colorado continually faces the problem of severe overcrowding in its prisons. In 1985 the state legislature, reacting to a surge in citizen concern about increasing crime rates, passed laws providing for mandatory prison sentences and longer sentences for persons convicted of violent crimes. The result was more convicts going to prison and staying for a longer period of time. The prison system soon was overloaded and overcrowded with violent offenders.[24] From 1985 to 1993 Colorado went from slightly over 3,500 prisoners in state prisons to nearly 10,000. Moreover, the average length of stay rose from 32 months in 1985 to an average stay of almost 57 months in the early 1990s.

In Colorado's Fourth Judicial District (El Paso and Teller counties), sixty convicted felons were being held in the county jails in 1990 because there was no room for them in the state penitentiary in Canon City. At the same time, over four hundred Colorado prisoners had to be housed temporarily in a prison in Missouri because there was no space for them in the Colorado prison system.

One solution being tried in Colorado in the early 1990s to relieve prison overcrowding is more effective use of probation and probation officers. At the time of sentencing, judges can elect to place a convicted felon on probation rather than sending him or her to state prison. A prisoner on probation is required to check in periodically with a probation officer. In most cases a convict on probation also is required to refrain from destructive behavior, such as taking drugs or drinking too much alcohol.

In most states the probation program is administered by the governor.

Colorado, however, is one of a small number of states that have placed criminal probation in the state court system. In the late 1980s Joseph R. Quinn, then chief justice of the Colorado Supreme Court, ordered probation administrators in four of Colorado's twenty-two judicial districts to begin experimenting with ways to make probation a more widely used and more effective alternative to prison sentences.

One of the most successful new probation techniques being tested is *risk-needs assessment*. Under this program, probationers are extensively tested and interviewed by probation officers and then evaluated according to their "risk" to society, that is, the extent to which they are likely to commit a violent crime against the public in the future. Probationers are then classified into one of three risk categories—maximum risk, medium risk, and minimum risk.

This classification system enables the probation office to assign extra time and attention to maximum-risk probationers, thereby reducing the likelihood that they will commit a serious crime while on probation. Judges, knowing that maximum-risk probationers will be supervised more closely, thus are more likely to give probation in place of a prison sentence.

At the same time probationers are evaluated in terms of risk, they are also analyzed in terms of their personal needs. Probationers with alcohol problems are placed into alcohol consumption control programs. Probationers with drug problems are placed in drug control programs, such as methadone substitution programs for heroin addicts.

Even more innovative, and still in the testing stage, is *intensive-supervision probation*. This experimental program doubles or triples the amount of supervision given to maximum-risk probationers. Instead of checking in with the probation officer once a week, intensive supervision probationers are required to check in two or three times a week. Instead of being visited at home an average of once a month by the probation officer, they are visited at home once a week, often in the late evening to make certain the probationer is conforming to the standard 9 P.M. to 5 A.M. "at home" curfew. Similar to risk-needs assessment, intensive-supervision probation was designed to permit the sentencing judge to place on probation convicted criminals who would otherwise be sent to prison.[25]

Judicial Performance Evaluation Commissions

When Colorado judges come up for reelection and run against their own record, the voting public receives little information on how the various judges have performed on the bench. Retention elections, moreover, usually generate little interest and low voter turnout, although at least twenty judges at the district and county court levels have been removed by voters by means of retention elections since 1968. To remedy this situation, the Colorado legislature passed legislation in 1988 establishing judicial performance evaluation commissions for both the statewide courts and the twenty-two district courts.

Each commission consists of ten members (four lawyers and six non-lawyers)—three appointed by the governor, three appointed by the chief justice of the Colorado Supreme Court, two appointed by the president of the state Senate, and two appointed by the speaker of the state House of Representatives. The commission studies and evaluates the record of a judge coming up for reelection. Judges are rated on such qualities as integrity, preparation, knowledge of law, handling of proceedings, and sentencing practices. Commissioners interview jurors, prosecutors, defense attorneys, and court personnel.

The goals of judicial performance evaluation are twofold: first, to provide persons voting on the retention of justices and judges with fair, responsible, and constructive information about judicial performance, and second, to provide justices and judges with useful feedback on their own performance for the purposes of self-improvement.

The judicial performance evaluation commission can make one of three recommendations—FOR retention of the judge, AGAINST retention, or NO OPINION. Although NO OPINION was not intended as a negative evaluation of a judge, early tests of the program indicated that voters were interpreting NO OPINION as a somewhat negative evaluation.

Prior to the formulation of a final narrative profile and recommendation, the appropriate commission on judicial performance supplies the judge under evaluation with a draft of its evaluation. The judge then has the opportunity to meet with the commission or at least to respond to its draft within a few days. If such a meeting takes place or a reasonable response is made, the commission may revise its evaluation and recommendation.

Judicial performance evaluation commissions represent a serious attempt to have more realistic judicial retention elections. Beginning with the November 1990 elections, the public received more information about the various judges, and the information was provided by a diverse and professional group of commission members.[26] In 1992, for example, voters were urged to retain seventy sitting judges but to reject at least three judges. Judicial performance evaluation commissions are a useful addition to maintaining a quality judiciary in Colorado, though some critics urge that these commissions should release to the public their specific rankings and not just their general ratings.[27]

Colorado's "Make My Day" Law

Colorado lawmakers attracted national publicity for another controversial innovation in 1985. They enacted legislation to provide protection from prosecution or civil suits to homeowners who might use force, even deadly physical force, against intruders into their homes who they believe are committing or intend to commit a crime. In many ways this was merely an effort to strengthen existing laws. But prosecutors and the Colorado District Attorneys' Council lobbied against it. The National Rifle Association lobbied for it. Governor Richard Lamm tried to get prosecutors and conservative legislators to fashion a compromise—which they eventually did.[28]

The nickname "Make My Day" law was given to the "Home Protection" bill and gave it a notoriety it probably did not deserve.[29] It also polarized opinion toward the bill. Still, the legislation had substantive consequences as well as high symbolic value. The symbolism was clear: it was an effort by legislators to communicate to law-abiding homeowners that they, too, have rights, and that too much attention in the courts and elsewhere had been paid to the rights of criminals.

But the legislation, which plainly had wide popular appeal, has raised a number of important issues: Does a homeowner have the right to use force against uninvited law enforcement officials? What force can a homeowner use against unarmed, harmless, or fleeing intruders? This Colorado law differs from laws elsewhere in that the law provides that property crimes, not just violent crimes, are grounds for use of force, shades perhaps of the state's frontier heritage. These and other concerns, often raised by prosecutors, have led to suggestions for modifying the Colorado "Make My Day" law.[30]

CONCLUSION

Colorado has a reasonably progressive state judicial system. The statewide reorganization of the court system and the Missouri Plan for appointing judges, both adopted in the 1960s, have given Colorado a state judiciary that is generally admired.

In the three decades from the 1960s to the 1990s, Colorado has continued to approach judicial problems in an imaginative and experimental fashion. Whether it is studying gender bias in the courtroom, working to make proba-

254 Judges and Justice

tion a more successful alternative to a prison sentence, or searching for new ways of measuring judicial performance, Colorado can be viewed as having one of the more innovative state judicial systems.

The Bureau of Justice Statistics in the U.S. Department of Justice reported that in a comparison of the fifty states, Colorado ranked sixteenth in per capita spending for criminal and civil justice. In 1988 the Centennial State spent more than $212 per Coloradan on criminal justice operations, including prosecutors, courts, and prisons. For many citizens that is too much. But whether Coloradans like it or not, they will have to pay judges more. The state will also need more prison capacity, and, most important, the state must find better ways of eradicating the root sources of crime.

The judicial system and the quality of justice in Colorado are continually being tested. The reforms of the past generation do not make the Colorado judicial system perfect. Nothing will accomplish that lofty task. Yet the reforms have made the system work better in recent years.

CHAPTER ELEVEN

The Important Role of
Local Government

State government and state politics get the lion's share of attention in state newspapers as well as in this book. Yet there are 1,934 other governments in Colorado, and the number grows. In addition to the state government and, of course, the large presence of the federal government, there are 63 counties, 267 cities and towns, and at least 1,428 special districts for libraries, schools, fire departments, and other services. There are some Native American tribal governments as well.

Does Colorado have too many local governments? Many people believe it does. Yet local and county governments enjoy staunch loyalty from constituents. For the most part, the local governments are here to stay, even though they are constitutionally dependent on the state government. As noted in chapter 5, Colorado citizens look at their local governments in a more favorable light than their state and national governments. Coloradans think of the local governments as having been first in the state and consider them more responsive.

The history of governmental life in Colorado has been a history of strong, tenacious local governments. They generally perform the same services in this state as are performed elsewhere, yet somehow the political clout of local officials (mayors, city council members, sheriffs, district attorneys, and county commissioners) is stronger in Colorado. These officials and their lobbyists in the statehouse are often viewed as one of the most influential voices in state lawmaking. Further, in recent years, program cuts and tax cuts at both the state and federal levels have greatly increased the responsibilities and tax burdens of local levels of government.

Gold was discovered in July of 1858 near the area where Cherry Creek flows into the South Platte River. Within weeks the town of St. Charles was organized on the east bank of Cherry Creek, and its founders hurried back to Kansas Territory to promote the new community and gain a charter for the town from the territorial legislature. Thus, close behind the gold prospectors and miners came those who hoped to profit from the new gold discoveries by organizing and, they hoped, controlling local government in this new frontier.

By October of 1858, barely three months after the first gold strike, the rival town of Auraria was organized on the west bank of Cherry Creek. Then, in mid November of 1858, General William Larimer arrived in the area with a group of Kansas men, several of whom carried commissions as officers of Arapahoe County. The Kansas territorial legislature had created Arapahoe County on paper in 1855, but General Larimer and his party were the first group to succeed in organizing a county government. Arapahoe County at this time encompassed a vast area, all of Kansas Territory west of the 103rd meridian.

To solidify their position, Larimer and his friends decided to acquire control of the St. Charles town site. A man left to guard the fledgling community later claimed the Larimer party convinced him to surrender the property by getting him drunk. Whatever happened, General Larimer took control of the east side of Cherry Creek and renamed the town for the territorial governor of Kansas, General James W. Denver. A short time later, Auraria and Denver were combined to form what is now the city of Denver.

Most of the members of Larimer's group, particularly the would-be officials of Arapahoe County, had come to the Cherry Creek area gold diggings, not to mine gold, but to promote a town, organize a county government, and hold office. They had come to "mine the miners" rather than do any of the risky and tiring work of prospecting and digging themselves.[1] One important result of their political inclination was the domination of Denver and the Denver region over Colorado government and politics, which has remained, with only an occasional minor challenge, ever since.

FRONTIER GOVERNMENT

Because gold was first discovered on the Front Range of the Rocky Mountains, most of the new settlements in what is now Colorado were in Kansas Territory. Thus the central government was remote and also largely ineffective. In some areas "mining districts" were organized, which were formal governments, with written constitutions and elaborate systems for legalizing mining claims. Since water was an essential part of both agriculture and mining, water rights were also established.

In the valleys, "claim clubs" were organized to protect agricultural land claims until the federal government could clear the Native American title to the land and offer it for sale at public auction. The El Paso Claim Club, organized in August of 1859, established and sought to protect claims on eighty square miles in the Fountain Creek and Monument Creek area near present-day Colorado Springs. "Claim clubs" had constitutions, elected officers, and provided "due process of law" in settling claim disputes.

In immediately setting up formal local governments, often with written constitutions, the first miners, merchants, and farmers in Colorado were simply carrying on a great American tradition. Beginning with the Pilgrims, who negotiated and signed their Mayflower Compact before landing on Plymouth Rock in 1620, Americans have tended to rely on written constitutions to structure democratic and representative forms of government, even in frontier areas. Exactly as their predecessors had done when the East Coast and the Middle West were first being populated, the citizens who rushed to Colorado following the first gold strikes near Cherry Creek set up self-manufactured governments that were, in most respects, quite democratic.[2]

LEGAL LOCAL GOVERNMENT

None of these instant local governments would be legitimate, however, until the U.S. Congress passed a law making Colorado a territory. An early resident described the situation: "This Rocky Mountain Country . . . has received just about as much legislative aid at Washington as the Fe Gee Islanders. No mail service for the next twelve months that can be relied on; no extinguishment of the [Native American] title; no territorial organization, and, in fact, no sort of governmental recognition for the advancement of our interests here . . . so we are compelled to adopt the squatter sovereignty doctrine, making our own laws."[3]

Colorado became a territory early in 1861. A territorial legislature was elected, which divided Colorado into seventeen counties during its first legislative session. Legal local government was thus underway in Colorado. When the territory became a state in 1876, provisions for local government, both counties and cities, were included in the state constitution.

It is important to appreciate that local government existed in Colorado, in the form of "mining districts" and "claim clubs," before the territorial government and, subsequently, the state government came into existence. As a result, Colorado citizens formed the habit of relying more on local units of government than on state government for providing local and regional services. In 1986 Colorado ranked forty-ninth among the fifty states and the District of Columbia in terms of state taxes per $1,000 of personal income. Colorado ranked sixth, however, in terms of local taxes (city and county) per $1,000 of personal income.[4] Coloradans have long done as much as possible at the local level and as little as possible at the state level.

Local government plays a large role in Colorado, and with the federal government also playing such a prominent role, state government is reduced to a lesser role in Colorado than in most other states. As one state government official in Colorado expressed this idea: "In one sense, there really is no such thing as a state of Colorado. It is more a collection of powerful local governments. One additional reason for this is that Colorado is a large and geographically difficult state. State legislators mainly come to the capitol in Denver to represent their local governments [city councils, county commissioners, local school boards, etc.] rather than to strongly pursue statewide concerns."[5]

GOVERNMENT OF DENVER

"City Hall War"

In the early days the Colorado legislature exerted strong control over the capital city of Denver, where the city administration was an integral part of the state government. The governor, not the mayor of Denver, appointed the members of the various boards and commissions that set administrative policy for the city.

In March of 1894 reform-minded Governor Davis Waite inaugurated a campaign to reduce what he considered to be an excessive amount of drinking, gambling, and prostitution in Denver. He began by firing two members of the Denver Fire and Police Board, a three-member administrative board that operated the Denver fire and police departments and issued liquor licenses. Waite argued that the governor could fire board members because the governor had the power to appoint them. The two fired board members felt differently, however, and refused to give up their jobs. They locked themselves in their offices in the Denver city hall, daring Governor Waite to remove them forcefully.

Soon the city hall was surrounded by supporters of the two defiant board members. Many people in Denver, including some prominent businessmen, profited from illicit activities such as gambling and prostitution and did not want to see them curtailed. Many supporters were armed with pistols and rifles and appeared to be ready to fire at anyone who tried to get the two board members out of city hall.

Not to be intimidated, Governor Waite ordered the state militia to move on city hall and enforce his removal order. The troops dutifully marched into Denver and pointed Gatling guns and small cannon at Denver's city hall. The situation was further complicated by large crowds of onlookers who came downtown to see what was going to happen. For an entire day, the two heavily armed groups stared warily at each other and waited.

Under pressure from city leaders not to turn downtown Denver into a bloody battlefield, Governor Waite ordered the troops to withdraw, ending Denver's "City Hall War" without a single shot being fired. Waite then appealed the case to the Colorado Supreme Court, which ruled the governor had the right to fire the two board members but had no power to remove them from city hall with military force. Faced with a court order, the two board members relinquished their posts. Governor Waite then appointed reform-minded replacements. The incident successfully defended the power of the state of Colorado to control local affairs in Denver.[6]

Urban Reform

By 1904, however, conditions in Denver were again producing public outrage. Gambling houses and saloons flourished. On election day, a corrupt political machine allegedly was buying the votes that kept its supporters in office. A major cause of the trouble, reformers believed, was that the governor and the state legislators continued to have direct control over the bureaus and governing boards of the municipality. City reform leaders then devised a series of proposals to separate Denver's government from state government and make the new city government simple and streamlined.

The first step in the plan was a constitutional amendment giving Denver the right to establish a home-rule city government. Instead of having their city structured and run by the state legislature, the voters of Denver would write and adopt a city charter creating their own unique form of city government. The proposed amendment would give Denver a wide range of local powers, enough so that the people of Denver would look to their city government, rather than state government, to solve problems and provide a large number of basic services.

The second step was to make Denver a single city and county. At that time Denver was located in Arapahoe County. Some local government functions were carried out by the city and some by the county. The reformers decided to reduce confusion and eliminate overlapping governmental jurisdictions by creating one body politic, the City and County of Denver. Arapahoe County would continue to exist, but as a suburban and rural county outside of Denver.

The third step in the reform plan was to give Denver strong annexation powers. As new neighborhoods developed immediately outside the city limits in the future, Denver would be able to expand its city limits and annex these new neighborhoods into the city.

In a stunning victory for progressive local government, all three of the reforms were adopted at the 1904 general election. The principle of home rule for local government, although limited to Denver at first, became firmly established in the Colorado constitution. Denver would no longer be directly under the thumb of state government. A subsequent constitutional amendment extended strong home-rule powers to Colorado cities other than Denver, and over the years all the major cities in the state adopted their own city charters and became home-rule cities.

The adoption of the constitutional amendment granting home-rule powers to Denver in 1904 probably was the most significant event in the history of local government in Colorado. It firmly established municipal home rule as the norm, rather than the exception. This broad grant of power, later extended to almost every city in the state, put Colorado cities in a position to be major policymakers and service providers. Equally important, Colorado cities were given broad powers to raise revenue through property taxes and sales taxes, thus enabling them to raise the money required to make government really effective at the local level.

Center of an Urbanized State

People, including many from Colorado, often think of Colorado in terms of beautiful mountain ranges and spacious prairies. Their image of the state is one of freedom and "wide open spaces" in an essentially rural setting. In many ways, however, Colorado is one of the more urbanized states in the country. The vast majority of its citizens live in relatively large and densely populated cities and suburbs, mainly in the Denver-Boulder metropolitan area.

The Denver-Boulder metropolitan area consists of six counties—Adams,

Arapahoe, Boulder, Douglas, Jefferson, and the City and County of Denver. In recent years, the population of Denver has remained stable while the population of the surrounding suburban counties has been growing rapidly. If post–World War II trends continue, by the year 2000 Arapahoe County and Jefferson County *each* will have a larger population than the City and County of Denver.

The City and County of Denver

Similar to large cities in many states, Denver has unique status in Colorado local government. It is the only combined city and county government in the state (making it similar to Philadelphia and San Francisco, which are also simultaneously cities and counties). Instead of having city officials and county officials, Denver has just one set of officials and administrators. Although technically local government is created and controlled by state government, Denver's unique status is provided for in the Colorado constitution. As a result, Denver's basic structure and home-rule powers cannot be easily changed by the legislature. In fact, more than five pages of the Colorado constitution are devoted to setting up the structure and home-rule governing powers of the City and County of Denver.

Because it is a city and a county government combined, Denver has more authority and power than any other municipal government in the state. Unlike other cities in Colorado, Denver does not have to deal with, or compete with, a separate county government. It is the only city in Colorado that has virtually all local government functions (except for schools) under its direct control.

The Denver city charter provides for a mayor-council form of city government—which means it has a strong mayor who is separately elected by the voters and not selected from among city council members, as in many city governments. The legislative power is vested in a thirteen-member city council, of which eleven members are elected from single-member districts and two members are elected by the entire city. As of 1990, city council members received an annual salary of $28,000.

The mayor of Denver is elected by the entire city to a four-year term of office. The mayor is the undisputed head of the city's executive branch. The only other elected official is the auditor, whose duties are limited to auditing city accounts. The mayor has total control over the executive budget, and the votes of nine of the thirteen council members (a two-thirds vote) are required to change an item in the mayor's budget. These strong budgetary powers lead most observers to characterize Denver as having a "strong mayor" form of city government.

City elections are nonpartisan in Denver, so there are no party primaries. Republicans and Democrats alike run against each other in the primary, and the top two finishers, regardless of party affiliation, run against each other in the general election. If one candidate gets a majority of the vote in the primary, he or she is elected, and a runoff election is not held.

The mayor of Denver is almost always a Democrat, and Democrats customarily enjoy a large majority on the city council. Periodically, however, a strong Republican candidate comes along and makes a serious challenge to the Democratic party for control of the mayor's office. Because 60 percent of the residents of Colorado live in the Denver metropolitan area, the mayor of Denver can become a highly visible and influential figure in Colorado politics. In recent decades, however, no mayors or former mayors of Denver have run for governor.

Leadership Initiatives

Denver has long been the largest and most densely populated city in Colorado. Not surprisingly, it is usually the first local government in the state to encounter "urban problems." Typical are deteriorating roads and bridges, high crime rates in downtown neighborhoods, and hot debates over whether to provide city subsidies in order to attract new industry. Denver is also usually the first local government to propose solutions to such problems. As one member of the city council expressed it: "Denver is on the cutting edge of city problems in Colorado. For instance, Denver was the first city in the state to identify an air pollution problem from people burning wood in home fireplaces. Our law controlling wood burning in home fireplaces was the first one in Colorado and was soon copied by many other cities and counties in the state."[7]

Due to its historical role as a powerful local government in Colorado, Denver traditionally has taken the initiative in providing various public facilities that serve all of the state rather than just Denver. The Denver Convention Center, Mile High Stadium (where professional football is played), McNichols Arena (where professional basketball is played and rock concerts are performed), Coors Stadium (where professional baseball is played), and Stapleton Airport (the hub airport for the entire Rocky Mountain West) are all examples of projects initiated by the city and county of Denver that benefit all of Colorado.

Another example of Denver's leadership role in the growth and development of Colorado is the new Denver airport. By the mid 1980s the city's Stapleton Airport had become one of the busiest regional airports in the United States. Unable to be expanded because of an adjacent federal government facility, the Rocky Mountain Arsenal, Stapleton was becoming overcrowded, particularly on bad weather days.

Denver officials took the lead in developing the new Denver International Airport (opened in late 1993) for the region. Located twenty miles northeast of Stapleton Airport on vacant land in Adams County, the new airport has sufficient space to accommodate anticipated air-traffic growth in the Denver area during the early years of the twenty-first century. Although both the federal and state governments contributed funds to begin the construction of the new airport, the major planning, financing, and promoting of the project, the largest public works project in Colorado history, were all undertaken by Denver.

The "City-State" of Denver

With 60 percent of the population of Colorado living in the Denver metropolitan area, and with Denver providing such strong governmental leadership in the metropolitan area, it could be argued that Colorado is not really a state but is actually the "city-state" of Denver. This viewpoint holds that the state government does not provide leadership—it is Denver that decides what will and will not be happening of significance in the Centennial State.

A 1990 editorial in the the *Denver Post* waxed ecstatic over the leadership provided to Colorado by the citizens of metropolitan Denver. The newspaper noted that the following projects, most of which would benefit the entire state, were approved by voters and elected officials in the Denver area:

Planning and building the world's largest airport

Constructing one of the finest convention facilities in America

Financing major improvements in the city's main library and its branches

Providing tax funds to support museums, the city zoo, community theaters, musical groups, and other artistic organizations throughout the metropolitan area

Authorizing a major bond issue to finance better roads and public facilities

Agreeing to pay a metropolitanwide sales tax to build a major league baseball stadium for Denver's new National League team, the Colorado Rockies

Attracting the nation's best retailers into a massive new regional mall

Working hard to clean up the air, which previously had been known as some of the most polluted in the United States

Investing nearly $200 million in the Denver core city school system.

With the boosterism expected of a hometown newspaper, the *Denver Post* concluded: "No other city [and its suburbs] in the nation has so dramatic a record of believing in itself."[8]

Metropolitan Problems

Denver was given annexation powers when it was first created in the early twentieth century. Metropolitan population growth was so rapid, however, that by the early 1960s more than half the residents of the Denver area lived in surrounding suburbs. In many cases these suburban populations were living in incorporated cities, such as Arvada, Aurora, Boulder, Englewood, Evergreen, Golden, Lakewood, Littleton, and Westminster, which were immune from being annexed by Denver.

Denver thus came to develop what are known as "metropolitan problems": the problems that occur when a central city is called upon to solve regional economic and social problems yet has no way to force surrounding suburban communities to help pay for their solution.

By the 1960s Denver had significant numbers of minorities (primarily blacks and Hispanics) living within the city limits, but the surrounding suburbs were predominantly Anglo. Further, groups that required expensive city services, such as elderly persons with health problems and unmarried mothers with small children, were concentrated in Denver, severely burdening the city's social service agencies. Out in the suburbs, however, most of the people moving in were married couples with solid incomes who required relatively few services and could easily pay property and sales taxes.

The metropolitan situation in Denver became more complicated in the late 1960s and early 1970s when United States courts ordered school busing to achieve racial and ethnic balance in the Denver public schools. Since the Denver school district is coterminous with the City and County of Denver, this meant that there would be school busing within Denver itself, but there would not be school busing in the surrounding suburbs or between Denver and its surrounding suburbs.

Many Denver residents, upset at the prospect of having their children bused out of their residential neighborhood to more distant schools, solved the problem by moving out of the city into one of the surrounding suburbs, where school busing was not required. The net result of court-ordered school busing in Denver, therefore, was to accelerate the movement of middle-class families with school-age children to the suburbs.

In the early 1970s, a citizen-initiated constitutional amendment was passed by Colorado voters. Now known as Poundstone One, it required a favorable vote of the people living in an area before that area could be annexed to Denver. Because many suburban dwellers had come to associate Denver with unwanted big-city problems, the likelihood of those residents voting to annex themselves to Denver was low. In effect, the adoption of Poundstone One put an end to Denver's ability to annex its surrounding suburbs.[9]

There is one way Denver can still annex, however. If a single property owner, or a small group of property owners, agrees to be annexed by Denver, then the annexation can take place. In some cases, owners of large tracts of vacant land have been willing to annex themselves to Denver in order to get city services, primarily water and sewer services.

Denver, to be sure, has lost most of its annexation powers, and it has many of the metropolitan problems associated with large cities in the eastern and midwestern United States. Denver, however, has many assets that have enabled it to maintain its position as the most important city in the Rocky Mountain West. It is still located at the center of its metropolitan area. Despite all the suburban growth, the primary public facilities associated with an urban center, such as art museums, performing arts theaters, and sports arenas, still are all located in the "central city." Further, Denver is still the state capital, and the majority of state offices and state employees are there. Denver has a large downtown composed of new high-rise office buildings, successful restaurants and nightspots, and a popular pedestrian walking and shopping mall. Thus, while Denver has its share of problems, no other city in the state can come close to challenging its position as the "Colorado Big Apple."[10]

OTHER CITIES AND TOWNS

Denver is the only city specifically provided for by name in the Colorado constitution. All the other cities and towns are provided for by general legislation passed by the legislature, or by a general grant of home-rule power to cities and towns contained in the state constitution.

Cities and towns that organize under laws passed by the state legislature are called statutory cities and towns. If less than 2,000 citizens in a community in Colorado want to incorporate, they are required by state law to form a town. If more than 2,000 citizens want to incorporate, they are required to form a city. These statutory towns and cities have a government structure and an array of city government powers that have been predetermined by the state legislature in Denver.

Instead of becoming statutory cities, however, most major cities in Colorado have chosen instead to become *home-rule* cities. Under the home-rule provisions of the state constitution, a charter commission is elected to write a city charter that structures a city's own particular form of government. The proposed charter is then adopted by a majority vote of the citizens of the city.

Towns

There are 186 statutory towns in Colorado. By state law, they are governed by a six-member town council and a mayor elected by all the voters of the town. The mayor presides at council meetings but has none of the executive powers associated with a strong mayor form of government. The council hires the executive officials needed to run the government, such as the town clerk and the town marshall.

Theoretically the town council could hire a professional town manager to administer the town government, yet there is no specific provision for this in state law. Although there is a provision in the state constitution for home-rule towns, virtually all of the towns in Colorado have chosen to remain statutory towns.

Cities

Only 17 of Colorado's 267 cities are statutory cities. The other 250 cities have opted for home rule, adopting their own particular structure of city government. The principal cities in Colorado other than Denver, such as Boulder, Colorado Springs, Fort Collins, Greeley, Lakewood, and Pueblo, have all adopted a variation of the council-manager form of city government.

Under the council-manager form, legislative power is held by a small city council, usually composed of from seven to nine council members. In some cases council members are elected from single-member districts. In other instances they are elected at large by all the voters in the city.

The responsibility for running the city government is given to a city manager, a trained professional who hires all other employees required to provide city services. The city manager is hired by the city council and can be fired by the city council. The council enacts the city's laws and sets general city policies. It is the city manager's job to enforce the laws and implement the council's policies.

In most home-rule cities in Colorado, a mayor is elected to preside over city council meetings. In some cases the mayor is elected by the voters. In other instances the city council elects one of its own members to be mayor. Under the council-manager form of municipal government, however, the mayor has no executive or administrative powers. The day-to-day responsibility of running the city government belongs to the city manager, not to the mayor.

The mayor's power and visibility can be significant, however. Often the mayor in a council-manager city will take the lead in building support for important programs—reducing crime, undertaking major public improvements such as performance halls and sports stadiums, luring new industry and jobs to the city, and so on.

Perhaps the most important characteristic of home-rule cities in Colorado is their broad grant of governing power which is imparted to them by the state constitution and which gives them all powers over "municipal affairs." In effect, this means that Colorado home-rule cities rarely need to go to the state legislature to obtain a grant of power to solve a new problem or undertake a new program of action.

Equally important, the broad grant of power to home-rule cities contained in the Colorado constitution limits the ability of the state legislature to interfere in city matters. The Colorado courts decide when an action is "municipal" in character or when an action is of "statewide concern" and thus subject to regulation by the state legislature. By and large, Colorado courts have interpreted the term "municipal affairs" broadly, encouraging home-rule cities to govern themselves and reducing attempts by the state legislature to make policy for home-rule cities.

According to James Colvin, city attorney for Colorado Springs, "Colorado probably has the strongest home-rule provision for cities in the entire nation." As a result, Colvin said, "Colorado cities feel they have real control over municipal affairs and do not think of themselves as under the thumb of the state legislature," which is the case in many other states. To prove his point, Colvin cited a recent decision of the Colorado Supreme Court which struck down a state law concerning employee residency requirements in Denver. The state legislature had attempted to override with state law a Denver law which required Denver employees to reside inside the Denver city limits. The state high court ruled that employee residency requirements were a matter of municipal, not statewide, concern and declared the state law unconstitutional.[11]

In practice, home-rule cities are an important element in Colorado gov-

ernment. With their broad grant of power firmly anchored in the state constitution, they have the ability to solve a wide range of problems at the city
level. As a result, the average city dweller in Colorado is more likely to turn
to city government, rather than state government, to solve local problems.

Adding to the power and influence of home-rule cities is the Colorado
Municipal League, the lobbying organization that represents the interests of
Colorado's cities at the legislature. The Colorado Municipal League is
widely recognized as one of the most powerful lobby groups at the state capitol. Because most Coloradans live in a city, the Municipal League speaks
for the vast majority of the state's population, and governors and legislators
appreciate this.[12] The Colorado Municipal League works particularly hard to
see that the broad grant of power to home-rule cities is not eroded, either by
interference from the state legislature or by popularly initiated constitutional
amendments.

An argument can be made that municipal government is the most important form of local government in Colorado. About 2.5 million of Colorado's
3.5 million citizens live in municipalities.[13]

Annexation Powers

In 1965 the state legislature enacted a law giving strong annexation powers to
Colorado cities. The law gave a city the power to annex any adjacent parcel
of land (not located in another city or town) if one-sixth of the boundary line
of the parcel was contiguous to the city boundary line. In the case of large
parcels of land that failed to meet the one-sixth contiguity requirement, these
parcels could be broken up into smaller parcels that did have one-sixth contiguity and then could be annexed parcel by parcel.

Because Colorado is a semiarid state, land cannot be developed for
homes, stores, office buildings, and factories unless water is available. In
Colorado, domestic water systems are mainly owned and controlled by the
cities. Thus landowners who want to develop their land are most anxious to
have it annexed into a city, thereby guaranteeing them access to city water
supplies and sewer services.

The liberal annexation law in Colorado coupled with the desire of land
owners to get city water and sewer service resulted in a wave of urban annexations in the late 1960s and the 1970s. Except for Denver, Colorado's major
cities rapidly annexed surrounding vacant land. Land owners, after getting
the land annexed, developed it for housing, shopping centers, and office
parks.

Because of this ability to annex their surrounding suburbs (when property owners want to be annexed), most Colorado cities do not have the metropolitan problems associated with Denver and many other large cities. Through the annexation process, they have been able to increase their property tax income and sales tax income by absorbing the housing projects and commercial establishments developing on their periphery.

As a result of liberal city annexation laws, by the early 1980s Colorado's cities contained, within their city limits, most of the people living in the metropolitan area. Instead of being surrounded by uncooperative suburbs, these cities had long since annexed these communities. This meant that many Colorado cities outside of Denver could take a "metropolitan" approach to solving problems because most of the people living in the metropolitan area also lived inside the city boundary line.

The 1965 annexation law also provided that when a Colorado city surrounds a parcel of land on three sides, that parcel can be annexed *without a vote of the people living in the area to be annexed*. This particular annexation law enabled cities to annex "enclaves," parcels of developed land that were almost completely surrounded by the city but were not yet part of it.

The power of cities to annex such enclaves unilaterally no longer exists in Colorado. In the late 1970s the voters of Colorado adopted Poundstone Two, a constitutional amendment requiring a vote of the people whenever land is annexed to a city, even if the city surrounds the land to be annexed on three sides. While it was in existence, however, Colorado's enclave annexation law permitted a number of Colorado cities to annex already developed and occupied housing developments which the cities had begun to encircle. For example, just before the Poundstone Two constitutional amendment took effect, the city of Colorado Springs annexed Broadmoor and Skyway, two long-established and well-known suburban communities, without a vote of the people being annexed.

As was expected, the Colorado Municipal League vigorously opposed the Poundstone Two constitutional amendment. Although most Coloradans live in cities and might have been expected to vote to preserve city annexation powers, the vote did not turn out that way. According to Municipal League officials, giving their fellow citizens "the right to vote" was more appealing to a majority of Colorado voters than preserving the strong annexation powers of cities.[14]

Although the Poundstone Two constitutional amendment somewhat limited urban annexation in Colorado, annexation remains a powerful part of urban policymaking in the state. Cities can no longer annex established communities without a favorable vote of the people to be annexed, but cities can annex surrounding property owners who want to come into the city. Because most property owners are going to need city water and sewer services at the time they develop their land, the great majority will continue to seek annexation. This will mean that most Colorado cities, except for Denver, will continue to expand their boundaries, to add to their population, and to expand their property tax and sales tax base. Colorado's annexation laws are making a major contribution to keeping the state's cities, other than Denver, financially healthy.

COUNTIES

Colorado has sixty-three counties, more than two states that are much larger in population, California and New York. Perhaps the major characteristic of Colorado counties is their diversity. Hinsdale County, located in southwestern Colorado, has only about 400 residents. In contrast, Denver has almost 500,000 residents, more than 1,000 times as many as Hinsdale County. Neither Hinsdale County nor Denver is an extreme case. Colorado has sixteen counties with less than 4,000 residents each. At the other end of the spectrum, nine counties have over 100,000 residents each.

In Colorado, as in many other states, counties were intended to be administrative units of the state and were organized according to laws passed by the legislature. Except for Denver, which has extensive home-rule powers, Colorado counties enforce and administer state laws and do not enact legislation in their own right. As in many other states, however, counties in Colorado have evolved into something more than "administrative units of the state." For the large number of rural Coloradans who do not reside in a city or a town, their county government is viewed as "local government" rather than a branch of state government.

The state legislature has given Colorado's sixty-three counties plenty of work to do. They finance and operate the district courts, providing courtroom and jail facilities. The district attorney's office, which supplies the prosecutors for district courts, is financed by counties. County governments also conduct state elections, title automobiles and sell license plates, build and maintain county roads, and administer state welfare programs.

Most Colorado counties are administered by a three-person board of county commissioners elected in partisan elections. Both political parties successfully elect commissioners, though there are slightly more Republican than Democratic county commissioners. In 1990, for example, there were one-hundred Republican county commissioners in Colorado, eighty-eight Democrats, and two county commissioners who listed themselves as unaffiliated. On the thickly populated Front Range, however, twenty-one county commissioners were Republicans and only 9 were Democrats.[15] It should be kept in mind, however, that the mostly Democratic thirteen-member city council in the City and County of Denver serves as the county commissioners within that jurisdiction.

County commissioners in Colorado serve a four-year term of office with no limit on the number of times they can be reelected. Counties with over 70,000 residents can expand the board of county commissioners to five members, yet only El Paso County, which contains the city of Colorado Springs, has chosen to do so.

The Colorado constitution requires each county to have a number of elected officials, including the county clerk, sheriff, treasurer, surveyor, assessor, and coroner. The county attorney may be elected or appointed. If it wishes, a county may elect a superintendent of schools to supervise public education in the county, although the schools will be directly administered by elected local school boards.

A limited form of county home rule is available in Colorado. An elected charter commission draws up a proposed county charter, which is then approved or disapproved by county voters. County home rule in Colorado, however, only allows for county citizens to determine the *structure* of county government. It does not increase the power and authority of county government or give home-rule counties the power to pass county laws. Only three of the sixty-three counties have voted to become home-rule counties and structure their own form of county government.[16]

One of the major problems with county government in Colorado is that the state legislature passes the same laws for counties with more than 100,000 residents as it does for counties with less than 4,000 residents. This is particularly difficult when the small counties often are rural and the large counties are suburban and located on the Front Range.

What often happens is that large counties will try to get legislation passed by the state legislature, while the small counties will oppose the legislation. A case in point is personnel policy—the hiring, promotion, and firing of county employees. The legislature has never granted authority to county governments to create civil service systems. The large counties, with large numbers of employees, would like to institute such systems but cannot do so until the legislature gives them permission. The small counties, however, do not want the added expense of setting up and operating civil service systems. Throughout the 1980s, the small counties, with the aid of key legislators from the small counties, prevailed on this issue. The state legislature never gave Colorado counties the authority to create county personnel systems.

In some cases the legislature appears to be capricious or, at worst, neglectful in the powers it grants to county governments. For example, it has given Colorado counties the power to regulate and control barking dogs, yet it has not given them the power to regulate and control attacks by vicious dogs on human beings.[17]

Reforms are always being proposed for county government in Colorado. Thus, it has occasionally been proposed that small counties—in the rural areas on the eastern plains, in the San Luis Valley, and in the western mountains—be combined in order to create governmental units that will have a larger tax base and thus be able to provide a higher level of services. Under the present system, each small county has its own set of elected officials and its own county court house and county maintenance facilities. Combining small counties would reduce this unnecessary duplication of county officials and facilities in underpopulated areas.

Combining small counties in Colorado, however, will be difficult to arrange. The state constitution says no county boundaries can be changed without voter approval in the counties involved. In those counties that would lose their county seat and county courthouse when combined, it is improbable that the citizens would vote to approve county consolidation. In addition to courthouse jobs, there would be a loss in area pride and area social and political importance.

We should note too that many of the smaller counties are working more and more in fruitful collaborative efforts. Thus Park, Lake, and Chaffee counties, for example, have a regional jail. Other counties share an airport or have fashioned a rural health delivery system. More and more counties have joint efforts as well as public-private partnerships.

Another reform suggested for county government in Colorado is to reduce the number of elected county officials, particularly those who are in low visibility positions that involve little policymaking. The county coroner, the county surveyor, and the county assessor are currently elected in Colorado, yet these jobs might better be filled by appointment by the board of county commissioners.

Many observers believe county government could be improved in Colorado if it had strong home-rule powers. Supporters of this proposal contend counties should be given the same extensive home-rule powers that home-rule cities in Colorado possess. In other words, exactly as home-rule cities in

Colorado are given all power over "municipal affairs," county governments should be given all power over "county affairs."

Such a broad grant of power would eliminate the need for counties to seek authority from the state legislature every time they want to solve a new problem or take on a new governmental function. Strong home-rule powers would be particularly helpful to the large, urbanizing counties on the Front Range that are trying to service large populations with a form of county government designed for small rural counties.

County governments are represented in Denver by Colorado Counties. This lobbying organization has to serve both the large and the small counties at the same time, but it generally takes a position in favor of urging the state legislature to modernize county government. According to one Colorado Counties official, "county government is the most archaic form of local government in Colorado. When it comes to reforming and modernizing county government, the Colorado state legislature needs to be dragged kicking and screaming into the twentieth century."[18]

CITY-COUNTY RELATIONSHIPS

It is impossible to fully comprehend local government in Colorado without looking at the way city and county governments relate to each other.

One reason the state legislature has not modernized county government is the tacit assumption that as urban populations develop within Colorado counties, those urban populations will be incorporated into new cities or will be annexed into existing cities. In other words, county governments do not need to be given the power to solve urban problems because, under Colorado's strong municipal incorporation and annexation laws, all significant urban populations in the state will eventually be living in cities.

There is no question that city and town annexations are a key element in city-county relations in Colorado. In most instances, county governments register no complaints about the annexation of urbanizing portions of a county into a city. There are times, however, when county and city interests conflict over annexation. Some cities carry out "flagpole annexations" that reach far away from the city line to take in a new shopping center or other large tax-paying facility. The county government is left to plan and solve urban problems in the large land area "skipped over" by the flagpole annexation.[19]

In some cases county governments face the problem of cities racing each other to see which city can annex the most land. Instead of growing in a logical and well-timed fashion, cities begin annexing large amounts of raw land for no other purpose than to make certain that a competing city does not annex it. Under such conditions, it is very difficult for a county government to plan competently for future population growth in the county.

The biggest problem with city-county relationships in Colorado is that many of the urbanizing areas are not being annexed by cities and are having to be served by archaic county governments. In some cases real estate developers want to develop county land that is not adjacent to an existing city. The developers go ahead and build on the land, adhering to county plans and zoning rules. The result is the creation of a highly urbanized area that needs urban services but that will have to be served by the county government.

Many counties in Colorado, particularly those on the Front Range and near resort communities in the Rocky Mountains, are beginning to experience a phenomenon known as *low-density urban sprawl*. People are building homes on large lots, five acres and larger, and then are living urban lives in what appear to be rural environments. In some cases real estate developers are building and selling large subdivisions composed of homes on five-acre lots. Far from any city that might annex them, these "urban" developments have to be served by county government. On the eastern plains adjacent to the Front Range, such developments are called "ranchurbia." In the foothills and mountains near Colorado's major ski areas, they are referred to as "resort sprawl."

The people moving into these low-density communities want a rural lifestyle but also demand high-quality urban services, such as roads cleared of snow in the winter, fire and police protection, and more. If the county commissioners are not already providing such urban services in these urban-style developments, they soon find themselves under political pressure to provide them.

Colorado counties, particularly those on the Front Range and in the ski resort areas in the mountains, will continue to experience urban development that is not incorporated or annexed into cities. This means that these counties, designed mainly to govern rural agricultural areas, will increasingly engage in the provision of urban services to large urban populations. In order to permit Colorado counties to provide such services adequately, the state legislature should modernize county government as quickly as possible.

SCHOOL DISTRICTS

Public schools in Colorado are governed by elected school boards that are completely separate from city and county government. Local school boards not only set school policies but also are in charge of raising the required revenues to support the local school system. School boards thus determine the school portion of local property tax rates and, with the approval of local voters, float bond issues for the construction of new schools and school facilities.

School board members are elected in nonpartisan elections to a four-year term of office. They are considered citizen volunteers and serve without pay. A president of the school board is elected from among its own membership, but the president's only responsibility is to preside at school board meetings. The board hires a salaried administrator to take charge of the day-to-day operation of the school system.

As has been the case in most other states, there has been a movement in recent years to reduce the number of school districts in Colorado. In many counties school districts have been combined into larger districts, and at the same time schools have been consolidated into a smaller number of larger schools. In some instances there is only one school district for an entire county. In 1993 Colorado had 181 school districts spread over its sixty-three counties.

In the 1960s the Colorado legislature significantly increased the amount of state aid distributed to public schools. At the same time, the legislature developed a formula for distributing additional funds to the less affluent school districts in the state. Both of these trends—increased state aid for public schools and the use of state aid to equalize per pupil expenditures from one school district to another—were supported by the legislature throughout the 1970s and 1980s.

In 1977 a group of parents of school children filed suit in state courts challenging the concept of local financing of schools through separate school districts. The suit contended it was unfair to finance schools locally because the district system resulted in there being rich school districts and poor school districts. A district court decided in favor of the parents and ruled that local financing of schools through school districts violated the Colorado constitution.

In 1982 this decision was reversed by the Colorado Supreme Court, although the state high court did indicate that more equality is needed in school financing. As a result of this decision, however, the public schools continue to be controlled and financed by local school boards.

In order to provide a measure of continuity among the various public school systems in Colorado, there is a seven-member State Board of Education. Each of the state's six congressional districts elects one member of the state board. The seventh is elected by all the voters. The State Board of Education appoints a state commissioner of education, gives advice and circu-

lates educational data to the local school districts, and makes recommendations to the legislature concerning statewide school policies and financing.

Under state law, Coloradans can organize to provide themselves specific
government services by creating "special districts." These districts provide
such services as water supply, sewage treatment, agricultural irrigation, fire
protection, and library services.

Citizens who wish to form a special district begin by circulating a petition
that describes the boundaries of the district and the services it will provide. If
a sufficient number of citizens sign the petition, a special election is held in
which the proposed district must be approved by a majority of the voters living within it. If created, the special district is governed by a five-member
elected board of directors.

Special districts are often used to provide water systems for rural housing
developments, particularly in resort areas in the Colorado mountains. Housing developers organize the water districts, and then, after the homes are
built and sold, the residents of the housing development take over the management of the special district. In some instances sales lag in the housing development, and the developer pulls out. When this happens, the special district providing water either goes bankrupt, or the limited number of people
who have moved into the development pay excessively high water charges.
Colorado gained an unwanted national reputation for fiscal irresponsibility
in the early 1990s when a large number of special districts in the state went
bankrupt.

METROPOLITAN GOVERNANCE

A number of efforts have been made to solve problems on a metropolitan
basis, particularly in the Metro Denver area. Denver and its surrounding
suburbs have undertaken a number of joint efforts to provide needed services
and cultural amenities throughout the entire Denver region.

The best example of metropolitan government in Denver is the Regional
Transportation District (RTD), a special district that operates the bus system.
Known and promoted as "The Ride," the RTD provides bus service from
downtown Denver to surrounding suburban communities. The RTD has the
authority to collect taxes throughout the metropolitan area to finance its bus
services.

Other examples of metropolitan government in Denver are the Metropolitan Denver Sewage Disposal District, which handles sewage treatment and disposal throughout the Denver area, and the Urban Drainage and Flood Control District, which works to reduce and control flooding on the South Platte River as it flows through the Denver region.

Most of the major metropolitan areas in Colorado have a regional "council of governments" that works to coordinate government services in the area. The council of governments, or COG as it is often called, is particularly involved in the process by which federal aid is distributed to city and county governments within a metropolitan area. During the 1980s, as the amount of federal aid to city and county governments declined, the importance of councils of government simultaneously declined. Two of the larger COGs in Colorado are the Denver Regional Council of Governments (nicknamed "Doctor COG" because of its initials, DRCOG) and the Pike's Peak Area Council of Governments (PPACG) in Colorado Springs.

One of the best-known examples of metropolitan government in Colorado is the Pueblo Council of Governments. This COG is structured to represent every major local government in the Pueblo region. The executive director of the Pueblo COG in the 1960s and 1970s was Allan Blomquist, who pursued a strategy of using the COG as an instrument for mobilizing political leadership for the entire Pueblo region. The result was metropolitanwide political support for a number of civic projects—a fine arts and conference center, redevelopment of the business section of downtown Pueblo, a biker-hiker trail running through the community along Fountain Creek and the Arkansas River, and development of city and state parks in connection with the construction of Pueblo Reservoir, the largest recreational body of water in Colorado. A national study of metropolitan government concluded that the Pueblo COG "is one of the most successful examples anywhere of voluntary political integration of the government institutions of the civil community."[20]

METROPOLITAN GOVERNMENT FOR DENVER: A DEBATE

In the summer of 1990 the then mayor of Denver, Federico Pena, proposed the adoption of a uniform sales tax throughout the Denver metropolitan area. In addition, Mayor Pena suggested that a single unified water system be developed, arguing that a regionwide water system would be less expensive and less environmentally damaging than having each local jurisdiction provide for its own water needs. No immediate action was taken on either of Mayor Pena's proposals, but the fact that he presented them showed there is sentiment for metropolitanwide solutions to governmental problems in the Denver area.

In mid 1991 a panel of twenty-seven local leaders appointed by the Denver Regional Council of Governments (DRCOG) unveiled two metropolitan-area governance proposals. Their most sweeping idea called for a single metropolitan county that would combine the Denver area's six counties into one giant metropolitan community that could provide traditional county services, such as transportation, solid-waste disposal, and regional recreation areas and parks. Their less sweeping and politically more pragmatic proposal called for a metropolitan-area council in charge of regional planning. Modeled after a plan in use in the Minneapolis–St. Paul area, this umbrella agency would permit cities and counties to perform most of their traditional functions but would require them to implement planning policies adopted by the metropolitan-planning council.[21]

All of these proposals, and they surface in new forms every few years, provoke heated arguments over whether the Denver region needs a strengthened metropolitan-wide government. Supporters of metropolitan governance say major local government problems, such as water supply, air pollution, and highway congestion, are not limited to one or two local jurisdictions but plague the entire area. The logical way to solve these problems, they claim, is to create a metropolitan government that will have the power, and the tax sources, to solve metropolitanwide problems.

Advocates of strengthened metropolitan governance arrangements say the area has to have bold leadership to provide vision and long-term planning for the whole region. Moreover, they say, economies of scale can be achieved that will result in substantial savings.

Supporters also contend creating a metropolitan government in Denver will *not* mean the end of local government. Local problems, such as neighborhood zoning and school safety, will still be handled by the existing city and county governments. Only problems of metropolitanwide impact would be turned over to the new metropolitan government.

Critics of this proposal counter that metropolitan government will be a "monster" that is too big to be representative of the people. Neighborhood values will be discarded, and policies will cater to only the interests of the "giant" metropolitan government. In the name of "metropolitan traffic improvement," opponents argue, new highway construction will slash through thriving existing communities that will have no way of protecting themselves from the "metropolitan monolith."

Opponents point to Two Forks Dam, the large water-supply project which failed to be approved by the Environmental Protection Agency, as the classic example of the evils of metropolitan government. The various governmental units in the Denver area worked together to plan Two Forks, and in the manner of a large regional government paid no attention whatsoever to the needs of the little guys, the fishing enthusiasts who wanted to preserve good trout fishing on the South Platte River and the environmentalists who did not want a beautiful river valley destroyed by flooding. If metropolitan government means mammoth regional projects similar to Two Forks Dam, then a large number of people in the Denver area do not want it.

Finally, many citizens fear that a metropolitan or regional government will merely mean *more* government and *more* taxes, both of which are rarely, if ever, liked much by typical Coloradans.

LOCAL GOVERNMENT AND THE STATE LEGISLATURE

Although home-rule city governments in Colorado have strong home-rule powers, they are not completely free from a measure of interference from the state legislature.

One problem cities have is the tendency of the state legislature to shift financial or service responsibilities from the state to the local level. Thus a few years ago the legislature mandated expensive retirement programs for city police and fire-fighting personnel and left it mainly to the cities to raise the money to pay for these expensive programs. "This was a disaster," said Mayor Robert Isaac of Colorado Springs. "They took our very solvent system and turned it into a very costly and underfunded system that caused all kinds of problems." Mayor Isaac used this as just one of many examples where the state legislature often did not understand the financial impact on cities caused by well-intentioned state mandates.[22] In the same manner, the legislature, under pressure from the U.S. Environmental Protection Agency, has set high water-quality standards for rivers and streams in Colorado but has mandated that local governments pay the cost of bringing the rivers and streams up to these high standards.[23]

At the same time that the legislature has been mandating that certain expensive services be performed by local governments, the legislature has been reducing the percentage of state funds allocated to local governments. An example is state allocations for city and county highway programs. The Colorado Municipal League charged that city allocations were reduced 56 percent and county allocations 45 percent by the state legislature in 1987.[24]

City and county officials in Colorado sarcastically refer to the state legislature's penchant for mandating expensive local services as "shift and shaft." [25] When mandating expensive local services is combined with cutting state aid to local governments, a good description of this "one-two punch" combination might be "shift and shrink."

Colorado Springs Mayor Robert Isaac said the state legislature has been better in recent years (late 1980s and early 1990s) as far as mandating expensive local programs is concerned. "But you have to watch them," Isaac notes, "and that is why we have a lobbyist up there who monitors what they are doing to us."

Mayor Isaac also said he has had generally good relations with recent governors. But occasionally the governor will make business arrangements involving the city, such as a deal with Apple Computer to locate a computer-manufacturing facility in Colorado Springs. In this case the governor announced the deal, got all the glory for creating new jobs in the local community, and then later told city officials they were going to have to pay for a new highway interchange or lower the company's taxes in order to make the deal work. Such actions do not sit well with Isaac, who has served as mayor of Colorado Springs for over twelve years. "Governor Romer is a great cheerleader," Isaac concluded, "but sometimes he gets out ahead of everyone else and forgets to do his homework." [26]

LOCAL GOVERNMENT AND LAND USE

Colorado is regarded by everyone as a beautiful place. The state is filled with mountains, rolling prairies, pine-forested foothills, river valleys, rocky buttes and mesas, and scenic canyons. As the population increases, however, housing developments and shopping centers continually encroach on and invade many of the most beautiful parts of the state. Because of this, land use is one of the most important, and controversial, political and governmental issues in Colorado.

Land use is the process whereby governments determine how land will be used. Through the twin processes of planning and zoning, governments adopt general plans for how land will be used and then zone specific parcels of land for specific purposes. The three most important zones are residential, which provides for constructing houses or apartments on the land; commercial, which permits shopping centers and retail stores; and industrial, which provides for manufacturing plants, office buildings, and the like. At the same time land is zoned for houses, stores, or factories, governments will usually designate which lands will be used for public purposes such as parks, schools, government buildings, and so on.

In Colorado, the responsibility for determining land use has been given to local government. Cities and towns make the major decisions for land use within their boundaries. County governments determine land use in those portions of the county that are not included in a city or town. Almost without exception, each city, town, and county in Colorado has a planning department, which has the job of proposing general land-use plans for the area and recommending specific zones for specific parcels of land. The city council members or the county commissioners will make the final decision as to what plans are adopted and what zones are placed on each specific piece of ground.

Given the rapid population increase in Colorado in recent years, and given the particular sensitivity on the part of many citizens of the state to preserving its natural beauty, land use has become a major political issue. Local citizens sensitive to environmental values will strenuously oppose zone changes that will result in construction in scenic areas. Before any form of construction occurs, citizen groups often urge city council members and county commissioners to purchase areas of local beauty for park land or open space. Even when development is permitted, environmentally sensitive citizens will call for lowering population densities and designating scenic areas, such as wooded stream valleys or pine-forested ridge tops, as private open space.

A number of Colorado cities have adopted innovative land-use programs. In the late 1960s Boulder adopted and implemented an extensive plan for buying a greenbelt of open land around the city. A Development Permit System has been implemented as a substitute for the traditional zoning process in rural Park County. Jefferson County, the large suburban county to the west of Denver, adopted a program for buying undeveloped land and constructing a countywide system of recreational bicycle trails. In the opinion of a former member of the Colorado Springs City Council, "land use is now the single most important issue in city and county government in Colorado. A tremendous amount of local government time now goes into it."[27]

The state government has tended to stay removed from land-use issues, leaving it to the city and county governments to decide how the significant natural beauty of Colorado will be integrated with the desire of private property owners to develop and build upon their property. By the early 1990s environmental concerns appeared to be growing in importance to many Colorado citizens. It was a trend that suggested that land use, the planning and zoning of growing communities, would continue to be the major local government issue.

CONCLUSION

Local government is of central importance in the Centennial State. Because home-rule cities, including Denver, have such strong powers, cities often take the lead in terms of initiating major governmental projects. Denver, through such projects as the new convention center, the new Denver International Airport, and the new Coors Stadium for baseball scheduled to open in 1995, has been particularly aggressive in undertaking projects that should benefit most Coloradans.

Because of the strong home-rule powers of cities, and because at least three out of every four Coloradans live in a city, city governments have generally been able to fend off attempts by the state legislature to interfere in city affairs. County governments, because they do not enjoy the broad grant of home-rule powers that cities possess, are more subject to control by the legislature than are the cities.

Strong city annexation laws are another important characteristic of local government in Colorado. As long as Colorado cities are able to annex most of the urban growth in their general area, they will continue to have strong financial resources and will be able to provide effective local government. The inability of Denver to undertake significant annexations is one of the major drawbacks to local government in Colorado.

City government in the Centennial State is conducted very much in the tradition of the moralistic political culture, particularly in Denver. More than any other group in state and local government in Colorado, home-rule cities initiate government projects that add to the "commonwealth" of the people. In their zeal for building parks, performing arts centers, airports, museums, zoos, and convention centers, the larger cities usually best fulfill the moralistic political tradition in Colorado.

CHAPTER TWELVE

Policy Concerns and Opportunities

Colorado citizens and policymakers face an unending stream of planning, budgeting, tax, and policy choices. Precisely what should be done in Colorado about education, the environment, promoting economic growth, creating more jobs, health insurance, tourism, and guaranteeing the integrity of representative government? How should Colorado deal with the issues of water, transportation, pollution, substance abuse, illiteracy, AIDS, crime, and overcrowded prisons? Who should be elected to office in Colorado? How can the state ensure enlightened leadership for the next generation? Decisions on these and similar matters are made all the time. Below are some proposals for changing policy and process that might help make Colorado a better state.

COLORADO'S ASSETS

Any "report card" on Colorado must begin by highlighting the Centennial State's numerous advantages.[1] It is, as everyone agrees, a state with majestic beauty and natural resources. Its economy is diverse. Its work force is well educated, is younger than the national average, and enjoys living in Colorado. Racial and ethnic tensions are low. Tourism is a guaranteed cushion for the economy. Colorado does not have political machines or political bosses, and its politics are relatively honest. Political scandals are an exception rather than the rule. Coloradans, taken as a whole, are moderately conservative yet also pragmatic and concerned about environmental protection.

Colorado is a small enough state that people in public life either know one another or can easily get to know one another. Further, there is a general legacy of honesty and good government personified by the state's several recent governors—Stephen McNichols, John Love, Richard Lamm, and Roy Romer—all of whom were dedicated, hardworking, and accessible.

Colorado is no longer a frontier. Denver is striving to become an international city, and its citizens are slowly yet surely developing a global perspective. Greater Denver is major league in more ways than merely having major league football, basketball, and baseball teams. True, Denver is not New York, Los Angeles, Philadelphia, Miami, or Chicago, but in some ways this is as much an asset as a liability.

POLICY AND BUDGET REALITIES

Those who listen to debates in the state legislature, attend city council meetings, or watch candidates being interviewed on the campaign trail will come face-to-face with people who plead for better schools, who demand better highways or mass transit systems, who are outraged by increased taxes, who insist on tougher approaches to crime prevention, who yearn for good jobs at good wages, who are irate about toxic waste dumps near their homes, who insist that Colorado does (or does not) need yet another major dam, or who want Colorado to have a first-class symphony or opera, and on and on.

Most public policies require money if they are to be carried out adequately. And, in many ways, the main public policy and state planning document a state has is its annual budget. In Colorado, as noted, both the governor and the legislature prepare a budget, but the more fiscally conservative legislative budget usually prevails.

For the 1993–94 fiscal year Governor Roy Romer issued a "Governor's Budget" calling for a 5.9 percent increase in spending over the previous year. Each year the governor says his budget reflects a strategic effort to deploy the state's limited resources in a few key policy areas. The governor's priorities, as reflected in his proposed budgets in recent years, paralleled his campaign promises when he first ran for governor in 1986 and ran for reelection in 1990:

—A strong package of business promotion and economic development initiatives.

—A major commitment to elementary, secondary, and postsecondary education, to ensure that all Coloradans can be successful participants in the state's work force.

—A program to maintain and strengthen Colorado's incomparable quality of life.

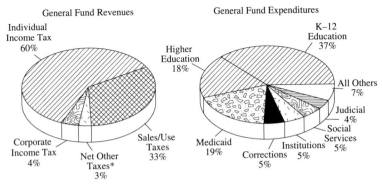

Figure 13. State of Colorado General Fund, Fiscal Year 1993–94

* Net Other Taxes are all other taxes less rebates and expenditures.
(*Source:* Governor's Executive Budget Plan, Fiscal Year 1993–94)

—An effective and humane support system for disadvantaged Coloradans that provides opportunities for moving out of the cycle of poverty
and dependency.
—Continued support for strong public protection, adequate public infrastructure, and prudent but innovative state government.[2]

Figure 13 indicates the general sources of state revenue and highlights the
purposes and programs for which state general funds are spent. These were
the projections Governor Roy Romer's budgeting and planning staff made
for the 1993–94 fiscal year.

The Colorado legislature and its Joint Budget Committee generally share
the governor's priorities. But they prefer to accomplish these goals by redi-
recting resources from existing programs and by more productive use of
existing instruments in these policy areas. A majority of the legislators in recent legislative sessions have not been as interested as the governor in programs that would result in higher taxes.

Centennial State legislators, as previously noted, prefer to keep taxes reasonably low. "In one policy area after another," writes Colorado State University political scientist John Straayer, "the legislature seems to fund programs at a level falling somewhere around the median for the fifty states. But
in relation to the state's fiscal capacity, Colorado's effort is very low, and
much of the funding is shunted down to the local units."[3] This is how most
Colorado legislators want it.

An important part of the job that citizens ask of their governor and legislators is determining the levels of investment in the various policy and pro-

gram areas. Is too much spent on education? Should more be spent building prisons? Are funds being spent efficiently? Are better facilities or higher teacher salaries the best way to promote more effective learning? Does Colorado need more prison cells or better job-training and rehabilitation programs if the state wants to prevent the increase of career criminals? State policymakers are painfully aware of the fact that they must live and make these decisions in a world of scarce resources.

PLANNING STRATEGICALLY

Coloradans periodically need to assess their state's assets and liabilities and think strategically about its competitive advantage vis-à-vis other states in the United States. There is increasingly intense competition for nearly every business, tourist, research scientist, professional sports team, nonprofit headquarters, and ski championship. As a result, a strategy is essential for the state to gain a sustainable edge over its competitors.

Colorado citizens need to have the best possible brainpower, in both the private and public sectors, devising plans that can help the state position or reposition itself competitively in the international market. State budget planners, though asked to project ahead, know they have to prepare and negotiate year-to-year budgets. The governor's office has planning and research staffs, but they are too small and spread too thin to do much long-term stategic planning.

Part of the problem surrounding the planning capacity of state government, or the lack of such capacity, arises because not everyone believes in planning. And many who do believe in planning think it should be done primarily at the city or county level. After all the needs of Denverites are different from the needs of people on the eastern plains or on the western slope. "Other than protecting our state water interests and trying to get more corporations to relocate here," one person commented, "the various parts of Colorado do not have that much in common that needs planning."

Coloradans of the individualistic political culture are also suspicious of planners and planning. They correctly suspect planners who have a reformist orientation. Moreover, planners try to discern a desirable future and then steer the state toward that desirable future. Skeptical individualists are never sure that the planners' conception of a desirable future will be the same as theirs. And even if it is, they are concerned about the cost of moving from the present to the future and about the possible loss of freedom that might come as part of the process.

A 1973 Colorado legislative committee concluded that the need for adequate long-range governmental planning was the most unfulfilled need of state government. "Such planning is not presently performed on a continuous or government-wide basis by any state agency or group of state officials," the report stated. "In fact, the state budget document must serve in most cases as the state planning document."[4] Some seventeen years later, in 1990, a new legislative committee, this one called the Subcommittee on Long-Range Planning for State Government, was still trying to sort out a sensible planning process for Colorado. A proposed State Long-Range Planning Commission, which would have been chaired by the governor and would have included state legislative leaders as well as several at-large members appointed by the governor, was considered but not approved by the legislature.

One of Colorado's leading business organizations, the Colorado Association of Commerce and Industry (CACI), has for several years put together helpful policy blueprints for Colorado. Designed to stimulate economic growth, CACI's policy blueprints acknowledge there are no quick solutions. But CACI believes the effort of putting forth specific recommendations on a whole range of policy choices is a much needed exercise in building a statewide consensus. Their efforts have been funded by several of the state's leading businesses and foundations. Their documents emphasize a vision of what business officials hope Colorado can be.

CAMPAIGN FINANCE REFORM

Coloradans say political contributors have too much influence on the political and policy decisions of their state. "Colorado's current campaign finance rules are the kind that make fat cats [big political contributors] purr," editorializes the *Rocky Mountain News*. "There are no limits on individual, corporate or political action committee donations. And disclosure requirements for contributors are laughable."[5]

Influential special interest groups, businesses, and wealthy individuals have poured millions of dollars into bankrolling Colorado's recent legislative and gubernatorial campaigns. A feature story in the *Denver Post* in 1983 said these contributions "have meticulously molded a Republican-dominated legislature friendly to their interests."[6] Business lobbyists acknowledge business political action committees were begun in Colorado in the 1970s because they wanted more business-oriented people in the state legislature. Their efforts have helped mainly incumbents of both political parties.

Campaign contributions, it is sometimes said, do not buy votes, yet most people believe contributions do open doors and give access to those who contribute. Former Colorado House Republican leader Ron Strahle of Fort Collins said he would have been much more comfortable if he had never had to ask for campaign money. "The whole area of contributions is a difficult one for me," noted Strahle. "If someone has been generous with you, you are predisposed to their cause," he said. "You wonder if, on a close vote, that might not affect your thinking."[7]

A few dozen lobbyists control much of the flow of political action committee (PAC) contributions. Under Colorado law it is legal for lobbyists to solicit virtually unlimited funds for legislators and even to run fund-raising events for them during the legislative session. Moreover, most legislators rely on these same lobbyists to provide critically needed information on legislation. Thus lobbyists in Colorado often control half or more of the funds for a legislator's campaign as well as half or more of the information legislators receive.

Former Governor Dick Lamm calls the growing dependence on campaign contributions the new corruption of our time, "where money in politics doesn't talk—it demands, it insists and dictates." Lamm argues both parties are far too dependent on these big contributors: "In representative government, politicians are supposed to represent the people. I think a strong case can be made that, in many cases, politicians represent money, not people, and that this process very definitely distorts the function of government."[8]

Former state Senator Terry Considine, a Republican from suburban Denver who also was the 1992 Republican candidate for U.S. senator, said the way campaigns are financed in Colorado has made most voters "feel alienated from government and feel it exists for other people, for insiders . . . and for fat cats that [live] outside [legislative] districts."[9]

Although some legislators agree with Considine that the legislature is too beholden to narrow business interests, many others deny this. As one legislator said: "My own experience has been that in general my Political Action Committee (PAC) contributions have never been tied to any kind of specific request but rather have been with the thought of buying into a philosophy with which the contributor feels comfortable."[10]

Colorado Common Cause and legislators like senators Regis Groff, Pat Pascoe, and Jack Fenlon have introduced legislative proposals to set limits on the size of individual, PAC, and political party campaign contributions. They also have urged strengthened requirements for disclosing campaign contributions, and would prohibit the shift of funds from one campaign to others. In addition, reformers favor establishing a bipartisan election commission to administer campaign laws and regulations in Colorado.

Minnesota, New Jersey, Michigan, and Wisconsin now have partial public financing of campaigns for governor and attorney general, and in some cases will phase in the public financing of state legislative campaigns as well. Public financing has worked in several states.[11] It has had the beneficial effect of encouraging strong challengers and of lessening candidate dependency on a score of well-heeled interests. And if done properly, it can also help strengthen the political parties, which is a desirable end in itself.

This is not the place to spell out how to finance and implement a program of partial public financing of Colorado elections. Useful blueprints are available.[12] The point is that public financing is a possible means of increasing faith in representative government in the state of Colorado.

MORE COMPETITIVE ELECTIONS

Elected and party officials in Colorado also need to encourage the creation of competitive congressional districts and state legislative districts. One reason for low voter turnout and for cynicism about the electoral and representative government processes is rooted in the decline of competitiveness in some districts. Party officials in both parties often agree to deals that protect incumbents and carve up "safe seats" for their respective parties. These practices have weakened the two-party system and encouraged the 1990 state constitutional amendment imposing term limits on elected officials. The lack of real choices in candidate elections has also led issue-oriented groups to launch initiative and referendum campaigns with greater frequency. If there is no real contest among the candidates of the two political parties, citizens either will be turned off or will turn to alternative means of expressing themselves.

STRENGTHENING THE GOVERNOR'S APPOINTMENT AUTHORITY

Colorado governors, the authors believe, should be able to appoint agency heads (division directors), either from within the government or from outside of state government. This proposal has won the support of leading officials in both parties and makes sense if Colorado is to hold governors accountable for the efficiency, productivity, and responsiveness of the state's executive departments.

Coloradans should also consider having the University of Colorado Board of Regents appointed by the governor rather than being elected by the people. Here again, these elections attract little attention and thus are not very responsive to the popular will. Making the governor, the state's most visible and responsive executive official, responsible for the setting of university policies is the better way of maintaining public control over the state university. In the same manner, serious consideration should be given to having the governor appoint the state Board of Education rather than having that body be popularly elected.

STRENGTHENING THE GOVERNOR'S BUDGET AUTHORITY

The most important power the Colorado governor needs, however, is an increase in influence over the state budget. The present budget process in Colorado is somewhat out of balance. Both the legislature and the governor need to have a reasonable and shared influence over budget decisions. The legislature, through the Joint Budget Committee, does an effective job scrutinizing departmental budget requests. Legislators justifiably pay attention to certain existing or proposed programs when the executive branch may overstep its boundaries or interfere with legislative prerogatives. But the governor's budget authority and influence can be modestly increased without diminishing the creative role the legislature currently plays. Under the leadership of state Senator Mike Bird and others, the Joint Budget Committee and the Governor Romer–led Office of State Planning and Budgeting have worked more closely. The process also has been noticeably more open. Yet the balance could still be shifted a bit more toward the governor.

LEGISLATIVE VACANCIES

Colorado should reform the process by which legislative vacancies are filled. Special primary and general elections should be held to fill such vacancies. Currently, a vacancy committee appoints someone of the same political party as the person vacating the legislative seat. The result is that a handful of party loyalists pick a fellow party loyalist. This might make sense if there are only a few weeks left in the vacating legislator's term, but not when there is a year or more left to serve. The policy decisions made by a state legislator are too important for vacancies to be left to a few party leaders. Voter interest and turnout would probably be low in special elections to fill vacancies, yet the voters in both parties would at least have the chance to vote their preferences.

COUNTY POWERS

The state legislature, the authors believe, should give more power to county governments in Colorado. This reform is particularly needed in view of the fact that the pattern is to give the county governments plenty of work to do. County governments should be given the same power over local affairs that home-rule cities enjoy. The need for county governments with more authority and freedom to operate is particularly pressing in those counties, close to major cities, that are experiencing rapid suburban population growth.

The state legislature also needs to face up to the fact that fast-growing suburban counties need to be treated differently from the small rural counties. It makes little sense to give the same laws and powers of government to rural counties with less than 1,000 residents that are given to large suburban counties with 500,000 residents.

CITY-COUNTY COMBINATION

The Colorado state legislature should also provide a mechanism by which county governments can be combined with city governments. In a number of the populous counties in Colorado, one large city contains most of the population of the county, and it would save considerable taxpayer money and eliminate government overlapping and duplication if the county and city governments could be combined into a single, more efficient government. Such city-county combinations would have to be approved, of course, by a vote of the people in both the city and the county. Examples of possible city-county combinations are Fort Collins and Larimer County, Boulder and Boulder County, Colorado Springs and El Paso County, and Pueblo and Pueblo County.

IMPROVING THE COLORADO BUSINESS CLIMATE

Despite Colorado's many lifestyle advantages and its growing maturity, the state faces tough questions from those who might consider relocating large companies here. What follows is a paraphrased summary of a conversation one of the authors had with a top executive of a major U.S. corporation. This person has had to decide, on several occasions, where to move major subsid-

iary operations. He prefers to remain anonymous. He was asked how he
went about assessing a state like Colorado and its business climate:

> Well, there is a list of things we look for—political stability, economic
> health and economic stability, favorable weather and environmental condi-
> tions (floods, earthquakes, water availability, etc.), quality public schools and
> excellent higher education institutions, a top transportation system (high-
> ways, airports, etc.) and the availability of a quality work force. Cultural and
> recreational opportunities are also important. Market considerations are a fac-
> tor too, depending on whether our facility is an R&D operation, manufactur-
> ing, or a regional sales headquarters.
>
> We don't have any offices or divisions in Colorado now, and I doubt we
> will. Colorado has a history of political instability, stemming right back to
> those labor disputes in the late ninetenth and early twentieth century. Also,
> Colorado is not exactly known as a place of economic booms in recent times.
> And it is also a long way away from most population centers.
>
> Our employees always list quality health-care facilities as their number one
> requirement when they look at a new area. It seems also that they want excel-
> lent schools for their children and high-quality colleges and universities, ei-
> ther to further their own education or so they might teach part-time. Many of
> our executives enjoy part-time teaching in some of the higher education pro-
> grams where we are now located. They are also keenly interested these days in
> the availability of jobs for their spouses. Then, too, they want recreational and
> cultural opportunities.
>
> Frankly, Colorado has not been on their lists, though I know many people
> enjoy skiing in your state.
>
> And from a corporate standpoint, Colorado does not compare with [a num-
> ber of other states] where there is a record of economic and political stabil-
> ity—and a better recognized entrepreneurial or business climate.
>
> Another drawback for Colorado is the lack of corporate headquarters there.
> We do not like to be the only or just one of a few major corporate headquarters
> in a state or urban area. If you are in that position, you are constantly turned to
> by every charity and by governments, schools, and so on to take the lead or
> make the major donations. Colorado does not really have corporate headquar-
> ters in the same way [other cities and states] clearly have.

This interview may portray Colorado's situation as more negative than it
is. Some of the comments about Colorado, however, have been validated by
an "industrial climate" rating made by Grant Thornton, a Chicago-based
national accounting and management consultant firm. North Carolina, Ver-

mont, and Wisconsin were all rated highly in their survey. Colorado ranked near the bottom. The study weighed sixteen factors, such as wages, taxes, workers' compensation insurance, unemployment insurance, fuel and energy costs, and the like.[13]

Colorado's mixed business and economic climate vis-à-vis other states is further illustrated by the comparative evaluation rankings of the Corporation for Economic Development, a Washington, D.C., economic development research group. Using seventy-eight factors that assess current and future state economic growth, Colorado comes out very well on its human and capital resources and amenities to attract people. But it fares quite poorly on economic performance and state policies supportive of business. Table 9 displays this report card, which in the aggregate earns Colorado about a C grade.

These evaluations of Colorado's economic competitiveness are not intended to offend anyone. They are merely frank studies of Colorado's competitive disadvantages. Their results pose a challenge to Colorado.

BALANCING ECONOMIC GROWTH AND ENVIRONMENTAL
PROTECTION

Colorado's first and greatest asset is its environment. Colorado is a place where quality-of-life issues are vitally important. Yet state leaders also have to expand the number of jobs in the state. In the past few years Colorado officials have stepped up the pace of trying to lure business prospects. Enormous efforts went into luring a major league baseball team (successful), a major maintenance facility for United Airlines (unsuccessful), the Super Conductor Super Collider project (unsuccessful), an Apple Computer plant (successful), and dozens of other firms or projects. Indeed, during the Romer years, criticism mounted in some circles that the state was trying "too hard" to bring in new industry.

Countless organizations, state and local officials, and economic development councils around the Centennial State have plotted strategies to ensure reasonable economic growth. These efforts have not been without debate and division. For example, certain interests mainly want to assist existing companies. Colorado Springs businessman Steve Schuck, criticizing Governor Roy Romer for his many travels to Europe and Asia, argued the best way to help the state's economy was to help local companies expand their operations.

Table 9. The 1990 Development Report Card

	Economic Performance Index[a]	Business Vitality Index[b]	Development Capacity Index[c]	State Policy Index[d]
Alabama	D	B	D	C
Alaska	C	C	B	C
Arizona	C	C	C	F
Arkansass	D	C	F	C
California	B	B	B	B
Colorado	**D**	**B**	**A**	**F**
Connecticut	A	B	A	B
Delaware	A	C	A	C
Florida	B	B	D	C
Georgia	C	A	D	C
Hawaii	A	D	B	C
Idaho	C	D	C	C
Illinois	D	C	B	B
Indiana	B	B	C	A
Iowa	C	D	D	A
Kansas	C	D	D	B
Kentucky	F	B	F	C
Louisiana	F	F	F	D
Maine	B	A	D	C
Maryland	A	A	A	A
Massachusetts	A	B	A	B
Michigan	C	C	C	A
Minnesota	B	C	A	A
Mississippi	D	C	F	C
Missouri	C	C	C	B
Montana	D	D	C	D
Nebraska	C	D	C	F
Nevada	A	C	C	F
New Hampshire	A	A	C	F
New Jersey	A	A	A	B
New Mexico	F	C	C	C
New York	C	A	B	A
North Carolina	C	A	C	D
North Dakota	D	F	D	D
Ohio	B	D	C	A

Table 9. The 1990 Development Report Card (continued)

	Economic Performance Index[a]	Business Vitality Index[b]	Development Capacity Index[c]	State Policy Index[d]
Oklahoma	D	F	D	A
Oregon	C	B	A	B
Pennsylvania	B	B	A	A
Rhode Island	A	C	B	B
South Carolina	C	D	D	D
South Dakota	D	C	C	D
Tennessee	D	A	D	D
Texas	D	C	B	D
Utah	B	C	A	C
Vermont	A	A	B	D
Virginia	B	A	B	B
Washington	C	C	A	C
West Virginia	F	D	F	C
Wisconsin	B	D	C	A
Wyoming	C	F	C	D

a. Economic Performance—employment growth, income per capita, equity, job quality, and quality of life.

b. Business Vitality—competitiveness of existing businesses and ability to spawn new ones.

c. Development Capacity—human and capital resources, infrastructure capacity, amenities to attract and retain talent.

d. State Policy Strength—effectiveness of governance and regulation, tax policy, commitment to enabling capital mobilization, improved education and research, and help for distressed communities.

Source: Corporation for Enterprise Development, *The 1990 Development Report Card for the States* (Washington, D.C., 1990), p.1. Reprinted with permission

There is a lot of wisdom in this approach. Along these lines the authors endorse a recent recommendation from the Colorado Association of Commerce and Industry, which advised that teams of locally elected officials, government administrators, and business peers make organized visits to existing employers. The goal of these visits would be to identify opportunities for job growth, to eliminate local obstacles to expansion, and to help link Colorado employers with Colorado subcontractors and suppliers.[14] Much of this work needs to be done by local economic development organizations.

But the governor's office and its Office of Economic Development need to be further strengthened to tackle this assignment on a statewide basis. And their efforts need to be focused clearly on Colorado's real economic needs, not on the political reputation of the governor.

An alternative and similarly important strategy is to recruit new businesses to relocate or start up operations in Colorado. Most business leaders believe this assignment is logically the responsibility of local and regional economic development agencies, yet statewide assistance also is needed. Colorado needs to attract more corporate headquarters. "Colorado has been very successful in recent years in recruiting the national headquarters of dozens of nonprofit organizations such as Junior Achievement, the National Civic League, and the Olympic Coordination Committee," said William J. Hybl, chairman of the state's leading charitable foundation, the El Pomar Foundation.[15] But the state has been far less successful recruiting corporate headquarters.

A private-public partnership is needed to assess Colorado's strengths and weaknesses and to think strategically about the long-term opportunities for attracting corporate operations. State leaders also need to commission a group of the existing corporate chief executive officers to travel elsewhere in the nation and help market Colorado as a prime place to which to move important business operations.

Colorado has an established International Trade Office (created in 1983) that is directed by the legislature to promote the export of Colorado goods and services and to attract job-creating foreign investments. It has also opened an office in Japan to further these objectives. Colorado's major export markets are in Japan, Canada, West Germany, and the United Kingdom, and exports to Mexico are increasing. Indeed, international trade has increased significantly in recent years.

The International Trade Office assists exporters with market research, with trade leads, and at trade fairs. It also counsels Colorado firms and identifies Japanese companies looking for investment opportunities and joint venture possibilities in Colorado. This trade office, if properly directed and funded, will pay rich dividends.

Morgan Smith, who has directed the International Trade Office, said virtually every governor and legislator across the United States now understands the need for each state to have its own international trade policy, especially with Japan. Smith notes that Colorado lacks the financial incentives some states can offer, yet he is optimistic about enhanced recruitment of foreign investments because Colorado "does have a highly educated workforce, scenic beauty and great opportunities for recreation and tourism, a major new international airport, . . . world-class technology companies supported by superb research universities, and a welcoming political and business climate."[16]

Finally, any plans for promoting the state's economy must recognize that Colorado's first and greatest asset is its environment. Environmental integrity must always be placed with economic development at the top of the policy agenda. A state with scarred mountainsides, smoggy and polluted urban areas, decaying cities, and extensive urban sprawl will turn away businesses. It will also turn away the top professionals the state wants to lure to Colorado to work in existing businesses, government agencies, and universities.

In dealing with environmental issues, it is important to remember that urban as well as rural environmental protection is crucial for Colorado. Coloradans should be equally clear about what they want to become and what they want to avoid becoming, and this will require not only the existence of statewide area-planning units but also the leadership and funds so that environmental tragedies can be averted.

Economic development and environmental protection efforts need to be addressed together, and business leaders and environmentalists need to find a common ground to talk together and negotiate their interests. A failure to do so spells long-term tragedy for the Centennial State.

CREATING A SUPERIOR EDUCATIONAL SYSTEM

In the early 1990s Colorado's Office of Business Development placed a colorful advertisement in airline magazines and elsewhere in which a young blond child is hoisting a Colorado flag in a schoolyard. In bold print the half-page ad says: "It's 8:00 A.M. and we know where our children are." The reader surmises the children are all in school and that Colorado is a state where education is a top priority. Then this Madison Avenue–styled script says that Colorado's economy will be a sound place in which to invest because Coloradans care about families and children. The ad goes on to say that Colorado's "schools, daycare programs, neighborhoods and environment . . . continue to rank among the top in the nation."

Curious about claims that Colorado's educational and learning systems ranked "among the top in the nation," one of the authors called the telephone number provided in the ad and asked about the high rankings of Colorado's educational system used in the promotional ad. The call was referred to a "business development representative" who laughed as if the ad were amusing. When asked about the school rankings to which the ad referred, he said he did not have them. Several questions later it had become plain that the Colorado Office of Business Development could not back up the claims of its promotional advertising.

The lesson is clear: Colorado should make accurate claims. Further, if Colorado wants to boast about its high-ranking schools, then it will have to continue to restructure its schools and human capital learning systems so they earn top rankings. Currently, Colorado can at best say its overall educational record is about average, yet not in the top dozen states.

Colorado usually ranks slightly above average among the states on broad educational indicators, such as test scores, ratios of graduating-nongraduating seniors, drop-out rates, pupil-teacher ratios, and spending for public schools and colleges and universities. Colorado did rank thirteenth among forty states that were compared on eighth-grade assessment tests in 1990.[17] Disturbing, however, was a Western Governors' Association Report that criticized Colorado for:

• Having a significant, general shortfall of investment in the learning needs of the adult workforce, especially for those needing basic education.
• Having no comprehensive policy or coordination mechanism to manage the entire portfolio of learning investment in the state.
• Having very little accountability for achievement of results from existing investments. The great majority of funds are distributed to schools and colleges by formula, with relatively few state requirements.
• Having no statewide program to increase the capital/labor ratio, modernize the technology, or generally improve the productivity of education and training institutions.
• Having an overly institution-oriented approach rather than a consumer-orientation, thereby causing an absence of consumer choice and competition among the providers of education, training, and related services.
• Having the lion's share of state investments in human capital development directed to a predominantly and increasingly unproductive sector.[18]

Colorado ranks high among states for the amount of formal schooling the average adult has completed, yet 40 percent of Colorado employers report having employees who cannot apply basic reading and math skills. The Public Service Company of Colorado fails nearly half of those who apply for jobs to read meters. The Safeway food chain fails at least one third of their applicants because of deficient basic skills.

The Colorado Adult Literacy Commission found that while the state spends over $16,000 a year to keep an inmate in prison and over $10,000 a year to keep a family on welfare, Colorado is one of only a few states providing no funds for literacy development to the general adult population. Less than 10 percent of adult Coloradans needing literacy assistance are being served, the commission said. "Ideally, we'd like to eradicate illiteracy in the state," says Tom Howerton, who served as chair of the Adult Literacy Commission sponsored by the state Board of Education. "Economically, it's a vital issue. Colorado needs its citizens to be literate in order for our state to compete in the world's economy."[19]

Colorado, like many other states, has had a continuing debate over whether parents and students should be able to pick their schools. This is often called the "school choice" or "voucher debate." Libertarians and conservatives in Colorado, led by John Andrews, the unsuccessful 1990 Republican nominee for governor, KOA radio talk-show host Michael Rosen, and former state senators Hugh Fowler and Terry Considine, have urged a major voucher or choice plan for Colorado. The Colorado Education Association, which represents most of the kindergarten through twelfth-grade public school teachers, and various school board organizations have opposed these ideas.

In 1990 the Colorado state legislature approved a modest school-choice bill that allows parents to choose among the various public schools in the school district where they live, provided the selected school has room. An experimental section of this new law even permits limited movement of students between school districts.

This recognition of choice may be a step in the right direction. Colorado, in a modest way, is joining school systems in Minnesota, Wisconsin, Oregon, and Arkansas that have pioneered consumer- and student-oriented educational investments. "To survive, each school would have to carve out a clientele of parents and students to which it had special appeal. Some might specialize in educating the gifted, while others may focus on kids with learning disabilities. Most would probably specialize by curriculum, some emphasizing math and science, some the dramatic arts, and so on."[20]

More voice, choice, and competition might help revitalize Colorado school systems. Choice means schools will have to perform well or risk losing their students. A certain infusion of the marketplace concept might help lead to a results-based, rather than an input-based investment option for learning. It should be noted, however, that Coloradan voters in the November 1992 elections decisively defeated a proposed voucher plan that would have allowed parents to use state funds at church and private schools as part of a major "choice" program.

Top colleges and universities not only help to lure big and small businesses to the state, but brainpower in the form of leading-edge research and development are vital to the invention of new technologies and products. California, Massachusetts, North Carolina, and Texas have been leaders in high-tech business activities in large part because of the synergistic relationship between industry and world-class higher educational institutions. To the state's credit, Colorado is investing much more than it once did in higher education, yet in 1992 Colorado ranked an embarrasing forty-sixth in the nation in spending per college and university student.[21]

TOWARD A BALANCED TAX SYSTEM

No policies in Colorado are more debated and criticized than tax and spending issues. Coloradans in general have low state taxes and relatively high local property and sales taxes. Local governments have borne the burden of providing most services. Many economists and business leaders believe there should be a more even balance between state and local financing in Colorado.

Similar to many other states, Colorado has numerous individuals and businesses that owe money to the state. There should be a stepped-up and aggressive overhaul of tax collections, tax inspections, and audits. The Colorado Department of Revenue needs added authority and enforcement leverage in order for it to earn respect and become more efficient. A recent tax amnesty program worked well and should be tried again.

Perhaps the most heated debate of the past decade in Colorado has revolved around whether citizens should be granted the right to approve at the ballot box any tax increases that are to be imposed on Colorado taxpayers. As noted in chapter 4, Colorado voters came close in 1990 to adopting a constitutional amendment that would require a vote of the people on both state and local tax increases. In 1992 Colorado voters approved this measure, Amendment 1, which will force the state to submit any new taxes to the voters for their approval. This amendment will have major implications for state financing and tax politics.

Coloradans, obviously, do not like taxes, and Colorado's elected officials are tax-conscious. On balance, Colorado taxes, state and local combined, are at the national mean. "While Colorado public opinion is in favor of tax limitation, its views are not strongly held," said pollster and political consultant Floyd Ciruli.[22] Colorado voters will occasionally vote to approve added special taxes for such services or amenities as libraries, museums, zoos, or a major league baseball stadium, but only if they are persuaded about the genuine merits of the service in question. The voters in 1992 voted against a one-cent increase in taxes earmarked for Colorado public schools, a measure advocated by Governor Roy Romer and the state teachers organizations— apparently because voters believed taxes were already too high and the schools could somehow make do.

Coloradans need to learn more about taxes and how and for what purposes their taxes are spent. Tax education should be part of the high school curriculum as well as the work of the media and civic and party organizations. A good tax will always be one "that the other fellow has to pay." Still, Coloradans need to know more about local mill levies, excise taxes, fishing license fees, and the twenty-two cents on the gallon Coloradans pay every time they fill up their gas tanks (one of the nation's highest gas tax rates).

What is the best tax? What is fair? These and many related questions should be part of the new civics in social studies programs at all levels. This will not end grass-roots tax-limitation movements, but it would elevate the quality of the debate and get more citizens involved in making some of the hard choices about taxing and spending.

PROMOTING TOURISM

Colorado's state and local governments as well as its tourism industries try to be creative in convincing tourists to make Colorado a destination for vacations. Year-round tourism is vital to Colorado's economic future. Yet in recent years California's Disneyland alone has spent more than four times as much to attract visitors to the amusement park than the state of Colorado spends on promoting tourism.

Most experts agree that it is not just how much money is spent to promote tourism—it is how the money is spent. Colorado needs to think strategically about its tourism opportunities. "Investments in roads, airports, clean air and water, advertising, and promotion will pay handsome dividends for generations to come," says *Denver Post* editorial page editor Chuck Green. "The state's natural beauty remains its people's greatest asset, and it needs more attractive care."[23]

Colorado's Tourism Board is financed by a modest tourism sales tax of .002 percent on lodging, restaurant food and drinks, ski lift and admission tickets, private tourist attractions, rental vehicles, and tour buses. (This tax and the Colorado Tourism Board will expire because their legislative term will be up in mid 1993. If the tax is to be continued, it will have to win voter approval pursuant to Amendment 1 passed by voters in 1992.) Colorado is only sixteenth among the states in what is spent to lure tourists, even though tourism is the state's number two industry.

The Tourism Board is trying to lure more foreign tourists, and is promoting more than just skiing. The board has set up welcome centers at state entry points in Trinidad, Fruita, Cortez, and Burlington.[24] Staffed mostly by volunteers, the centers are designed to encourage those visitors just driving through Colorado to stay longer, visit more locations, and, most importantly, spend more money. Preliminary results indicate that these welcome centers are having positive results.

The vitality of the tourism industry in Colorado depends on much more than government promotion, however. The tourism industry itself has to advertise as inventively as possible. And it has to appreciate that bad quality is a broken promise. The tourism industry has to ensure that it is offering a quality product. Public-private collaborations also make sense, such as the joint efforts to xeriscape (landscape without using much water) open land in downtown Denver near I-70, I-25, and Colfax Avenue.

If Colorado is going to compete in the intensive tourist-luring competition with other states and nations, it will have to:

> Replace the dull brown welcome signs at the state's borders. These signs say, ''Welcome to Colorful Colorado,'' but are singularly colorless themselves.
> Improve highway signs in rural areas of the state to point out mountain ranges and provide better indication of distances between locations.
> Provide more markers for historic and scenic points of interest at or near major points of interest.
> Promote mountain climbing and cycling in Colorado as well as its nearly two-hundred golf courses.
> Encourage more and better hiking, biking, and horseback-riding trails throughout the state.
> Help publicize tourist attractions in the less visible regions of the state, such as the Shrine of Sangre de Cristo in San Luis and the Guadalupe Church in Conejos.[25]

These are merely illustrative of a range of opportunities both the public and private sectors must exploit to ensure Colorado's role as a tourist attraction.

Infrastructure is a relatively new and perhaps overly fancy term for what used to be called "public works." Infrastructure refers to public facilities such as streets, highways, bridges, dams, reservoirs, water and sewer lines, and airports.

Major work always is needed to update the over 75,000 miles of state highways, county roads, and city streets in Colorado. The state has nearly 4,500 bridges, and as many as 500 more may have to be built in the late 1990s. Perhaps as many as 1,500 of the existing bridges may become structurally deficient in the next twenty-five years.[26]

Infrastructure-rebuilding efforts are needed for public safety, for making Colorado competitive for economic development, and for promoting tourism. Business visitors and tourists are quick to judge a state by the quality of its airports, roads, and similar facilities. Congested highways in and around Denver are a deterrent to business and tourist promotion.

Colorado needs a top-quality infrastructure, most of all to serve its own citizens. If Coloradans themselves admire their own public facilities, that in itself is a desirable goal—and in the long run that will promote the tourism and business climates that are also important to the economic health of the state. It makes sense to create a state Department of Transportation (CODOT) to provide the needed integration of some of these efforts.

Colorado also will need more water storage projects. Giant dams such as the much-debated Two Forks are less likely to be approved and funded in the near future. But no one doubts, even with the most stringent conservation efforts, Colorado's real need for additional water storage facilities. These must be planned and built in advance of their actual need. Here again, long-term strategic planning is essential.

HUMAN RESOURCES

Many Coloradans want the state to be able to provide care and services for those who cannot provide for themselves. Everyone should have access to quality medical care, it is often argued, as well as to prevention programs and rehabilitation services. While as many people as possible should be encouraged to be self-reliant, it is a mark of a civilized society that communities take care of their truly needy.

Those of a moralistic political culture, as that term has been used in this book, are clearly more committed to the compassionate vision of the state than are those of the individualist persuasion. Individualists emphasize the need for individuals to take care of themselves; if that fails, then their families, churches, or similar volunteer and charitable organizations should tend to these needs. The state should enter in only as a last resort, according to individualists.

Yet there are those who point out that there are thousands of forgotten children, children at risk, children and adults with disabilities, adults who cannot read above the fourth-grade level, alcohol and substance abusers, and victims of mental illness, AIDS, and other ailments. These are just a few of the people for whom private and public social policies are a must.

Every state, and Colorado can be no exception, has to behave as if its most precious resources are human beings. And a society that is committed to encouraging equal opportunities and ensuring that all young people develop their abilities as far as is possible has to provide the investment in human capital to make this a reality.

PUBLIC SAFETY

Colorado needs a stepped-up war on drugs. Most Coloradans said they are willing to pay slightly increased taxes if the governor and the legislature earmark such revenues for a coherent and specific war to eradicate dangerous drugs from the state. Yet Coloradans would pay these additional taxes only if they were convinced drug abuse would be significantly reduced.

Prison inmate literacy and substance-abuse programs are needed. Most inmates in Colorado prisons have had serious alcohol or drug habits. Most also are unable to read above the fourth-grade level. Peer-tutoring programs can help some. If properly done, investments in upgrading, educating, and training the prisoners and juvenile offenders of the state will pay rich dividends in lowered crime rates, decreased welfare costs, and an improved work force. Investments in the corrections budget are among the least popular with taxpayers. Yet again, the mark of an enlightened society is whether or not it treats its lawbreakers with decency and a chance for rehabilitation.

At the same time, the rights of victims of crime need to be continually kept uppermost in everyone's mind. The state and local governments in Colorado have the enormous and costly responsibility of ensuring that law enforcement officials at all levels of government are well-trained and well-equipped to prevent as many crimes as possible and that they swiftly apprehend lawbreakers. The public is justifiably discouraged by the low percentages of lawbreakers who are arrested and properly penalized. Crime prevention has to be everyone's business, and police and sheriff departments can be significantly helped by neighborhood crime watch programs and related citizen assistance efforts.

HUMAN RIGHTS IN COLORADO

Colorado, like most states, has had its share of intolerance and chauvinism. Native Americans, Latinos, Asian Americans, Catholics, African Americans, immigrants, and more recently gays have all been victims of intolerance and sometimes even violence directed at them in Colorado. Coloradans in the mid-1990s think of themselves as reasonably tolerant and as generally respecting other people's privacy, liberty, and freedoms. But intolerance in at least limited degrees endures here as elsewhere in the United States.

Coloradans need to respect religious, ethnic, and sexual-orientation differences. The passage of Amendment 2 in 1992 once again reminded everyone in the Centennial State that tolerance is never wholly guaranteed. The 1992 anti-gay sentiment that flared up as a result of the passage of Amendment 2 is doubtless evidence of a more general failure of Coloradans to treat one another with respect and an appreciation for diversity. Coloradans, just as all Americans, have to keep fighting intolerance and bigotry whenever they arise. And this issue must be an especially important priority for elected officials, educators, business leaders, religious leaders, and the media.

Governor Roy Romer rightly urged in 1993 that all Coloradans, whether churchgoers or not, "spend less time trying to determine what it is we ought to legislate about the morality of others and spend more time trying to determine how we can create communities where each of us can grow."[27]

CONCLUSION

Colorado is a rich state, blessed with wondrous beauty and talented people. Its aspirations are high, and its civic and political leaders are trying to devise policies and programs that lead in even more positive directions.

The institutions of government in Colorado are, on balance, responsive and efficient. Most elected officials care deeply about making Colorado an attractive and responsible state. Elected and unelected leaders alike are forever trying to strike a balance between economic growth and preserving the glorious natural beauty that has long made Colorado famous.

Battles over water, taxes, and education will always play a central role in

Colorado politics and government. A continuing tug of war will doubtless remain among contending factions: between advocates of the status quo and reformers, between metropolitan-area residents and rural or resort-area residents, between environmentalists and developers, between Republicans and Democrats, between the governor and the legislature, between city and county interests, and between the state and the "feds."

The state's assets plainly outweigh its liabilities. Most of its problems are solvable. Improvements in the governmental and political system, some of which are discussed in this book, are needed. And when these and similar improvements are made, they will further unlock the talents and energies of the people of Colorado.

Suggestions for Further Research
and Reading

Colorado has a number of libraries that contain a rich lode of source material on the state's history and politics. The University of Colorado at Boulder has an excellent collection, as does the University of Denver. Particularly useful are the master's theses and doctoral dissertations on Colorado history and politics that are kept at the political science department at Boulder.

Convenient to researchers in southern Colorado is the Colorado Room in the Tutt Library at Colorado College in Colorado Springs. This special collection of books, photographs, and other memorabilia about Colorado in general and Colorado Springs in particular is both helpful and accessible.

Useful materials are also available at the State Historical Society, which has its own building and museum one block southwest of the state capitol in Denver. The original copy of the state constitution is kept at the historical society, but it is not on display to the general public.

Both the *Denver Post* and the *Rocky Mountain News* file clippings of their major newspaper articles and allow scholars to peruse them. Much of the material prior to the 1980s is on microfilm, so readers must search for a story in the filmed whole newspaper (after locating it in an index) rather than reading an actual clipping. The *Colorado Statesman* is a weekly newspaper published in Denver for those particularly interested in Colorado politics and government. It also is a rich source of gossip about politicians, lobbyists, and political consultants.

There are several daily newspapers published in the smaller cities on the Front Range, such as the *Colorado Springs Gazette Telegraph*, the *Boulder Daily Camera*, and the *Pueblo Chieftain*, and these provide occasional analyses of state as well as local politics.

Considerable polling is now done in Colorado, and many of the pollsters will allow scholars to study the results of previous polls. Talmey-Drake Associates in Boulder and Floyd Ciruli and Associates in Denver are two of the more prominent polling firms in Colorado. The *Denver Post* has an extensive archive of past Colorado poll results (mainly conducted in the 1980s and 1990s by the Talmey organization).

Official election results for Colorado statewide and national elections are available from the Office of the Colorado Secretary of State, which is located about one block northwest of the state capitol in Denver. Registration data is also available from the same source.

The Centennial State still is small enough that most high-ranking state officials are willing to give interviews to scholars, researchers, and students. These often can be arranged directly or through the public relations offices of the various departments of state government.

The staff of the Legislative Council (located in the northwest corner of the basement of the capitol) is generally helpful to scholars, has a great deal of information about Colorado immediately at hand, and usually knows which particular division of state government is responsible for which governmental and political functions. The state geographer has a wealth of information about Colorado's physical features. The state demographer, in the Department of Local Affairs, can provide population data.

Researchers will find it useful to interview current and retired journalists who have covered Colorado politics and government for the Associated Press, the Denver newspapers, and related media.

There are a dozen or so experts on the history and politics of the Centennial State who teach at the state's colleges and universities. Among the especially well informed are historian Duane Smith at Fort Lewis College in Durango, political scientist Robert Lorch at the University of Colorado at Colorado Springs, political scientist John Straayer at Colorado State University in Fort Collins, and political scientists Conrad McBride and Dan Sloan at the University of Colorado at Boulder.

Nor should one overlook former governors, retired judges, and former state legislators, particularly former legislative leaders. Although their expertise is concentrated in particular time periods, these former participants in the political process often can provide invaluable perspectives.

The careful student of Colorado politics and government will want to examine the standard writings. We provide, on the following pages, a listing of the many works we consulted for our research. We have not included everything that is available, yet we have tried to include the most important bibliographic materials. We have also included a list of the master's theses and doctoral dissertations on Colorado subjects that we consulted in the course of our own research. Again, these are selective and not exhaustive bibliographies.

Selected References on Colorado History, Politics, and Government

BOOKS

Abbott, Carl, Stephen J. Leonard, and David McComb. *Colorado: A History of the Centennial State*. Rev. ed. Boulder: Colorado Associated University Press, 1982.

Athearn, Robert G. *The Coloradans*. Albuquerque: University of New Mexico Press, 1976.

————. *Rebel of the Rockies: A History of the Denver and Rio Grande Western Railroad*. New Haven: Yale University Press, 1962.

Atwood, Wallace W. *The Rocky Mountains*. New York: Vanguard Press, 1945.

Baker, James H., and Leroy R. Hafen, eds. *History of Colorado*. Vols. 1–5. Denver: State Historical Society of Colorado, 1927.

Blakey, Roy G. *The United States Beet-Sugar Industry and the Tariff*. New York: Longmans, Green and Co., 1912.

Borneman, Walter R., and Lyndon J. Lampert. *A Climbing Guide to Colorado's Fourteeners*. Boulder: Pruett Publishing Co., 1984.

Cassels, E. Steve. *The Archeology of Colorado*. Boulder: Johnson Books, 1983.

Chalmers, David M. *Hooded Americanism: The First Century of the Ku Klux Klan, 1865–1965*. New York: Doubleday and Co., 1965.

Colton, Ray C. *The Civil War in the Western Territories: Arizona, Colorado, New Mexico and Utah*. Norman: University of Oklahoma Press, 1959.

Cronin, Thomas E. *Direct Democracy: The Politics of Initiative, Referendum and Recall*. Cambridge: Harvard University Press, 1989.

Davis, Kenneth S. *Kansas: A History*. New York: W. W. Norton and Co., 1984.

Donnelly, Thomas C., ed. *Rocky Mountain Politics*. Albuquerque: University of New Mexico Press, 1940.

DeVoto, Bernard, ed. *The Journals of Lewis and Clark*. Boston: Houghton Mifflin Co., 1953.

Ehrenhalt, Alan. *The United States of Ambition: Politicians, Power, and the Pursuit of Office*. New York: Random House, 1991.

Elazar, Daniel J. *American Federalism: A View from the States*. 2d ed. New York: Thomas Y. Crowell, 1972.

———. *Cities of the Prairie: The Metropolitan Frontier and American Politics*. New York: Basic Books, 1970.

———. *Cities of the Prairie Revisited: The Closing of the Metropolitan Frontier*. Lincoln: University of Nebraska Press, 1986.

Ellis, Elmer. *Henry Moore Teller: Defender of the West*. Caldwell, Id.: Caxton Printers, 1941.

Ellis, Richard N., and Duane A. Smith. *Colorado: A History in Photographs*. Niwot, Colo.: University Press of Colorado, 1991.

Garnsey, Morris E. *America's New Frontier: The Mountain West*. New York: Alfred A. Knopf, 1950.

Goldberg, Robert Alan. *Hooded Empire: The Ku Klux Klan in Colorado*. Urbana: University of Illinois Press, 1981.

Gonzales, Rudolfo. *I Am Joaquin*. New York: Bantam Books, 1972.

Greenbaum, Fred. *Fighting Progressive: A Biography of Edward P. Costigan*. Washington, D.C.: Public Affairs Press, 1971.

Gulliford, Andrew. *Boomtown Blues: Colorado Oil Shale, 1885–1985*. Niwot: University Press of Colorado, 1989.

Hafen, Le Roy R. *Colorado: The Story of a Western Commonwealth*. Denver: Peerless Publishing Co., 1933.

Harmon, Robert Bartlett. *Government and Politics in Colorado: An Information Source Survey*. Monticello, Ill.: Vance Bibliographies, 1978.

Harvey, Lashley G., and Frank C. Spencer. *Colorado: Its Government and History*. Denver: Herrick Book and Stationery Co., 1934.

Hogan, Richard. *Class and Community in Frontier Colorado*. Lawrence: University Press of Kansas, 1990.

Hollister, Ovando J. *Boldly They Rode: A History of the First Regiment of Colorado Volunteers*. Lakewood, Colo.: Golden Press, 1949.

Hollon, W. Eugene. *The Lost Pathfinder: Zebulon Montgomery Pike*. Norman: University of Oklahoma Press, 1949.

Hosokawa, Bill. *Thunder in the Rockies: The Incredible Denver Post*. New York: William Morrow and Co., 1976.

Hrebenar, Ronald J., and Clive S. Thomas, eds. *Interest Group Politics in the American West*. Salt Lake City: University of Utah Press, 1987.

Hundley, Norris, Jr. *Water and the West: The Colorado River Compact and the Poli-*

tics of Water in the American West. Berkeley and Los Angeles: University of California Press, 1975.

Jackson, Donald. *Thomas Jefferson and the Stony Mountains: Exploring the West from Monticello*. Urbana: University of Illinois Press, 1981.

Jackson, Helen Hunt. *A Century of Dishonor*. New York: Harper and Row, 1965.

James, Frank H., ed. *Politics in the American West*. Salt Lake City: University of Utah Press, 1969.

Johnson, Frank T. *Autobiography of a Centenarian*. Denver: Big Mountain Press, 1961.

Josephy, Alvin M., Jr. *The Civil War in the American West*. New York: Alfred A. Knopf, 1991.

Kelly, George V. *The Old Gray Mayors of Denver*. Boulder: Pruett Publishing Co., 1974.

King, Clyde L. *The History of the Government of Denver with Special References to Its Relations with Public Service Corporations*. Denver: Fisher Book Co., 1911.

Lamm, Richard D. *The Lamm Administration: A Retrospective Summary*. Denver: Office of the Governor, 1986.

Lamm, Richard D., and Michael McCarthy. *The Angry West: A Vulnerable Land and Its Future*. Boston: Houghton Mifflin Co., 1982.

Lamm, Richard D., and Duane A. Smith. *Pioneers and Politicians: 10 Colorado Governors in Profile*. Boulder: Pruett Publishing Co., 1981.

Langdon, Emma F. *The Cripple Creek Strike*. Denver: Great Western Publishing Co., 1904.

Larson, Charles. *The Good Fight: The Life and Times of Ben B. Lindsey*. Chicago: Quadrangle Books, 1972.

Larson, Robert W. *Populism in the Mountain West*. Albuquerque: University of New Mexico Press, 1986.

Lavender, David. *Bent's Fort*. Garden City, N.Y.: Doubleday and Co., 1954.

Limerick, Patricia Nelson. *The Legacy of Conquest*. New York: W. W. Norton and Co., 1987.

Lindsey, Benjamin B. *The Beast*. New York: Doubleday, Page and Co., 1910.

Lorch, Robert S. *Colorado's Government*. 5th ed. Niwot, Colo.: University Press of Colorado, 1991.

McGovern, George S., and Leonard F. Guttridge. *The Great Coalfield War*. Boston: Houghton Mifflin Co., 1972.

Marin, Christine. *A Spokesman of the Mexican American Movement: Rodolofo "Corky" Gonzales and the Fight for Chicano Liberation, 1966–1972*. San Francisco: R and E Research Associates, 1977.

Martin, Curtis W. *Colorado Politics*. Denver: Big Mountain Press, 1960.

Martin, Curtis W., and Rudolph Gomez. *Colorado Government and Politics*. 3d ed. Boulder: Pruett Publishing Co., 1972.

Michener, James A. *Centennial*. New York: Random House, 1974.

Morris, John R. *Davis H. Waite: The Ideology of a Western Populist*. Washington, D.C.: University Press of America, 1982.

Ormes, Robert M. *Guide to the Colorado Mountains*. 7th ed. Colorado Springs: Robert Ormes, 1979.

Parkman, Francis, et al. *Chronicles of Colorado*. Boulder: Roberts Rinehart, 1984.

Pepper, Henry C. *County Government in Colorado*. Fort Collins: Colorado Agricultural College, 1934.

Peirce, Neal R. *The Mountain States of America*. New York: W. W. Norton and Co., 1972.

Proceedings of the Constitutional Convention to Frame a Constitution for the State of Colorado. Denver: Smith-Brooks Press, State Printers, 1907.

Osborne, David. *Laboratories of Democracy*. Boston: Harvard Business School Press, 1988.

Powell, John Wesley. *Report on the Lands of the Arid Region of the United States*. Washington, D.C.: United States Government Printing Office, 1878.

Reisner, Marc. *Cadillac Desert: The American West and Its Disappearing Water*. New York: Penguin Books, 1987.

Reisner, Marc, and Sarah Bates. *Overtapped Oasis: Reform or Revolution for Western Water*. Washington, D.C.: Island Press, 1990.

Rohrbough, Malcom J. *Aspen: The History of a Silver Mining Town, 1879–1893*. New York: Oxford University Press, 1986.

Rosenthal, Alan, and Maureen Moakley, eds. *The Political Life of the American States*. New York: Praeger, 1984.

Shockley, John S. *The Initiative Process in Colorado Politics: An Assessment*. Boulder: Bureau of Governmental Research and Service, University of Colorado, 1980.

Shoemaker, Joe. *Budgeting Is the Answer: A Story of a Unique Committee, the JBC of Colorado*. Denver: World Press, 1977.

Smith, Duane A. *The Birth of Colorado: A Civil War Perspective*. Norman: University of Oklahoma Press, 1989.

———. *Horace Tabor: His Life and Legend*. Boulder: Colorado Associated University Press, 1973.

Sprague, Marshall. *Colorado: A History*. New York: W. W. Norton and Co., 1984.

———. *Massacre: The Tragedy at White River*. Boston: Little, Brown and Co., 1957.

———. *Money Mountain: The Story of Cripple Creek Gold*. Boston: Little, Brown, 1953.

Stegner, Wallace. *Beyond the Hundredth Meridian: John Wesley Powell and the Second Opening of the West*. Introduction by Bernard DeVoto. Boston: Houghton Mifflin Co., 1954.

Stone, William Fiske, ed. *History of Colorado*. Chicago: Clark Publishing Co., 1918.

Straayer, John A. *The Colorado General Assembly*. Niwot, Colo.: University Press of Colorado, 1990.

Suggs, George C. *Colorado's War on Military Unionism: James H. Peabody and the Western Federation of Miners*. Detroit: Wayne State University Press, 1972. Reprint, with a new preface. Norman: University of Oklahoma Press, 1991.

Summer, Helen L. *Equal Suffrage: The Results of an Investigation in Colorado Made for the Collegiate Equal Suffrage League of New York State*. New York: Harper and Brothers, 1909.

Ubbelohde, Carl, ed. *A Colorado Reader*. Rev. ed. Boulder: Pruett Publishing Co., 1964.

Ubbelohde, Carl, Maxine Benson, and Duane Smith. *A Colorado History*. 6th ed. Boulder: Pruett Publishing Co., 1988.

Vandenbusche, Duane, and Duane A. Smith. *A Land Alone: Colorado's Western Slope*. Boulder: Pruett Publishing Co., 1981.

Walton, Roger Alan. *Colorado: A Practical Guide to Its Government and Politics*. Revised ed. Lakewood, Colo.: Colorado Times Publishing Co., 1991.

Waters, Frank. *The Colorado*. 1946. Reprint. Athens, Ohio: Swallow Press, 1984.

Whitford, William Clarke. *Colorado Volunteers in the Civil War*. Glorieta, N.M.: Rio Grande, 1974.

Wilbanks, William. *The Make My Day Law: Colorado's Experiment in Home Protection*. Lanham, Md.: University Press of America, 1990.

Wilkinson, Charles F. *Crossing the Next Meridian: Land, Water, and the Future of the West*. Washington, D.C., and Covelo, Calif.: Island Press, 1992.

Woodbury, David O. *The Colorado Conquest*. New York: Dodd, Mead and Co., 1941.

Woodword, Phyllis. *The Adventure in the State House*. Denver: Colorado Department of Education, 1980.

Wright, James Edward. *The Politics of Populism: Dissent in Colorado*. New Haven: Yale University Press, 1974.

DISSERTATIONS

Fox, Leonard P. "Origins and Early Development of Populism in Colorado." Ph.D. diss., University of Pennsylvania, 1916.

Hensel, Donald W. "A History of the Colorado Constitution in the Nineteenth Century." Ph.D. diss., University of Colorado, 1957.

Hjelm, Victory S. "The Colorado State Legislator: Tenure and Turnover." Ph.D. diss., University of Colorado, 1967.

Hogan, Richard L. "Law and Order in Colorado: 1858–1888." Ph.D.diss., University of Michigan, 1982.

Huber, Frances Ann. "The Progressive Career of Ben B. Lindsey, 1900–1920." Ph.D. diss., University of Michigan, 1963.

Knautz, Harlan E. "The Progressive Harvest in Colorado: 1910–1916." Ph.D. diss., University of Denver, 1969.

Knott, Robert H. "State Growth Management Policy: The Development of the Colorado Revenue Process." Ph.D. diss., University of Colorado, 1982.

Olson, Laura L. K. "Power, Public Policy and the Environment: The Defeat of the 1976 Winter Olympics in Colorado." Ph.D. diss., University of Colorado, 1974.

Pisciotte, Joseph P. "The Colorado State Legislator: Entry into the Legislative Process." Ph.D. diss., University of Colorado, 1967.

Stealy, Wallace R. "The Politics of the Colorado Department of Game, Fish and Parks." Ph.D. diss., University of Colorado, 1968.

Suggs, George. "Colorado Conservatives vs. Organized Labor: A Study of the Peabody Administration." Ph.D. diss., University of Colorado, 1964.

Wickens, James F. "Colorado in the Great Depression: A Study of New Deal Policies at the State Level." Ph.D. diss., University of Denver, 1964.

MASTER'S THESES

Atcheson, Carlo Joan. "Nativism in Colorado Politics." Master's thesis, University of Colorado, 1970.

August, Stephen M. "Resolution of Water Regulation Conflict in the Colorado River Basin: The Interstate Compact." Master's thesis. University of Colorado at Colorado Springs, 1972.

Bence, Gregory Alexander. "The Knights of Labor in Colorado." Master's thesis, University of Northern Colorado, 1974.

Bird, Leah M. "The History of Third Parties in Colorado." Master's thesis, University of Denver, 1942.

Davis, James E. "The Rise of the Ku Klux Klan in Colorado, 1921–1925." Master's thesis, University of Denver, 1963.

Decker, Gerhart J. "Early Colorado Statehood Movements and National Politics (1860–1867)." Master's thesis, University of Denver, 1943.

Fisher, Gary K. "A Political Analysis of the Enactment of H.B. 1041 (A Colorado Land Use Act), 1974." Master's thesis, Colorado State University, 1975.

Girran, Robert B. "Carl Whitehead and the Socialist Party of Colorado, 1930–1955." Master's thesis, University of Denver, 1967.

Hornbein, Marjorie. "Colorado's Amazing Gubernatorial Election Contest of 1904." Master's thesis, University of Denver, 1967.

Kobs, Katherine M. "The Political Career of William Lee Knous." Master's thesis, University of Colorado, 1972.

Kolomitz, Jon. "The Influence of the K.K.K. in Colorado Politics." Master's thesis, University of Colorado, 1962.

Kountze, Harold J., Jr. "Davis H. Waite and the People's Party in Colorado." Master's thesis, Yale University, 1944.

Manlsis, George P. "A History of the Early Life and Gubernatorial Administration of Governor George A. Carlson, 1915–1917." Master's thesis, University of Denver, 1963.

McCarty, Patrick F. "Big Ed Johnson of Colorado—A Political Portrait." Master's thesis, University of Colorado, 1958.

Mischke, Bert B. "Judicial Interpretation of the Constitutional Powers of the Governor of Colorado." Master's thesis, University of Denver, 1947.

Olson, Lynn Marie. "The Essence of Colorado Populism: An Analysis of the Populists and the Issues of 1892." Master's thesis, University of Northern Colorado, 1971.

Rhodes, Robert B. "Governor John Evans." Master's thesis, University of Denver, 1952.

Roussalis, Mary. "The Administration of Colorado's Governor Fredrich W. Pitkin, 1879–1883." Master's thesis, University of Denver, 1962.

Shelly, Walter L. "The Colorado Party: The Formative Years, 1861–1876." Master's thesis, University of Colorado, 1963.

Simmons, Thomas Hood. "The Electoral System of the Colorado General Assembly, 1972–1980." Master's thesis, University of Colorado at Boulder, 1981.

Starr, Paul D. "The Initiative and Referendum in Colorado." Master's thesis, University of Colorado, 1958.

Strovas, Frank C. "Rural Precinct Committeemen in Colorado: A Study of Elbert, Lincoln and Washington Counties." Master's thesis, University of Colorado, 1972.

Welch, Gerald D. "John F. Shafroth, Progressive Governor of Colorado, 1910–1912." Master's thesis, University of Denver, 1962.

Wells, Cyrus E. "Eugene D. Millikin: A Senator's Senator." Master's thesis. University of Colorado, 1962.

Zerlenga, Antoinette U. "The Governor's Veto in Colorado." Master's thesis, University of Colorado, 1935.

Notes

CHAPTER ONE

1 John Gunther, *Inside U.S.A.* (New York: Harper and Brothers, 1947), p. 213.

2 For useful revisionism of the cowboy and mountain-men legends, see Patricia Nelson Limerick, *The Legacy of Conquest* (New York: Norton, 1987).

3 Bruce Driver, *Western Water: Tuning the System,* report to the Western Governors' Association, July 7, 1986. MINCO, Denver, Colorado, p. 1.

4 Adopted from comments made by state Representative Renny Fagan, Democrat, House district 22 (Colorado Springs), July 15, 1990.

5 Edward Abbey, quoted in Miriam Horn, "The New Old West," *Rocky Mountain News Sunday Magazine,* July 15, 1990, p. 13–M.

6 Colorado Association of Commerce and Industry Educational Foundation, *Blueprint for Colorado: A Look at the 90s,* June 1990, p. 15.

7 Richard D. Lamm and Michael McCarthy, *The Angry West: A Vulnerable Land and Its Future* (Boston: Houghton Mifflin, 1982), p. 277.

8 Thomas H. Simmons, "Colorado," in Alan Rosenthal and Maureen Moakley, eds., *The Political Life of the American States* (New York: Praeger, 1984), p. 64. See also Daniel J. Elazar, *Cities of the Prairie: The Metropolitan Frontier and American Politics* (New York: Basic Books, 1970), p. 348–51.

9 James C. Pierce, director, Colorado Endowment for the Humanities, telephone interview by T. Cronin, Denver, June 1990.

10 Duane Vandenbusche and Duane A. Smith, *A Land Alone: Colorado's Western Slope* (Boulder: Pruett Publishing, 1981).

11 Gunther, *Inside USA,* p. 213. See also Neal R. Peirce, *The Mountain States of America* (New York: Norton, 1972), chap. 2.

12 Paul Talmey, pollster and political analyst, interview by T. Cronin, Boulder, June 7, 1990.

13 Bob Ewegen, *Denver Post* editor, interview by T. Cronin, Denver, July 1990.

14 Patricia Nelson Limerick, *The Legacy of Conquest* (New York: Norton, 1987).

15 Walt Klein, political consultant, telephone interview by T. Cronin, Winston-Salem, N.C., June 14, 1990.

16 Author notes from John Andrews–Roy Romer debate, Colorado Municipal League, Sheraton Hotel South, Colorado Springs, June 20, 1990.

17 James A. Michener, *Centennial* (New York: Random House, 1974), p. 926.

18 James Edward Wright, *The Politics of Populism: Dissent in Colorado* (New Haven: Yale University Press, 1974), p. 191.

19 See Robert Alan Goldberg, *Hooded Empire: The Ku Klux Klan in Colorado* (Urbana: University of Illinois Press, 1981).

20 Shawn Slater, quoted in Dirk Johnson, "Colorado Klansman Refines Message for the '90s," *New York Times* (national edition), February 23, 1992, p. 16.

21 Richard D. Lamm and Duane A. Smith, *Pioneers and Politicians: 10 Colorado Governors in Profile* (Boulder: Pruett Publishing, 1984), p. 132.

22 Richard D. Lamm, former governor, interview by T. Cronin, Denver, August 7, 1990.

23 See Elazar, *Cities of the Prairie,* chap. 6, and Daniel J. Elazar, *American Federalism: A View from the States,* 2d ed. (New York: Thomas Y. Crowell, 1972), pp. 84–126. See also John Kincaid, ed., *Political Culture, Public Policy and the American States* (Philadelphia: ISHI press, 1982), and a special issue of *Publius: The Journal of Federalism* 21 (spring 1991).

24 Talmey, interview, June 7, 1990.

25 See Ronald J. Hrebenar and Clive S. Thomas, eds., *Interest Group Politics in the American West* (Salt Lake City: University of Utah Press, 1987).

26 Miller Hudson, "Lobbyists Use Financial Clout," *Colorado Statesman,* May 25, 1980, p. 8.

1 See Carl Abbott, Stephen J. Leonard, and David McComb, *Colorado: A History of the Centennial State* rev. ed. (Boulder: Colorado Associated University Press, 1982), pp. 19–25.

2 Carl Ubbelohde, Maxine Benson, and Duane A. Smith, *A Colorado History* 5th ed. (Boulder: Pruett Publishing, 1982), p. 18.

3 Ibid., p. 60.

4 Duane Vandenbusche and Duane A. Smith, *A Land Alone: Colorado's Western Slope* (Boulder: Pruett Publishing, 1981), p. 77.

5 See Duane A. Smith, *Horace Tabor: His Life and Legend* (Boulder: Colorado Associated University Press, 1973).

6 Emma F. Langdon, *The Cripple Creek Strike* (Denver: Great Western Publishing, 1904), p. 16.

7 Robert G. Athearn, *Rebel of the Rockies: A History of the Denver and Rio Grande Western Railroad* (New Haven: Yale University Press, 1962), p. 101.

8 See Marshall Sprague, *Money Mountain: The Story of Cripple Creek Gold* (Boston: Little, Brown, 1953).

9 See George S. McGovern and Leonard F. Guttridge, *The Great Coalfield War* (Boston: Houghton Mifflin, 1972).

10 Vandenbusche and Smith, *A Land Alone*, p. 124.

11 Marshall Sprague, *Colorado: A History* (New York: Norton, 1984), p. 137.

12 Ubbelohde, Benson, and Smith, *A Colorado History*, p. 174.

13 Ibid., p. 331.

14 John Parr, letter to T. Cronin and R. Loevy, February 9, 1991.

15 For a range of views, see Richard D. Lamm and Michael McCarthy, *The Angry West: A Vulnerable Land and Its Future* (Boston: Houghton Mifflin, 1982), and the novels of Edward Abbey.

CHAPTER 3

1 Duane A. Smith, *The Birth of Colorado: A Civil War Perspective* (Norman: University of Oklahoma Press, 1989), p. 20.

2 The current state historical marker at Glorieta Pass simply reads: "The decisive battle of the Civil War fought in New Mexico was fought at the summit of Glorieta Pass on March 28, 1862. Union troops won the battle when a party of Colorado Volunteers burned the Confederate supply wagons, thus destroying Southern hopes for taking over New Mexico." The marker is located about a mile off present-day I-25. For background see Smith, *The Birth of Colorado*, p. 20; and Marc Simmons, *New Mexico: An Interpretative History* (New York: Norton, 1977). We also consulted a memoir of Benjamin Franklin Ferris, who fought in the First Colorado Volunteers, on file at the Civil War Museum at Glorieta Pass, New Mexico.

3 Alvin M. Josephy, Jr., *The Civil War in the American West* (New York: Alfred A. Knopf, 1991), pp. 76–86. Josephy entitled his chapter on the Battle of Glorieta Pass "Gettysburg of the West."

4 Smith, *The Birth of Colorado*, p. 210.

5 Carl Ubbelohde, Maxine Benson, and Duane A. Smith, *A Colorado History*, 5th ed. (Boulder: Pruett Publishing, 1982), p. 223.

6 Oliver Knight, "Correcting Nature's Error: The Colorado–Big Thompson Project," *Agricultural History* (October 1956): 157–69.

7 See Fred Greenbaum, *Fighting Progressive: A Bibliography of Edward P. Costigan* (Washington D.C.: Public Affairs Press, 1971).

8 See Andrew Gulliford, *Boomtown Blues: Colorado's Oil Shale, 1885–1985* (Niwot, Colo.: University Press of Colorado, 1989).

9 These environmental costs were claimed by the Sierra Club in *Peak and Prairie*, December 1987/January 1988, p. 3TF.

10 Richard D. Lamm, quoted in *Denver Post Magazine*, June 22, 1986, p. 17.

11 *Denver Post*, June 9, 1988, p. 6B.

12 See, for example, "Water Board Spokesman Rips Federal Regulation," *Rocky Mountain News*, June 3, 1990, p. 24.

13 Useful background essays are John Aloysius Farrell, "Denver Plays Its Water Card," *Denver Post Magazine*, June 22, 1986, pp. 17–23; Tim Wirth, "Water Equation Is Still Unsolved in the Formula for Colorado's Future," *Denver Post*, May 13, 1989, p. 7B; and Bill Hornby, "Mountain Water Is Vital to Front Range," *Denver Post*, June 12, 1990, p. 7B.

14 Mike Bird, Republican, state Senate district 9 (northern Colorado Springs and northern El Paso County), interview by R. Loevy, Denver, February 5, 1992. See also Dan Njegomir, "Bird Believes Medicaid Has Got to Go," *Colorado Springs Gazette Telegraph*, January 2, 1992, p. B1.

15 "Federal Expenditures in Colorado—1988," *A Colorado Taxpayer Report*, vol. 36, no. 5 (October 6, 1989), issued by the Denver-based Colorado Public Expenditure Council.

16 Richard D. Lamm and Michael McCarthy, *The Angry West: A Vulnerable Land and Its Future* (Boston: Houghton Mifflin, 1982); this account represents a populist resentment of outsider control, whether it be by absentee-landlord corporations or the U.S. government. Theirs is both an individualistic and moralistic lament.

CHAPTER 4

1 For a fuller discussion of the passage of the 1875 enabling act for Colorado statehood, see Robert E. Smith, "Thomas M. Patterson, Colorado Statehood, and the Presidential Election of 1876," *Colorado Magazine* 53(2): 153–62.

2 A good analysis of the bill of rights of the proposed Colorado Constitution of 1875–76 appears in Mort Stern and Albert F. Frantz, "Making the Colorado Constitution Good for Another 100 Years: Taking a New Look at the Colorado Constitution," *Denver Post*, October 10, 1976; reprinted in *The Colorado Constitution: Is It Adequate for the Next Century?* Report of the Citizens' Assembly on the State Constitution, Boulder, August 27–29, 1976, pp. 44–46.

3 See Zeke Sher, "When Women Won Colorado," *Denver Post Empire Magazine*, March 4, 1979.

4 The expression "Supreme Ruler of the Universe" probably is a paraphrase of the reference in the U.S. Declaration of Independence to the "Supreme Judge of the World."

5 Donald Hensel, "A History of the Colorado Constitution in the Nineteenth Century" (Ph.D. diss., University of Colorado at Boulder, 1957), p. 106.

6 In the 116 years from 1876 to 1992, there were fifty-nine general elections. A total of 253 constitutional amendments were proposed during this period, 122 of which were approved by the voters. This is a success rate of 48 percent. Updated from data provided by the Legislative Council Library of the Colorado General Assembly.

7 Curtis W. Martin and Rudolph Gomez, *Colorado Government and Politics,* 3d ed. (Boulder: Pruett Publishing, 1972), p. 29.

8 As originally adopted in 1910, the Colorado initiative required signatures equal to 8 percent of the number of voters for Colorado secretary of state. The signers were not required to be registered voters, however, which made authentication of the signatures more difficult. A 1980 constitutional amendment, referred by the state legislature, stipulated that signers be registered voters, but in an effort to compensate for this tougher requirement, it reduced the number of signatures required from 8 percent of the number of voters for Colorado secretary of state to 5 percent.

9 John F. Shafroth, quoted in *Rocky Mountain News,* February 12, 1910.

10 Editorial, *Denver Republican,* October 4, 1910.

11 Amendment No. 3, 1974 general election.

12 See Amendment No. 4 in Colorado General Assembly, Legislative Council, *An Analysis of 1988 Ballot Proposals,* Research Publication no. 326, Denver, 1988, p. 7.

13 Amendment No. 3, 1972 general election.

14 Amendment No. 6, 1976 general election.

15 See Amendment No. 1 in Colorado General Assembly, Legislative Council, *An Analysis of 1988 Ballot Proposals,* pp. 1–3.

16 Ibid., pp. 2–3.

17 Colorado Secretary of State, *1988 Colorado Campaign Reform Act Summary: Contributions and Expenditures,* Denver, 1988, p. 53.

18 Amendment No. 7, Colorado General Assembly, Legislative Council, *An Analysis of 1988 Ballot Proposals,* pp. 16–19.

19 Colorado Secretary of State, *1988 Colorado Campaign Reform Act Summary,* p. 56.

20 Amendment No. 10, 1976 general election. The quotations describing the propo-

nents of the amendment are from R. D. Sloan, Jr., *Proposed Amendments, Referred and Initiated, to the Colorado Constitution, 1946–1976,* Bureau of Governmental Research and Service, University of Colorado at Boulder, n.d., pp. 43–44.

21 R. D. Sloan, Jr., *Proposed Amendments, Referred and Initiated, to the Colorado Constitution in 1978 and 1980,* Bureau of Governmental Research and Service, University of Colorado at Boulder, 1981, p. 4. This short update article can be found in a pocket at the back of recently purchased copies of R. D. Sloan, Jr., *Proposed Amendments 1946–1976.*

22 Amendment No. 6, Colorado General Assembly, Legislative Council, *An Analysis of 1988 Ballot Proposals,* pp. 11–16; Colorado Secretary of State, *1988 Colorado Campaign Reform Act Summary,* pp. 54 56.

23 *Colorado Springs Gazette Telegraph,* November 8, 1990, p. A3.

24 Data on Colorado constitutional amendments provided by the Legislative Council Library of the Colorado General Assembly.

25 See Thomas E. Cronin, *Direct Democracy: The Politics of the Initiative, Referendum and Recall* (Cambridge: Harvard University Press, 1989), p. 197.

26 Lyle Kyle, president, Colorado Expenditure Council, and former director, Legislative Council of the Colorado General Assembly, interview by T. Cronin, Denver, June 30, 1989.

27 *Grant v. Meyer,* June 1988.

28 Donetta Davidson, elections officer, Office of the Colorado Secretary of State, interview by R. Loevy, Denver, June 30, 1989.

29 Citizens' Inquiry into the Colorado Constitution, *The Colorado Constitution: Is It Adequate for the Next Century?* p. 1.

30 Ibid.: governor's powers, pp. 20–22; legislative sessions, p. 25; city and county government, p. 32; finance, p. 40.

31 Model Constitutional Convention, *Summary of the Proceedings,* September 11–13, 1987, Denver, pp. 6–7.

32 Ibid., p. 8.

33 Marshall Kaplan, dean of the Graduate School of Public Affairs at the University of Colorado at Denver, expressed disappointment in the legislature's failure to hold hearings on the convention's report, yet he understood the political pragmatism characterizing the legislative leaders at the time. Interview with T. Cronin, Denver, June 19, 1990.

34 David Hite, deputy director, Legislative Council of the Colorado General Assembly, interview by R. Loevy, Denver, June 28, 1989.

35 The *Denver Post* poll, conducted by Talmey and Associates of Boulder, March

1988, N=508 statewide. Thirty-eight percent agreed, 13 percent were neutral, 16 percent disagreed, and 33 percent said they didn't know or had no ideas on this matter.

36 Editorial columnist Bill Hornby and the editorial board of the *Denver Post* appeared to be calling for writing a new constitution, but we suspect they mainly wanted to eliminate out-of-date sections and perhaps also strengthen the role of the governor vis-à-vis the legislature. See "Colorado Needs a Compass for Its Second Century," *Denver Post,* July 5, 1987, p. 6F; and Bill Hornby, "Let's Clean Up Our Constitution," *Denver Post,* July 19, 1987, p. 6F. For the view of most legislators and lobbyists, see the thoughtful article by Roger Alan Walton, "A Dissenting View," *Denver Post,* July 5, 1987, editorial page.

37 The same mixed sentiments exist in most other states, too. See the useful overview essay by John Kincaid, "State Constitutions in the Federal System," in *The Annals of the American Academy of Political and Social Science* (March 1988), pp. 12–22.

CHAPTER 5

1 Our thanks to state demographers Reid Reynolds and Jim Westkott for sharing a variety of demographic studies. We also thank political analysts Floyd Ciruli and Paul Talmey, who shared poll data with us. We took advantage of the collections of polls in the editorial/newsroom files of the *Denver Post.* We wanted additional data on Coloradans and their political views and thus designed our own poll, which we call the Colorado College–Colorado Citizens Poll. We commissioned the poll, and it was ably conducted by Talmey-Drake Research and Strategy of Boulder in September 1990. We are indebted to Paul Talmey for his thoughtful assistance in the design of our questions. We funded this statewide telephone poll of 614 adult Coloradans through monies provided for the McHugh Professorship at Colorado College by the McHugh Family Foundation of Denver.

2 Harold L. Hodgkinson, *Colorado: The State and Its Educational System* (Washington, D.C.: Institute for Educational Leadership, 1990), p. 1.

3 Colorado College–Colorado Citizens Poll, conducted by Talmey-Drake, September 1990, N=614. Poll results are reported throughout the chapter.

4 See Henry Dubroff's analysis of the *1990 Lifestyle Market Analysis* in "Skiing Hot, Clothes Not in Denver," *Denver Post,* June 22, 1990, pp. 1C–2C.

5 Average annual wage and salary income as reported by Colorado Department of Labor and Employment, Denver.

6 Carl Miller, former editor, *Denver Post,* interview by T. Cronin, Denver, June 26, 1990.

7 Vincent Carroll, editor, *Rocky Mountain News,* interview by T. Cronin, Denver, August 11, 1990.

8 Colorado Voter Poll, conducted by Ciruli and Associates for 9-News and *Rocky Mountain News,* mimeo, August 7–10, 1990, N=548.

9 Talmey and Associates poll for the *Denver Post,* September 1984, N=520.

10 *New York Times–CBS News Poll,* mimeo, October 1990.

11 Unnamed citizen, interview by T. Cronin, Crawford, August 9, 1990.

12 "Poll: Voters Like City Government but Not Taxes," *Colorado Springs Gazette Telegraph,* December 26, 1991, p. B4.

13 As reported in the *Denver Post,* January 8, 1989, p. 13A.

14 *Denver Post,* June 22, 1986, p. 11A.

15 For more on this longstanding debate, see Thomas E. Cronin, *Direct Democracy: The Politics of the Initiative, Referendum and Recall* (Cambridge: Harvard University Press, 1989).

16 Talmey Research and Strategy poll, March 1990, courtesy of Paul Talmey.

17 Carl Miller, "Many Coloradans Not Sure of Official IDs," *Denver Post,* June 15, 1986, p. 1B.

18 Paul Talmey, pollster and political analyst, interview by T. Cronin, Boulder, October 4, 1990.

19 As reported in the *Denver Post,* January 8, 1990, p. 8B.

20 See Fred Brown, "Amend 2 Boycott Spurs Backlash," *The Denver Post* (January 3, 1993), p. 1, p. 4. Poll data are from tables on p. 4.

21 Pollster Paul Talmey, quoted in *The Talmey-Drake Report,* vol. 1, no. 5. September 1992, p. 1.

22 "Forget Family Values; The Only Way to Win Voters' Hearts Is to Claim Someone Is Out to Get Them," ibid., p. 2.

23 See, for example, Bruce E. Keith, David B. Magleby, Candice J. Nelson, Elizabeth Orr, Mark C. Westlye, and Raymond E. Wolfinger, *The Myth of the Independent Voter* (Berkeley and Los Angeles: University of California Press, 1992).

24 *New York Times–CBS News Poll.*

25 Colorado Voter Poll, p. 4.

CHAPTER 6

1 Floyd Haskell, former senator, telephone interview by T. Cronin, August 16, 1990.

2 Martha Ezzard, quoted in Carl Miller, "Ezzard Says Right-Wingers Forced Her to Leave GOP," *Denver Post,* August 15, 1987, p. 6B.

3 Duane Woodard, quoted in Neil Westergaard and Jeffrey A. Roberts, "Woodard

Quits GOP to Join Dems," *Denver Post,* October 24, 1987. Also in interview conversations with T. Cronin in 1988 and 1989.

4 Bob Kirscht, quoted in Daniel Taylor, "Kirscht Defects to GOP in Wake of Job Ouster," *Rocky Mountain News,* January 15, 1981, p. 5. See also Thomas H. Simmons, "The Electoral System of the Colorado General Assembly, 1972–1980" (master's thesis, University of Colorado, 1981).

5 Linda Shaw, former mayor, Lakewood, telephone interview by T. Cronin, August 16, 1990.

6 Technically speaking, when the county convention is nominating candidates for state and local offices, it is known as the county *assembly.* When it is nominating delegates to go to the state convention and vote on delegates to the party national convention, it is known as the county *convention.*

7 The same nomenclature applies to the state convention that applies to the county convention. When nominating candidates for state offices, the state convention is technically known as the state *assembly.* When electing delegates to the party national convention (at which the party candidate for president of the United States is nominated), the state convention is officially the state *convention.*

8 Mary Estill Buchanan did so poorly at the 1980 Republican state convention that she did not even get enough delegate votes to qualify for the primary election ballot. She put her name on the primary election ballot by getting a sufficient number of Republican signatures on a petition.

9 See T. Cronin and R. Loevy, "The Case for a National Preprimary Convention Plan," *Public Opinion,* December 1982/January 1983, pp. 50–53.

10 Gene R. Nichol, "Legislative Reapportionment Panel Should Also Set Congressional Lines," *Denver Post,* February 8, 1992, p. 7B. Nichol is dean of the University of Colorado Law School and vice-chair of the Colorado Reapportionment Commission.

11 Comparisons between counties are made in terms of *average vote margins* rather than *average vote percentages* because margins tell more about the real voting power of a particular county. For instance, Hinsdale County votes 64.3 percent Republican, but Hinsdale County is so small in population that 64.3 percent produces a Republican margin over the Democrats of only 78 votes. El Paso County, on the other hand, votes just 59.7 percent Republican, somewhat less than Hinsdale County, but El Paso County has such a large voting population that 59.7 percent produces a Republican margin over the Democrats of 16,321 votes. It is vote margins, not vote percentages, that win elections.

12 John P. McIver and Walter J. Stone, "Stability and Change in Colorado Politics," article forthcoming in 1993, p. 71. McIver and Stone see Colorado participating

in a general realignment of the mountain states from the Democratic party to the Republican party.

CHAPTER 7

1 John Sanko, "Campaign Trail Is No Primrose Path." *Rocky Mountain News,* August 5, 1990, p. 28.

2 Robert S. Lorch, *Colorado's Government,* 3d ed. (Boulder: Colorado Associated University Press, 1983), p. 180.

3 Because Senate terms are staggered, with one-half of the senators elected every two years, the Colorado Reapportionment Commission has the additional task of designating which Senate districts are scheduled for election in which election years. This job is more important than it might first appear. An incumbent state senator originally elected to a four-year term of office could have to run for reelection after only two years if the reapportionment commission designates his or her Senate district to be elected at the next election.

4 Dick Freese, chair, Colorado Democratic party, interview by R. Loevy, Denver, December 21, 1989.

5 Carl Miller, "Correcting a Decade of Power Abuses," *Denver Post,* April 16, 1989.

6 Renny Fagan, Democrat, state House district 22 (Colorado Springs), interview by R. Loevy, Colorado Springs, December 19, 1989. Hank Hahne, political coordinator, Colorado Republican Committee, interview by R. Loevy, Denver, December 29, 1989.

7 Freese, interview, December 21, 1989.

8 Hahne, Denver, December 20, 1989.

9 John A. Straayer, "Elections and the 1992 Legislature in Colorado," notes on the new legislative districts distributed at the annual meeting of the Colorado/Wyoming Political Science Association, Southern Colorado University, Pueblo, April 10, 1992. Straayer, a professor of political science at Colorado State University, Fort Collins, has studied the Colorado state legislature extensively.

10 Gene Nichol, "Legislative Reapportionment Panel Should Also Set Congressional District Lines," *Denver Post,* February 8, 1992, p. 7B.

11 According to a study by Colorado Common Cause, eighteen of the incumbent Colorado legislators who ran for reelection in 1986 had no opposition. Eleven of these legislators with "super safe" seats were Republicans and seven were Democrats. See Colorado Common Cause, *"PACed" Houses II: Common Cause Reports on Campaign Financing in Colorado,* Denver, January 1988, p. 21.

12 Freese, interview, December 21, 1989.

13 John Britz, director, House Democratic Majority Fund, interview by R. Loevy, Denver, December 21, 1989.

14 Hahne, interview, December 20, 1989.

15 A master's thesis analyzed Colorado legislative elections for the period 1972–80 and reached a similar conclusion. It noted: "Since most districts [in Colorado] tend to be safe havens for one of the major parties, legislative control depends on the outcome of races in the one-fifth of Senate districts and one-quarter of House seats that are competitive." Thomas Hood Simmons, "The Electoral System of the Colorado General Assembly, 1972–1980" (master's thesis, University of Colorado at Boulder, 1981), p. 82.

16 Data on Colorado legislative elections gathered and analyzed by M. Trevithick, May 31, 1990. Data provided by the Office of the Colorado Secretary of State, Denver. This study focused only on two-party—Democratic and Republican—competition. Third-party candidates were excluded, as were primary election defeats of incumbent party members by members of their own political party. Following legislative redistricting and reapportionment in 1971 and 1981, all candidates were considered *not* to be incumbents.

17 Wayne Knox, Democrat, state House district 3 (south central Denver), interview by R. Loevy, Denver, December 21, 1989.

18 During the 1960s, the Colorado legislature was under orders from U.S. courts to reapportion the state legislature so that the populations of legislative districts were substantially equal. The legislature had great difficulty meeting the court requirements for equal apportionment, particularly in the Senate. The result was that some legislative elections during the 1960s were conducted with multimember districts and some with single-member districts. The exact chronology was as follows: 1960, multimember districts; 1962, multimember districts; 1964, single-member districts; 1966, multimember districts; and 1968, single-member districts. The Democrats won a landslide victory in Colorado in 1964, winning a majority of seats in the state House of Representatives. Because single-member districts were in use in that election, the Democrats failed to gain control of the state Senate despite the great size of their electoral sweep.

19 Knox, interview, December 21, 1989.

20 Lyle Kyle, former director, Colorado Legislative Council, and former president, Colorado Public Expenditure Council, interview by R. Loevy and M. Trevithick, Denver, July 18, 1989.

21 Malcolm E. Jewell, *Metropolitan Representation: State Legislative Districting in Metropolitan Counties* (New York: National Municipal League, 1969), p. 20.

22 Colorado Common Cause, *"PACed" Houses II*, p. 1.

23 Ibid., p. 7.

24 Ibid., p. 2.

25 Ibid., p. 10.

26 Fagan, interview, December 19, 1989. Representative Fagan's view that the Democrats would continue to gain seats in the Republican suburbs of Denver was strongly supported by Wayne Knox, interview, December 21, 1989.

27 Hahne, interview, December 20, 1989.

28 Terry Considine, "Should Colorado Limit Terms for Its Elected State and Federal Officials—Yes," *Denver Post,* June 2, 1990, p. 7B.

CHAPTER 8

1 John A. Straayer, *The Colorado General Assembly* (Niwot, Colo.: University Press of Colorado, 1990), p. 12.

2 Chuck Berry, speaker of the House, Colorado House of Representatives, notes by R. Loevy on speech to Taft Institute, Colorado Springs, June 27, 1991.

3 Alan Ehrenhalt, *The United States of Ambition: Politicians, Power, and the Pursuit of Office* (New York: Random House, 1991), p. 197.

4 Colorado Legislative Council Staff, memorandum on *The Legislative Process,* Denver, December 1, 1988, p. 8. The complete list of legislative occupations as presented by the Legislative Council staff for 1987–88 was as follows: lawyers (20%), educators (15%), other (14%), business/industry (12%), full-time legislators (12%), farmers/ranchers (10%), real estate (6%), marketing/public relations (6%), executives (5%).

5 Quoted in Ehrenhalt, *The United States of Ambition,* p. 199.

6 Mike Bird, Republican, state Senate district 9 (northern Colorado Springs and northern El Paso County), interview by R. Loevy, Colorado Springs, December 19, 1989.

7 As an additional way to follow the tight legislative schedule, Colorado legislators can "prefile" bills before the legislative session begins. The news media cooperates by giving prefiled bills the same amount of news coverage given to bills introduced during the session.

8 David Hite, deputy director, Colorado Legislative Council staff, interview by R. Loevy, Denver, June 28, 1989.

9 Wayne Knox, Democrat, state House district 3 (south central Denver), interview by R. Loevy, Denver, December 21, 1989.

10 Ibid.

11 Straayer, *The Colorado General Assembly,* p. 155.

12 Ben Wear, "Berry Takes a New Tack in House," *Colorado Springs Gazette Telegraph,* May 19, 1991, p. B1. The Democrat quoted is Representative Peggy Kearns of Aurora.

13 Berry, June 27, 1991.

14 Jana Mendez, Democrat, state Senate district 18 (Longmont-Boulder), interview by R. Loevy, Denver, December 22, 1989.

15 Colorado Legislative Council Staff, memorandum on *The Legislative Process,* p. 32.

16 Even when House committees and Senate committees have different names, the differences are slight. For instance, the House has the Agriculture, Livestock, and Natural Resources Committee. The equivalent committee in the Senate is the Agriculture, Natural Resources, and Energy Committee.

17 "Lawmaking Process to Undergo Reforms," *Denver Post,* November 9, 1988, p. 3AA.

18 Knox, interview, December 21, 1989.

19 Bird, interview, December 19, 1989.

20 For a fuller discussion of the conservative effects of the majority party (Republican) caucus, see Straayer, *The Colorado General Assembly,* p. 157–58.

21 "GOP Won't Say 'Cheese' for Dems' Videotaping," *Denver Post,* April 11, 1989, p. 5B.

22 Quoted in "GOP Admits Trying to Get Vote Commitments on Budget," *Denver Post,* April 6, 1989, p. 3B; "GOP Won't Say 'Cheese' for Dems' Videotaping," p. 5B.

23 The Binding Caucus Is All But Dead," *Denver Post,* April 5, 1989, p. 3B.

24 Chris Paulson, quoted in "Lawsuit Filed under GAVEL May Ax Budget," *Denver Post,* May 25, 1989, p. 1A.

25 Berry, June 27, 1991.

26 For more detail on legislative committees and the legislative process, see the very helpful study by Straayer, *The Colorado General Assembly.*

27 Alan Rosenthal, director, Eagleton Institute, Rutgers University, quoted in "Lawmakers' Control of State Budget Limits Influence of Colorado Governor," *Denver Post,* January 29, 1989, p. 1B.

28 When one party controls one house of the Colorado legislature and the other party controls the other house, the Joint Budget Committee is evenly split between the two parties. This was the situation in 1975–76, when the Republicans were the majority in the state Senate and the Democrats were the majority in the state House of Representatives. The Joint Budget Committee had two Republicans from the Senate and one Republican from the House, one Democrat from the Senate and two Democrats from the House.

29 Shoemaker was so enthusiastic about the JBC that he wrote a book about it. See Joe Shoemaker, *Budgeting Is the Answer: A Story of a Unique Committee—The Joint Budget Committee of Colorado* (New York: World Press, 1977).

30 Mendez, interview, December 22, 1989.

31 Alan Rosenthal, *Governors and Legislatures: Contending Powers* (Washington, D.C.: Congressional Quarterly Press, 1990), p. 139.

32 Bird, interview, December 19, 1989.

33 Ibid.

34 Fred Brown, "Legislative Staff Grows and Grows," *Denver Post,* March 10, 1990, p. 3B.

35 Stewart Bliss, governor's chief of staff, interview by T. Cronin, Denver, August 1, 1990.

36 Richard D. Lamm, former governor, interview by T. Cronin, Denver, August 7, 1990.

37 Mendez, interview, December 22, 1989. John Straayer agrees with Senator Mendez's view: "The system is incremental in nature. For the most part, each budget represents adjustments from past budgets and is not the embodiment of the vision of a new governor or even a new legislature. In this respect, therefore, Colorado budgets are like most others—marginal adjustments to the status quo, year after year." Straayer, *The Colorado General Assembly,* p. 237.

38 Colorado Legislative Council Staff, memorandum on *The Legislative Process,* p. 44.

39 Shoemaker, *Budgeting Is the Answer,* p. 59.

40 Bird, interview, December 19, 1989. See also Mike Bird, "The Budget May Need Some Reforms, but the Process Doesn't," *Colorado Statesman,* March 11, 1988, p. 8 and p. 11.

41 Bob Kirscht, quoted in Fred Brown, "A Fine Mess They've Gotten Us Into," *Denver Post,* January 15, 1992, p. 7B.

42 Ibid.

43 "Defamation of Vegetable," *Washington Post* (national weekly edition), April 1–7, 1991, p. 27.

44 John Sanko, "Strickland Wants to Keep Closer Tabs on Lobbyists," *Rocky Mountain News,* January 22, 1992, p. 18.

45 Roger Alan Walton, interview by T. Cronin, at "the Walton table," Profile Restaurant, Denver, June 1990. See also the informative article by Sam Lusky, "Lobbyists, Lobbyists, Lobbyists," *Colorado Statesman,* June 1, 1990, p. 1 and p. 11.

46 Roger Alan Walton, *Colorado: A Practical Guide to Its Government and Politics* (Fort Collins: Publisher's Consultants, 1983), p. 85.

47 Sanko, "Strickland Wants to Keep Closer Tabs on Lobbyists," p. 18.

CHAPTER 9

1 These statements all came from a panel discussion with four former governors held at the University of Northern Colorado in the spring of 1990 and video-recorded for KRMA-TV, Channel 6 in Denver, 1990.

2 "Lawmakers' Control of State Budget Limits Influence of Colorado Governor," *Denver Post,* January 29, 1989, p. 1B.

3 The governor's budget does not include the budgets of the secretary of state's office, the treasurer's office, or the attorney general's office. Because these state officials are elected by the people rather than being appointed by the governor, they submit their budgets directly to the state legislature.

4 Joseph A. Schlesinger, chap. on "Governors" in Herbert Jacob and Kenneth Vines, eds., *Politics in the American States: A Comparative Analysis* (Boston: Little, Brown, 1965).

5 See Thad Beyle, "Governors," chap. 6 in Virginia Gray et al., *Politics in the American States* (Glenview, Ill.: Scott, Foresman/Little, Brown, 1990), pp. 228–29. The study was completed prior to the Colorado governor being limited to two four-year terms in office.

6 "Lawmakers' Control of State Budget Limits Influence of Colorado Governor," *Denver Post,* January 29, 1989, p. 1B.

7 Ibid.

8 Eugene Petrone, former executive director, Colorado Office of State Planning and Budget, interview by R. Loevy, Denver, January 19, 1990.

9 Larry Kallenberger, executive director, Colorado Department of Local Affairs, interview by R. Loevy, Denver, January 26, 1990.

10 Petrone, interview, August 1, 1990.

11 Stewart Bliss, governor's chief of staff, interview by T. Cronin, Denver, August 1, 1990.

12 Richard D. Lamm, former governor, interview by T. Cronin, August 7, 1990.

13 Ibid.

14 Wade Buchanan, policy analyst for Governor Roy Romer, interview by R. Loevy, Denver, November 16, 1990.

15 Kallenberger, interview, January 26, 1990.

16 Ibid.

17 Colorado College–Colorado Citizens Poll, conducted by Talmey-Drake, September 1990, N=614.

334 Notes to Pages 215–233

18 B. J. Thornberry, deputy chief of staff to Governor Roy Romer, interview by R. Loevy, Denver, January 22, 1990.

19 Petrone, interview, January 19, 1990.

20 Kallenberger, interview, January 26, 1990.

21 Roy Romer, quoted in "Lawmaker's Control of State Budget Limits Influence of Colorado Governor," *Denver Post,* January 29, 1989, p. 1B.

22 Charles Roos, veteran capitol reporter for the *Rocky Mountain News,* interview by T. Cronin, Denver, May 24, 1990.

23 Richard D. Lamm and Duane A. Smith, *Pioneers and Politicians: 10 Colorado Governors in Profile* (Boulder: Pruett Publishing, 1984), p. 153.

24 John A. Love, quoted in ibid., p. 165.

25 Richard D. Lamm, quoted in Carl Ubbelohde, Maxine Benson, and Duane A. Smith, eds., *A Colorado History* (Boulder: Pruett Publishing, 1982), p. 369.

26 Richard D. Lamm, quoted in *Newsweek,* September 17, 1979.

27 See, for example, the provocative volume Lamm coauthored: Richard D. Lamm and Michael McCarthy, *The Angry West: A Vulnerable Land and Its Future* (Boston: Houghton Mifflin, 1982).

28 Lamm and Smith, *Pioneers and Politicians,* p. 4.

29 Governor Roy Romer, comments to Taft Institute Seminar, Denver, June 27, 1988.

30 Lamm and Smith, *Pioneers and Politicians,* p. 4.

31 See T. Cronin, "New I-25 Governors Have a Tough Road to Travel," *Rocky Mountain News,* January 24, 1987, p. 67.

CHAPTER 10

1 James MacGregor Burns, J. W. Peltason, and Thomas E. Cronin, *State and Local Politics* (Englewood Cliffs, N.J.: Prentice-Hall, 1990), pp. 131–32.

2 We have adapted several of these pro and con arguments from the useful *Analysis of the 1966 Ballot Proposals,* Research Publication no. 110, produced by the Legislative Council, Colorado General Assembly, 1966, pp. 13–15.

3 Joseph R. Quinn, chief justice, Colorado Supreme Court, interview by R. Loevy, Denver, February 9, 1990. For a similar view, see Charles Roos, "Colorado System among the Best for Selecting Qualified Judges," *Rocky Mountain News,* August 4, 1990, p. 90.

4 Jean E. Dubofsky, former justice, Colorado Supreme Court, interview by T. Cronin, Boulder, June 7, 1990.

5 Ralph A. Cole, former state senator, Republican (Littleton), interviewed by T. Cronin, Denver, July 10, 1990.

6 Richard D. Lamm, quoted in John Sanko, "State High Court Shifts Back to Center," *Rocky Mountain News,* August 4, 1991, p. 8.

7 John E. Gallagher, former district judge, Fourth Judicial District, interview by T. Cronin, Colorado Springs, August 21, 1990.

8 "Colorado Loses in Battle to Tax Drug Loot," *Colorado Springs Gazette Telegraph,* February 21, 1990, p. A3.

9 Quinn, interview, February 9, 1990.

10 Luis D. Rovira, quoted in John Sanko, "The Place Where Justice Is Done," *Rocky Mountain News,* August 4, 1991, p. 34.

11 Ibid.

12 Luis D. Rovira, chief justice, Colorado Supreme Court, interview by T. Cronin, Denver, February 27, 1992.

13 Dubofsky, interview, June 7, 1990.

14 Charles Larsen, *The Good Fight: The Life and Times of Ben B. Lindsey* (Chicago: Quadrangle Books, 1972), see also Lindsey's own story, *The Beast* (New York: Doubleday, Page, 1910).

15 See the spendid study by Anthony Lewis, *Gideon's Trumpet* (New York: Vintage, 1964).

16 David L. Wood, cochair, Colorado [Supreme Court] Gender Bias Task Force, interview by R. Loevy, February 20, 1990. Wood is an attorney in Fort Collins, Colorado. See also Rebecca Virtue Smith, "The Colorado Supreme Court Task Force Examines Gender Bias," *Colorado Lawyer* 19 (July 1990): 1291–96. The task force report is available from the Office of the State Court Administrator, Denver.

17 Katherine Tamblyn, cochair, Colorado [Supreme Court] Gender Bias Task Force, interview by R. Loevy, February 22, 1990.

18 Quinn, interview, February 9, 1990.

19 Douglas Haxton, district administrator, Fourth Judicial District, interview by R. Loevy, February 13, 1990.

20 Quinn, interview, February 9, 1990.

21 Elaine Menter and Rodney Patula, "Arbitration, Mediation: Two Proven Alternatives," *Denver Post,* July 2, 1990, p. 2C.

22 See, for example, Robert Bronstein, "Mediation and the Colorado Lawyer," *Colorado Lawyer* 11 (September 1982): 2315–23.

23 Quinn, interview, February 9, 1990.

24 John Suthers, district attorney, Fourth Judicial District, interview by R. Loevy, Colorado Springs, February 22, 1990. See also John Suthers, *Letter to Legislators, Judges, Law Enforcement Officials, etc.,* Office of the District Attorney, Fourth Judicial District, Colorado Springs, February 2, 1990.

25 This information on innovations in the Colorado judicial probation program was collected by R. Loevy at a joint interview in Colorado Springs with probation officials in Colorado's Fourth Judicial District (El Paso and Teller counties) on February 22, 1990. Participants in the joint interview included Kenneth W. McClelland, chief probation officer, Art Osier, supervisor of probation officers, Jerrye Gilmore, probation officer 3, and Linda Zeller, administrative secretary. See also Colorado Judicial Department, *Colorado Intensive Supervision Probation Program—Annual Management Report—FY 1989,* Denver, November 1989.

26 Anne Rankin Mahoney, "Citizen Evaluation of Judicial Performance: The Colorado Experience," *Judicature* 72 (December 1988–January 1989): 212. See also State Commission on Judicial Performance, "Commissions on Judicial Performance: The First Report on the Judicial Performance Evaluation Program," presented to the Colorado General Assembly, January 31, 1991.

27 See, for example, Bob Ewegen, "Commission on Judicial Performance's Secrecy Keeps Voters in the Dark," *Denver Post,* November 2, 1992, p. 7B.

28 See William Wilbanks, *The Make My Day Law: Colorado's Experiment in Home Protection* (Lanham, Md.: University Press of America, 1990).

29 The expression "Make My Day" came from a scene in a popular film of the mid 1980s, *Sudden Impact.* The film's star, Clint Eastwood, has his revolver pointed at the head of a criminal, and when the criminal appears as though he may try to escape, Eastwood says, "Go ahead. Make my day!" The implication is that it is acceptable to shoot lawbreakers who are threatening you or endeavoring to escape.

30 Wilbanks, *The Make My Day Law,* chap. 10.

CHAPTER 11

1 Carl Ubbelohde, Maxine Benson, and Duane A. Smith, *A Colorado History* 6th ed. (Boulder: Pruett Publishing, 1982), p. 64.

2 Ibid., pp. 95–99.

3 Ibid., p. 102.

4 Data provided by the Colorado Public Expenditures Council.

5 Douglas G. Brown, director, Legislative Legal Services, interview by the authors, Denver, July 18, 1989.

6 For a sympathetic biography of Governor Waite that discusses this episode, see John R. Morris, *Davis H. Waite: The Ideology of a Western Populist* (Washington, D.C.: University Press of America, 1982).

7 Cathy Reynolds, at-large member, Denver City Council, interview by R. Loevy, Denver, December 6, 1989.

8 "Credit Belongs to the People for Exerting Can-Do Spirit," *Denver Post,* August 19, 1990, p. 2H.

9 The Poundstone One constitutional amendment was named for its principal author and supporter, Frieda Poundstone, a well-known lobbyist at the Colorado state legislature.

10 The name "Big Apple" is often applied to New York City to symbolize its position as one of the most important cities in the United States. To call Denver the "Colorado Big Apple" is to imply that Denver remains, by far, the most important city in Colorado.

11 James Colvin, city attorney of Colorado Springs, interview by R. Loevy, Colorado Springs, February 7, 1992. The Colorado Supreme Court case cited by Colvin is *City and County of Denver v. State,* 788 P.2d 764 (Colo. 1990).

12 Kenneth G. Bueche, executive director, Colorado Municipal League, interview by R. Loevy, November 22, 1989.

13 Updated from *Colorado Municipal League Newsletter,* Denver, September 15, 1989, p. 1–2.

14 Bueche, interview, November 22, 1989.

15 Information on political party membership of Colorado county commissioners provided by Colorado Counties. Data assembled by M. Trevithick.

16 Home-rule counties include Pitkin County, which includes the city of Aspen, and Weld County, which includes the city of Greeley.

17 Harry Bowes, chief executive officer, Colorado Counties, interview by R. Loevy, November 21, 1989.

18 Ibid.

19 The term *flagpole annexation* comes from how the annexation appears on a map. The "flagpole" is a thin strip of annexed land reaching out from the current city boundary line. The "flag" is the large piece of ground at the end of the "flagpole," some distance from the city boundary line, that is the main area being annexed. Flagpole annexations must be designed in such a way that they meet the one-sixth contiguity requirements of Colorado's municipal annexation law.

20 Allan Blomquist, former executive director, Pueblo Council of Governments, interview by R. Loevy, February 12, 1992. Also see Daniel J. Elazar, *Cities of the Prairie Revisited: The Closing of the Metropolitan Frontier* (Lincoln and London: University of Nebraska Press, 1986), pp. 61, 120–21, 189–90.

21 Eric Anderson, "Mega-County Pushed for Denver Metro-Area," *Denver Post,* July 17, 1991, p. 1B.

22 Robert Isaac, mayor of Colorado Springs, interview by T. Cronin, Colorado Springs, August 2, 1991.

23 Colorado Municipal League, *Fiscal Fair Play: The Need for a State-Municipal Partnership,* undated policy statement, Denver, p. 3.

24 Ibid., p. 4.

25 Bueche, interview, November 22, 1989.

26 Issac, interview, August 2, 1991.

27 Michael Bird, former vice-mayor and city council member of Colorado Springs, interview by R. Loevy, Colorado Springs, November 10, 1989.

CHAPTER 12

1 We are indebted to Marshall Kaplan, dean of the Graduate School of Public Affairs, University of Colorado at Denver, for suggestions we used here.

2 *Governor's Budget,* Fiscal Year 1990–91, p. 1., and *Governor's Budget,* Fiscal Year 1992–93, pp. 1–11. See also *Governor's Executive Budget Plan,* Fiscal Year, 1993–94.

3 John A. Straayer, *The Colorado General Assembly* (Niwot, Colo.: University Press of Colorado, 1990), p. 285.

4 Legislative Council, Interim Committee on the Organization of State Government, December 1973.

5 Editorial, "State's Campaign-Finance Laws Put Influence on Sale," *Rocky Mountain News,* October 20, 1989, quoted in Straayer, *The Colorado General Assembly,* p. 205. See also Charles Roos, "Big Dollar Dynamos Aren't Exactly Newfound Friends," *Rocky Mountain News,* August 17, 1990, p. 88.

6 Cindy Parmenter, "Special Groups Put Stamp on Assembly," *Denver Post,* September 18, 1983, p. 1.

7 Ron Strahle, quoted in ibid., p. 12A.

8 Richard Lamm, quoted in ibid.

9 Terry Considine, quoted in Eric Anderson, "Considine Tips Ship of State," *Denver Post,* July 28, 1991, p. 1A.

10 Letter from unnamed legislator to authors, January 1991.

11 See the comprehensive survey of state expenses in Herbert E. Alexander, "Public Financing of State Elections," paper presented at State of the States Symposium, Eagleton Institute of Politics, Rutgers University, December 1989.

12 See ibid.; and David B. Magleby and Candace J. Nelson, *The Money Chase: Congressional Campaign Finance Reform* (Washington, D.C.: Brookings Institution, 1990). See also Larry Sabato, *Paying for Elections: The Campaign Finance Thicket* (New York: Priority Press, 1989).

13 "N[orth] Carolina Rated Tops for Industrial Climate," *Rocky Mountain News,* August 17, 1990, p. 78.

14 Adapted from Colorado Association of Commerce and Industry, *Blueprint for Colorado: A Look at the 90's,* Denver, June 1990, p. 4.

15 William J. Hybl, chair, El Pomar Foundation, interview by T. Cronin, Colorado Springs, August 22, 1990.

16 Morgan Smith, "Colorado Forging Strong Economic Alliance with Japan," *Rocky Mountain News,* July 27, 1990, p. 67.

17 "A Dismal Report Card," *Newsweek,* June 17, 1991, p. 65.

18 Lewis J. Perelman, *Human Capital Investment for State Economic Development: A Case Study of a State Government "Portfolio"* (Denver: Western Governors' Association, July 1988).

19 Tom Howerton, quoted in Janet Bingham, "Illiteracy Costing Colorado Millions," *Denver Post,* June 14, 1990, p. 5B.

20 John E. Chubb and Terry Moe, "Reform Can't Be Left to the Educational Establishment," *New York Times,* August 26, 1990, Op-Ed page. See also their book *Politics, Markets and American Schools* (Washington, D.C.: Brookings Institution, 1990); Joe Nathan, "Prime Example of School-Choice Plans," *Wall Street Journal,* April 20, 1989, p. A14; and David T. Kearns and Dennis P. Doyle, *Winning the Brain Race—A Bold Plan to Make Our Schools Competitive* (San Francisco: Institute for Contemporary Studies, 1988.

21 Cited in J. Sebastian Sinisi, "Would-be Regents Focus on Finances," *Denver Post,* October 1992, p. 1.

22 Floyd Ciruli, "Some Tax Limitation Inevitable Here," *Colorado Statesman,* July 6, 1990, p. 6.

23 Chuck Green, "Up Close, It's a Different Colorado," *Denver Post,* June 24, 1990, p. 3H.

24 Kathryn Nielson, "Colorado Tourism Industry Facing Global Competition," *Rocky Mountain News,* June 24, 1990, p. 1B.

25 See Steve Hinchman, "San Luis Chooses Christ over Gold," *High Country News,* June 4, 1990, p. 15.

26 Figures updated and adapted from *Hard Choices: A Report on the Increasing Gap between America's Infrastructure and Our Ability to Pay for Them,* Appendix 3. Colorado: A Case Study Prepared for the Use of the Subcommittee on Economic Goals and Intergovernmental Policy of the Joint Economic Committee, U.S. Congress, Washington, D.C., 1984.

27 Romer, quoted in John Sanko and Fawn Germer, "Romer Seeks Unity on Spending Limits," *Rocky Mountain News,* January 15, 1993, p. 8.

Index

Fort Lewis College, 207
Fort Lyon, 56
Fort St. Vrain, 35
Fort Wise. *See* Fort Lyon
Forty-niners, 37
Fountain Creek, 257, 277
Fourteeners, 5
Fowler, Hugh, 299
France, 3, 14, 32, 33, 34
Fraser River, 78
Free market, 51, 60
Freese, Dick, 161
Free silver, 61, 62, 146
Free speech, 241
Frontier, xv, xvii, xx, xxi, xxii, xxiv, 4, 7, 19, 56, 59, 90, 227, 284; agricultural, 37; cattle growers', xxii; metropolitan-technological, xxi, xxiii; mining, xxii, xxiii; mountains, 7, 34; rural-land, xx, xxi, xxiv, 37; rurban-cybernetic, xxi, xxii, xxiii; suburban, xxi; sunbelt, xxii; urban-industrial, xx, xxi, xxiii, 37, 42; settlement, xxiii; Western, xxii
Front Range, xxiii, 5, 8, 10, 12, 15, 16, 17, 30, 36, 41, 42, 43, 44, 45, 47, 48, 50, 51, 67, 71, 72, 78, 137, 148, 153, 154, 155, 221, 256, 271, 273, 274
Fruita, 302
Frying Pan–Arkansas Project, 68
Frying Pan River, 68
Fur trade, xxii, 7, 34, 36, 227

Gallagher, John F., 234, 235
Garfield, 6
GAVEL amendment, 100, 186, 187, 188, 189, 190
Gays, 24, 305. *See also* Homosexuals
Gender bias, 246–48, 253
General Assembly, 18, 89, 117, 171, 176, 177, 198, 201. *See also* Legislature
Geography, xxiv, xxx, 3, 5, 6, 7, 8
Geology, 5

Georgia, xv, xviii, 36, 208
Georgetown, 38
Germany, 120, 296
Gettysburg of the West, 57
Ghost towns, 4, 31, 49, 53, 62
Gideon v. Wainwright, 245
Gilpin, William, 55, 56, 57
Glenwood Springs, xxxi, 72, 244
Glorieta Pass, Battle of, 56, 57, 58
God (in the Colorado Constitution), 90, 92
Gold, 7, 33, 36, 37, 42, 46, 48, 49, 51, 53, 57, 61, 84, 85, 256; camps, 43, 45, 47; mining, 4, 25, 38, 43, 49, 56, 60, 62, 63, 68, 256; rush, xxii, xxx, xxxi, 16, 25, 36, 227; standard, 62; strikes, 36, 37, 42, 44, 45, 47, 48, 257
Golden, 36, 46, 84, 264
Goldwater, Barry, 143, 157
Good government associations, 28, 95
Governor: appointive powers of, 27, 100, 206–10; authority of, 177, 194, 208, 210, 214, 289, 290; and the budget, 27, 194, 195, 207, 212, 285; and business support, 18, 280; Constitutional provisions for, 89, 208; elections, 22, 43, 86, 133, 139, 142, 144, 145, 170; and the issues, 23, 79, 84, 99, 116, 159, 215, 216, 259; leadership by, 17, 24, 27, 95; and party politics, 29, 129, 148, 155, 160, 162, 212–14; and policy, 26, 70, 71; and relations to the judiciary, 207, 226, 229–35; 237; and relations to the legislature, 4, 182, 192, 197, 198, 199, 201, 202, 203, 204, 213, 214, 306; territorial, 55, 57, 85, 86; voter support of, 19, 21, 111
"Governor Gloom," 222
Governor's Mansion, 205, 206, 218
Granby, 6
Grand Junction, 17, 32, 60, 65, 66, 72, 74, 154